D1029726

New Quantitative Techniques
for Economic Analysis

This is a volume in
ECONOMIC THEORY, ECONOMETRICS, AND MATHEMATICAL
  ECONOMICS

A Series of Monographs and Textbooks

Consulting Editor: KARL SHELL

A complete list of titles in this series appears at the end of this volume.

New Quantitative Techniques
for Economic Analysis

Edited by   GIORGIO P. SZEGÖ

Department of Mathematics and Statistics
University of Bergamo
Bergamo, Italy

 1982

ACADEMIC PRESS
A Subsidiary of Harcourt Brace Jovanovich, Publishers

New York   London   Toronto   Sydney   San Francisco

ACADEMIC PRESS, INC.
111 Fifth Avenue, New York, New York 10003

United Kingdom Edition published by
ACADEMIC PRESS, INC. (LONDON) LTD.
24/28 Oval Road, London NW1 7DX

Library of Congress Cataloging in Publication Data
Main entry under title:

New quantitative techniques for economic analysis.

   (Economic theory, econometrics, and mathematical
economics)
   Includes bibliographical references·
   1. Economics, Mathematical--Addresses, essays,
lectures. 2. Economics--Mathematical models--Addresses,
essays, lectures. I. Szegö, G. P. II. Series.
HB135.N48   330'.0724   81-17576
ISBN 0-12-680760-4   AACR2

PRINTED IN THE UNITED STATES OF AMERICA

82 83 84 85   9 8 7 6 5 4 3 2 1

jwe 3-17-83

Contents

List of Contributors   xi
Preface   xiii

Part I MODELS AND REALITY

**Mathematical Methods for Economic Analysis:
A Biased Review**

G. P. Szegö

1.	Historical Background	3
2.	Chaos and Order	6
3.	A Reappraisal of Established Techniques	9
4.	Conclusions	14
	References	14

Dynamic Econometric Models: A System-Theoretic Critique

R. E. Kalman

1.	Background	19
2.	Definition of ''Model'' in System Theory	21
3.	Some Properties of Models	22
4.	Results of Realization Theory	24
5.	Conclusions concerning Stage (1)	25
6.	Stage (2): Parametrization	26
7.	Conclusion	27
	References	28

Economics: Past and Future

Siro Lombardini

1.	Introduction: The Case of Economics	29
2.	The Positivist Approach to Economics	31
3.	The Neopositivist Approach to Economics	32
4.	Economics between Ideology and Praxeology	34
5.	Physical Systems and the Economic System	36
6.	The Cognitive Process by Which the Economic System Is Envisaged	41
7.	The Ideological Prejudices (Fallacies) of the Neoclassical Definition of the Economic System	44
8.	How Can We Assess Preanalytic Knowledge?	47
9.	Some Fundamental Properties of the Economic and the Social Systems	49
10.	Connections between the Social and Economic Systems	52
11.	Equilibrium Model and Economic Theory	54
12.	The Normal Structure and the Law of Motion of the Economy	57
13.	Efficiency and Equilibrium	58
14.	Aggregation in Economic Models	59
15.	Normative Models in Economics	61
16.	Individual and Social Choices	63
17.	Theory and Observation	65
18.	Diachronic Stability and Historical Stability	67
19.	Catastrophe Theory and Structural Changes in the Economic System	69
20.	The Role of Expectations and Some Possible Discontinuities in the Economic Process	70
21.	Quantitative Changes and Evolution	70
22.	Knowledge and Behavior	71
	References	71

Part II NEW QUANTITATIVE TECHNIQUES AT WORK

Ergodicity for Economists

Joseph Ford

1.	Introduction	79
2.	A Two-Dimensional Mapping Model Exhibiting Chaotic Behavior	80
3.	Integrable Systems	83
4.	The Transition from Integrable to Chaotic Behavior in Conservative Systems	86
5.	Ergodic and Mixing Systems and C Systems	89
6.	K Systems and B Systems	91
7.	Statistical Description of Chaotic Systems	93

8. Closing Remarks   95
   References   96

Catastrophe Theory in Banking and Finance

Thomas Ho and Anthony Saunders

1. Introduction   97
2. Catastrophe Theory   99
3. Catastrophic Bank Failure   102
4. Conclusions and Summary   112
   References   113

Order by Fluctuation and the Urban System

P. M. Allen

1. Introduction   115
2. Interurban Dynamics   117
3. Conclusion   151
   References   152

The Qualitative Analysis of Nonlinear Dynamic Economic Systems by Structural Methods

F. J. Evans and G. Fradellos

1. Introduction   153
2. Aspects of Systems Structure   155
3. The Nature of Nonlinear Oscillatory Behavior   157
4. Economic Models   161
   References   179

Part III A REAPPRAISAL OF ESTABLISHED METHODS

Optimal Consumption Plans—A Dynamic Programming Approach

Martin J. Beckmann

1. Consumption Planning under Certainty   183
2. Section 2   184

3.	Section 3	184
4.	Section 4	185
5.	Section 5	188
6.	Section 6	189
7.	Section 7	189
8.	Section 8	193
9.	Risk	194
10.	Section 10	195
11.	Section 11	197
	References	197

Generalized Separation Property for Dynamic Portfolio Models

Piera Mazzoleni

1.	Introduction	199
2.	Revised Merton Model	200
3.	A Complete Separation Theorem for Alternative Risks	205
	Appendix. A Brief Outline of Stochastic Control	210
	References	214

Hierarchical Control and Coordination in Dynamical Systems

Krzysztof Malinowski

1.	Introduction	215
2.	Hierarchical Optimization by Price Coordination	216
3.	Price Coordination and Optimization of Complex Systems with Inventory Couplings	219
4.	Two-Level Control Structure with Price Coordination for Systems with Inventory Couplings	222
	References	228

Discontinuous Solutions in n-Person Games

G. P. Szegö and G. Gambarelli

1.	Introduction	229
2.	Weighted Majority Games	230
3.	The Case of Three-Person Games	232
4.	Constant-Power Sets	237
5.	Share Trading	238
6.	The Generating Algorithm	241
7.	Further Outstanding Problems	242

8. Conclusions   242
References   243

Part IV   SPECIAL PROBLEMS

Elementary Properties of Nonnegative Matrices   **247**

Giulio Cesare Barozzi

References   253

**Optimal Control of Econometric Models: Some
Experimental Results for the Italian Monetary Sector**

Corrado Corradi

1. Introduction   255
2. The Computational Scheme   257
3. Experimental Results   260
Appendix   262
References   263

**Stability and Instability in a Two-Dimensional
Dynamical System: A Mathematical Approach
to Kaldor's Theory of the Trade Cycle**

Franco Cugno and Luigi Montrucchio

1. Section 1   265
2. Section 2   266
3. Section 3   267
4. Section 4   273
5. Summary   277
References   278

Competitive Equilibrium and Indivisible Commodities

Aldo Montesano

1. Introduction   279
2. The Problem of the Existence of a Competitive Equilibrium in an
Economy with Unique (or Indivisible) Commodities   281

3. Competitive Pseudoequilibrium in an Economy with Unique
    (or Indivisible) Commodities   293
    References   300

New Results for a Competitive Equilibrium   **301**

Piera Mazzoleni

References   318

List of Contributors

Numbers in parentheses indicate the pages on which the authors' contributions begin.

P. M. Allen (115), *Université Libre de Bruxelles, 1050 Bruxelles, Belgium*

Giulio Cesare Barozzi (247), *Institute of Applied Mathematics, University of Bologna, Bologna, Italy.*

Martin J. Beckmann (183), *Department of Economics, Brown University, Providence, Rhode Island 02912, and Institute of Statistics, Technical University, Munich, West Germany*

Corrado Corradi (255), *Institute of Economic Science and Institute of Applied Mathematics, University of Bologna, Bologna, Italy*

Franco Cugno (265), *Cognetti de Martiis Laboratory of Political Economy, University of Turin, Turin, Italy*

F. J. Evans (153), *Department of Electrical and Electronic Engineering, Queen Mary College, University of London, London, England E1 4NS*

Joseph Ford (79), *School of Physics, Georgia Institute of Technology, Atlanta, Georgia 30332*

G. Fradellos (153), *Department of Electrical and Electronic Engineering, Queen Mary College, University of London, London, England E1 4NS*

G. Gambarelli (229), *Department of Mathematics and Statistics, University of Bergamo,* via Salvecchio, 19, *24100 Bergamo, Italy*

Thomas Ho (97), *Department of Finance, Graduate School of Business, New York University, New York, New York 10012*

R. E. Kalman (19), *Swiss Federal Institute of Technology, Zurich, Switzerland, and University of Florida, Gainesville, Florida 32611*

Siro Lombardini (29), *Cognetti de Martiis Laboratory of Political Economy, University of Turin, Turin, Italy*

Krzysztof Malinowski (215), *Institute of Automatic Control, Technical University of Warsaw, 00-665 Warsaw, Poland*

Piera Mazzoleni (199, 318), *Institute of Mathematics, University of Venice, Venice, Italy*

Aldo Montesano (279), *Laboratorio di Economia Politica, Università di Venezia, Venezia, Italy*

Luigi Montrucchio (265), *Mathematics Institute, Turin Polytechnic, Turin, Italy*

Anthony Saunders (97), *Department of Finance, Graduate School of Business, New York University, New York, New York 10012*

G. P. Szegö (3, 229), *Department of Mathematics and Statistics, University of Bergamo,* via Salvecchio, 19, *24100 Bergamo, Italy*

Preface

During June 1977 in order to celebrate the tenth anniversary of the Summer School on Mathematical System Theory and Economics, which took place at the Villa Monastero in Varenna, Italy, June 1–12, 1967, a restricted seminar on New Quantitative Techniques for Economic Analysis was organized, again at the Villa Monastero in Varenna.

This seminar was financially supported by CNR Comitato Scienze Matematiche and was attended by P. Allen, M. Beckmann, A. Cellina, B. Cornet, F. Evans, M. Feigenbaum, J. Ford, H. Kuhn, E. Llorens, K. Malinowski, P. Mazzoleni, C. Sutti, G. P. Szegö, R. Thom, and G. Treccani. It was immediately followed by a more applied session held in Bressanone, which was attended by G. Barozzi, A. Cellina, C. Corradi, A. Montesano, H. Kuhn, and G. P. Szegö, among others. Interest in the discussion was such that many of the participants decided to meet again at the University of Bergamo in June 1978 on the occasion of the Italo-Polish Symposium on the Application of System Theory to Economic Problems. The symposium was financially supported jointly by the Comitati Ingegneria, Scienze Economiche Sociologiche e Statistiche and Scienze Matematiche of CNR.

It was decided that this symposium should have a follow-up in 1979. This took place in Varenna in June 1979 and was mostly devoted to the major questions that were left undecided at the 1978 symposium and in particular those on the validity of models. This final part of the symposium was attended by F. Aftalion, F. Archetti, M. Beckmann, P. Ferri, G. Gambarelli, R. E. Kalman, S. Lombardini, L. Pawlowski, and G. P. Szegö, among others.

The topics discussed in this sequence of three yearly meetings were as follows: a critical appraisal of the results, the limits, and the developments of such well-established quantitative techniques as optimal control, dynamic programming, stochastic optimization theory, theory of games, theory of hierarchical systems, and a detailed analysis of the new quantitative techniques for economic analysis.

This volume is divided into four parts. The first part, devoted to general questions concerning models and model making, contains three papers by G. P. Szegö, R. E. Kalman, and S. Lombardini.

The second part is concerned with the presentation of the main results and of various interesting economic applications of some quantitative techniques that in spite of their promising potential, have not been widely used in the economic field. These techniques are ergodic theory, irreversible thermodynamics, and catastrophe theory. In this part we present four papers by J. Ford, P. Allen, F. J. Evans and G. Fradellos, and T. Ho and A. Saunders.

The third part contains four papers devoted to a critical analysis of already well-established techniques by M. Beckmann, G. Gambarelli and G. P. Szegö, K. Malinowski, and P. Mazzoleni.

The fourth and last part of the book is devoted to special problems. This part contains five papers: by G. Barozzi, C. Corradi, F. Cugno and L. Montrucchio, P. Montesano, and P. Mazzoleni.

Part I

MODELS AND REALITY

Mathematical Methods for Economic Analysis: A Biased Review

G. P. Szegö

1. HISTORICAL BACKGROUND

Early attempts to quantify economic phenomena and to propose suitable mathematical models were based on the analytical and quantitative techniques used in the investigation of mechanics. These techniques, which had proved successful in the description and study of the properties of the physical world, were then acritically adapted to the study of economic phenomena. Clearly no claim was ever made about an identity of economics with mechanics. Indeed, no basic principle of mechanics, and in particular of dynamics, was ever shown to hold for economic phenomena involving one or more decision makers. Contrary to the situation in mechanics, no invariant law of conservation or variational principle seems to hold for economic systems.

On the other hand, disregarding the doctrinal aspects, the mechanics approach seemed to produce very satisfactory, promising results in a variety of special cases.

Furthermore, in spite of the lack of a general theory, these early scattered results had the positive effect of inducing a certain quantification in economic thought and allowing the slow emergence of more generally valid theories, the derivation of more realistic models, and, most importantly, the formulation of more relevant, correct, and precise questions.

About 50 years ago it was finally recognized that economic phenomena had certain characteristics that were totally different from those of the physical world, which made them in certain cases completely unsuitable for

3

descriptions of a mechanical nature. This is because a single economic agent behaves not only according to past and present values of certain variables but, contrary to what happens in the physical world, also according to his or her own (possibly not rationally justifiable) expectations about the future values of these quantities. This unique property makes the phenomena that occur in economics and social sciences quite different not only from phenomena taking place in the mathematical world but also from biological phenomena, since the living cell does not seem to have anticipatory and learning properties.

The difficulties in describing economic phenomena can therefore be better appreciated by realizing that in the life sciences the existing models do not seem to give a totally satisfactory description of reality either, and that new techniques and approaches are now being proposed.

A first ad hoc theory for the description and formalization of situations of conflict in games with uncertain outcomes was developed by von Neumann and Morgenstern in their seminal work [70]. The concepts of strategy, utility function, and payoff, which are essential in a modern description of economic phenomena, received the first unitary systematization in their work. By considering optimization problems with only one decision maker as a particular case of games, they showed that the basic theory of optimization was in a sense a particular case of the theory of games. In the work of von Neumann and Morgenstern the computational aspects had not yet been developed. That was the focus of the contributions of G. Danzig, L. Kantorovich, and T. Koopmans, who, almost simultaneously with von Neumann and Morgenstern, devoted themselves mostly to the computational aspect of a very important class of static optimization problems: the so-called linear programming problem.

From the viewpoint of the validity of the model, these optimization problems can quite legitimately be applied to classes of (mostly micro) economic problems with one decision maker and a simple, deterministic, linear objective. It may, however, be less realistic to try to extend the approach to larger aggregates, since in this latter case the existence of a linear, deterministic, objective function may be difficult to prove.

A major step toward the formulation of dynamic economic problems and their solutions was application of the theory of automatic control and, more precisely, of the theory of optimal control to economic systems. Now that through the existence of common numerical solution techniques and a better understanding of the underlying principles, control theory and programming theory have essentially merged, the origin, motivations, and background of these two theories are drastically different. Mathematical programming was essentially the product of an extensive research effort in mathematics and computer science to obtain the solution of well-defined static problems arising in management science; on the other hand, control theory is the formalization of a long line of engineering problems dealing with automatic control and electronics. In this context it took quite a few years to reach a universally accepted formulation of the synthesis problem in the form of optimization of a functional subject to constraints both in the form of differential equations and of algebraic inequalities. We shall discuss in detail the evolution of optimal control theory in Section 3 of this chapter. Here we just recall that the formalization of dynamic economic problems within the framework of optimization methods took place only in the late 1960s, about 25 years after the formulation and solution of the static programming problem. The theory of optimal control thus gave rise to an important new branch of economic theory, in both its deterministic and stochastic frameworks.

Dynamic optimization theory was also applied to the case involving more than one decision maker, i.e., the case of differential games.

In spite of the successful new theoretical developments, recent years have witnessed criticism and soul-searching among scholars. The criticism has in particular stressed the problems of the validity of the models as suitable representations of the real economic world and of the construction of the model.

A complete discussion of the problems connected with the significance of models in economics is presented in the chapter by S. Lombardini.

The basic criticism that has been advanced concerns the need for a suitable method of accounting for the discontinuities and irreversibilities present in many economic phenomena. The need to include these two unconventional factors in analytic models is present not only in economic thought but in other branches of knowledge as well, in particular, physics, chemistry, and biology.

Various theories have been proposed for trying to overcome these difficulties. Among them the most significant in our opinion are the catastrophe theory developed by Thom [66] and irreversible thermodynamics, which was the creation of the Nobel laureate I. Prigogine and his school in Brussels [55]. We shall further discuss these theories in Section 3.

Another important line of thought that applies to the case of some systems characterized by a rather particular mathematical structure is ergodic theory. This mathematical theory deals with some very simple deterministic equations, which rather surprisingly give rise to solutions characterized by highly erratic behavior.

For such systems, as shown in the chapter by J. Ford, it is questionable whether it is feasible to obtain an analytic solution and, if such a solution is obtained, whether it is of any use. Thus the most important aspect of ergodic theory, which is also of interest in economic sciences, is provided by statistical techniques for predicting the behavior of a system regardless of the fact that the system itself is deterministic.

In addition to the problem of providing new, more precise models, there are still some basic questions concerning model making that must be answered. In the chapter by R. E. Kalman the traditional approach to model making in economics is challenged. In the traditional approach first a model structure connecting the variables is hypothesized, then as a second step it is possible to derive from the data the coefficients of the model and reach a conclusion on the validity of the model identified in this way. Kalman points out that a set of input–output data, i.e., of values of exogenous and endogenous variables, gives rise to only one canonical realization, i.e., a model that reproduces exactly the dynamic relationship connecting the data. While this statement is perfectly correct from the mathematical viewpoint, its implications for economic modeling ought to be most carefully weighed. If we analyze the procedure more closely, in traditional economic theory, model making is essentially a three-step procedure. The first two steps are the choice of the variables and the assumptions about the structure of the models; the third step is the identification of the parameters. Thus the first two steps are the fruit of purely speculative hypotheses, and the third step is the outcome of statistical analysis. Through Kalman's approach the three steps are the same, but only the first (choosing the variables) is arbitrarily decided by the model maker, while the next two are the outcome of the mathematical method that from the dynamic evolution of the chosen variables fully identifies the canonical realization. The only decision of the model maker is then the selection of the variables; clearly, the more variables are included in the analysis, the more the model is adherent to reality within numerical error. The choice of the variables is therefore dictated by the aim and the finality of the model; clearly it cannot be the process of an exact objective method, but more of a subjective analysis.

Having made this short presentation of what we feel are the major problems in the area of quantitative methods in economics, we shall proceed in the next sections to a more detailed discussion of two important topics: synergetics and the development and application of the theory of optimal control to economics. This latter classical subject has not been treated elsewhere in this volume. We felt that the volume would not be complete without an account of the evolution and development of this important area.

2. CHAOS AND ORDER

Most classical theories used to describe the behavior of economic systems and to synthesize optimal solutions were witness to the mechanical origin of the models and are essentially suited to continuous systems and solutions. Notable exceptions are the so-called bang-bang solutions of time optimal control problems. Also in the case of certain games, such as two-person differential games of chase and pursuit and multiperson coalition games, the solutions have discontinuous behavior. With the exception of this latter case, all preceding situations involving discontinuous solutions had very little relevance to economic problems. On the other hand, there is still a large number of cases in economic problems that show a lack of smoothness, both because of the adding up of a set of elementary discontinuities in the behavior of single decision makers (for instance, in the formation of public opinion) and the sudden variation in the structure of the whole system, as in the case of bankruptcies. These examples show the need for a theory that allows a description of discontinuous behavior in economics and the social sciences. A possible technique for describing such phenomena is provided by the catastrophe theory developed by R. Thom. A presentation of the fundamental results of this method appears in the chapter by T. Ho and A. Saunders in which this theory is applied to the particular case of catastrophic bank failures.

Catastrophe theory has been applied to the investigation of a variety of problems from stock market price jumps to the prediction of revolutions and other turmoil in large social structures. A collection of different applications is proposed by Zeeman [71]. While the presentation of the results and of the underlying theory is fascinating, we must point out that questions have been advanced by some scholars regarding the practical possibility of predicting the occurrence of catastrophes and their relative typologies.

Modern English usage attaches to the word "catastrophe" the negative meaning of unexpected disaster, while in the intention of Thom it had the original sense of a sudden event of abrupt, deep structural variation. As pointed out by Thom, this deep, sudden variation within the system, called a catastrophe, in many circumstances was intended as a natural defence of the system against excessive pressure that could destroy the whole structure. For instance, in this framework, bankruptcy of a firm, which is a rather interesting event not only from the mathematical but also from the financial point of view, is essentially a procedure that induces a discontinuity in the financial structure of the company. Through bankruptcy, in fact, debt and stockholders of the firm agree or are forced to alter their respective roles. The "rules of the game" of the financial markets that allow a bankruptcy procedure to be forced on the stockholders of a company if certain circumstances arise can indeed be interpreted as safeguards of the financial market as a whole. Thus bankruptcy has the institutional purpose of preventing a financial crisis originating within a certain company from affecting the whole market, thus ensuring that the consequences of the financial loss may be if possible strictly confined within the company itself. This financial tool therefore operates with the same finality as the fuse in an electrical system, which has the purpose of inducing a local catastrophic event in order to save the system.

Other important discontinuities, so far identified only in the static context, have been identified in most multiperson games. These discontinuities occur when, following a continuous variation in the data of the problem (for instance, in the payoff of a game) an abrupt variation in the structure of the coalition takes place. This result, which has been known for years, has been emphasized by the development of a recent technique allowing efficient computation of the value of the game and therefore identification of the optimal strategies and coalitions as the structure of the game changes. A summary of these results and of the relative basic theory is presented in the chapter by G. Gambarelli and G. P. Szegö.

In this chapter the results are applied to the problem of formation of the controlling majority of a corporation. The interesting point on which we comment here concerns the validity of models, their degree of adherence to reality, and the nonessentiality of discontinuities in the description of economic situations. First, we must recall that models of the evolution of the controlling majority of corporations having a simpler structure than the one we have outlined do not show the jumps, as pointed out in the simple game-theoretical model, due to the sudden exchange of ownership of blocks of shares. On the other hand, if one makes the game-theoretical model itself more precise and adherent to the real situation by considering the market effect induced by actual trading of the block of shares and the relationship between the number of shares traded, their "value," and their price, the pattern will again change. In this more precise model these market effects will tend to smooth out the jumps in such a way that the discontinuous behavior shown in the simpler model disappears.

This case illustrates that systems are not intrinsically continuous and that continuity or discontinuity in their behavior is a property that emerges or disappears according to the properties of the model, i.e., ultimately depending on its finalities.

In the physical world there are many similar examples of situations that can be described by different models showing either continuous or discontinuous behavior according to the particular situation one wants to investigate and to the properties the analyst wants to highlight.

An important attempt to develop a unifying theory of all the phenomena that show an unstable structure is provided by a new discipline for which the name *synergetics* has been proposed by H. Haken. This discipline brings to light the profound analogies among systems of various natures as a change in external parameters forces into the system a variation in operating mode. The analysis of the similarities among systems of quite different nature in changing over from an old stable structure to a new, possibly oscillating structure is quite impressive. The declared aim of synergetics is to apply a variety of tools ranging from catastrophe theory to irreversible thermodynamics to general system theory to "contribute to the mutual understanding and further development of seemingly completely different sciences." The contribution of these techniques to economics and the social sciences have so far not been overly exciting, but the approach is very promising. The proposed techniques of describing the formation of public opinion, i.e., the generation of order from chaos in a social environment, may provide a completely new framework for economic modeling (see Haken, 1978).

3. A REAPPRAISAL OF ESTABLISHED TECHNIQUES

During the last 15 years it has been recognized that many important dynamic economic problems can be formulated in a standard mathematical form called dynamic optimization, or optimal control. This is a well-defined problem consisting of three elements: the objective function, the state relationships, and the constraints.

Dynamic optimization in which both the theoretical and the numerical aspects are relevant has been the subject of a recent book edited by Dixon and Szegö [22], from which most of the following remarks are taken.

While most new as well as older quantitative techniques of economic analysis have been discussed in at least one article in this collection, optimal control, which is the major established analytical tool in this area, has not been treated at all. For this reason we shall devote this section to a brief summary of the historical developments of the accomplishment and of the recent evolution of this technique. Dynamic optimization is a technique of finding the values of decision (or control) variables that optimize the objective function and satisfy the constraints. The state relationships that provide the structure of the problem can be viewed as the main constraints of the problem and serve as a connection between the decision and state variables. The constraints consist of additional equations or inequalities which must be satisfied by the decision and state variables. The objective function may depend on both sets of variables, though this double dependence is often disguised in the formulation of the problem.

The static version of the problem is normally termed the linear or non-linear programming problem, depending on the nature of the objective function and the constraints. In such problems the objective is usually a differential function of the optimization variables. In contrast, in dynamic optimization the objective function is usually a functional and frequently a time integral along the trajectory. The problem is still not complete until the initial conditions on the state variables are given and the final desired state specified.

It is very difficult to trace the first attempts to solve the dynamic optimization problem or to assess the preliminary formulation of more recent times.

From one point of view, the mathematical problem could be viewed as having been solved in the 1930s by the contributions of the Chicago school of the calculus of variations.

One of the early statements of an applied problem in the dynamic optimization framework is given in Flügge-Lotz [25], in which many earlier results published by this author in German from 1943 to 1948 are also presented. In this monograph the state equations are assumed to be linear, hence the control discontinuous, and for this problem the standard terms of optimal control theory such as switching points, starting points, and end points for discontinuous solutions are introduced and the phenomenon of "chattering" described. In particular, the case of an increasing switching frequency leading as $t \to \infty$ to a point in two-dimensional phase space that is not the desired equilibrium point is considered. Although no real optimal solution is given, according to the author, "the theory is sufficiently developed to allow the design of discontinuous control systems with optimum efficiency."

Further similar publications appeared in the same year by Bushaw and La Salle [15], and further mathematical refinements and results appeared in Bellman *et al.* [6], where the problem is formulated exactly as a minimum time control problem and a complete solution provided for the linear case. At approximately the same time the works by Gamkrelidze [27, 28] and Krassovski [37] appeared, mostly devoted to the time optimal control problem.

A complete formulation of the optimal control problem and a critical discussion of the previous results are contained in the monograph by Tsien [67], in which for the case $n = 2$ the optimal control problem is formulated in its full generality (see Section 14.7, p. 212, of Tsien's monograph) and correctly regarded as a calculus of variations problem with a differential equation (the state equation) as an auxiliary condition. The problem is treated there as a "problem of Bolza" solvable by the Euler–Lagrange technique, but it is recognized by Tsien that no analytical solution can be achieved, and a numerical approach is proposed.

A complete presentation of the optimal control theory via the classical results of the calculus of variations was presented in the papers of Berkowitz [7], who referred in particular to the results of Valentine [68]. Valentine had investigated a problem very similar to the modern optimal control problem that even contained hard inequality constraints on the control functions. A presentation of the classical calculus of variation approach to optimal control is given in the book by L. Markus and E. B. Lee (1967) and a more extensive investigation in the volume by Pontryagin *et al.* [56, Chap. V].

The Soviet scientists at that time investigated the mathematical aspect in great depth and rigorously proved that, when the control set U is an open set, the optimal control problem is equivalent to the Lagrange problem of the calculus of variations, but that the calculus of variations is ill-equipped to deal with the case when U is a compact set. To handle this case, the famed maximum principle was introduced by L. Pontryagin *et al.* in 1962; the only available papers in the West containing the detailed proof were the translations of a series of three papers by Rozonoer [58].

The existence of an optimal control should of course be proved before attempting its identification, and an existence theory was proposed by Kalman [35] and termed controllability. Kalman derived controllability conditions for linear state equations, and these are extended to nonlinear systems in Lee and Markus [42, Chap. 6].

Prior to the proof of the maximum principle, a totally different approach to the optimization of dynamic systems, termed dynamic programming, was proposed by the American mathematician R. Bellman. The theory was developed at the RAND Corporation in the early 1950s and first presented in systematic form in monograph by Bellman [3]. While the maximum principle may be regarded as an outgrowth of the Hamiltonian approach to variational problems, the method of dynamic programming may be viewed as related to the Hamilton–Jacobi approach to variational problems. Indeed, we may quote Bellman [4, p. 66], who stated, "The classical approach corresponds to Fermat's principle in optics and the dynamic programming approach to Huygen's principle." Further discussions on this matter can be found in the papers by Fortet [26] and Dreyfus [23] and in the monograph by Bellman and Kalaba [5, Chap. 2]. The central axiom on which the theoretical basis of dynamic programming is constructed is the following principle of optimality: "An optimal policy has the property that whatsoever the initial state and conditions, the remaining decisions must constitute an optimal policy with regard to the states following from the first decision."

This principle and therefore dynamic programming apply only to Markov decision processes, i.e., processes that can be fully defined by the state of the system at the kth instant and by subsequent decisions.

The structure of the dynamic programming formulation is quite different from that of the maximum principle and leads to different numerical approaches, as will be seen in Section 4.

Proceeding with our historical presentation of the main contributions to the theory of optimal control, we now turn to the theoretical foundation of the more general modern analysis, namely, that which views the optimal control problem as an optimization problem in infinite-dimensional space and allows its solution by taking a finite-dimensional approximation. The rigorous formulation of this approach is due to the efforts of Balakrishnan [1, 2], Halkin [31–33], and Neustadt [53, 54] between 1961 and 1966. Many numerical proposals for algorithms for solving the problem were also made in these pioneering years of numerical algorithms, and the proposals by

Bryson and Denham [14], Breakwell *et al.* [13], Merrian (1964), McGill and Kenneth (1964), Kopp and Moyer [36], and Mitter [51] deserve mention and illustrate the way many of the early optimization principles were adapted in an attempt to solve that important problem. As conditions that guaranteed the convergence of a numerical iterative process to a stationary point of an unconstrained optimization problem were not available until the papers of Wolfe [69], it is not surprising that many of these early attempts were either inefficient or frequently failed to converge. The extension of Wolfe's results to general constrained optimization is still in progress; many of the algorithms currently in use for that problem do not possess the twin properties of convergence from any starting point and a fast rate of convergence near the solution. However, with the advent of differentiable exact-penalty functions, it is predictable that such algorithms will soon be available and will be rapidly applied in the optimal control area.

In spite of the fact that in the early 1960s most of the applications of optimal control were devoted to practical aerospace and automatic control problems, immediately after publication of the English translation of Pontryagin's book, the same techniques were applied to the study of economic problems. Thus we can regard the theory of optimal control as a major factor in the development of dynamic economics, i.e., of the development of dynamic modeling of economic systems.

In particular, the most significant application of optimal control theory to macroeconomic theory has been the theory of growth, the branch of economic theory that investigates the optimal policy for economic growth given limited resources. In this area too the basic result has been an analytic solution around which the whole field of Hamiltonian economic systems has been developed [18, 38, 61]. While the book by Kuhn and Szegö is a collection of the papers presented at the 1967 Conference on Mathematical Systems Theory and Economics, the more recent volume by Cass and Shell [18] presents a more up-to-date view of the field.

More recently governments faced with a shortage of energy have commenced to model the complete energy systems of nations in an effort to predict the effects of sudden changes in fuel prices and to optimize investment in new equipment. Early results with these models emphasize once again the fact that predictions obtained by such models are highly dependent on the accuracy of the model. If important relations are left out or modeled inaccurately, or certain possibilities not included, then very misleading forecasts can occur.

For this reason in any such exercise the complementary problem of identifying the structure of the system and then the parameter values must be investigated thoroughly before any dynamic optimization can be attempted. Mathematically the state equations of the system must be known before the problem can be solved. In many problems this identification stage is by far the more difficult, though frequently this can itself be posed as a dynamic optimization problem in terms of likelihood functions.

In econometric and ecological areas the problem is still usually to understand the system. While models of the economy of many countries have been built, most econometricians are more concerned with investigating their accuracy and introducing perturbations into the models and studying their effects, rather than attempting to optimize among them. Indeed, it would be difficult, if not impossible, to obtain agreement on an objective function for a national economy, and many economists claim, with good reason, that it is impossible to construct a utility function (i.e., an objective function in an uncertain world) for any group of individuals.

Smaller-scale economic problems, such as investment allocation and portfolio selection under uncertainty, lead to better-defined optimization problems. Those problems can be formulated as stochastic optimal control problems, and in many cases an analytic solution can be obtained. From this analytic solution the whole theoretical framework of these problems can be better understood and the numerical solutions obtained for more difficult problems of the same nature better appreciated.

Practically simultaneously with the development of deterministic optimal control we have witnessed development of the theory of stochastic optimal control, both in the maximum principle version (see again Pontryagin *et al.* [56]) and in the dynamic programming approach (see, for instance, Dreyfus [23]). It was only after a complete theoretical systematization of stochastic calculus and in particular of stochastic differential equations (see Itô and McKean [34], McKean [44], and Kushner [40]) that the theory of stochastic optimization reached a state of development and completeness suggesting its application to the analysis of economic problems. This took place in the area of finance (see Merton [46] and Samuelson [59]) with the solution of a continuous-time portfolio selection problem. Since then this technique has been applied to a wide variety of financial problems ranging from a more complete solution of the portfolio selection problem [47], to a theory of rational option pricing [10, 48, 62] to a theory of multicurrency portfolio selection [63], to an analysis of the demand for indexed bonds [24], to identification of the optimal demand of insurance [57], to analysis of optimal investment decision under uncertainty [60], and finally to the basic problem of the optimal financial structure of a firm [49].

The results obtained by means of this powerful technique are of great theoretical interest and could be applied to a whole range of dynamic economic problems under uncertainty.

The chapter by P. Mazzoleni provides an elegant new mathematical presentation of that technique.

4. CONCLUSIONS

From the point of view of the application of mathematical models, it must be clear that no problem can be considered solved when only a local (or global solution) of the mathematical model has been found. The data used in the mathematical problem are almost certainly subject to error. Since the mathematical solution of the problem varies according to the value of the parameters, there exists in general a strong dependence between the data and the solution. The value of the objective function in the neighborhood of the optimal solution may in practice vary much more with some variables than with others and, if the optimal solution must be implemented, it is necessary to know which variables must be more tightly measured and continuously observed. These "sensitivity" problems of the optimal solution are of crucial importance in any possible application of optimization theory to mathematical models of socioeconomic systems.

The sensitivity problem is related to another basic question also discussed in the chapter by S. Lombardini: that of stability. Everyone is aware that the traditional definition of stability of a solution with respect to perturbations may not be ideally suited for the investigation of economic problems. The major difficulty is the scale of the time parametrization along a solution. Indeed, given a perturbation of a solution, the evolution of the distance between the first "reference" solution and the perturbed solution, given a finite observation time that is short with respect to the solution time scale, the stability properties of this evolution may be nonrecognizable, and in particular it may be impossible to distinguish empirically the case in which the solution is stable with respect to the perturbation from the case in which it is stable. Thus the general mathematical definition of stability that applies to all possible perturbations in a neighborhood and to the case of infinite observation time, even if rather strict and independent from the time parametrization of the solutions, may not be completely adherent to the actual problem to be solved. On the other hand, the use of ad hoc definitions and criteria of finite-time stability, while it may help the formulation of more realistic questions, may pose unsolvable problems in construction of the models.

REFERENCES

1. Balakrishnan, A. V., Optimal control problems in Banach spaces, *SIAM J. Contr. Optim.* **1** (1963).
2. Balakrishnan, A. V., and Neustadt, L. W. (eds.), "Computing Methods in Optimization Problems." Academic Press, New York, 1964.
3. Bellman, R., "Dynamic Programming." Princeton Univ. Press, Princeton, New Jersey, 1957.

4. Bellman, R., "Adaptive Control Processes, A Guided Tour." Princeton Univ. Press, Princeton, New Jersey, 1961.
5. Bellman, R., and Kalaba, R., "Dynamic Programming and Modern Control Theory." Academic Press, New York, 1963.
6. Bellman, R., Glicksberg, I., and Gross, O., On the "bang-bang" control problem, *Q. Appl. Math.* **14** (1956).
7. Berkovitz, L. D., Variational methods in problems of control and programming, *J.M.A.A.* **3** (1961).
8. Berkovitz, L. D., On control problems with bounded state variables, *J.M.A.A.* **4** (1962).
9. Bhatia, N. P., and Szegö, G. P. Stability theory of dynamical systems, "Grundlehren der Mathematisches Wissenschaften," Vol. 104. Springer-Verlag, Berlin and New York, 1970.
10. Black, F., and Scholes, M., The pricing of options and corporate liabilities, *J. Political Econ.* **81**, 637–659 (1973).
11. Boltyanskii, V. G., Gamkrelidze, R. V., and Pontryagin, L. S., On the Theory of optimal processes, *Dokl. Akad. Nauk SSSR Vol.* **110** (1956).
12. Boltyanskii, V. G., Gamkrelidze, R. V., and Pontryagin, L. S., The theory of optimal processes I. The maximum principle, *Izv. Akad. Nauk SSSR, Ser. Mat.* **24** (1960).
13. Breakwell, J. V., Bryson, A. E., and Meyer, A. L., Optimization and control of nonlinear systems using the second variation, *SIAM J. Contr.* **1**, No. 2 (1963).
14. Bryson, A. E., and Denham, W. F., A Steepest Ascent Method for Solving Optimum Programming Problems, *A.S.M.E.* (1962).
15. Bushaw, D. W., Differential Equations with a Discontinuous Forcing Term. Stevens Institute of Technology, Rep. 469 (1953).
16. Bushaw, D. W., Optimal discontinuous forcing terms, *in* "Theory of Nonlinear Oscillations" (S. Lefschetz, ed.), Vol. IV. Princeton Univ. Press, Princeton, New Jersey, 1958.
17. Cannon, M., Cullum, J., and Polak, E., "Theory of Optimal Control and Mathematical Programming." McGraw Hill, New York, 1970.
18. Cass, D., and Shell, K., "The Hamiltonian Approach to Dynamic Economic." Academic Press, New York, 1977.
19. Dierker, E., "Topological Methods in Walrasian Economics," Lecture Notes in Economics and Mathematical Systems, Vol. 92. Springer-Verlag, Berlin and New York, 1972.
20. Dixon, L., and Szegö, G. P. (eds.), "Towards Global Optimization." North-Holland Publ., Amsterdam, 1975.
21. Dixon, L., and Szegö, G. P. (eds), "Towards Global Optimization, II." North-Holland Publ., Amsterdam, 1978.
22. Dixon, L., and Szegö, G. P. (eds.), "Numerical Optimization of Dynamic Systems." North-Holland Publ. Amsterdam, 1980.
23. Dreyfus, S., "Dynamic Programming and the Calculus of Variations." Academic Press, New York, 1965.
24. Fischer, S., The demand for index bonds, *J. Pol. Econ.* **83**, 509–534 (1975).
25. Flügge-Lotz, I., "Discontinuous Automatic Control." Princeton Univ. Press, Princeton, New Jersey, 1953.
26. Fortet, R., Remarques sur la programmation dynamique, *Ann. Fac. Sc. Univ. Clermont*, **2** (1962).
27. Gamkrelidze, R. V., On the theory of optimal processes, *Dokl. Akad. Nauk SSSR* **116** (1957).
28. Gamkrelidze, R. V., The theory of time-optimal processes in linear systems, *Izv. Akad. Nauk SSSR Ser. Mat.* **22** (1958).
29. Glansdorff, P., and Prigogine, I., "Thermodynamic Theory of Structure, Stability and Fluctuation." Wiley, New York, 1971.

30. Haken, H., "Synergetics: an Introduction." Springer-Verlag, Berlin and New York, 1978.
31. Halkin, H., "Optimal Control as Programming in Infinite Dimensional Spaces." CIME, Bressanone, Italy, 1961.
32. Halkin, H., An abstract framework for the theory of process optimization, *Bull. Am. Math. Soc.* **72** (1966).
33. Halkin, H., and Neustadt, L. W., General necessary conditions for optimization problems, *Proc. Nat. Acad. Sci.* **56** (1966).
34. Itô, K., and McKean, H. P., Jr., "Diffusion Processes and Their Sample Paths." Academic Press, New York, 1964.
35. Kalman, R. E., *Bol. Soc. Mat. Mex.* **5**, 102 (1960).
36. Kopp, R. E., and Moyer, H. G., Trajectory optimization techniques, "Computing Methods in Optimization Problem," Vol. II. Academic Press, New York, 1964.
37. Krassovski, N. N., On the theory of optimal regulation, *Automat. Telemekh.* **18** (1957).
38. Kuhn, H. W., and Szegö, G. P., "Mathematical Systems Theory and Economics," Vols. I and II, Lecture Notes in Op. Res. & Mathematic Economics Vol. 11 & 12, Springer-Verlag, Berlin, 1969.
39. Kuhn, H. W., and Szegö, G. P. (eds.), "Differential Games and Their Applications." North-Holland Publ., Amsterdam, 1971.
40. Kushner, H. J., "Stochastic Stability and Control." Academic Press, New York, 1967.
41. La Salle, J. P., Study of the Basic Principle Underlying the "Bang-Bang" Servo. Goodyear Aircraft Co., Rep. GER 5518 (1953).
42. Lee, E. B., and Markus, L., "Foundations of Optimal Control Theory." Wiley, New York, 1969.
43. McGill, R., and Kenneth, P., Solution of variational problems by means of a generalized Newton-Raphson operator, *J.A.I.A.E.* **2** (1964).
44. McKean, H. P., Jr., "Stochastic Integrals." Academic Press, New York, 1969.
45. Merriam, C. W., III, "Optimization Theory and The Design of Feedback Control Systems." McGraw-Hill, New York, 1964.
46. Merton, R. C., Lifetime portfolio selection under uncertainty: The continuous-time case, *Rev. Econ. Statist.* **51**, 247–257 (1969).
47. Merton, R. C., Optimum consumption and portfolio rules in a continuous time model, *J. Econ. Theory* **3**, 373–413 (1971).
48. Merton, R. C., An intertemporal capital asset pricing model, *Econometrica* **41**, 867–887 (1973).
49. Merton, R. C., On the pricing of corporate debt: The risk structure of interest rates, *J. Finance* **29**, 449–470 (1974).
50. Merton, R. C., On the Microeconomic Theory of Investment under Uncertainty, WP 958–77. Sloan School of Management, MIT (October 1977).
51. Mitter, S. K., Successive approximation methods for the solution of optimal control problems, *Automatica* (January 1966).
52. Moser, J. J., "Stable and Random Motions in Dynamical Systems." Princeton Univ. Press, Princeton, New Jersey, 1973.
53. Neustadt, L. W., Optimal control problems as extremal problems in a Banach space, *Proc. Pol. Inst., Brooklyn Symp. Syst. Theory* (1965).
54. Neustadt, L. W., An abstract variational theory with applications to a broad class of optimisation problems, I and II, *SIAM J. Contr.* **4** (1966).
55. Nicolis, G., and Prigogine, I., "Self-Organization in Non-Equilibrium Systems." Wiley, New York, 1977.
56. Pontryagin, L. S., Boltyanskii, V. G., Gamkrelidze, R. V., and Mishchenko, E. F., "The Mathematical Theory of Optimal Processes." Wiley (Interscience), New York, 1962.

57. Richard, S., Optimal consumption, portfolio and life insurance rules for an uncertain lived individual in a continuous-time model, *J. Financial Econ.* **2**, 187–204 (1975).
58. Rozonoer, L. I., The L. S. Pontryagin maximum principle in the theory of optimal systems, I, II and III, *Automat. Telemekh.* **20** (1959).
59. Samuelson, P., Lifetime portfolio selection by dynamic stochastic programming, *Rev. Econ. Statist.* **51**, 239–246 (1969).
60. Scheffman, D., Optimal Investment under Uncertainty, Univ. of Western Ontario (1975) (unpublished).
61. Shell, K., "Essays on the Theory of Optimal Economic Growth." MIT Press, Cambridge, Massachusetts, 1967.
62. Smith, C., Option pricing: A review, *J. Financial Econ.* (forthcoming).
63, Solnik, B., "European Capital Markets." Lexington Books, Lexington, Massachusetts, 1973.
64. Strauss, A., "Theory of Optimal Control," Lecture Notes in Operations Research, Vol. 10. Springer-Verlag, Berlin and New York, 1968.
65. Szegö, G. P., "Optimization Algorithms Mathematical Theory and Computer Results." Academic Press, New York, 1972.
66. Thom, R., "Structural Stability and Morphogenesis." Benjamin, New York, 1975 (French version, 1972).
67. Tsien, H. S., "Engineering Cybernetics." McGraw Hill, New York, 1954.
68. Valentine, F. A., "The Problem of Lagrange with Differential Inequalities as Added Side Conditions, Contributing to the Calculus of Variations 1933–37." Univ. of Chicago Press, Chicago, Illinois, 1937.
69. Wolfe, P., *SIAM Rev.* **11**, 226–235 (1969). **13**, 185–188 (1971).
70. Von Neumann, J., and Morgenstern, O., "Theory of Games and Economic Behaviour." Princeton Univ. Press, Princeton, New Jersey, 1944.
71. Zeeman, E. C., Applications of Catastrophe Theory. Mathematics Institute Univ. of Warwick (1973).

DEPARTMENT OF MATHEMATICS AND STATISTICS
UNIVERSITY OF BERGAMO
BERGAMO, ITALY

Dynamic Econometric Models: A System-Theoretic Critique

R. E. Kalman

1. BACKGROUND

Econometrics was born in the 1920s in the hope that economics could be made into a quantitative science by following the then extremely successful example of physics, which seemed to provide a self-evident recipe for understanding the perceived world. So a two-stage process was envisaged:

(1) Economic laws and interrelations are written down as dynamical equations (recall Newton's laws).

(2) The coefficients of these equations are determined quantitatively by extracting statistically relevant information from real data.

The progress in econometrics in terms of yielding scientific insight into economic phenomena has been disappointingly little in the nearly 60 years that have elapsed, at least in comparison with the progress in physics after Newton in the late seventeenth and early eighteenth centuries, even if we allow ourselves the illusion that things are happening as slowly now as they were 250 years ago.

The thesis of this chapter, hardly subject to debate among the "hard" sciences, is that economics is not at all like physics and therefore that it is not accessible by a methodology that *was* successful for physics. Far from being governed by absolute, universal, and immutable laws, economic knowledge, unlike physical science, is strongly *system* (context) *dependent*; when economic

19

insights are taken out of the temporal, political, social, or geographical context, they become trivial statements with little information content. Thus, for example, contemporary debates about Keynesianism and global monetarism have little to do with economic issues but should be viewed as (rather clumsy) attempts to grasp some of the real system aspects of contemporary economic life (see Whitman [14]).

Since economic "laws" do not possess the attributes of physical laws, writing down equations, in the style of physics, to translate economic statements into mathematics is not a productive enterprise. I should add that this objection is not relieved by increasing the number of variables, quite to the contrary. System theory provides a simple but hard suggestion: Do not write equations expressing assumed relationships; deduce your equations from real data. In fact, the process,

$$\text{data} \rightarrow \text{model},$$

is one of the important problems of modern system theory, and it is a problem on which research has yielded highly nonelementary results. To put it differently, there will never be a Newton in economics; the path to be followed *must* be different.

As regards the second stage of the econometric process, the situation is even worse. A parameter has absolute significance only if it relates two quantities that are both concrete and explicitly measurable. Thus, in Ohm's law, resistance is surely such a parameter, since the reality and quantitative nature of voltage and current are today no longer subject to debate. Economists have often dreamed of imitating the simple situation characterized by Ohm's law just by hoping for the best, for example, by assuming that such a law (the Phillips curve) exists between inflation and unemployment. But unemployment and inflation, in any quantitative sense, are fuzzy and politically biased attempts to replace complex situations by (meaningless) numbers; consequently any hope that two such concepts can be tied to one another by a single coefficient is barbarously uninformed wishful thinking. System theory provides a rigorous analytical framework that spells out why this is so. Any economist having doubts about the reasoning or empirical validity may refer to innumerable examples in applied physics, technology, and biology. (For a discussion of evidence for the Phillips curve, see Fellner [1, p. 48].)

For a somewhat more detailed development of these austere arguments— which of course call for and should have a far more thorough analysis—the reader is referred to Kalman [2, 6]. Here we shall attempt mainly to explain the (mathematical) inevitability of the facts of life in modeling and in the parametrization of models; explicit connections with concrete econometric problems will be treated in Kalman [7].

2. DEFINITION OF "MODEL" IN SYSTEM THEORY

It is not an exaggeration to say that the development of system theory since the early 1960s is directly related to the acceptance of rigid, mathematically precise definitions of what should be called a *system* (or, especially for people in the more applied fields, *model*). Evidently no deep critique of modeling is possible without agreement on the point of definition. The question of whether the model "fits" reality will not be at issue in this chapter; we do emphasize, however, that the concept of a system presented below has had a long evolution, beginning roughly with Newtonian mechanics; its relevance today is attested to by the success of many applications to highly diverse fields.

In defining a model one cannot be too general, because then the ideas become unfocused; one also cannot be too specific, because then the philosophical and practical relevance of the exercise tends to vanish quickly. So the definition of a class of models must use some simple and empirically verifiable "organizational principle."

The one organizational principle for which system theory has provided (seemingly) total understanding is the concept of *linearity*. (Physicists sloppily and incorrectly call it the "principle of superposition.") I know of no comparable principle in economics that serves the same purpose. Optimality has been claimed to be such a principle, but optimization is too complicated a task to be performed daily in most activities considered "economic." In time-series analysis, which is vital to stage (2) of the econometric program, the implicit assumption is almost always linearity; yet the logical consequences of this fact are rarely realized by econometricians or even by time-series theorists (see Kalman [7]).

A second, less important, organizational principle, *finite dimensionality*, is unavoidable for purely practical reasons. Progress in dealing with real-life situations can nowadays be made only with the help of data digestion involving digital computers, and the latter, operating with finite amounts of data, are abstractly always finite-dimensional devices.

In modern notation, a *finite-dimensional linear system* is given by the discrete-time relations, for $t = \ldots, 0, 1, 2, \ldots$,

(1) $$x_{t+1} = Fx_t + Gu_t \quad \text{and} \quad y_t = Hx_t,$$

where u_t (input), x_t (state), and y_t (output) are finite-dimensional vectors and F, G, H are corresponding matrices. Thus the system Σ is really given, as regards the actual numbers needed to define it, by the matrix triple $\Sigma = (F, G, H)$. (I shall omit any discussion of the possibly time-dependent nature of (F, G, H)—the *nonconstant* case—because this detail is irrelevant for the theoretical discussion presented below.)

Once a precise definition of a system has been given, all conceptual or intuitive questions concerning system problems can be precisely investigated by translating such questions into mathematical problems concerning the triple (F, G, H).

We shall talk indifferently about (linear) systems or models, always meaning thereby the mathematical setup given by (1).

3. SOME PROPERTIES OF MODELS

Let us now list some typical questions of this sort, with a nontechnical discussion of the corresponding mathematical conclusions.

(a) When are two models given by different triples, $\Sigma = (F, G, H)$ and $\hat{\Sigma} = (\hat{F}, \hat{G}, \hat{H})$, effectively the same? If so, we say that $\Sigma \cong \hat{\Sigma}$, i.e., that Σ and $\hat{\Sigma}$ are *equivalent*.

The answer is that x and $\hat{x}$ must be related by a nonsingular linear transformation T, that is, $\hat{x} = Tx$, where T is some (arbitrary) nonsingular matrix. Consequently, Σ and $\hat{\Sigma}$ must be bound by the relations

(2) $\hat{F}T = TF, \qquad \hat{G} = TG, \qquad \hat{H}T = H.$

These relations are rather complicated and cannot be determined by inspection except in (uninterestingly) trivial cases.

Evidently we cannot assign an absolute meaning to the basic explanatory variables given by the state vector x; what the components of x are depends on the coordinate system chosen, i.e., on the transformation T. This is quite different from physics, because there each component of x has a definite and system-independent measurable meaning; for example, $x_1 = $ position, $x_2 = $ momentum, $x_3 = $ angle. Economic (or biological) quantities cannot be measured with such absolute certainty. This follows from the system-theoretic point of view. We can only *postulate* the x of our model and must therefore allow the ambiguity that a different x may in fact occur in an equivalent model.

Even more unpleasantly, none of the parameters (numbers) in (F, G, H) have absolute meaning. If two collections of such numbers satisfy (2), then either set of numbers, quite different, still defines effectively the same model. Only the model itself has intrinsic significance, not the numbers defining it.

(b) What part of a model can be inferred from empirically given input/output data, that is, from $u_0, u_1, \ldots$ and $y_0, y_1, \ldots$? (This is, in fact, the problem of time-series analysis—constructing a model that behaves like the data.)

It is better to answer the question in the complementary sense.

That part of the model which is not reachable or which is not observable *cannot* be inferred from input/output data.

The *reachable* part of a model is that part whose internal variables $\bar{x}_t$ can be arbitrarily affected by a suitably chosen input u_t. The *observable* part of the model is that part whose internal variables $\hat{x}_t$ can be explicitly determined from knowledge of the observables y_t. The intersection of the reachable and observable parts of a model is always a model (system); this model is called *canonical* and denoted by Σ^{can}.

By a process called *reduction*, every model can be replaced by the canonical subsystem contained in it. Thus if we start out with a model Σ that does not have the desirable properties of reachability plus observability (i.e., is not canonical), we can always obtain from it a better and smaller model $\hat{\Sigma}$ that does have these properties.

The trouble is that the process of reduction requires mathematics and computation; it is not at all intuitive or easily visualized.

Because reduction is nontrivial, it is safe to claim that most models (perhaps 90%) used in practice, especially in econometrics, are not canonical. They are therefore, with high probability, invalid, because it can be shown that every noncanonical model, in addition to explaining its own input/output behavior [all possible sequences u_t and y_t computed using (1)], contains certain other elements not dependent on input/output data but mirroring the prejudices of its modeler.

Not all prejudices are wrong; for example, Newton's assumption of "conservative dynamics" gives a model where momentum is conserved; hence the model is nonreachable and therefore noncanonical. I shall not argue against conservation of momentum, yet I do not know of *any* situation in economics where noncanonical models can be justified in this way. But then most modelers are not Newtons.

It would be interesting to apply the preceding analysis to all theoretical models of economics, beginning with the nineteenth century, and to check which theories are equivalent to canonical models and where the prejudices are. This process has only barely begun. (See the interesting treatment of Livesey [9] concerning observability in Leontief-type input/output models.)

The preceding statements about system equivalence and canonicalness have a kind of universal and immutable validity, resembling (in this respect only) Newton's laws, but of course on a much more abstract level. Two sensible-sounding objections to this conclusion can and should be immediately demolished.

(a)   One cannot object to the input/output point of view, because Newton's and Ohm's laws are also concerned with such a notion. In fact, system theory generalizes such laws in the sense that a directly measurable relationship between input and output is not assumed; instead of determining a single parameter, such as a resistance, system theory is concerned with the much more general question of determining a system.

(b)   One can also not object to using the organizing principle "linear" or "finite-dimensional." In fact, Sontag and Rouchaleau [11] have proved that all the preceding statements are also valid for so-called *polynomial* systems, where "polynomial" is regarded as the precise notion of "finitely nonlinear." See also Sontag [10]. Unfortunately, polynomial is not as useful an organizing principle as linear, because it is too general. Yamamoto [15] has shown that finite-dimensional is not a restrictive assumption for the preceding statements; this is done by defining an organizing principle for a subclass of infinite-dimensional linear systems.

One question that does require detailed discussion, however, is whether the fact that a noncanonical system *cannot* be determined from input/output data can be turned into a positive statement: *Do* input/output data determine a canonical system? This is, intuitively enough, called the *problem of realization*, to which we shall now turn.

4.   RESULTS OF REALIZATION THEORY

Up to the present, the main achievement of system theory has been the so-called uniqueness theorem for canonical realizations. The following informal statement of the theorem should clarify its implications for modeling and econometrics.

Theorem   (i)   *Any (finitely produced) input/output data S have a canonical realization Σ_S, that is, a system Σ_S that will reproduce exactly the given data S.*

(ii)   *There is effectively only one canonical realization. Any two canonical realizations are equivalent in the sense of relations (2).*

(iii)   *A canonical realization is always the simplest possible; it cannot be reduced further without losing some of its explanatory power in terms of reproducing the data that went into its construction.*

(iv)   *Whether a realization is canonical can be tested easily by applying various simple tests for reachability and observability.*

(v)   *A canonical realization can be easily computed from the input/output data.*

(vi)   *A finite amount of such data will suffice; in fact, the uniqueness of the realization is a check for knowing whether the data are complete; a nonunique realization can arise only if there are incomplete data.*

For a more technical discussion of the classical (complete) realization problem we refer the reader to Kalman [4]. For the newer partial (incomplete) realization problem Kalman [5] should be consulted.

Let us consider briefly the conceptual consequences of the mathematical facts outlined above. (They are also valid for polynomial systems; see Sontag [10].)

That any (finitely generated) data have a canonical realization, as stated in (i), means that the modeling process can be reduced to a mechanical procedure. (More succinctly: Newtons are no longer needed.) Of course, since the model is finite, a similar restriction must be imposed on the data, but this is not a serious practical restriction, since "real data" does not imply "infinite data."

Claim (i) also means that the collection and cleansing of data are more basic than the model-building process. Few practicing economists would dispute such a claim.

Claim (ii) has a brutal implication. It means that two teams of modelers *must* come up with the same (equivalent) models if they use the same data. There cannot be 100 models for the same data but only one. On the other hand, this result also protects modelers from accusations of prejudice; after all, the model comes from the data—the modeler only pushes the button on the computer that takes care of computing the realization [see (v)].

Supervising the modeling process is easy, because, by (iv), the check for canonicalness is one of the simplest modeling computations. (This provides a much needed management tool for coping with the proliferation of models, modelers, and modeling organizations.)

Simplicity of explanation (sometimes called "parsimoniousness" in modeling) is subject to a rigid critique: (iii) shows how far a model can be simplified and still retain its required explanatory functions. (As Einstein said, every explanation in science should be as simple as possible, but not simpler. Now we know exactly what he meant by "possible.")

Perhaps the most important thing is that (vi) also lets us deal with the situation of not having enough data. *Some* properties of the model can always be inferred from the data. I do not sympathize with the usual complaints of economists and econometricians about lack of data, about impossibility of experiments, etc. This is surely not the main issue, as insisted on long ago, e.g., by von Neumann [13]. A similar conclusion can be reached by strict mathematical reasoning from the above theorem. Of course, no amount of system-theoretic sophistication will free the economist from the necessity of worrying about which data are relevant. In fact, the principal unsolved problem in realization theory is the treatment of noisy (inaccurate) data.

5. CONCLUSIONS CONCERNING STAGE (1)

This completes our discussion of the system-theoretic situation concerning stage (1) of the econometric program. The conclusions are clear.

If we are dealing with a complex system-determined situation, as seems to be practically always the case in economics, then equations must be induced from data and cannot be assumed on the basis of prior theory. Realization theory shows that the latter procedure (usually) merely produces prejudiced, hence invalid, models. Moreover, there are, at least in principle, two perfectly clean ways of obtaining unprejudiced models. Either we take a given model and squeeze out the prejudice by reducing it to a canonical one, or we induce the model directly from the data. According to our theorem, the result is always the same.

What this discussion emphasizes is that the essential thing is not writing equations but obtaining a canonical model. This is more subtle than just obtaining a set of numbers (seemingly the main object of the econometric enterprise in stage (2)), because relations (2) define a system as an equivalence class of sets of numbers.

So the following questions arise. How can a system, as an abstract object, be parametrized by numbers? What is the meaning of the quantities so obtained? Do they have direct economic significance like the value of a resistor appearing in Ohm's law?

6. STAGE (2): PARAMETRIZATION

Here the situation is more difficult and much less explored. One thing, however, is clear. A system, even a linear one, is a *nonlinear object*. The ordinary notion of the parameter presupposes a linear situation; in fact, Newton's and Ohm's laws are essentially linear relationships. When the problem shifts from determining a single parameter (such as resistance) to determining a system, because direct measurements of the individual system components are impossible, then the problem changes from linear to nonlinear. This is not at all surprising; even though an electrical device such as a transistor obeys Ohm's law in its microstructure, in its usual applications it appears as a system to the user and the simplicity of the linear description wanes. (A good model for a transistor is a quite complicated nonlinear problem!)

What kind of an object is the system (1)? It was first shown in Kalman [3] that it is a point on a (quasi-projective) algebraic variety; it follows from this that it is in general not possible to globally parametrize linear systems except those having only one input and one output (like the resistor). A modern mathematical treatment of these facts was given recently by Tannenbaum [12] in the framework of algebraic geometry.

The implications of this situation for econometric strategy are devastating. Since the problem is to identify a system and since systems cannot be described in general by globally definable parameters, the whole idea of a parameter loses its (uncritically assumed) significance. The application of quantitative methods to economics is *not* just a matter of determining numbers. For example, if the earth is regarded as a system, it is clear that a geographic position cannot be determined by just giving two numbers; we must also arbitrarily agree on a coordinate system, which involves putting an axis through two *ad hoc* defined geographic poles and fixing, even more arbitrarily, $0°$ with reference to Greenwich, England. (This is an interesting example of the use of power politics to resolve a mathematical problem, a phenomenon not unknown in economics!) The preceding is a wholly oversimplified analogy with respect to problems encountered in econometrics, but it does illustrate the impossibility of giving an absolute intuitive meaning to parameters that have only local definition.

Turning now to economic problems, system theory shows that it is futile to think, for example, of the unemployment-versus-inflation situation in terms of a single parameter having economic significance. To model this situation, it is necessary to consider many other related factors; if the modeling is successful, we may of course project the results on the unemployment-versus-inflation plane and obtain the famous Phillips curve. But just because we compute a certain relationship in our model, it would be extremely foolish to conclude that there is a *direct* relationship between unemployment and inflation, in the sense that there indeed is such a relationship between current and voltage in the case of Ohm's law. Regarding the results of such a projection as a deep and intrinsic discovery to which the name of Phillips must be duly attached is a conceptual absurdity.

If we did assume such a direct relationship, we would simply inject prejudice into the modeling process without conveying thereby any scientifically useful information. Indeed, exactly the same kind of prejudice is imposed on the problem if, as in standard econometric procedures (see Koopmans [8]), we assume that certain matrices have 0s, 1s, or undetermined parameters. Such a procedure simply reinterprets a system which is already identified in terms of a more convenient set of parameters whose relevance to economic questions is a matter of assumption, not a property of the data. See Kalman [7] for details.

7. CONCLUSION

The *Jugendtraum* of econometrics, determining economically meaningful parameters from real data via dynamical equations supplied from economic theory, turns out to have been a delusion. It will not provide new insights, because the theory may be itself prejudiced as reflected by the models it supplies and because dynamical models are not susceptible to unambiguous parametrization unless the parameters are accessible to direct measurement— in which case there never was a problem at all.

So the system-theoretic critique will eventually force a total revision of econometrics as a viable field of research. This is not a question of the quality of insights, theories, or experience so far gathered in economics, but simply a matter of the logic of what modeling means. It is also not primarily a question of statistics, since statistics can meaningfully begin only after the logical (noise-free) situation has been clarified.

REFERENCES

1. Fellner, W., "Towards a Reconstruction of Macroeconomics." American Enterprise Institute, Washington, D.C., 1976.
2. Kalman, R. E., Comments on the scientific aspects of modeling, in "Towards a Plan of Actions for Mankind (M. Marois, ed.), pp. 493–505. North-Holland Publ., Amsterdam, 1974.
3. Kalman, R. E., Algebraic-geometric description of the class of linear systems of constant dimension, *Proc. 8th Annual Princeton Conf. Informa. Sci. Systems* 189–191 (1974).
4. Kalman, R. E., Realization theory of linear dynamical systems, in "Control Theory and Functional Analysis," Vol. II, pp. 235–256. International Atomic Energy Agency, Vienna, 1976.
5. Kalman, R. E., On partial realizations, transfer functions, and canonical forms, *Acta Polytech. Scand. Math. Comput. Sci. Ser.* **31**, 9–32 (1979).
6. Kalman, R. E., System-theoretic critique of dynamic economic models, *Policy Analys. Informat. Syst.* **4**, 3–22 (1980).
7. Kalman, R. E. Identification of linear relations from noisy data *in* "Developments in Statistics" (P. R. Krishnaiah, ed.), Vol. 4, Academic Press, **New York,** 1982.
8. Koopmans, T. (ed.), "Statistical Inference in Dynamic Economic Models." Wiley, New York, 1950.
9. Livesey, D. A., A minimal realization of the Leontief dynamic input/output model, in "Advances in Input/Output Analysis" (K. R. Polenske and J. V. Skolka, eds.), pp. 527–541. Ballinger, Cambridge, Massachusetts, 1976.
10. Sontag, E. D., "Polynomial Response Maps" (Springer Lecture Notes in Control and Information Sciences No. 13). Springer, New York, 1979.
11. Sontag, E. D., and Rouchaleau, Y., On discrete-time polynomial systems, *J. Nonlinear Analysis* **1**, 55–64 (1976).
12. Tannenbaum, A., "Lectures on Moduli and Parametrization of Linear Systems" (Springer Lecture Notes in Mathematics, Vol. 845). Springer, New York, 1981.
13. von Neumann, J., The impact of recent developments in science on the economy and on economics (speech before the National Planning Association, Washington D.C., in December 1955). "Collected Works," Vol. VI, pp. 100–101, Pergamon Press, 1963.
14. Whitman, M. v. N., Global monetarism and the monetary approach to the balance of payments, Brookings Papers on Economic Activity, 1975, pp. 491–555.
15. Yamamoto, Y., to appear (1981).

SWISS FEDERAL INSTITUTE OF TECHNOLOGY
ZURICH, SWITZERLAND
    AND
UNIVERSITY OF FLORIDA
GAINESVILLE, FLORIDA

Economics: Past and Future

Siro Lombardini

1. INTRODUCTION: THE CASE OF ECONOMICS

Most of the current problems in the philosophy of science are particularly relevant to economics. If epistemologists had been better acquainted with economics, these problems would have been faced long ago. Most economists, on the other hand, do not seem to be aware of such methodological problems: Either they argue over their theoretical models—concerning hypothetical economies (Walras versus Sraffa, Sraffa versus Marx)—in their ivory towers isolated from the real world, or they adopt a naive pragmatic attitude (every model is valid provided it is of some practical use in being able to forecast some particular future development).

While most economists claim that economics is free of, or can be rescued from, value judgments, the results of their analyses are used to make specific ideologies acceptable or, at least, more appealing. Empirical models are built by using pieces of various theories and by making structural hypotheses that entail a set of specific mathematical relations. By properly choosing distributed lags, temporary trends, and slack variables almost any model can be adjusted to fit the empirical data. This suffices to prove the inadequacy of the neopositivist approach to economics. Yet most economists still cleave to it more or less consciously. It is for this reason, but not only for this reason, that the epistemological debate is of paramount importance to economists. On the other hand, some reflections on the methodological problems raised by recent developments in economics may contribute to the clarification of some issues of the debate. Some of the epistemological problems that are more particularly discussed deserve special mention:

(a)   The problem of "ideology" versus "scientific explanation";
(b)   The problem of casual explanation versus teleological explanation (see, in particular, Braithwaite [8], Chap. 8);
(c)   The problem of the social role of science and of the role of society in the development of science;
(d)   The problem of how evolution and discontinuous change can be dealt with by a scientific theory and, in connection with this problem, that of the cognitive value of stochastic models.

The principal methodological problems raised by the development of economic analysis are connected with these epistemological problems in various ways.

For several decades economists have been talking about *revolutions*, the Keynesian and the Sraffa [94] revolutions being the better known. Behind the lively debate raised by Keynes's and Sraffa's contributions, we can easily perceive a common *disciplinary matrix*, in Kuhn's sense [36], in spite of the different ideologies. Yet substantial divergencies would have come to the surface had economists consciously faced the epistemological problems that have just been mentioned: Their solution would have made some of the methodological problems raised by the development of economics much easier to solve. In fact neither of the two concepts of scientific growth, as a cumulative or as a discontinuous and disconnected process, seems to apply to economics. Marginalism has been rescued by "planometrics," which was developed to solve problems of planning in socialist countries, after having been used to prove that such economies were necessarily inefficient. Classical economics has not been superseded: In order to deal with the problems of economic development economists have to revert to the classics. Therefore there are many reasons why epistemologists should give more attention to the methodological problems economists have to face. This chapter is intended as a contribution to a debate that may be of benefit to both sides.

In Sections 1–4 I shall recall some of the features of the development of economic analysis that are more relevant to our debate. Then in Sections 5 and 6 I shall dwell on the differences between physical systems and the *economic system* as it is analyzed by economists. It will thus be easier to understand the peculiarities of developments in economics compared with developments in other sciences, and of the methodological problems that economists face (or should face). In Sections 7–10 some of the problems will be considered that should be at the center of the debate that interests both economists and epistelmologists: the role of preanalytic knowledge (and therefore of ideology in particular), together with some logical problems that are raised when one wants to isolate the economic system from the social system. In Sections 11–16 we shall reconsider the economist's *model*, in the Kuhn [36] sense,[1] that hinges on the notion of equilibrium. Some reflections will then be made on the use of equilibrium models for forecasting and normative purposes. In Sections 17–22 we shall make a few comments on the unsolved problem of how to deal with evolution and with the discontinuities in the process of development.

2. THE POSITIVIST APPROACH TO ECONOMICS

Economic analysis was born with a normative aim. The title of Adam Smith's work [93]—*An Inquiry into the Nature and Causes of the Wealth of Nations*—expresses its purpose: knowledge of the economic processes to be used to induce or at least facilitate behavior suited to increasing the nation's wealth. After the capitalist system became consolidated, research more and more clearly pursued apologetic aims, not usually explicitly stated. This process was paradoxically facilitated by the acceptance, also among economists, of the positivist approach derived from the development of physical science.

According to this approach the main purpose of economics is believed to be explanation of the economic system. Such a purpose can be attained because the fundamental properties of the system are assumed to be independent of its history (more precisely, it is assumed that all history is summarized by the initial conditions). It is because of these properties that explanation of the system entails visualization of its rational structure. The normal (rational) structure of the system can be represented by a system of simultaneous equations that can be arrived at by an axiomatic theory akin to that of celestial mechanics. Some of the postulates on which such a theory is based are, in fact, as we shall see later, ideological prejudices. Since a normal or rational structure is by definition a structure that is able to last forever, stability analysis is not a search for a property the system might or might not have, but an assessment of a property the model must display if it is to be a valid scientific interpretation of the real economy. This opinion is shared by economists of various (and even antagonistic) schools; it can be

---

[1] In the following discussion the word "model" will be italicized when used in the Kuhn sense. In a different context "model" refers to a semantic interpretation of a theory (see Aris [2]).

regarded as an element of the disciplinary matrix of economics in Kuhn's sense.[2]

In economic analysis all teleological schemes are banished (on this point Weber agrees with the positivist approach): The operators' acts are interpreted by relations whose nature is essentially causative. In the marginalist theory of general equilibrium, these relations are arrived at by assuming optimizing behavior. In other theories, like the Keynesian, behavioristic relations are immediately assumed. In both, however, consumers' decisions are considered facts that can be put in relation to others (for instance, price variations). Therefore a problem of empirical verification arises. The assumption of optimizing behavior leads to the discovery of some properties of the relations by which the economic system is described—properties that should then be confirmed by observation.

Since the positivist approach exalts the criterion of empirical observability, only facts produced by individual choices are considered scientifically relevant. Facts that reflect collective choices are in general unique events; therefore we cannot express them by aggregate variables that can be statistically estimated. This is why the marginalist statement that the goal of the economic system is the satisfaction of individual needs begs the question. In Pareto's formalization, based on the postulate of noncomparability of individual utilities, such a goal suffices to envisage the purpose of economic analysis. Pareto's formalization has been proved unacceptable by Bergson [6]; the assumption that the goals of the system are also the result of collective preferences does not entail the comparability of individual utilities. Collective choices are, in all ways, facts as well as individual choices.[3]

3. THE NEOPOSITIVIST APPROACH TO ECONOMICS

Affirmation of the neopositivist concept has not been without consequences on economic analysis—not all of them favorable. The preconception that the theoretical model reflects the properties of the actual system has been

---

[2] It is worthwhile to recall a remark made by Gandolfo [14] on the assumption of a stable economic system: "To this approach we could object that it is not allowed to impose on the model the condition that equilibrium is stable: this at least does not seem logically satisfactory: the answer to such an objection is that, since . . . unstable equilibria are not meaningful from an economic point of view we are interested in analysing the properties of comparative statics only for stable equilibria." Gandolfo's view on the role of the stability assumption coincides with that of Garegnani [15] in spite of their different theoretical approaches, for Garegnani also assumes a priori the convergence of the real process toward equilibrium.

[3] Marx [51] substantially adheres to the view that individual needs are the goals of the economic system; social needs are essentially the aggregation of individual needs, which depends on income distribution (see Chapter X of Volume III of [51]).

abandoned. This has allowed the physicist wider freedom of movement without jeopardizing the usefulness of research, since in physics it has always been possible to verify experimentally the laws arrived at through scientific research and to utilize the results for operative purposes. In economics, the neopositivist approach has increased the gap between theoretical analysis and empirical research. The interest of economists was concentrated on formalization of the theory to clarify the axioms and the deductive methods to derive *meaningful theorems* (see Samuelson [86, p. 3]. The basis of the theory remains the concept of the economic system mentioned in Section 2. In fact, this concept has become more rigid: The tendency is associated with that of the relatively more autonomous development of empirical research, which was not asked to produce an explanation of the economic process (which could thus be *understood*) but to produce models to be employed essentially for forecasting purposes. The release of theorizing from empirical research was made easier and to some extent justified by Popper's [74] reformulation of the criteria of verification of scientific theories. Analysis of the logical structures of economic theories could therefore make great steps forward: Their coherence has been better assessed, the problem of the existence of a solution for the model of general equilibrium correctly posed, useful theorems of comparative statics correctly derived, and theoretically fruitful generalizations of the model obtained.

Yet the classical positivist *model* has remained unchanged: It has affected the choice and the solution of theoretical problems. On the other hand, the models that have been and are being applied for practical purpose are not mere specifications of the theoretical models: Their kinship with theory is in fact very loose and sometimes rather ambiguous. The empirical models can hardly supply the indications that empirical research is usually asked for to confirm the theory. This does not worry economists too much — neither the theoreticians nor the pragmatists. The former aim at justifying theory for the sake of theory: According to them the most that can be produced is *thought experiments* which in fact, if properly performed, can contribute to the development of scientific knowledge. The latter adopt a naive pragmatic attitude: Economic research must substantially pursue practical goals; we must be able to apply economic models in forecasting future develop- ments of the economy and possibly in determining the best forms of inter- vention by which we can change them in order to attain certain predetermined objectives. Such an approach can indeed yield practical results. In fact, when the economic process repeats in every period those characteristics, observed in the previous periods, that are considered essential (i.e., when the latent structure of the system is sufficiently stable), even merely predictive models—logically unable to provide indications that would verify the theory—can be effectively used for practical purposes. A careful assessment of the models employed and of the methods used in forecasting will lead us to admit that substantially what the economist discovers are merely *trends* (whether they are explicitly looked for or are disguised by the estimation of the parameters of structural models). Therefore the criticism that Popper has made of the historical forecasting entailed by Marxist theory can be extended to most of the forecasting models developed by economists.

"While we may base scientific predictions on laws, we cannot (as every cautious statistician knows) base them merely on the existence of trends. A trend ... which has persisted for hundreds or even thousands of years may change within a decade, or even more rapidly than that. It is very important to point out that *laws and trends are radically different things*" [73, p. 115].

4. ECONOMICS BETWEEN IDEOLOGY AND PRAXEOLOGY

The neopositivist approach, in providing more autonomy to a theory that had been mostly developed for its own sake, increased the freedom of empirical research. The consequence was twofold. On the one hand, the operative purpose of research was stressed: Econometrics was born. On the other hand, economists could accept in their scheme functions that were not "observed," such as the *social welfare function*, thus opening the way to *normative economics*.

The invariance of the essential features of a market economy is reaffirmed in terms weaker than those entailed by the classical theory and by other marginalist theories more open to positivist influence: For the market is considered compatible with the pursuit of social objectives. It thus becomes possible to reconcile political trends toward socialism with acceptance of the free market economy. Changes in income distribution and the use of economic resources for social needs can be justified on the basis of the results of economic analysis (welfare economics).[4] The essential features of the system continue to be assumed stable: They must be determined before the system is analyzed by means of models that, in their logical structure, are borrowed from physics. It is because of these features that the market can guarantee the coexistence of optimal individual decisions. What the new conception of the economic system makes possible is the visualization of a variety of rational structures of the economy among which society can—and according to some economists must—choose. In the neopositivist approach not only the

---

[4] Certain state interventions yielding an increase in welfare, as advocated by Smith and Mill (management of economic activities by public bodies), can be more rigorously justified through the notion of external economies and the analysis of the structural effects of a monopoly.

essential features of the system are assumed to be predetermined but also the set of the instrumental variables and of the controllable structural changes, namely, those variables and those changes that can be manipulated in order to attain social objectives in the most efficient way. Social objectives cannot be explained by economic theory: They originate from outside. What the economic model guarantees, given the goals the system has to pursue, its structure, and the initial conditions, is optimality of the social actions that must be realized. We will elaborate on the meanings of these terms later; see Section 15. What we need to observe now is that the economic model cannot guarantee that the pragmatic indication is valid; for that, two conditions are required. The first condition concerns goals; they must be meaningful, in a sense that we shall try to clarify later (Section 15). The second condition concerns the structure of the system; the validity of the assumptions made depends on empirical verification of the results. The nature of the operation does not differ from that defined for the descriptive models in spite of some particular difficulties that must be faced when the results are proposals for action. Therefore in the neopositivist approach the cognitive value of the normative models is the same as that of the descriptive models; it depends on their forecasting capabilities. This substantial homogeneity is granted by a fundamental postulate: Only the controller can affect the economic process in ways we can predetermine (by a planning or control model), since the behavior of the other operators can be defined by means of casual relations that can be formalized before the control problem is envisaged.[5]

In the development of economics in socialist countries we can find the same trends that the neopositivist conception fostered in the Western world. In socialist countries we notice two trends in the field of mathematical (formalized) economics: a theoretical trend and a practical one. The former is that shown for instance in Makarov's contribution [45]. It aims at defining the structural features considered unchangeable since they determine the necessary mechanism for the rationality of the system (i.e., efficiency in achieving the goals considered peculiar to the system). It tends to distinguish the objectives of the efficiency mechanism from the *goals* determined by political decisions. Some of the aims of social reform find

---

[5] The relationship between normative models and descriptive models depends on the logical process by which the former are obtained. There are two ways in which we can obtain a normative model: (a) We can start by defining the tools of the economic policy and thereby the variables and the relations that can be controlled through political decisions. Then, through empirical research, we can determine the relations between the controlled variables and the others that will be affected by such political decisions. (b) We can build a theory explaining the economic process; then we can classify the variables and the relations into two sets: the set of variables and relations that can be controlled and the set of uncontrollable variables and relations.

their scientific formulation in this way (in Marcarov's model these aims would not be the redistribution of income but rather certain ecological goals).

The latter trend is shown in the abundance of literature on programming models, generally worked out in relation to specific fields of special activities. These developments are linked with those of mathematical programming, control theory, cybernetics, and systems theory (see for instance Kantarovich [30]). Rather peculiar is the position taken by Novozhilov [66], according to which formalization of the theory of value changes during the historical development of the system.

5. PHYSICAL SYSTEMS AND THE ECONOMIC SYSTEM

In macrophysics, as well as in biology, theory is a set of propositions specifying a structural system that is isomorphic with an actual system present in the world. All actual systems before being observed must in fact be interpreted and, as Hanson [18] has rightly pointed out, all observations are "theory-laden." Yet when we talk of physical systems, as Scheurer [87, p. 44] has remarked, "we refer to a part of the inanimate nature that we arbitrarily isolate in order to observe it: the rest of the world will be thought of as wholly external and not integrated into the system." The hypothesis of structural stability is then verifiable empirically in relation to the physical perception of the system. In physics itself, though, when we analyze the structure of atoms and molecules, we no longer perceive with our eyes the physical objects of the system we want to analyze.[6] In astrophysics the hypothesis of structural stability is acceptable only in a first approximation (an approximation more than sufficient for practical purposes). The system has in fact a history that cannot be inferred from the structural features shown at present, since the analysis of such features is carried out with models that consider the system a relatively stable closed system. A sort of reverse relation is, however, true. Definition of the system and therefore explanation of its present structure could be improved by knowledge of the history of the universe. In fact, the history of the universe can be visualized only through a preconceptive imagination of what might have happened, which is acceptable in as much as it brings forth new definitions of the system that make it possible to acquire better knowledge of its working. Moreover, some *prejudices*—like those that led to acceptance of the Ptolemaic interpretation of the universe—are revealed and can be eliminated.

---

[6] Even in macrophysics similar remarks can be made if certain problems of measurement are considered.

In economics we find the difficulties mentioned in relation both to micro-physics and to astrophysics. The economic system, in fact, cannot be perceived directly: It cannot be "cut out" of the social world in the way that a physical system is cut out of the natural world. It is the product of a process of abstraction, having as its acknowledged aim the isolation of certain features of social processes that explain a system of relationships considered sufficiently stable and sufficiently independent of other relationships.

A physical system can often be individualized by means of a set of local laws that enable us to control, to utilize, or to manipulate the system for practical purposes. Each of these laws is formulated and verified independently of the others. Thus the set of laws, even if it can be considered satisfactory for the solution of quite a few practical problems, cannot provide a satisfactory explanation of the system considered as a whole that is included in a larger system. In many cases it is possible to derive local laws by interpreting the system by means of a model defining its optimal behavior.[7] Yet such interpretations of local laws are often considered mere superstructures that do not increase the cognitive value of the local laws that can be derived directly and verified separately. This is no longer true when the theoretical models enable us to formalize new laws or to generalize some of the local ones.

For physical systems there is another way in which we can individualize and describe them. It can be adopted when it is possible to isolate the system and make precise and repeated measurements of every input and output clearly defined. Such a procedure is offered to us by realization theory.[8] In the case of a linear system, it can be proved that on the basis of a congruous set of measurements we can obtain a model that for all possible values of the inputs gives us the corresponding values of the outputs. It can also be proved that such a model can be reduced to a minimal dimension: In a finite number of steps we can arrive at any state of the system from any initial condition. We can thus consider such a model a good *description* of the

---

[7] One example of local laws is Ohm's law relating resistance to voltage and current strength, which is sufficient for solving the problem of current distribution in a network. Yet such a problem can be framed as an optimization problem logically similar to the transport optimization problem well known in mathematical programming. By solving it we simply obtain Ohm's law.

[8] "A linear dynamic system may be defined via its *input–output* map—$f: \Omega \to \Gamma$—which tells us how an output function applied to the system is "transformed" into an output function . . . We may regard f as an experimental specification of the system, or as some idealized summary of known experimental input/output data. The system itself is then viewed as a "black box," and we are interested in deducing the internal equations of motion from f. This is the *problem of realization*" (Kalman [29, p. 42]).

system. But I do not think it can also be considered an *explanation* of the system.

The first way a system can be individualized is scarcely relevant for the economic system. According to Popper, even in economics laws have been discovered that are similar to the natural laws we have described above as *local*: Examples of such laws are, "You cannot introduce agricultural tariffs and at the same time reduce the cost of living," and "You cannot have full employment without inflation" [73, p. 62]. These laws are indeed quite different from the local laws in physics, since they are mere logical connections between variables in an ideal world that cannot be put in correspondence with a clear-cut set of empirical phenomena (for which reason these laws cannot be empirically tested; and they are characterized in their theoretical formalization, as Popper himself has recognized, by the peculiar nature of the parameters being changing variables). In fact, the economic system cannot even be described if we disregard the interaction between the system as a whole and its parts. The approach followed by economists (from Quesnay to Walras) has always been indeed a *system approach.*

There are two reasons why the second way in which a system is individualized and described in physics cannot be applied to the economic system (apart from the peculiar difficulties that the measurement of economic phenomena entails):

(a)   In economics we cannot assume that the system remains unchanged while we measure its inputs and outputs, and

(b)   We cannot always easily define even which are the inputs and the outputs; what is an input according to one theory may be an output according to another.[9]

In spite of the peculiarities of the subject, economists have adopted models akin to those developed in physics. As is well known, mathematics was developed mostly to solve physical problems: Also, in economics mathematical methods become quite soon equated with scientific method. In fact, in physics, in spite of its clear limitations as already pointed out in the past century, the mathematical experimental method has produced laws that are successfully applied in the solution of practical problems. "The most amazing thing," Toraldo di Francia explains," is that for the first time after the discovery of mathematics, a method the results of which have an 'intra-subjective' value, has been introduced" [97a, p. 23–24). The same cannot be

---

[9] In some descriptive models (adhering to neo-Keynesian theories), money is an output, while in some other models intended to be applied in normative economics, money is an input.

said of application of the mathematical method in economics. On Popper's assessment ("The success of mathematical economics shows that one social science at least has gone through its Newtonian revolution," [73, p. 60] we cannot but agree with Hutchinson's remark that "the mathematical 'revolution' in economics has been one mainly (or almost entirely) of *form, with very little or no empirical, testable, predictive content involved*" [28, p. 40]. We can add that at times its mathematical garb had limited the critical development of economic theory.

The fundamental reason for the different role played by the mathematical method in economics as compared with that in physical sciences can be clearly stated. In physics the protopostulate of the space–time invariability of the phenomena that are to be explained is justified to a satisfactory degree by observation: It was in fact used to define the field of physics. Such a proto-postulate in economics is only a convenient—for the neopositivist school, indeed a necessary—working hypothesis. In fact, owing to the peculiarities of the economic system the invariability protopostulate can be accepted as a first approximation in relation to a set of phenomena considered within well-defined time horizons, as was clearly perceived by Marshall. Even in physics the formulation of problems shows its debt to preanalytic knowledge, at least for the indisputable reason that any technical language develops out of common conventional language. Notwithstanding Bacon's statement, the physicist not only reads in the open book of nature but also asks nature specific questions. The questions may be suggested by more-or-less casual observations or by practical problems that are necessarily formulated in a precoded language which may change only very slowly in accordance with the results of scientific research.

The fact that attention was paid only to phenomena that admitted the protopostulate of space–time invariability (only a few of the latest develop-ments of physics have pushed analysis beyond its traditional boundaries) and the possibility that in physics we can test statements of theories by experimentation have allowed the development of physics to proceed through *accumulation* of the results of research. Every new theory, except in the case of parallel theories,[10] supersedes the previous theory. Yet at the same time it allows us to define the peculiar context in which the old theory can offer an interpretation of the concrete process, which can be considered satisfactory for some practical purposes that in such a context can be cor-rectly defined. Preanalytic knowledge, which plays by no means a minor role in the promotion of research, does not prevent the results of research from being generally accepted, at least for their practical usefulness. It is

---

[10] An example is the two theories on light: the particle and the wave.

also worth noting that in physics theories are of course valid in particular contexts within a limited range of conditions, which accounts for the inevitable approximation˜ of the theoretical results to the empirical data. Knowledge is never definitive, even in physics (which alone suffices to invalidate the Laplace *model*). As Bohm [7, p. 133] has pointed out, "There may exist an unlimited variety of additional properties, qualities, entities, systems, levels, etc., to which apply corresponding new kinds of laws of nature."

To adopt the scientific method the economic system must be conceived in a particular way that makes it possible to qualify the normal system as a rational structure; the operators of the economic system are assumed to be powerless and the market to behave as a physical system. The semantics specific to economics reflect to a large extent the conventional language in which the actual processes, qualified as economic processes, are described. A feature of the scientific method that must be mentioned is the continuity assumption. In economics, too, the relations between the variables are expressed by continuous functions or functionals. In physics the axiom of conservation of continuity has always been considered essential, any break in continuity being attributed to continuous variations perceived discontinuously. This was true before development of the quantum theory. It is on the postulate of continuity that Laplace's mechanical concept of the world is based. Since 1876, Maxwell had in fact acknowledged that the stability of systems—a concept we shall discuss later—could not be assumed a priori; in fact, in some systems singularities make it impossible to forecast a unique future development, for in the closeness of the singular points "influences whose magnitude is too small to be taken into account by a finite creature, can produce results of a relevant importance" [52, p. 443]. Maxwell thus challenged Laplace's concept, which will, however, continue to mold the language of physics and which, as we have seen, has been adopted by economists.

Only in the 1940s was the hypothesis of atomistic behavior, which allowed economists to apply the scheme of celestial mechanics to the economic system (by the theory of general equilibrium), challenged by the formulation and application to economics of the theory of games [102]. Edgeworth has already shown why the mechanical scheme cannot be used to explain market behavior in the case of oligopoly. The persistent identification of the scientific method with the method adopted in physics led Edgeworth to outline one possible consequence of the regime of monopolies and oligopolies: "Among those who would suffer by the new regime, there would be . . . the abstract economists, who would be deprived of their occupation, the investigation of the conditions which determine value. There would survive only the empirical school, flourishing in a chaos congenial to their mentality" [12, p. 130]. In spite of the new perspectives offered by the theory of games, models have generally been built according to the mechanistic concept of the economic system which has been made more flexible and less open to being invalidated by empirical data by a stochastic approach.

6. THE COGNITIVE PROCESS BY WHICH THE ECONOMIC SYSTEM IS ENVISAGED

According to Friedman [13, p. 15] "the relevant question to ask about the "assumptions" of a theory is not whether they are descriptively 'realistic,' for they never are, but whether they are sufficiently good approximations for the purpose in hand. And this question can be answered only by seeing whether the theory works, which means whether it yields sufficiently accurate predictions. The two supposedly independent tests thus reduce to one test." Assumptions do not fall from heaven: They are arrived at by a cognitive process that cannot escape critical evaluation. At the beginning of the process there is always a weltanschauung which can and must be reconsidered after the results of the scientific research. It was the positivist weltanschauung that caused the illusion that all cognitive processes could be resolved into scientific analysis. This illusion could not withstand the aporia of the abservational–theoretical distinction.[11] In fact, the two pillars that sustained the positivist weltanschauung, namely, the assumption that a definite logical system could be arrived at on which any other system could be based and the assumption that scientific development was resolvable into an accumulation of definitive results, have collapsed: The illusion that by the positivist approach we can get rid of any weltanschauung has thus become apparent. It is now clear that we cannot avoid uniting all the results of all cognitive processes into a systematic whole, as coherent as possible, which is always to some extent inherited and which cannot be resolved in a well-connected scientific theory. To admit that *pure* science does not exist does not mean to deny that it is impossible to define scientific criteria or to submit all ideological premises to critical assessment.

What we now need to emphasize is that all scientific theories entail some preliminary knowledge that can be qualified as *preanalytic*, since it cannot be previously confirmed by the application of scientific criteria: It has in fact some ideological content associated with a particular weltanschauung.

[11] As Quine [81, 42] suggests "It is nonsense, and the root of much nonsense, to speak of a linguistic component and a factual component in the truth of any individual statement. Taken collectively, science has its double dependence upon language and experience: but this duality is not significantly traceable into the statements of science taken one by one." See also Hempel [21] and Suppe [95].

Preanalytic knowledge is particularly relevant in economic analysis owing to the peculiar nature of the system economists propose to study. The underlying ideology may assume the form of *ideological prejudices:* This happens when it restricts the possibility of using the results of research to reconsider the preanalytic knowledge from which the research itself has started.

A few comments on the way the economic system is defined will clarify these general remarks.

The observation of social facts is justified on the grounds of certain weak hypotheses, formulated in conventional language, that allow us to envisage recurring and interconnected states of the social system and to describe them in terms of individuals, groups, and classes, of relationships between these elements, and of institutions in the wide sense of the word. Thus the description of the social systems entails some refining and restructuring of the common language.

Comte [9], who was the first to state the possibility of a *positive* study of the social system (by methods of course differing from those of the natural sciences), considered the social system something more than and different from the set of individuals that make it up. He thus anticipated the modern system approach, which we can find also in Spencer's analysis of the social system. Once the social system has been structured through the observation of social facts and with the help of the "understanding" of social-historical processes, we can proceed along two lines:

(1)   We can continue to consider the system an organic whole which we can envisage as having a sufficiently stable structure with respect to its essential goals, as can be inferred by comparing different societies. This is the sociological approach which can assume various forms according to

(a)   the importance attributed to the positive analysis of social actions considered *facts* (statistical uniformities or causal laws) compared with that ascribed to the search for the meaning of the action and function of the institution (teleological laws);

(b)   the cognitive value attributed to the comparison of different social systems;

(c)   the ways social changes are defined and the factors accounting for them are analyzed;

(d)   the relevance given to the conflicts internal to the system (this line of research has acquired particular importance in the structuralist approach);

(e)   the concept of man entailed by the concept of the economic system and thus the connections between the study of personality and that of social processes.

(2)   We can create a specific language that allows us to envisage sub-systems of the social system or specific *models* for the interpretation of it. It is by this approach that the fields and methods of other social sciences, those of economics in particular, are defined. For classical economists the economic system is a subsystem of the social system (according to Marx the subsystem that will eventually determine the evolution of the whole social system). Marginalists, on the contrary, consider *all* social phenomena the subject of economics, in as much as all these phenomena can be considered homogeneous from a specific standpoint; They all entail the use of scarce resources for the achievement of nonhomogeneous goals. (The field of economics is defined by a specific *model* for the analysis of social phenomena.) In fact, since not all social phenomena are considered by economists but only those in which the economic aspect is dominant, the set of phenomena analyzed by marginalists roughly coincides with the classical economic system: A difference remains in the way the system is considered.

Marginalists stress the metahistorical character of the economy, whose structure can be interpreted by a rational system that is universally valid. It then becomes harder to connect economics with sociology—apart from the different instruments used—as can be ascertained by comparing Pareto's [68] economic theory with his sociological theory [69].

We think it is better to conceive of a social system in a restricted sense, existing side by side with an economic system, both being inferred from the social system as a whole. This means that understanding of the social system is obtained through the study of both the economic system and the social system in the restricted sense (which we shall call the sociological system). The results of the two studies cannot be mechanically combined. They open the way to a dialectic cognitive process aimed at understanding the whole social system.

Envisaging the system in economics corresponds to *isolating* the system in physics. It is scientifically fruitful if it leads to a *new* description of the system, since it is required to produce the theory—thanks also to the creative imagination outlined by Hempel [20, p. 32]. The technical language by which the logical language (which makes possible formalization of the essential properties of the system) is interpreted can be definitely obtained. In speaking of the definition of the economic system we used the word "envisage" and not "find" or "single out" because the elements that de-termine the economic system cannot be considered real entities that can be directly perceived. Weber has warned us against the risk of hypostatizing the economic system. He viewed the social system as necessarily organic and functional, which makes the empirical knowledge *meaningful.*[12]

7. THE IDEOLOGICAL PREJUDICES (FALLACIES) OF THE NEOCLASSICAL DEFINITION OF THE ECONOMIC SYSTEM

There are significant differences between Weber's organic, functional view and that underlying the axioms on which classical and neoclassical economic theory is based. Marginal theory, compared with Weber's, [104] is essentially static, inasmuch as it assumes that the mechanisms that secure repetition of the relationships essential to the definition of the social system are taken as invariant in the historical process. Weber, on the contrary, is aware that the social system evolves, so that the features that are assumed as given in analyzing its functioning also change. The static marginalist concept is based on certain protopostulates that entail ideological prejudices (fallacies). Let us recall the fundamental ones:

(1) The essential function of any rational economic system is the most efficient use of resources for the satisfaction of individual needs which can logically be taken as preexisting the economic system. Rationality then appeared with the rise of the industrial system and the market economy. In fact, according to the marginal concept, for an economy to be rational it is sufficient that, through the market mechanism, it enables consumers to attain the highest level of satisfaction whatever the income distribution the system by its functioning may produce. Rationality does not entail any particular income distribution, nor is it regarded in its functional relations with the information process which in fact is determined to some extent by the economic system itself. The marginalist concept of rationality is certainly a very peculiar one. Were we to define rationality as the capability of a system

[12] In explaining the type of functional analysis that sociologists adopt, Weber argues that "for purposes of sociological analysis two things can be said. First this functional frame of reference is convenient for purposes of practical illustration and for provisional orientation. In these respects it is not only useful but indispensable. But at the same time if its cognitive value is overestimated and its concept illegitimately "reified," it can be highly dangerous. Secondly, in certain circumstances this is the only available way of determining just what processes of social action it is important to understand in order to explain a given phenomenon. But this is only the beginning of sociological analysis as here understood. In the case of social collectivities, precisely as distinguished from organisms, we are in a position to go beyond merely demonstrating functional relationships and uniformities. We can accomplish something which is never attainable in the natural sciences, namely, the subjective understanding of the action of the component individuals" [103, p. 102–103].

to ensure a stable life for all individuals, we would find that some tribal societies are more rational than capitalist economies.

(2) All constraints on the consumer must operate through one factor only: income. Therefore, once the structure of the system has become established, relaxing the constraints for one individual means tightening them for at least one other. We can easily see that this is a fallacy: There are a number of constraints that cannot be taken into the reckoning of available income. In fact, the consumer's level of satisfaction is also limited by his or her imperfect and uncertain knowledge. We cannot say that the information available to consumers and its degree of uncertainty are exogeneous data, for the process by which information is communicated to consumers is to a large extent internal to the system, since it depends on the functioning of the market mechanism.

(3) The market is a mechanism that reconciles the decisions of the purchasers with the decisions of the sellers: All goods and services are treated as commodities that can be brought and sold in the market. There are three ideological prejudices entailed by such a concept of the market mechanism. The first is the assumption that the market operates in such a way as to bring about an equilibrium between demand and supply and that it is capable of producing such a result in a sufficiently short interval of time (for specific problems entailed by the dynamic approach, see Meade [53]). The second and third can be seen in the assimilation of the capital and labor markets to the market for commodities.[13] Sraffa's [94] approach avoids the third prejudice by leaving the model open to any exogenous explanation of income distribution (an exogenous explanation being possible, and indeed required, because the economic system is conceived on the basis of mere technical relations). Sraffa's theory also throws some light on the second prejudice by pointing out some of the logical contradictions caused by assimilation of the capital market to the commodities market. Some partial theories (like the well-known Phillips curve) have provided an explanation of a few peculiarities of the labor market, yet the third prejudice has impeded the integration of these theories into the more general theory of economic equilibrium.

(4) In the economic system individuals are without power, as they are all equally controlled by the market. On the other hand, the state is considered almost all-powerful, being conditioned only by technical constraints (like those imposed by the budget). Indeed, the task of economic policy is to determine the constraints that the state ought to accept and the ways in

---

[13] Such an assimilation can be found also in Marx' theory of value [51]. Yet Marx has outlined some of the peculiar features of the labor market in his analysis of the dynamics of the capitalistic economy.

which it should use its power in order to attain the most efficient satisfaction of social needs and produce the most favorable feedback on the economic system. In fact, the distribution of power in a capitalist system is far more complex: It renders the conflict endemic and makes it hard to analyze the relationships between individuals' decisions and group behavior.

Because of these fallacies it has been possible for neoclassical economists, following the neopositivist approach, to conceive of the economic system as being able to remain invariant. It is opportune at this point—even if it means anticipating ideas that we shall develop later—to remember the reasons why the system can change: because of changes in its essential relations, brought about by interaction between the economic system and the sociological system; and because of structural crises that can occur since the economic system is not structurally stable and can induce new forms of interaction between the two systems. In the neopositivist approach the first cause of change is ignored because the interactions between the two systems are considered negligible or irrelevant (for economics). The second cause is denied because the system is assumed a priori to be structurally stable. The system is then considered *invariant* and generally also as continuous, having properties that make it possible to use differential calculus to describe it.[14] The system is *open* only in so far as some inputs (labor in particular) come from outside; some data and some relations (consumers' tastes and technologies) are also considered exogenous and subject to exogenous change. The organizing structure of the system is the minimum required to ensure efficient allocation of resources. If the system one day enters a crisis—as Schumpeter thinks possible—it would mean the end of rationality. Peculiar in this respect is the position of Pareto [69], who thinks that the economic process diverges from a course characterized by conditions of maximum efficiency, since in their concrete actions individuals do not abide by the efficiency criterion. To explain the concrete processes we need to develop a line of sociological research aimed at analyzing the motivations and effects of *nonlogical actions*. Marginal economics will then be resolved into pure praxeology, as has been admitted by von Mises [100]. As we have seen, the neopositivist approach has made possible the twofold development of economics as a normative and a descriptive science: Bridging the gap between empirical research and theoretical analysis is becoming more and more difficult.

---

[14] In the modern formalization of the general equilibrium theory the application of topological theorems has made it possible to drop the differentiability assumption; the continuity assumption is still necessary to prove the existence of equilibrium. See Arrow and Hahn [4].

8.   HOW CAN WE ASSESS PREANALYTIC KNOWLEDGE?

As we have seen, the importance that preanalytic knowledge assumes in the construction of economic theory is such that it cannot be ignored. The problem we have to face is twofold. The first part of the problem concerns the validity of the preanalytic knowledge used to formulate the scientific theory in question, and the second part concerns the validity of such knowledge *per se*. To deal with the second part we must critically reconstruct the complex interaction between the production of weltanschauung and the development of scientific theories: We shall mention this problem in Section 22. Here we give some consideration to the first part so that we may better understand certain peculiarities of scientific method in economics and assess the similarities and the divergences among various economic theories. To clarify the nature of the first part of the problem let us suppose that we can define in some way the set of all observable social facts. Actually, as we have seen, there is no observation that does not presuppose to some extent theoretical knowledge more or less consciously elaborated, just as there is no theoretical knowledge that is not directly or indirectly connected with empirical observation.

When we build a theory, we isolate from the set of all facts that can be observed in the time interval $t_0 t (P_{tot})$ the subset F_{tot} that we think can be related to the system S_F with which we can associate the theory $T_{S_F^*}[A_P \rightarrow R]$ that (based on the primitive terms P and on the axioms A) produces a set of relations R by which we can interpret the system $S_F^* \supseteq S_F$. When $S_F^* = S_F$, we can say that the theory is merely descriptive.

The system S_F has been envisaged through the technical language available. Construction of the theory entails reformulation of the language that can interpret the logical language by which the structure of the system is analyzed. Once the definition of the subset F_{tot} and the formulation of the languages have been adjusted, we can represent the process by which the theory has been produced by the scheme

$$(1) \qquad P_{tot} \supseteq F_{tot} \leftrightarrow S_F \leftarrow T_{S_F^*}[A_P \rightarrow R].$$

The theory is considered valid as long as another theory $T_{S_F^*}'[A_P' \rightarrow R']$ is not produced that describes the system S_F^* more efficiently (i.e., with a smaller number of primitive terms and axioms or more primitive terms and axioms in common with other theories) or can explain a system $S_F^{**} \supset S_F^*$.

Let us now assume that some time has elapsed so that we are at t' ($t' > t$), and let us draw the subset $F_{tot'}'$ from the set of all facts that can be observed in the interval $t_0 t'$ with criteria similar to those applied in obtaining the subset F_{tot} and by using the technical language associated with the theory

$T_{S_F^*}$. Let $S'_{F'}$ be the system associated with $F'_{tot'}$ being $S'_{F'} \not\subset S_F^*$. Four cases can then arise:

(1) It is possible to define a transformation from the system S_F to the system $S'_{F'}$ and to build a theory that can explain both S_F and $S'_{F'}$ as well as the transition from the former to the latter: $T_{S^{\perp}_{F'}}^{\perp}[A_P^{\perp} \to R^{\perp}]; S_{F'}^{\perp} \supseteq S'_{F'}; S_{F'}^{\perp} \supseteq S_F^* \supseteq S_F$; and $S_{F'}^{\perp} \supseteq S_F \to S'_{F'}$.

We shall then say that S_F is historically unstable and that the theory $T_{S_F^*}$ can explain the system S_F but not its evolution and transformation into the system $S'_{F'}$. The limited cognitive value of the theory may be due to pre-analytic knowledge or to the methods applied in building it. It is possible that at time t other preanalytic knowledge not used in constructing the theory $T_{S_F^*}$, which has indeed produced theorems in contrast with it, has helped to visualize the crisis and the possible transformations of the system S_F outside of and in spite of the theory $T_{S_F^*}$. Such a situation can be detected in Marxist thought. The argument by which Marx [50] envisages the crisis of the capitalist system cannot be integrated into the theory of value by which the genetic and structural characteristics of the early capitalist system are explained.

(2) It is impossible to define and explain the transformation from S_F to $S'_{F'}$ within the new theory $T_{S^{\perp}_{F'}}^{\perp}[A_P^{\perp} \to R^{\perp}]$ by which we can explain the system $S_{F'}^{\perp} \supset S'_{F'}$. Yet by the new theory it is possible to explain S_F as well as S'_F, since $S_{F'}^{\perp} \supseteq S'_{F'}. S_{F'}^{\perp} \supseteq S_F$.

Let us assume that the new theory is semantically akin to the old one. Then we can define the set R^0 of the relations contained in $T_{S_{F'}^{\perp}}^{\perp}$ and not in $T_{S_F^*}$,

(2) $R^0 \equiv R^{\perp} - R^{\perp} \cap R,$

as the *cognitive shortcomings of the theory* $T_{S_F^*}$ as revealed at *time* t'.

Let us now consider the set R^e of the relations included in theory $T_{S_F^*}$ and not in theory $T_{S_{F'}^{\perp}}^{\perp}$ (namely, relations that were considered necessary to explain the system at time t and that are no longer required after production of the new theory):

(3) $R^e \equiv R - R \cap R^{\perp}.$

We can call R^e the *set of redundances and misunderstandings* of the theory $T_{S_F^*}$ as revealed *at time* t'.

(3) Both the first and the second cases are excluded, since the new theory is not semantically akin to the old one. Yet internal development of the old theory $T_{S_F^*}: T_{S_F^*} \to T'_{S_F^*}$ did occur such that it is possible to associate with $S'_{F'}$, suitably reinterpreted, the theory that has been attained semantically akin to $T_{S_F^*}$ or that can explain the transition from S_F to $S'_{F'}$. Then it is possible to evaluate the internal progress of the theory and single out the shortcomings

as well as the redundancies and the misunderstandings of the theory in its primitive formulation.

(4)   Even the third case is excluded. The two theories $T_{S_F^*}$ and $T_{S_F^\perp}$ are not comparable.

From these considerations it appears that to assess preanalytic knowledge that has been used to build the theory at time t we have to wait for observations that can be made on the behavior of the social system at a successive point in time t'. In a certain sense this is true. Therefore any theory involves a certain gnoseological risk.[15] Yet critical evaluation of preanalytic knowledge can be carried out without the acquisition of new observations. *Thought experiments* may make possible critical evaluation of preanalytic knowledge through critical assessment of the theory. Two final remarks should be made:

(a)   In the process of constructing a scientific theory we cannot eliminate all preanalytic knowledge: At least some of it is necessary to single out the system we propose to analyze.

(b)   The preliminary configuration of the system required to produce the theory entails some limitation of the cognitive value of the theory. The theory indeed cannot explain the changes that alter such a preliminary configuration of the system. This remark is particularly relevant to economics for the reasons already outlined in Section 5.

9.   SOME FUNDAMENTAL PROPERTIES OF THE ECONOMIC AND THE SOCIAL SYSTEMS

It is difficult to establish any logical connection between the concepts of the social system upon which sociological theories hinge and the definitions of the economic system accepted by economists (see, e.g., Parsons [70]).

---

[15] Such a risk becomes apparent if we consider the noncumulative character of the cognitive process. We often speak of revolution in scientific fields. In the natural science most revolutions have later proved to be appropriate generalizations of the theories they superseded. In other cases (the quantum theory versus the relativity theory), in spite of the epistemological problems raised, the revolutionary theory coexists with the previous theory. When we consider the development of physics, we are inclined to share Lakatos' [37] view that competing research programs ensure the continuous growth of scientific knowledge. The development of economics characterized by disguised revolutions and by revolutions that eventually appear not to have been such makes both Lakatos's [37] and Kuhn's [35] theories unsatisfactory. Further, in referring to economics, we cannot consider an essential feature of a mature theory its capacity to anticipate novel facts in the sense in which this can be said to occur in the natural sciences. If this criterion should be accepted contrary to what Lakatos seems to believe [37, p. 88], not only Marxism but all economic science cannot be qualified as mature science.

Sociological and economic theories look compatible if, having defined a global social system U_F we can, through congruous (reducing) transformations $\mathcal{T}_S$ and $\mathcal{T}_Z$, derive the economic (S_F) and the social (Z_F) systems (in a strict sense) from the global social system:

$$(4) \qquad\qquad S_F = \mathcal{T}_S(U_F),$$

$$(5) \qquad\qquad Z_F = \mathcal{T}_Z(U_F).$$

(It is, of course, impossible to derive the global social system in a mechanical way from the two specific system S_F and Z_F.)

To clarify some fundamental notions, let us assume that the social system can be interpreted by a set of relations between two sets of variables $x = [x_1, x_2, \ldots, x_m]$ and $y = [y_1, y_2, \ldots, y_n]$:

$$(6) \qquad\qquad y = u(x).$$

Let us now assume that m among the $n + m$ variables can be considered exogeneous. We are then left with a system (of as many equations as unknowns) by which the social system is isolated from the world in which it is conceived (one of the exogenous variables may, for instance, be the natural growth of the population if it can be considered independent of social processes). The isolated social system, considered in its synchronic structure (static system) may be:

Harmonious, if it has a finite number of solutions;
Indeterminate, if it has an infinite variety of solutions;
Contradictory, if it does not admit any solution.

As Vercelli [98] has reminded us, if we assume that the variables are functions of time, a contradictory system may become a harmonious system. Indeed, when we analyze a dynamic system, we must distinguish four cases:

(a) The system has a unique continuous solution: Then the possible contradictions of the associated static system are internal to the economic system which can be termed *dynamically determinate*.
(b) The dynamic system admits more than one solution: Then we can call it *dynamically indeterminate*.
(c) The dynamic system has bifurcation points: Then we can call it *structurally indeterminate* (see Section 18).
(d) The dynamic system is *contradictory*.

The last possibility is almost unknown in physics: In fact, should such a case occur, what it would reveal would be the inadequacy of the mathemati-

cal model in interpreting the associated real system; the reasons for such
inadequacy could then be easily detected. In the social sciences the peculiar
problems involved in the definition of the social system make case (d) far
from unusual; more likely, it is quite possible that we are unable to express
the law of motion (of change) of a social system in terms of a coherent
dynamic system.

Let us assume that there is an easy way of deriving, from the global social
system, the economic and sociological systems, each being defined by a subset of the x and y variables. Let the economic system be defined on the basis
of the variables $y_{(1)}$ and $x_{(1)}$ and the sociological system on the basis of the
variables $y_{(2)}$ and $x_{(2)}$:

$$(7) \qquad y = [y_{(1)}, y_{(2)}], \qquad x = [x_{(1)}, x_{(2)}]$$

(for simplicity we have assumed that the subsets are disjoint).

Let $y_{(\bar{2})}$, $x_{(\bar{2})}$ be the sociological variables that enter as exogenous variables
into the relations defining the economic system, and $y_{(\bar{1})}$, $x_{(\bar{1})}$ the economic
variables that enter as exogenous variables into the relations defining the
sociological system. Then we can write

$$(8) \qquad y_{(1)} = u_1(x_{(1)}, y_{(\bar{2})}, x_{(\bar{2})}),$$

$$(9) \qquad y_{(2)} = u_2(x_{(2)}, y_{(\bar{1})}, x_{(\bar{1})}).$$

From a harmonious social system we can derive a contradictory economic
system. The opposite is also possible, as it is possible that both system are
harmonious (or contradictory). It is more interesting to analyze the properties of a dynamic economic system derived from a dynamically determined
social system.

If the dynamic economic system is dynamically or structurally indeterminate, it means that the development of the economic system cannot be
visualized on the basis of mere knowledge of the economic system (we can
qualify these cases as Weberian cases).

Let us now revert to the case of a dynamically or structurally indeterminate
social system. Then there are two cases that need to be outlined: the case
in which the economic system is also dynamically or structurally indeterminate (we can describe such cases as Marxian) and the case in which the
economic system is dynamically determinate (it was this case that Schumpeter
[89] had in mind).

Worthy of comment are some noticeable properties of the social and
economic systems that, for the sake of simplicity, we shall write as

$$(10) \qquad y(t) = u[x(t)].$$

Two cases (each having two subcases) can be distinguished:

(1)   The m exogenous variables are constant in time:

(i)   As time tends to infinity the dynamic system tends toward the solution of the static system: $y = u(x)$; then we can say that the system moves toward a harmonious state.

(ii)   The system does not admit of any stationary equilibrium (the harmonious state); then we can say that the system is inherently dynamic.

(2)   The m exogeneous variables change in time according to a known law:

(i)   The system tends toward an equilibrium path of development (we shall clarify this notion in Section 12); then we can say that the exogenously induced dynamic state prevails.

(ii)   The system does not tend toward any equilibrium path; then we can say that the dynamic behavior of the system is determined by internal factors.

10.   CONNECTIONS BETWEEN THE SOCIAL AND ECONOMIC SYSTEMS

Let us now ask a fundamental question under the simplifying assumptions accepted in the previous section, namely, When are we entitled to disregard the complex relations of the global social system and to concern ourselves only with the economic system? The two systems are linked in various ways: by common inputs and by relationships of a cybernetic character. There is indeed one limiting case in which we can define the economic system as a completely autonomous system. If we assume that the relations of Eq. (10) are linear, the extreme case is obtained when the matrix of the system, which we shall indicate by U, can be written as a diagonal matrix or submatrix:

$$(11) \qquad\qquad U = \begin{bmatrix} U_1 & 0 \\ 0 & U_2 \end{bmatrix},$$

where U_1 represents the set of the economic relations and U_2 that of the social relations. In such case the systems are independent of each other (isolated). In such case—and indeed only in such an unrealistic case— the economic system can be studied apart from the social system. For Eqs. (8) and (9) can be written

$$(12) \qquad\qquad y^1 = U_1 x^1,$$

$$(13) \qquad\qquad y^2 = U_2 x^2,$$

where

$$(14) \qquad\qquad x = [x^1, x^2] \quad \text{and} \quad y = [y^1, y^2].$$

The hypothesis that the matrix of the social system is completely decomposable (and therefore that the economic system can be singled out as a subsystem of the social system isolated from the sociological system) is not acceptable. But the weaker hypothesis that the matrix U is *nearly decomposable* in the sense of Simon and Ando [92] can be accepted. What we assume is that the matrix U can be expressed in terms of an indecomposable matrix U^*, altered by adding the terms of an arbitrary matrix P of the same dimensions as U, multiplied by a very small real number ε:

$$(15) \qquad\qquad U = U^* + \varepsilon P.$$

More precisely, ε must be sufficiently small so that, for any root λ_i^* of the matrix U^* there exists a root λ_i of U such that

$$(16) \qquad\qquad |\lambda_i - \lambda_i^*| < \delta,$$

where δ is sufficiently smaller than δ^* defined by

$$(17) \qquad\qquad \min_{\substack{i,j \\ i \neq j}} |\lambda_i^* - \lambda_j^*| = \delta^*$$

(see the article by Simon and Ando [92, p. 116]).

Thus there is no confusion as to which root of U corresponds to any particular root of U^*.

Let

$$(18) \qquad\qquad y^{*1} = U_1 x^{*1},$$

$$(19) \qquad\qquad y^{*2} = U_2 x^{*2},$$

where

$$(20) \qquad x^* = [x^{*1}, x^{*2}] \quad \text{and} \quad y^* = [y^{*1}, y^{*2}].$$

For the nearly decomposable system we are examining we can then show that:

(a) In the short run the behaviors of y^1 and y^2 are very close to the behaviors of y^{*1} and y^{*2}, the time paths of y^1 being dominated by roots of U^{*1}; the behavior of y^1 is independent of y^2. All this means that in explaining the short-run processes, we can confine ourselves to study of the economic system.

(b) As time goes on, the interactions between the two systems affect the behavior of each of them. For each system the largest root will dominate all others; the behavior of the social system as a whole will depend on the behavior of both the economic system and the sociological system and will influence both systems.

11. EQUILIBRIUM MODEL AND ECONOMIC THEORY

Both the classical and the neoclassical conceptions of the economic system envisage a harmonious state that is eventually reached through a dynamic process (the Ricardo–Mill stationary state) or induced by a market mechanism (the Smith–Marshall system of natural or normal prices and the Walras–Pareto general equilibrium). Therefore economic analysis hinges on the notion of equilibrium.[16]

The first equilibrium model has been proposed by Quesnay [80], while the notion of equilibrium prices can be traced back to classical economics. In classical economics (Ricardo and Mill [82], in particular) an important role is played by the notion of *stationary equilibrium*: The economic process will eventually reach a state in which the structure of the economy will remain unchanged. The notion of equilibrium plays a different role in the neoclassical analysis: The purpose of equilibrium models is to envisage a normal structure of the economy that can be reached at any time and maintained forever, provided no changes occur in the exogenous data. Two approaches have been developed: the Marshallian *partial equilibria* approach and the Walras–Pareto *general equilibrium theory*. The partial equilibria approach aims to deal with a rather large set of economic processes that take various intervals of time to be completed, by distinguishing the short-period equilibrium from the long-period equilibrium. The cognitive values of these models are limited by the assumption that during the process of adjustment no change in any magnitude or parameter will occur except in variables defining the economic process being dealt with.

In fact, because of the *ceteris paribus* assumption, all statements in the Marshallian theory are *counterfactual statements*. Equilibrium theory is always a hypothetical description of the economy. Equilibrium is thus always *partial* even if we consider a multiple market economy, inasmuch as we have to assume that a set of factors accounting for the economic process will not operate (see, e.g., Morishima [58]).

In the Walras–Pareto theory, equilibrium model aims at envisaging a normal state of the whole economy that—because of the ideological prejudices recalled in Section 7—Pareto [68] was able to prove to coincide with one structure of the infinite variety of rational structures (Pareto optima) (see Koopmans [32]).

There have been two generalizations of the Walras–Pareto model:

(a)   The first, formalized by Hicks [22], visualizes the dynamic process as a succession of static equilibria, each being reached within a single period

---

[16] There are a few exceptions. See for instance Schumpeter [88], Myrdal [64], Lundberg [43], Hirshman [26], and Kornai [34].

also on the basis of expectations about the future development of the economy. If all the expectations are realized, then we can speak, after Hicks, of *intertemporal equilibrium* (unfortunately such an hypothesis is completely unrealistic when prices change and the system does not grow at a uniform and constant rate).[17]

(b)   The second, formalized by Malinvaud [46] (in some respect anticipated by Hayek [19]), defines equilibrium for a number of successive periods as the result of a set of simultaneously compatible plans, each being drawn for the entire succession of periods.

Equilibrium period analysis does not provide an explanation of the time development of the economy: "The static equilibrium entirely based upon current parameters"—as Hicks reminds us—"is, in strictness, irrelevant to the dynamic process" [24, p. 23] (see also Robinson [85]).

For equilibrium period analysis to be logically meaningful the equilibrium must be stable. To envisage the stability of an equilibrium a disequilibrium period analysis has to be applied. Then a question arises, similar to one that had to be tackled in nonequilibrium thermodynamics: How can we reconcile the relations that presuppose disequilibria with those based on the assumption of equilibrium? In fact, individual behavior is interpreted by two sets of relations: those expressing reactions to disequilibria and those expressing optimizing behavior. In thermodynamics this difficulty is overcome by considering systems indefinitely near equilibrium; in economics it has not received the attention it deserves.

To enable period analysis to explain the development of the economy, members of the Stockholm school [40, 64, 67] have proposed a disequilibrium method. *Ex post* variables may diverge from *ex ante*; divergences, causing reactions which by this method help to explain the system's inherent dynamics.

The greater flexibility of the disequilibrium approach makes it more suitable for *describing* actual processes. Yet the cognitive value of disequilibrium models, partly because of their mechanical formulation, remains doubtful. On the other hand, the models *à la* Malivaud are planning models that cannot be used to describe actual processes of development.

We can then say that, in spite of the above-mentioned generalizations, the marginalist approach to general equilibrium is unable to provide an explanation of the system's dynamics.

---

[17] In order to make the model capable of interpreting the real processes, the disequilibrium method has been adopted in period analysis; see Lindhal [40] and Lundberg [43]. The greater flexibility of the method makes it more suitable for describing the process but less capable of providing a clear-cut explanation of it.

There are two main factors accounting for economic development: entrepreneurial activity and accumulation. They cannot be adequately analyzed
within the marginalist theory of general equilibrium. Accumulation is indeed
considered a subproduct of consumers' and firms' decisions taken at a
given moment in time on the basis of expectations held at that time. How the
economic system can ensure that accumulation will be forthcoming according to the growth potential of the economy (and if not, what are the consequences) is not explained. Entrepreneurial activity is considered to be
exogenously given in spite of the arguments–later resumed by Schumpeter
—by which Marx proved that such activity interacts with the process of
economic development.

Only in the 1930s, with the contribution of von Neumann [101] was a
different meaning given to the notion of equilibrium: The equilibrium model
aims at envisaging not the structure of the economy at a given moment in
time but a *law of motion* of the economic system.[18] Equilibrium can exist at
any given moment in time only if it has always existed: Then it will go on
forever. Such a dynamic version of *equilibrium* can clarify some of the
structural properties of a growing system. Yet no explanation is offered of
the factors accounting for growth (see also Leontief [39] and Morishima
[60, 61]).

It is easy to prove that only a subset of the set of static equilibria is compatible with a dynamic equilibrium: precisely those static equilibria whose
initial and final conditions have some structural features in common.[19] We
must not be misled by the compatibility that under certain conditions
can be established between static and dynamic equilibria. The static equilibrium model aims at solving the problem of the efficient allocation
of given resources at a given moment in time; it cannot state the
conditions for equilibrium growth. The dynamic equilibrium model
states a law of motion for which we cannot establish an initial or final
moment.

The equilibrium models exclude a priori a set of possible laws of development of the system. In particular, it is denied a priori that

(a)   The economic system can be interpreted by means of "explosive
models," the fluctuations being forced into a "serpent" defined by the ceilings
and floors that constitute the structural characteristics of the system not
inglobable in the model (see Hicks [23]).

---

[18] For accumulation to be determined by an endogenous mechanism, special conditions are
required (see, e.g., Marx [50]): They have failed in modern capitalist economies. It is for this
reason that in such economies accumulation is to some extent *forced accumulation* induced by
political decisions.
[19] See Lombardini and Nicola [41].

(b)   The economic system, being tendentially explosive, will eventually undergo structural changes. It might be that, when some variables attain certain critical values or some parameters take on critical values, reactions occur that cause structural changes in the economic system. Such a possibility, which is disregarded in *positive economics*, when models are built to interpret the functioning of the system, is considered when problems of economic policy are posed. In fact, as is well known, one of the fundamental questions to be answered in the analysis of problems of economic policy concerns when a given economic policy must be reversed. The inability of the positive models to explain such discontinuities has created an *epistemological discontinuity*; as we shall see in Section 15, normative models cannot be resolved into *positive* models.

The ideological prejudices we mentioned in Section 7 are reflected in the way the equilibrium of the system is conceived in both the static and the dynamic models.

If we drop the prejudices mentioned in point 3 of Section 7, we can easily realize that the equilibrium mechanism of a capitalistic system is twofold. One equilibrium mechanism operates at the level of the system as a whole and guarantees that the distribution of incomes (wage dynamics in particular) is in harmony with the system's growth potential. As it is this mechanism that guarantees the preservation of certain properties of the system needed for survival of the capitalist system, it is preferable to speak of a *homeostatic mechanism*. The other equilibrium mechanism is that which operates in the commodities markets, in the various modalities theorized by neoclassical economists [49, 103]. The special role of money in a capitalist system does not permit the homeostatic mechanism to be resolved in the market equilibrium mechanism as pretended by the theory of general equilibrium (Walras' law). The models of general equilibrium are in fact inherently incapable of explaining the role of money (see Myrdal [62]).

12.   THE NORMAL STRUCTURE AND THE LAW OF MOTION OF THE ECONOMY

In the static equilibrium model there are as many equilibria (or sets of equilibria) as there are sets of initial conditions. In fact, what the model proposes to determine is the allocation of resources that is best for the given initial conditions. We then analyze how the equilibrium is changed when some of the parameters expressing initial conditions are changed (comparative statics). No analysis of this kind is logically possible when one deals with the dynamic version of general equilibrium.

The model of dynamic equilibrium indeed cannot tell us what will happen when some parameters characterizing the structure of the system are changed. What the model can tell us is what path of development would have occurred if the new values of the parameters had been realized in all past periods. Thus dynamic equilibrium models can only be used to compare the structure of an economy growing along an equilibrium path with that of another economy characterized by different values of the parameters (see Robinson [84]). It is then logically impossible to use the model of dynamic equilibrium to define and to measure the marginal productivity of capital (see Robinson [84]). The notion of the marginal productivity of capital can be rigorously defined only in a planning model such as the Malinvaud model. The notion can then be applied in analyzing the results of the variants in the plan.

Of the dynamic equilibria, those characterized by a constant and uniform rate growth have received special attention from economists. It is in this case that (a) we can easily state the conditions under which we can associate with a static equilibrium an equilibrium path of development of the system (see Lombardini and Nicola [41]); (b) the Marxian transformation problem can be solved, the conditions stated by Marx being granted (Morishima [59]): and (c) the expectation problem is easily solved (future development being rigorously determined by past development). Unfortunately the constant and uniform rate-of-growth equilibrium models are incapable of interpreting the process of development even under the ideal conditions that have to be assumed in building a theory because of (a) the existence of scarce resources, (b) technical innovations, and (c) the structural changes in final demand necessarily associated with an increase in income (see Pasinetti [71], Cozzi [10], Quadrio Curzio [79]). When these features of the system are taken into account, the role of expectations becomes of paramount importance.

13. EFFICIENCY AND EQUILIBRIUM

In spite of their intrinsic inability to describe the process of development of the system, equilibrium models are still considered by most economists as necessary in visualizing a normal state and a normal path of development of the economy: Should the economy be driven away from this state or path, a political decision is urged or some event is expected that may restore equilibrium and thereby make possible the full and rational utilization of resources. The equilibrium model is thus regarded as neither a planning model nor a descriptive model. It may be described as a *reference* model which helps us to visualize some fundamental economic problems that *have to be solved*. The latest contribution by Pasinetti [72] is in this sense. No doubt every system tends to perpetuate itself, and this tendency contributes to the efficiency of the system inasmuch as it entails preservation of efficient solutions of the problems faced in the past. The usefulness of the Pasinetti approach, which has the merit of freeing equilibrium analysis from most of the ideological prejudices discussed in Section 7, cannot be disputed. Yet equilibrium analysis must be considered only partial and preliminary, for the efficiency of the system results both from the tendency toward equilibrium and from certain disequilibrating processes, for instance, innovations. Moreover, some disequilibrating processes cause changes in the goals pursued by individuals or by society, which may make it either more difficult or easier for the system to reach equilibrium and thus to preserve efficiency. This is also the reason why actual efficiency can be effected in a positive way by disequilibrating processes, as was well known to Schumpeter [88] (see also Kornai [34] and Simon [91]).

A more radical consideration is put forward at this point. Only when the economy grows at a constant rate, because population or per capita consumption increases while individual and social preferences remain constant with time, does efficiency have a clear meaning. When the system does not grow at a constant rate and individual or social preferences change—partly because of the interactions between means provision and goals formation (see Preti [76, pp. 228-229])—a technical definition of efficiency in the economic sense becomes impossible.

The socially-minded neopostivist conception of the economic system makes it possible to use *models* hinging on the notion of equilibrium for comparison between economic and social systems that differ from one another because of different institutions and organizations (see Vinci [99], Koopmans and Montias [33], Holesovsky [27], and Montias [55]). This application too cannot be qualified as either descriptive or normative.

14. AGGREGATION IN ECONOMIC MODELS

All variables entering into any economic model are aggregated variables (i.e., each of them corresponds to a *set* of observations). The process of aggregation must be further pursued when we move on to macroeconomics (i.e., when the economic variables refer to the entire economy). We shall pass over the particular problems to be faced in determining the empirical observations that must be related to the theoretical variables and limit ourselves to some remarks on the logical process of aggregation.

In the Walras model of general equilibrium economic activities and goods are classified in *industries* and *commodities*; such an aggregation process raises some logical and methodological problems (see Robinson

[83], and Becattini [5]). Consumers' and firms' decisions are aggregated over intervals of time of predetermined length. Demand and supply functions for single commodities can thus be defined. The problem then arises as to whether we can assign to the aggregated variables properties found in the individuals' variables that result from an optimization procedure. In the case of consumers' demands and supplies the problem has been analyzed by Wold and Jureen [105]. In the case of firms we must assume competition and free entry, whereupon the assumption that firms are all alike in their structure and in their decisions looks reasonable (in a theoretical context that leaves no room for the analysis of innovation). More realistically, Marshall refers the average (aggregated) values to a representative firm.

What we wish to underline is the ideological character of some assumptions that are more-or-less consciously made when we face problems of aggregation. In the aggregation required in the model for general equilibrium of the Walras type the interference of ideology is noted in particular in the field of the demand function. The aggregation of consumers' decisions cannot be justified by a procedure such as that proposed by Simon and Ando and applied by us to state the conditions under which the economic system can be isolated from the social system. In fact, interactions between consumers' preferences and decisions are relevant in determining both the short- and long-run behavior of the markets. It is only for ideological reasons that such interactions are usually disregarded in the demand analysis by assuming that consumers' preferences are given and are independent of one another.

The interference of ideology is even more evident—and more pregnant of consequences—in the aggregations required to build macroeconomic models; this is particularly true when we want to define *capital* as an aggregate variable. Capital can be defined in three ways: as a set of capital goods, as a monetary measure of the capitalist's power (to which profits are referred), and as the monetary value of capital goods. Only if the economy grows along an equilibrium path at a constant and uniform rate does no contradiction arise among these definitions of capital. The monetary value of the capital goods, all fully employed, is computed at equilibrium prices and corresponds to the capitalist's capital. When we leave such an equilibrium path, only the increments in the capitalist's capital correspond to monetary values at the market prices of capital goods: precisely of capital goods purchased to implement investment programs. The contradictions that arise among the various definitions of capital reflect real contradictions in a capitalist economy entailing its inability to ensure stable and efficient growth.

One of the merits of Sraffa and his school has been their demonstration of the logical inconsistency entailed in any attempt to define total capital (in monetary terms) in marginalist schemes.

15. NORMATIVE MODELS IN ECONOMICS

The marginalist equilibrium models, as we have seen, have a twofold meaning: They represent the *normal* state of the economy induced by the competitive mechanism and the rational structure of the system, the rationality concept being constrained by the ideological prejudices mentioned in Section 7. We can thus have two versions of the equilibrium theory, the first being descriptive and the second normative. The reasons why the equilibrium model cannot be used to describe and explain actual processes have been pointed out in previous sections. Let us now discuss the role of normative models in economics.

A normative model differs from a descriptive model of the same set of economic processes inasmuch as it is intended to determine the value of certain variables (*controllable variables*) and the ways certain structural changes (*controlled structural changes*) can be performed. Both the variables and the structural changes are dealt with in the descriptive models as being exogeneously given. In the neopositivist approach the criterion applied in assessing the validity of a model is essentially the same whether it is a normative or a descriptive model; the validity of a normative model depends on the predictive value of the descriptive models it entails. Such an approach is indeed incapable of clarifying the relation between descriptive and normative models, since it raises the problems of causal explanation versus teleological explanation. A comparison between the use of models in solving practical problems in natural science and in economics may help to clarify the issue. In natural science models are also used to control certain processes. But this is possible by virtue of—and only by virtue of—the predictive value of the model. In economics normative analysis cannot be reduced to descriptive analysis. In fact, normative analysis entails a practical syllogism in the sense clarified by Anscombe [1]. All theorems of normative economics can be framed eventually as a syllogism of this kind:

Society pursues the goals *P* (it wants to obtain the result *P*) in the most efficient way.

It believes that in order to attain goals *P* (or to obtain the result *P*) action *A* is required.

Society is ready to implement action *A*.

Such a scheme requires, first, that *social action* can be defined as a well-determined set of social events that can be singled out in the social process. Epistemological problems then arise, which we need not discuss here. For practical purposes we can agree on what a social action is under given circumstances. It is sufficient to visualize a set of possible events that can materialize alternatively to other sets as a consequence of well-defined political decisions. Social action can thus be regarded as being the result of a *social choice*. It is of course a constrained choice, and economists do not always consider all the constraints. The abstraction involved in all theorizing leads to the neglect of some constraints (chiefly sociological and political constraints) that are particularly relevant when one wants to visualize the concrete alternatives and make valid suggestions to political operators.

Here we are not concerned with the applicability of the normative models (and therefore with the relationship between *welfare economics* and *economic policy*): We are interested in logical problems. What economists cannot validate are the major premise of the syllogism; they can only provide the minor premise. Society's goals are assumed by the economist to be given, in fact, the economist has to *simulate* them.

As we shall see, to speak of society's goals is rather problematic. Even more disputable is to state that society wants to attain these goals in the most efficient way and is capable of doing so.

Let us for the moment assume that the major premise of the syllogism is meaningful according to some criterion we do not now need to define. If the minor premise supplied by the economist is correct, the conclusion will follow. Can we say that it is empirically meaningful? We could answer this question if we could collect a set of observations for testing the validity of the practical syllogism by associating it with a scientific law: Society's decision to attain goals P leads to the effect E_A which is produced by action A under the hypothesis that the economic system can be described by the model T_E. In order that we may associate the practical syllogism with such a scientific law certain conditions must be fulfilled:

(a)   That the term "society" can refer to a concrete entity. Political decisions are in fact the results of complex processes that cannot be resolved by the choice made by a well-defined operator, even at the abstract level on which the matter is discussed. By means of the practical syllogism we can only envisage an abstract possibility of rational behavior and state some necessary conditions required for such a behavior to materialize (see, e.g. Morgenstern [56]). The economist's analysis may have some practical relevance, especially when it leads to a negative indication (the impossibility of obtaining certain results through certain procedures).

(b)   That the statement, "Society is ready to implement action A," implies "Society implements action A." Such a factual implication is questionable, apart from the difficulties mentioned under (a), for various reasons. First, even if we can consider society a well-defined operator, we cannot ignore the fact that the manifestation of intentions (the pointing out of goals), the willingness to act, and the carrying out of the action are separated in time. Intentions, as well as the conditions that justify an action, change with the passing of time. Second, we must note that operators willing to implement action may be hindered by many factors that economists cannot analyze. For all these reasons some economists (see Morgenstern [57, p. 50]) are convinced that economic policy is not a scientific discipline.

There is another important reason that makes it difficult to validate the practical syllogism. Let us suppose that, having assumed that society pursues goals P, we observe that effects E_A are obtained. Can we say on the basis of this observation that the practical syllogism is confirmed? I do not think that we can answer this question in the affirmative. We must in fact distinguish among four cases:

(a)   The goals at which society is actually aiming are coherent and actions are consciously implemented to attain these goals. In such a case, and only in such a case, the problem of empirical validation of the practical syllogism can be resolved into the problem of empirical verification of a scientific law, apart from the difficulties and ambiguities we have already mentioned.

(b)   Society's goals are not coherent. The action that is carried out, which we assume to be that indicated by the economist, is not consciously implemented in order to achieve the goals P. Empirical verification of the effects of action does not lead to validation of the practical syllogism.

(c)   The goals are coherent, but the action carried out does not coincide with the optimal action suggested by the economist. Then we cannot make any empirical verification; nor can we validate the practical syllogism.

(d)   The goals are not coherent, and the action carried out does not coincide with that suggested by the economist (the optimal action). In such a case the practical syllogism is practically irrelevant.

A final remark: Only for neopositivist economists is the problem of empirical verification of normative statements relevant (see e.g., Marschak [48]). For economists who are open to Weber's influence, normative statements can never be empirically confirmed. "To form the idea of economy," wrote Knight [31, p. 163], "or economizing, one must first know that the end of an action is in general more or less different from its empirical result. Economy involves an intention or intended result, which is not amenable to observation in any admissible use of that term." (See also Myrdal [63].)

16.   INDIVIDUAL AND SOCIAL CHOICES

In the field of normative economics the problem that has attracted the greatest attention concerns the relationship between goals pursued by individuals (individual preferences) and those pursued by society (collective preferences). Accepting the *model* suggested by the positivist and neo-positivist approaches, some economists have posed the problem of how to resolve collective preferences into individual ones. The problems amount, logically, to a problem of *aggregation*, which like those already mentioned involves, in a yet more evident and explicit manner, special ideological preconceptions. The neopositivist *model* suggests a modality for aggregating individual preferences: the principle of democracy. Arrow's brilliant analysis has clearly brought to light some logical difficulties which have been widely discussed and disposed of in various ways (see Sen [90]).

The practical problems concerning collective decisions are rather different from these theoretical problems. In empirical models collective decisions can be dealt with by assuming that some variables are exogenously given (predetermined). In planning models these variables become *instrumental variables* (see Tinbergen [97]). Yet such a procedure ignores the two most important problems that arise in connection with the relationship between society and individuals: (a) the peculiar nature of collective decisions in contrast to that of economic decisions taken in the market and to that of the individual decisions that contribute to the determination of social choices, and (b) the complex interplay the economic process induces between individual and collective decisions. In fact, the psychological mechanism that causes the individual to make decisions in the market is different from the psychological mechanism that leads him or her to take part in a collective decision. In taking part in social choices the individual makes a decision in the firm conviction that the collective decision resulting from those of all individuals will involve the same constraints for all and produce uniform effects for everybody. In the market, except in the oligopoly case, choices are made in an autonomous manner, and the individual does not interact with others whose decisions affect the objective conditions under which a choice must be made (prices, quantity rationing, etc.). In the market one pursues one's own interests; in taking part in social choices one always pursues some collective goals, selecting from among the possible goals those that create the most favorable conditions for maximizing one's own satisfaction, which depends not only on private consumption but also on the satisfaction of social needs.

Since individual preferences (as expressed when market choices are made) are heterogeneous compared with social preferences resulting from the interplay of individuals' decisions contributing to social choices, the genesis of social preferences cannot be analyzed in the way Arrow [3] and other economists following his approach have done. By properly posing the problem the economist can clarify the contradictions that can arise because of individual preferences coexisting with social preferences reflected in social choices.

Let us now revert to the problem of collective decisions in macroeconomic models. To express these decisions by means of macroeconomic variables (predetermined variables or instrumental variables) we need to achieve proper aggregation. To clarify some implications, let us consider a concrete example.

In macroeconomic models a set of collective decisions are aggragated in the variable: *public expenditure*. It is easy to verify that no unique relation can be established among the various levels of public expenditure and all possible sets of public decisions that cause such levels of expenditure to occur. In fact, the same level of public expenditure can be induced by various sets of public decisions. The effects of public expenditure do not depend only on the level but also on the structure that reflects the set of public decisions that have brought about the expenditure.

Some cognitive limits of macroeconomic models can thus be clearly understood. The manifold relations between levels of public expenditure and sets of public decisions may induce some asymmetry in the effects that increases in public expenditure have compared with those of reductions. An expansion of public expenditure can easily occur through the expansion of current expenditure because of the pressure of social groups and because of obstacles to the increase in investment expenditure. On the contrary, a reduction in public expenditure is more easily realized through the curtailment or postponement of investment expenditure. As it is well known, fluctuation in public expenditure causes changes in its structure that affect the relationship between public expenditure and the other aggregate variables.

The factors accounting for changes in the structure of public expenditure and the effects of such changes are not adequately analyzed both because of the macroeconomic approach and because of the belief, shared by most economists, that the task of the state concerns the level and not the structure of the final demand.

17. THEORY AND OBSERVATION

The still prevailing neopositivist approach to economics relies on empirical research being able to confirm theory. The economist can offer some relevant remarks concerning the debate on the observational-theoretical distinction.

In empirical research economists use models and not theories. It is worthwhile recalling that a model can be:

(a) Based on Tarki's definition, a specification of the theory (in general entailing more structural information than the theory, which is required to describe the actual economic process).

(b) A simplified version of the theory, such a version being deemed adequate to describe the process as it occurs in a specified historical context.

Models cannot be placed in a one-to-one correspondence with theories, not only because a theory can have various specifications and various simplified versions but also because the models used in empirical research are partial (or incomplete) models in the Marschak sense [47, p. 7]. The variety of models that can be built by economists to deal with the same set of processes make the problem of empirical verification of a theory more intricate in economics than in other sciences. In fact,

(1) The same observation may verify a variety of theoretical models. As we have already indicated, by manipulating lags and temporary trends we can make a large variety of models fit empirical data.

(2) The relations constituting a model applied for empirical research may be derived from various theories.

(3) Most of the great economic theories are *by their nature* incapable of producing models that can be empirically tested. What the theory can provide is logical implications of the hypotheses made on the structure of the economic system, the structure being defined under a set of conditions that cannot be met in the real world.

As we have noted, the aggregation processes required to build a model make these remarks still more relevant.

An economic theory can be neither confirmed nor rejected on the basis of the good or poor predictive value of a model supposedly derived from it. The cognitive value of a model is not a simple increasing function of its predictive value. It is not difficult to conceive of models with a high predictive value and a very low cognitive value. The converse is also true. The analysis of historical series can make it possible to build empirical models that, if the unknown structure of the system remains unchanged, can produce good forecasting. Yet this kind of model usually does not contribute to a better understanding of the economic system.

Examples can also be given of models having a high cognitive value and no predictive value. In meterorology the scientific laws are well known, yet they cannot be used to forecast the weather; forecasting is done by utilizing historical series by means of aggregate models.

The affirmation that empirical research cannot validate economic theory does not mean to deny the utility that indications derived from empirical investigations may have for the development of theory. Even more relevant is a reverse relation. Development of the theory can contribute to orientation and improvement of empirical research not by providing models that need only to be "estimated" and "tested" but by stimulating a preliminary cognitive process, preliminary to building the empirical model to be utilized for practical purposes (be it a descriptive model or a normative model).

The neopositivist approach to scientific research ignores the interaction between the development of knowledge and social conditions (in particular the structure of power). Scientific procedures and methods are affected by such interplay. Methodology cannot be depurated of its historical dimension. The *raison d'etre* and the validity criteria of a scientific discipline cannot be established from outside in such a way as to be valid for all disciplines. It is inside the discipline that we can define congruous procedure and proper criteria.

Most theorizing by economists is nothing more than a *thought experiment*. As rightly noted by Kuhn [36] from various kinds of thought experiments, "The scientist learns about the world as well as about his concept." It is my feeling that the debate has reached a point at which, in order to be fruitful, it needs to meet the challenge offered by open-minded reflections on the peculiarities of the crises of modern economies. Empirical research of the kind well known to economic historians may supply indications capable of reinvigorating the theoretical debate. When the inadequacy of the equilibrium models is recognized, economists will very likely become more aware of the ideological prejudices on which their *model* is grounded and of the need to develop a new *model* in order to deal in particular with the problem of the structural instability of (real) economic development.

18. DIACHRONIC STABILITY AND HISTORICAL STABILITY

Economic analysis—be it descriptive or normative—presupposes a *conservation principle* involving the essential features of the system necessary for the logical coherence of the theory itself. Only after this postulate has been granted can the problem of stability be faced (see, e.g., Lunghini [44] and Nicola [65]).

In studying the stability of a system S, the static or dynamic equilibrium of which has been defined, we must conceive of a different system S^* of which S, under particular conditions, can be considered a subsystem. The conservation postulate concerns the system S^* (for the relation between stability and regulation of the system, see Lange [38]).

The invariance of the system S^* with time can be questioned; then we face a problem of *structural stability*.

Let us pose the problem in its broadest terms. Of a given system let us consider the set $\mathbb{R}$ of the features that are not assumed "taken for granted" *a priori* (in the model by which the system is interpreted the set $\mathbb{R}$ is not included). They may be conditions of positivity for certain economic variables or certain relations among the variables (for example, we may regard the distribution of income according to certain relationships as essential for a capitalist system to be maintained).

Let us consider a set $\pi = (P', P'', \ldots)$ of parameters and relations of the model that can take different values or forms. Let $\Sigma(P)$ be the set of solutions of the model and let $\pi^c \subset \pi$ be the subset of parameters and relations having the following property: For each $P^c \in \pi^c$ there exists at least a solution for which the set $\mathbb{R}$ is verified. Let $\pi^c \neq 0$. Then we shall say that the model is *theoretically meaningful*. $\Sigma(P^c \in \pi^c)$ is the set of *congruous solutions*. If $\pi^c = \pi$, the model is *totally congruous*: otherwise it is *partially congruous*. When we deal with dynamic models, it may happen that some solutions are congruous only for a certain number of periods (or intervals of time) (see Lombardini [42]).

Let us assume that the model is theoretically meaningful and let us establish a suitable topology which allows us to define the distance between homogeneous elements of the set π. Let $\pi^s \subset \pi^c$ be the subset of parameters and relations having the following property: for each $P^s \in \pi^s$ there exists a neighborhood all included in π^c. We can qualify the solutions of the set $\Sigma(P^s \in \pi^s)$ as *diachronically stable*. If $\pi^s = \pi^c$, then the model is diachronically stable.

The concept of diachronic stability is linked with the concept of structural stability; because of the definition of the set $\mathbb{R}$, the former is more general than the latter, while the definition of the set π entails specification of the possible causes of structural changes.

When we consider a dynamic system (the set of solutions of the model being represented by the phase diagrams), we may be interested not only in establishing the diachronic stability but also in detecting special cases of indeterminacies. Let $\pi^b \subset \pi^c$ be the subset of parameters and relations having the following properties (besides being elements of π^c): When $P \in \pi^b$, the dynamics of the system change (i.e., changes occur in the trajectories expressed by the phase diagrams). If π^b is not nul, the model (system) has *bifurcation points*. A bifurcation implies indeterminacy. We do not wish to discuss here whether the structural indeterminacies (Section 9) are due to the incompleteness of a model that does not take into account all the structural properties of the economic system, to the interaction between the sociological and the economic systems, or to "real" indeterminacies.

It may be useful to note a difference between the usual notion of stability (which we could describe as synchronic) and that of diachronic stability. In analyzing synchronic stability we must define a more specific system as compared with that whose stability we wish to assess, having defined the static or dynamic equilibrium of the general system; the specific system coalesces with the general system under specific conditions (precisely those that represent the necessary and sufficient conditions for stability). In analyzing diachronic stability we need to define a more general system—as compared with that whose stability has to be assessed—in order to allow for structural changes that are theoretically admissible.

Let us now

(a)   Restrict the set π by considering only the structural changes deemed to be historically likely.

(b)   Enlarge $\mathbb{R}$ to include also the features of the economic system that we assume will be desirable to achieve at some time.

(c)   Require for a solution to be congruous that the "dated" features be obtained not later than the associated dates.

If the system has at least a congruous solution in this new context, we shall say that it is *historically valid*. In a similar way we can move from the concept of diachronic stability to the concept of historical stability. It is worth noting that the notions of historical validity and stability entail specifically made ideological assumptions, precisely the assumptions that enable us to restructure the sets π and $\mathbb{R}$.

19.   CATASTROPHE THEORY AND STRUCTURAL CHANGES IN THE ECONOMIC SYSTEM

In biology, ecology, and other sciences, the behavior of some entities, aiming at minimizing a potential function, depends on the values of some parameters, such dependence being formalized by a manifold function. Points of bifurcation are then possible; at such points small changes in the parameters may cause sudden and radical changes in behavior.

Thom [94], who has developed this theory, uses the term *catastrophe* to indicate these discontinuous changes. The French mathematician has thus provided a simplified theoretical framework for analysis of the structural stability of a large set of systems; the bifurcations that lead to catastrophes can all be classified into seven types. The catastrophe represents a transition phase between situations that are stable at the points of possible changes in the parameters (see Porton and Stewart [75]).

Catastrophe theory can have only a very limited application in economics, because (a)   the systems that are analyzed are seldom governed by potential functions, and (b)   interactions among the various subsystems constituting the economic system are too complex to be analyzed by this theory. For some interesting applications of catastrophe theory see Zeeman [106] and Goodwin [17]. Dynamic models entailing bifurcation points have been utilized in analyzing some economic systems (see Cugno and Montrucchio

[11]). It is useful to recall that discontinuities do not necessarily entail indeterminacies. The discontinuity assumption is a pure abstraction no less than the continuity assumption. The former may be more useful than the latter in analyzing some economic processes (such as changes in stabilization policy).

20. THE ROLE OF EXPECTATIONS AND SOME POSSIBLE DISCONTINUITIES IN THE ECONOMIC PROCESS

Discontinuities and possible structural instability may be due to the role that expectations have in the economic process. In fact, we must distinguish two kinds of expectations: (1) Expectations derived from all possible information about past development by means of an *implicit* model (which may be simulated by some psychological mechanism); we can qualify these as *rational* expectations. (2) Expectations that cannot logically be derived from the information available on the past development of the economy; these expectations are produced by a *creative imagination* and may be qualified as *disconnected anticipations*. When such anticipations are sufficiently strong and widespread, a discontinuity may occur in the process of development. Disconnected anticipations are more likely when the social (or economic) system is indeterminate (Section 9). Then the system may become diachronically (or even historically) unstable. In Keynes's analysis short-term expectations are in general considered rational expectations (to use the terminology just proposed), while long-term expectations are in general disconnected anticipations.

Some technical features of the system may also cause discontinuities (see Goodwin [16] and Medio [54]).

21. QUANTITATIVE CHANGES AND EVOLUTION

Even the dynamic model, entailing bifurcation points, presupposes a principle of conservation, in truth a weaker formalization of the principle, such as admitting a variety of structures (or of paths of development) having a set of features that will remain constant with time. Whenever laws of conservation are postulated, the theory provides a substantially static conception of the world; evolution, which presupposes a *direction*, cannot be explained. Yet conservation laws proved to be very fruitful in physics; the ideal of a static, nonevolutionary universe has not been superseded by the quantum theory (see Prigogine [78]). Attempts to overcome the mechanistic conception have been made with the use of stochastic models. Such models can indeed by fruitfully utilized when research has essentially practical goals.

Yet their cognitive value is doubtful. What they enable us to do is to associate with each value of a variable (or with each modality of given feature of the system or with each possible state of it) the values taken by another variable (or by another modality or state of the system). Since the nature of such an association, which can be expressed by relations of various kinds, is usually unknown, the model can hardly be considered capable of providing an explanation of the process that it can describe and to some extent foresee in its future occurrences.

When the process to be analyzed can be satisfactorily isolated and is recurrent, we can describe structural change by stochastic models (dissipative models), as proved by Prigogine [77]. The conditions that make it possible to apply dissipative models can scarcely be obtained in economics (the urbanization process is perhaps one of the few examples that can be dealt with by dissipative models). In fact, when the economist wishes to visualize the future, knowledge of the present system is not sufficient, as we have noted in Section 18; ideological premises must be stated. Unfortunately this is usually done in an unconscious way, which hampers critical assessment of the theory.

22. KNOWLEDGE AND BEHAVIOR

In economics there is a peculiar reason why we are unable to visualize the future through the mere application of formalized descriptive models: Knowledge of the present process is not without influence on its future development. For economics we could state a principle resembling the Heisenberg indeterminacy principle. In fact, knowledge of the process induces changes in the behavior of its operators, and therefore it causes changes in the process itself. A recent revival of microeconomics aims at making the market behavior more rational. Success of the theory consists in making the future different from what could be foreseen by mere application of the descriptive model. Quite often the connection between knowledge of the process and historical change is quite complex. The theoretical development may induce changes in social attitudes or in political projects and thereby cause changes in the economic process. (It may be sufficient to recall the role that, according to Marx, economic theory can have in fostering structural changes in the social system.)

REFERENCES

1. Abscombe, S. E. M., Intention. Oxford University Press (Blackwell), London and New York, 1957.
2. Aris, R., "Mathematical Modelling Techniques." Pitman, London, 1978.

3. Arrow, K., "Social Choice and Individual Values." Wiley, New York, 1951.
4. Arrow, K., and Hahn, F., "General Competitive Analysis." Holden-Day, San Francisco, California, 1971.
5. Becattini, G., "Il concetto di industria e la teoria del valore." Boringhieri, Torino, 1962.
6. Bergson, A., A reformulation of certain aspects of welfare economics, *Quart. J. Econ.* **52**, 310–334 (Feb. 1938).
7. Bohm, D., "Casuality and Change in Modern Physics," Routledge and Kegan Paul, London, 1957.
8. Braithwaite, R. B., "Scientific Explanation." Harper, New York, 1960.
9. Comte, A., "Cours de Philosophie Positive," Vols. I-VI. Paris, 1830–1842.
10. Cozzi, T., "Sviluppo e Stabilità della Economia." Fondazione L. Einaudi, Torino, 1969.
11. Cugno, F., and Montrucchio, L., "Structural stability and bifurcation in Goodwin's 1967 model. Paper presented at the *GES Meeting, Udine* (October 1978).
12. Edgeworth, F. Y., "Papers relating to Political Economy," Vol. 1. 1925.
13. Friedman, M., "Essays in Positive Economics." Univ. of Chicago Press, Chicago, Illinois, 1969.
14. Gandolfo, G. C., "Metodi di dinamica economica." ISEDI, Milano, 1977.
15. Garegnani, P., On a change in the notion of equilibrium in recent works on value and distribution, *in* "Essays in Modern Capital Theory" (M. Brown, K. Sato, and P. Zarembka, eds.). North Holland Publ., Amsterdam, 1976.
16. Goodwin, R., The nonlinear accelerator, *Econometrica* **19**, 1–17 (1951).
17. Goodwin, R., Wicksell and the Malthusian catastrophe, *Scand. J. Econ.* **80** (1978).
18. Hanson, N. R., "Patterns of Discovery." Cambridge Univ. Press, London and New York, 1958.
19. Hayek, F. A., "The Pure Theory of Capital," Vol. 4, Impression. Routledge and Kegan Paul, London, 1941.
20. Hempel, C. G., "Philosophy of Natural Science." Prentice Hall, Englewood Cliffs, New Jersey, 1966.
21. Hempel, C. G., On the standard conception of scientific theories, *in* "Minnesota Studies in the Philosophy of Science" (M. Radner and S. Winokur, eds.), Vol. IV. Univ. of Minnesota Press, Minnesota, 1970.
22. Hicks, J. R., "Value and Capital." Oxford Univ. Press (Clarendon), London and New York, 1939.
23. Hicks, J. R., "A Contribution to the Theory of the Trade Cycle." Oxford Univ. Press (Clarendon), London and New York, 1950.
24. Hicks, J. R., "Capital and Growth." Oxford Univ. Press, London and New York, 1965.
25. Hicks, J. R., "Capital and Time." Oxford Univ. Press, London and New York, 1973.
26. Hirschman, A. O., "The Strategy of Economic Development." Yale University Press, New Haven and London, 1963.
27. Holesovsky, V., "Economic Systems Analysis and Comparison." McGraw-Hill, New York, 1977.
28. Hutchinson, T. W., "Knowledge and Ignorance in Economics." Oxford Univ. Press (Blackwell), London and New York, 1977.
29. Kalman, R. E., Introduction to the algebraic theory of linear dynamic systems, *in* "Mathematical Systems: Theory and Economics I." Springer-Verlag, Berlin and New York, 1969.
30. Kantarovich, L. V., "The Best Use of Economic Resources." Pergamon, Oxford, 1965.
31. Knight, F. H., What is truth in economics? *In* "On the History and Method of Economics. Selected Essays." University of Chicago Press, Chicago, Illinois, 1956.

32. Koopmans, T. C., "Three Essays on the State of Economic Science." McGraw-Hill, New York, 1952.
33. Koopmans, T. C., and Montias, J. M., On the description and comparison of economic system, in "Comparison of Economic Systems" (A. Eckstein, ed.). Univ. of California Press, Berkeley, California, 1971.
34. Kornai, J., "Antiequilibrium on Economic Systems Theory and the Tasks of Research." North-Holland Publ., Amsterdam, 1971.
35. Kuhn, T. S., "The Structure of Scientific Revolutions," enlarged ed. Univ. of Chicago Press, Chicago, Illinois, 1970.
36. Kuhn, T. S., Second thoughts on paradigms, in "The Structure of Scientific Theory" (F. Suppe, ed.). University of Illinois Press, Urbana, Illinois, 1977.
37. Lakatos, J., "The Methodology of Scientific Research Programmes." Cambridge Univ. Press, London and New York, 1978.
38. Lange, O., "Introduction to Economic Cubernetics." Pergamon, Oxford and PWN Polish Scientific Publ., Warsaw, 1970.
39. Leontief, W., Dynamic analysis, in "Studies on the Structure of American Economy" (W. Leontief et al., eds.). Oxford Univ. Press, London and New York, 1953.
40. Lindahl, E., "Studies in the Theory of Money and Capital." New York, 1970.
41. Lombardini, S., and Nicola, P. C., Income distribution and economic development in Ricardian and Walrasian models, in Proc. of II Polish-Italian Conf. Appl. System Theory to Econon. Management and Technol. Rome, 1974.
42. Lombardini, S., Modern monopolies in economic development, in "The Corporate Economy" (R. Marris and A. Wood, eds.). Macmillan, London, 1971.
43. Lundberg, E., "Studies in the Theory of Economic Expansion." Kelley and Millman, Inc. New York, 1955.
44. Lunghini, G., Analisi qualitativa, determinatezza e stabilità, Industria. Lunglio-settembre (1966).
45. Makarov, V. L., L'esistenza di equilibrio economico in un modello con innovazione, Resoconti Accad. Sci. URSS 231, No. 1 (1976). Italian translation (mimeographed).
46. Malinvand, E., 1952, Capital accumulation and efficient allocation of resources, Econometrica 21, No. 2, 233–268 (1953).
47. Marschak, J., "Statistical inference in economics: An introduction, in "Statistical Inference in dynamic Economic Models" (T. C. Koopmans, ed.). Wiley, New York, 1950.
48. Marschak, J., Economic measurements for policy prediction, in "Studies in Econometric Method" (W. C. Hood and T. C. Koopmans, eds.). Wiley, New York, 1953.
49. Marshall, A., "Principles of Economics." Macmillan, New York, 1920.
50. Marx, K., "Theories of Surplus Value." International Publ., New York, 1952.
51. Marx, K., "Capital. A Critical Analysis of Capitalist Production." Lawrence and Wishart, London, 1974.
52. Maxwell, J. C., Does the progress of physical science tend to give any advantage to the opinion of necessity (or determinism) over that of contingency of events and freedom of will? in "The Life of J. C. Maxwell with a Selection From His Correspondence and Occasional Writings and a Sketch of His Contribution to Science" (L. Campbell and W. Garnett, eds.). Macmillan, New York, 1882.
53. Meade, J. E., "The Controlled Economy." Allen and Unwin, London, 1971.
54. Medio, A., "Teoria non lineare del ciclo economico." Il Mulino, Bologna, 1979.
55. Montias, J. M., "The Structure of Economic Systems." Yale Univ. Press, New Haven, Connecticut, 1976.
56. Morgenstern, O., When is a problem of economic policy solvable, in "Wirtschafsteorie und Wirtschaftspolitik testscrift fur Alfred Amonn." Francke Verlag, Bern, 1953.

57. Morgenstern, O., "The Limits of Economy." Hodge, London, 1937.
58. Morishima, M., "Walcras Economics. A Pure Theory of Capital and Money." Cambridge Univ. Press, London and New York, 1977.
59. Morishima, M., "Marx's Economics. A Dual Theory of Value and Growth." Cambridge Univ. Press, London and New York, 1977.
60. Morishima, M., "Equilibrium Stability and Growth." Oxford Univ. Press (Clarendon), London and New York, 1964.
61. Morishima, M., "Theory of Economic Growth." Oxford Univ. Press (Clarendon), London and New York, 1969.
62. Myrdal, G., "L'equilibre monetaire." Paris, 1950.
63. Myrdal, G., "Objectivity in Social Research." Duckworth, London, 1970.
64. Myrdal, G., "Economic Theory and Underdeveloped Regions." London, 1957.
65. Nicola, P. C., "Equilibrio generale e crescita economica." Il Mulino, Bologna, 1973.
66. Novozhilov, V. V., Cost-benefit comparisons in a socialist economy, in "The Use of Mathematics in Economics" (V. S. Nemchinov, ed.). Oliver and Boyd, London, 1964.
67. Ohlin, B., Some notes on the Stockholm theory of savings and investments, Econ. J. (1937).
68. Pareto, V., "Corso di Economia Politica," 1st ed., 1896 (republished by Einaudi, Torino, 1943).
69. Pareto, V., "Trattato di sociologia generale." Edizione Comunità, Milano, 1964.
70. Parsons, T., "The Social System." Free Press, Glencoe, Illinois, 1951.
71. Pasinetti, L. L., A new theoretical approach to the problems of economic growth, in "Study Week on the Econometric Approach to Development Planning." Amsterdam and Chicago, 1965.
72. Pasinetti, L. L., "Structural change and economic growth." Cambridge Univ. Press, London and New York, 1980 (forthcoming).
73. Popper, K., "The poverty of historicism," 2nd ed. Routledge and Kegan Paul, London, 1961.
74. Popper, K., "Conjectures and Refutation." Routledge and Kegan Paul, London, 1969.
75. Porton, T., and Stewart, J., "Catastrophe Theory and its Applications." Pitman, London, 1978.
76. Preti, G., "Praxised Empirismo." Einaudi, Torino, 1957.
77. Prigogine, I., Allen, P. M., and Herman, R., The evolution of complexity and the laws of nature, A contribution to the 3rd generation report to the Club of Rome. Goals for a Global Society (mimeographed).
78. Prigogine, I., Allen, P. M., and Herman, R., Metamorphoses de la science; Culture et science aujourd'hui (mimeographed).
79. Quadrio Curzio, "Rendita e Distribuzione in un Modello Economico Plurisettoriale," Milano, 1967.
80. Quesnay, F., "Tableau Economique des Physiocrates." Paris, 1969.
81. Quine, W. V. O., "From a Logical Point of View." Harper, New York, 1963.
82. Ricardo, D., "Principles of Political Economy and Taxation, (O. MacCullochs, ed.). London, 1821.
83. Robinson, J., "The Economics of Imperfect Competition." Macmillan, New York, 1933.
84. Robinson, J., The unimportance of reswitching, Q. J. Econ. February (1975).
85. Robinson, J., History versus equilibrium, in "Contribution to Modern Economics." Oxford Univ. Press (Blackwell), London and New York, 1978.
86. Samuelson, P., "Foundations of Economic Analysis." Harvard Univ. Press, Cambridge, Massachusetts, 1948.
87. Scheurer, P. B., Simmetria ed evoluzione dei sistemi fisici, in "La Simmetria" (E. Agazzi, ed.). Il Mulino, Bologna, 1973.

88. Schumpeter, J. A., "The Theory of Economic Development." Oxford Univ. Press, London and New York, 1969.
89. Schumpeter, J. A., "Capitalism, Socialism and Democracy." Harper, New York, 1947.
90. Sen, A. K., "Collective Choice and Social Welfare." Holden Day, San Francisco, California, 1970.
91. Simon, H. A., "Models of Man Social and Rational, Mathematical Essays on Rational Human Behaviour in a Social Setting." Wiley, New York, 1967.
92. Simon, H. A., and Ando, A., Aggregation of variables in dynamic systems, *Econometrica* **29**, No. 2 (1961).
93. Smith, A., "The Wealth of Nations." Methuen, London, 1950.
94. Sraffa, P., "Production of Commodities by Means of Commodities." Cambridge Univ. Press, London and New York, 1960.
95. Suppe, F., The search for philosophical understanding of scientific theories, *in* "The Structure of Scientific Theories" (F. Suppe, ed.), Univ. of Illinois Press, Chicago, Illinois, 1977.
96. Thom, R., "Stabilité Structurelle et Morphogenèse." Benjamin, New York, 1972.
97. Tinbergen, J., "On the Theory of Economic Policy." North-Holland Publ., Amsterdam 1952.
97a. Toraldo di Francia, G., "L'indagine del Mondo Fisico," Einaudi, Torino, 1976.
98. Vercelli, S., Equilibrio e dinamica del sistema economico. Semantica dei linguaggi formalizzati e modelli Keynesiani, *in* "Quaderni dell'Istituto di Economica della Facoltà di Science Economiche e Bancarie di Siena," No. 4 (1979).
99. Vinci, F., "Gli ordinamenti economici," Vols. I and II. Giuffrè, Milano, 1944–1945.
100. Von Mises, L., "Epistemological Problems of Economics." D. Van Nostrand Co. Inc, Princeton, New Jersey, 1960.
101. Von Neumann, J., A model of general economic equilibrium, *Rev. Econ. Stud.* **13** (1945–1946) (the essay was published in German in 1938).
102. Von Neumann, J., and Morgenstern, O., "Theory of Games and Economic Behavior." Princeton Univ. Press, Princeton, New Jersey, 1944.
103. Walras, L., "Elements of Pure Economics" (W. Jaffè, translator). Allen and Unwin, London, 1954.
104. Weber, Max, "The Theory of Social and Economic Organization." The Free Press, New York, 1947.
105. Wold, H., and Juréen, L., "Demand Analysis: A Study in Econometrics." Wiley, New York, 1952.
106. Zeeman, E. C., "Catastrophe Theory." Addison Wesley, Reading, Massachusetts, 1977.

COGNETTI DE MARTIIS LABORATORY
  OF POLITICAL ECONOMY
UNIVERSITY OF TURIN
TURIN, ITALY

Part II

NEW QUANTITATIVE TECHNIQUES AT WORK

Ergodicity for Economists*

Joseph Ford

1. INTRODUCTION

A number of recent papers (see, for example, May [20]) have emphasized the wildly erratic solution behavior that can occur in even simple mathematical models for systems of interest in economics, ecology, biology, and various areas of physics. Even the simple difference equation model

(1) $$X_{n+1} = aX_n(1 - X_n),$$

where $0 \leq X \leq 1$, is sufficient to illustrate this wild behavior, and the properties of this equation have been studied recently by workers in a variety of scientific disciplines [20].

The behavior now known to occur for such models offers both a hope and a challenge for economists. There is now reason to expect that the wildly fluctuating data characteristic of many systems in economics, ecology, and physics merely reflect the chaotic behavior inherent in the underlying deterministic equations rather than errors in data gathering or omission of crucial variables. But at the same time, one is faced with the challenge of providing an adequate statistical description of the chaotic behavior that occurs in these deterministic models. It is to this latter challenge that this chapter is addressed. In physics, statistical mechanics has, since the turn of the century, been vitally concerned with providing a theory for the stochastic

* Work supported in part by National Science Foundation Grant DMR 76-11966.

behavior experimentally observed in the motion of physical systems pre-
sumed completely deterministic. However, especially during the past
15 years, a combination of rigorous analytic and "empirical" numerical
(computer) studies has dramatically increased our general understanding
of dynamical systems, particularly in regard to chaotic behavior. Unfortunately from the economics point of view, much of the current progress
has been in the theory of conservative systems without dissipation. Nonetheless, we present here, beginning in Section 3, a very brief outline of this
recent work on conservative systems in order to illustrate a general approach
that may have much relevance to many scientific disciplines, including
economics.

2. A TWO-DIMENSIONAL MAPPING MODEL
   EXHIBITING CHAOTIC BEHAVIOR

Before turning to the general theory of conservative systems, let us discuss
a two-dimensional, nonconservative mapping which is, loosely speaking, a
generalization of the nonconservative, one-dimensional mapping specified
by Eq. (1). Quite generally for nonconservative (dissipative) systems, all
solutions tend to some steady-state limiting solution. For example, all
solutions for the damped harmonic oscillator tend to the motionless equilibrium point [22] of the system, while dissipative anharmonic oscillator
systems can possess periodic limit cycles [22] (for which input equals loss
during each cycle) which are asymptotically approached by all solutions.
Such limit cycles dominate the behavior of Eq. (1) [20]. However, as has
been recently discovered [18, 26], it is possible for all solutions of a dissipative
system to approach asymptotically an aperiodic limiting solution having
highly chaotic properties, which is called a strange attractor. Moreover, this
aperiodic limiting solution appears to mimic the chaotic motion discussed
in theories of turbulence and weather prediction [18, 26].

M. Henon has suggested [13] that the nonconservative mapping

(2a) $X_{n+1} = Y_n - aX_n^2 + 1,$

(2b) $Y_{n+1} = bX_n,$

where a and b are constants, exhibits such a strange attractor, and he has
presented [13] strong computer evidence in support of this conjecture.
In addition, Henon establishes that Eqs. (2a,b) are the most general quadratic
mapping having a constant Jacobian, here equal to $-b$, which means that,
upon each iteration, small area elements change in size by the constant
factor b. For the parameter values $a = 1.4$ and $b = 0.3$ in Eqs. (2a,b), a
computer may be used to determine the shape of the strange attractor

solution shown in Fig. 1 which involves 10^4 mapping iterates. It has been numerically verified that any initial point in the region "trapped" by the attractor, after the initial transient behavior dies, may be expected to generate the attractor solution shown in Fig. 1. In this figure, one notes that the "curves" have an obvious "thickness." On magnification of the region interior to the small square shown in Fig. 1, one obtains the fine structure shown in Fig. 2, which involves 10^5 mapping iterates. On further magnification of the small square in Fig. 2, one obtains the fine structure shown in Fig. 3, which is identical to that in Fig. 2. Moreover, another magnification (not shown here) of the square in Fig. 3 again reveals the same structure. This evidence strongly suggests that the mapping of Eqs. (2a,b) indeed possesses a strange attractor, that is, a limit set which is the product of a one-dimensional manifold and a Cantor set. For those unfamiliar with the notion of a Cantor set, a simple example may be obtained as follows: Start with the unit interval and delete the middle third; then delete the middle third of the then two remaining intervals; next delete the middle third of the remaining intervals; and so on; the points that remain at the end of this infinite process form a typical Cantor set.

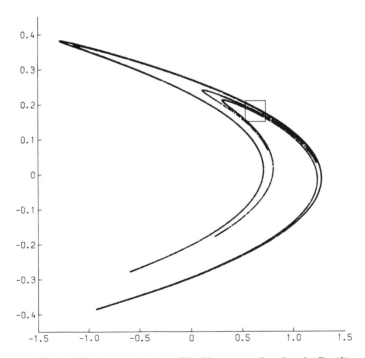

Fig. 1.   The strange attractor of the Henon mapping given by Eq. (2).

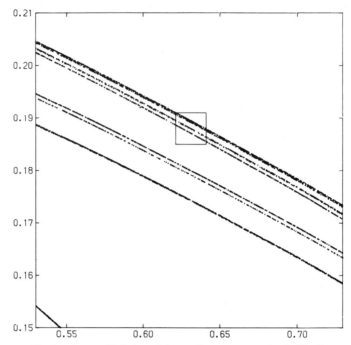

Fig. 2. A magnified view of the small square appearing in Fig. 1.

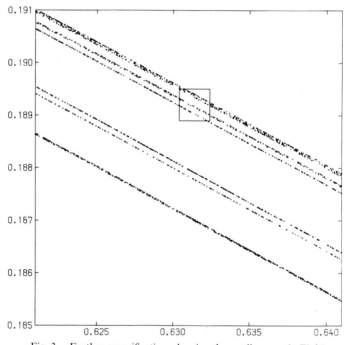

Fig. 3. Further magnification, showing the small square in Fig. 2.

Within the strange attractor, almost all solutions are expected to densely and aperiodically cover the attractor curve; in short, the solutions are ergodic within the attractor. The virtue of Henon's model over previous ones is that, for it, one may accurately compute "trajectory" behavior for long time intervals and one may hope to obtain analytic proofs for such a simple model. For the purposes of this exposition, however, Eqs. (2a,b) provide an especially simple example of the pathological behavior that can occur in deterministic, dissipative systems.

3. INTEGRABLE SYSTEMS

The deterministic, conservative systems of classical mechanics exhibit the full spectrum of behavior from completely integrable to completely stochastic. This brief survey begins with the simplest: the integrable systems. Even though integrable systems yield only a limited type of statistical behavior, they nonetheless form a logical basis of comparison for the more chaotic systems discussed later.

A classical Hamiltonian system having $2N$ degrees of freedom is said to be integrable [2] provided it possesses N single-valued, analytic constants of the motion Φ_k whose pairwise Poisson brackets[5] $[\Phi_j, \Phi_k]$ are all zero, thus ensuring that these constants are functionally independent. All the known, analytically solvable problems of classical mechanics have precisely this property. For an integrable system, these N constants of the motion Φ_k confine all phase space trajectories to lie on N-dimensional surfaces which for bounded motion, the only case we consider here, may be shown [2] to be N-dimensional tori bearing trajectories that are periodic or multiply periodic functions of the time. Finally, the Hamiltonians for an integrable system can always, by a change of variables, be written as a function of the momenta P_k alone, where the P_k are merely the Φ_k in the new variables.

These rather abstract (hence perhaps vague) notions can be made concrete by considering the bounded motion for an integrable, two degrees of freedom Hamiltonian $H = H(q_1, q_2, p_1, p_2)$. Here we may put the Hamiltonian in the form

$$(3) \qquad H = H(J_1, J_2),$$

where J_1 and J_2 (rather than P_1 and P_2) are the momentum variables, using the usual physics notation. In these variables, the equations of motion are $\dot{J}_k = 0$ and $\dot{\phi}_k = \Omega_k(J_1, J_2)$, where the dot denotes a time derivative, the ϕ_k are position variables, and the $\Omega_k \equiv \partial H / \partial J_k$. We may then immediately integrate to obtain $J_k = J_{k0}$ and $\phi_k = \Omega_k t + \phi_{k0}$, where J_{k0} and ϕ_{k0} are the initial conditions. Here all trajectories must lie on one or another

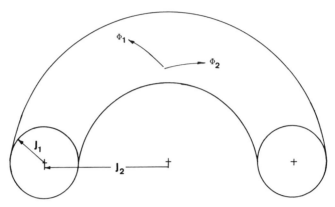

Fig. 4.   A cross-sectional view of a typical torus.

two-dimensional doughnut (torus) surface in phase space. Figure 4 shows one such torus, where the constants of the motion J_1 and J_2 may be regarded as the radii of the torus with the position variables ϕ_1 and ϕ_2 being angle variables on the torus. The Ω_k are then clearly angular frequencies and, since they depend on the constant J_k, a given torus bears either strictly periodic or else multiply periodic trajectories. Phase space for these integrable systems is thus seen to be especially simple, being filled with nested two-dimensional tori bearing periodic or multiply periodic trajectories. The generalization of these notions to integrable, N degrees of freedom Hamiltonians is straightforward though more difficult to visualize.

For the integrable, two degrees of freedom Hamiltonians of $H = H(q_1, q_2, p_1, p_2)$, we may graphically survey the bounded motion in a simple way that will be particularly useful in later sections on nonintegrable Hamiltonians. Since the energy for such systems is a constant of the motion, we may draw its trajectories in the three-space (q_1, q_2, p_2), since p_1 may be determined from $H(q_1, q_2, p_1, p_2) = E$. If we now graph in the (q_2, p_2) plane the intersections each three-space trajectory makes with the (q_2, p_2) plane where $q_1 = 0$, we obtain a set of nested curves that are nothing more than a cross-sectional view of the nested tori lying in the full phase space. For this reason such graphs were called surfaces of section [2, Appendix 31] by Poincaré. These surfaces of section are highly useful since they can be obtained via numerical integration even in the absence of any prior knowledge concerning the Hamiltonian. Here for each selected orbit, we have only to determine numerically those (q_2, p_2) coordinates of orbit points at which $q_1 = 0$.

For example, consider the Hamiltonian system

(4) $H = \frac{1}{2}(p_1^2 + p_2^2 + p_3^2) + e^{-(q_3 - q_2)} + e^{-(q_2 - q_1)} + e^{-(q_1 - q_3)} - 3,$

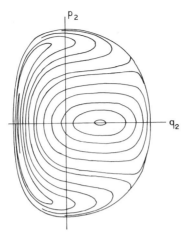

Fig. 5. A surface of section for Hamiltonian (4) at $E = 1$.

which is of both mathematical [6, 25] and physical [28] interest and which was first studied by Toda [31]. Without entering into the technical details here, let us merely remark that one may discard the uninteresting translation degree of freedom for Hamiltonian (4), thereby reducing it to a two degrees of freedom Hamiltonian for which one may numerically compute (q_2, p_2) surfaces of section. Figures 5 and 6 present these surfaces of section at

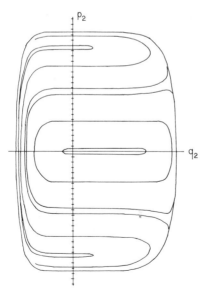

Fig. 6. A surface of section for Hamiltonian (4) at $E = 256$.

energies $E = 1$ and $E = 256$. From these figures, we immediately observe that, to computer accuracy, Hamiltonian (4) is integrable and that the shape and positions of the nested toroidal surfaces (here seen in cross section) are easily surveyed. Indeed, all the allowed motion for the integrable [5, 8, 10, 12, 15, 19] Hamiltonian (4) is included in these figures since (q_2, p_2) points lying outside the outermost curve would require unphysical, negative values for p_1^2. This surface of section technique is particularly valuable for Hamiltonian (4) since, even though it is integrable, the solutions are quite complicated elliptic functions and therefore are not very informative even when written out explicitly.

Although the trajectories in phase space for integrable systems are quite smooth and well behaved, they nonetheless exhibit a limited type of statistical behavior. If we project the multiply periodic motion on a given torus onto a single, judiciously chosen axis in phase space, this projected motion can yield a function of time strikingly similar to that of a stationary stochastic process. This type of limited statistical behavior has been discovered and rediscovered by many workers. (Some excellent work along these lines is described by Cukier *et al.* [4]. Also see the older review article by Mazur and Montroll [21].) However, more recent studies have revealed systems whose phase space trajectories themselves wander chaotically through phase space. It is toward such truly chaotic systems that we now move.

4. THE TRANSITION FROM INTEGRABLE TO CHAOTIC BAHAVIOR IN CONSERVATIVE SYSTEMS

Consider now the ubiquitous, conservative systems described by Hamiltonians having the form

$$(5) \qquad\qquad H = H_0 + V,$$

where H_0 is integrable and V is some small perturbing term. Kolmogorov, Arnold, and Moser (KAM) provided one of the most significant advances in classical dynamics of this century by rigorously establishing [1, 16, 23] sufficient conditions under which the motion generated by H lies (for the most part) near the motion of H_0. Under suitable conditions, KAM prove that most tori of H_0 persist, being only slightly distorted by the small V. These preserved tori, while they fill most of the allowed phase space, nonetheless form only a pathological, nondense set. Moreover, the dense, but small, regions of destroyed H_0 tori contain highly erratic and chaotic trajectories [24]. Thus, in order to obtain chaotic trajectories over most of phase space, one must violate one or more of the KAM conditions. We may illustrate this transition, without entering into many of the sophisticated details [9], by considering a simple, two degrees of freedom system. Let us examine the Hamiltonian

(6) $$H = \tfrac{1}{2}(p_1^2 + p_2^2 + q_1^2 + q_2^2) + q_1^2 q_2 - q_2^3/3,$$

which was first studied by Henon and Heiles [14]. Here $H_0 = \tfrac{1}{2}(p_1^2 + p_2^2 + q_1^2 + q_2^2)$, while $V = q_1^2 q_2 - q_2^3/3$. When the total energy E is sufficiently small, V is also small and the motion should be of the near-integrable type predicted by the KAM theorem. Following Henon, we now discuss the change in the character of the motion as the total energy and hence V increase. In particular, we numerically integrate the equations of motion for Hamiltonian (6) at fixed energy E and graph a (q_2, p_2) surface of section. An orbit lying on a torus in phase space will yield intersection points lying on a curve in the (q_2, p_2) plane, but an erratic trajectory no longer confined

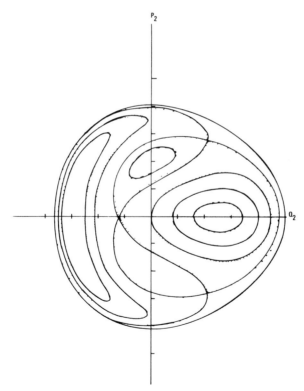

Fig. 7. A surface of section for Hamiltonian (6) at $E = 1/12$; 1 scale division $= 0.10$.

to a torus would be expected to yield a set of "random"-looking dots as it intersects the (q_2, p_2) plane.

In Fig. 7, we show a numerically integrated surface of section at energy $E = \frac{1}{12}$. Here curves apparently exist everywhere, although improved integration accuracy (not shown) reveals small regions of chaotic trajectories. Indeed, in Fig. 8, a region of erratic trajectories has become sufficiently broad to be observed by the computer at the accuracy used. The random set of dots in Fig. 8 was generated by a single trajectory. Finally, in Fig. 9 we observe that most of the allowed phase space is filled with chaotic orbits because, again, all the dots in Fig. 9 were generated by a single orbit. For the sake of brevity, let us conclude this discussion of Hamiltonian (6) by remarking that the chaotic trajectories shown in Figs. 8 and 9 exhibit many of the properties characterizing the rigorously ergodic and mixing systems discussed in Section 5.

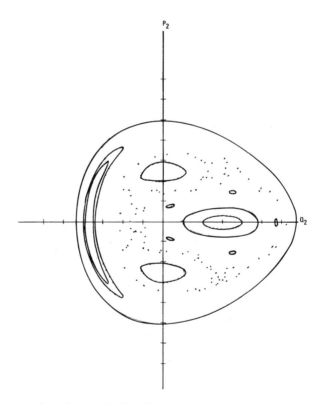

Fig. 8.   A surface of section for Hamiltonian (6) at $E = 1/8$; 1 scale division $= 0.10$.

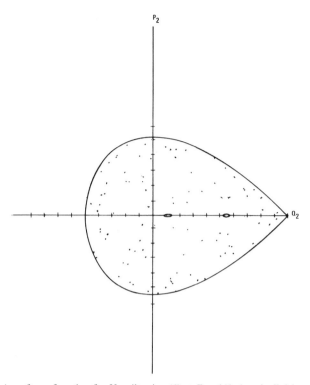

Fig. 9.   A surface of section for Hamiltonian (6) at $E = 1/6$; 1 scale division $= 0.10$.

5.   ERGODIC AND MIXING SYSTEMS AND C SYSTEMS

For isolated, conservative Hamiltonian systems, there now exists a well-defined [17] hierarchy of increasingly chaotic behavior. In this section, we discuss ergodic systems, mixing systems, and C systems, while in Section 6, we introduce K systems and B systems. Finally, in Section 7 we discuss the statistical properties of these chaotic but deterministic systems. In all these sections, we shall consider only systems whose trajectories lie on closed, bounded energy surfaces (or hypersurfaces) and whose trajectory flow, generated by the equations of motion, preserves area on the energy surface. Such behavior is generic to isolated, conservative Hamiltonian systems. The following discussion is somewhat intuitive; rigor is provided by review texts such as Arnold and Avez [2, Chapters 2 and 3].

A system is said to be ergodic, loosely speaking, provided each (and almost every) system trajectory uniformly and densely covers the energy surface under the flow. Ergodicity thus requires chaotic behavior for individual trajectories, but it does not specify what happens to initially close trajectories, that is, whether they remain close for all time or separate. This question is left to the stronger property of mixing, which requires that each small, nonzero area element on the energy surface eventually flow into a very thin, elongated filament densely covering the energy surface. Mixing thus requires chaotic behavior for initially close bundles of trajectories, but it states nothing about how rapidly the trajectories must separate. This is left to C systems which have the strongest chaotic trajectory behavior. For C systems, almost all initially close orbits must at least exponentially separate under the flow; for them each initial area element grows exponentially in at least one direction while shrinking exponentially in at least one other, while, of course, preserving area.

Perhaps the most interesting known physical system having all these properties is the hard sphere (or disk) gas [29, 30], but for simplicity we here illustrate these ideas by considering a system whose "energy surface" is the unit square and whose equations of motion are given by the plane, area-preserving mapping

$$(7) \qquad (X_{n+1}, Y_{n+1}) = \Phi(X_n, Y_n) = (X_n + Y_n, X_n + 2Y_n),$$

where n is regarded as an integral, discrete time variable and where any point (X_{n+1}, Y_{n+1}) carried outside the unit square by Eq. (7) is returned there by repeatedly subtracting unity from each coordinate as necessary. A reader tempted to regard this area-preserving mapping as a highly artificial illustration is advised that the surfaces of section shown in Figs. 5–9 are area-preserving mappings generated by the Hamiltonian system flows discussed earlier. For the mapping of Eq. (7), Fig. 10 shows the havoc wreaked on the unit square after only two iterations of the mapping.

In order to appreciate what happens to small area elements of the unit square, let us differentiate Eq. (7) to obtain

$$(8) \qquad (dX_{n+1}, dY_{n+1}) = (dX_n + dY_n, dX_n + 2dY_n).$$

A simple rotation of axes brings Eq. (8) to the form

$$(9) \qquad (d\zeta_{n+1}, d\eta_{n+1}) = (\lambda d\zeta_n, \lambda^{-1} d\eta_n),$$

where $\lambda = 2^{-1}(3 + 5^{1/2}) > 1$. Thus on each iteration, every area element expands by the factor λ in the ζ direction and compresses by the factor λ^{-1} in the η direction. Thus it is this sequential, exponential C-system behavior that is responsible for the obvious mixing (and thus ergodic) behavior shown in Fig. 10. Despite the simplicity of this transparent mapping system, it nonetheless exhibits the chaotic trajectory behavior that can

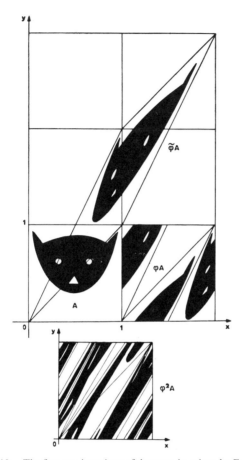

Fig. 10.   The first two iterations of the mapping given by Eq. (7).

occur in more sophisticated systems. In particular, trajectories in the chaotic regions for Hamiltonian (6) appear to possess exactly these properties.

6. K SYSTEMS AND B SYSTEMS

Ergodic, mixing, and C systems are usually defined in terms of the chaotic behavior of their trajectories. K systems (after Kolmogorov) and B systems (after Bernoulli), on the other hand, are for our purpose more conveniently discussed in terms of the truly statistical behavior they can exhibit in sequences of experimental measurements made of a system observable. Ultimately their chaotic behavior can also be related to highly erratic trajectories but not in such an obviously simple and direct way. Suppose we make sequential (at 1-sec intervals, say) measurements of finite accuracy on any system observable G from $t = -\infty$ to $t = +\infty$, yielding a doubly infinite, denumerable sequence $\{G_k\}$. Then a K system is one so chaotic that knowledge of the $\{G_k\}$ sequence from $k = -\infty$ to $k = n$, for any finite integer n, does not precisely determine the next value G_{n+1}. Stated in terms of trajectories, the precise system orbit is, at best, determined only once the whole $\{G_k\}$ sequence is known. In short, each measurement provides additional information (see, for example, Billingsley [3]) about the system, and a K system may be defined as one that yields a strictly positive average amount of information per measurement. A B system is even more chaotic in the sense that, for it, observables exist whose sequential measured values are, statistically, completely independent. This means that there exist $\{G_k\}$ sequences for deterministic systems indistinguishable from those generated by an honest roulette wheel.

We may illustrate such system behavior again using a simple, area-preserving mapping, the so-called baker's transformation sketched in Fig. 11. Here the unit square is stretched to a rectangle of length 2 and height $\frac{1}{2}$; then the rectangle is cut vertically and the right half placed on top of the left to reform the unit square. Obviously, each small initial small area element is sequentially (and exponentially) stretched in the horizontal x direction and shrunk in the vertical y direction. Clearly then, this mapping is a C system and hence ergodic and mixing, but of greater interest in this section is the fact that it is also both a K system and a B system, as we now show.

In Section 7, we shall give the algebraic equations defining the baker's transformation. Here we choose to present a numeric representation that

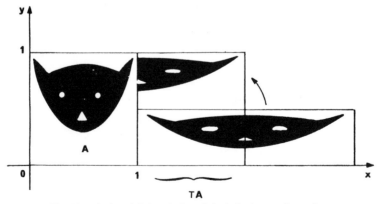

Fig. 11.   A pictorial description of the baker's transformation.

renders its K-system and B-system properties transparent. Let (x_0, y_0) be any time zero mapping point in the unit square and express both x_0 and y_0 as binary decimal numbers. Then write x_0 to the right of the decimal in the usual way, but write y_0 backward to the left of the same decimal, forming a double infinite sequence of zeros and ones with a single decimal in the middle. For example, if $x_0 = 0.10101010\ldots$ and $y_0 = 0.001001001\ldots$, then we would write

(10) $\ldots 100100100.10101010\ldots$

Now moving the decimal sequentially to the right gives the sequential forward mapping iterates of (x_0, y_0) since each rightward movement of the decimal doubles x and halves y; moreover, it also properly accounts for the cutting and folding of the baker's transformation. Backward iterates are similarly obtained by moving the decimal to the left. This ingenuous binary representation of each (x_0, y_0) point thus specifies the whole baker's transformation orbit passing through that (x_0, y_0).

Now let us observe that the first digit to the right of the decimal at each iteration determines whether or not the mapping point at that iteration lies to the right or the left of $x = \frac{1}{2}$. Thus if, for a precise (but unknown) orbit, we sequentially measure the system observable G which takes the value 1 if $x \geq \frac{1}{2}$ and 0 if $x < \frac{1}{2}$ from $k = -\infty$ to $k = +\infty$, we thereby precisely determine the binary representation for (x_0, y_0) and thus the precise orbit. Quite clearly we do not determine the precise orbit until the whole sequence is measured; moreover, each measurement clearly produces a better approximation to (x_0, y_0) and thus provides positive new information at each step. Hence the baker's transformation is obviously a K system. Finally, since x_0 and y_0 are in general both irrational, the sequence of zeros and ones in each measured $\{G_k\}$ set is completely random in the sense that most of the $\{G_k\}$ sets will be completely indistinguishable from doubly infinite sets of zeros and ones generated by flips of an honest coin. This means that the baker's transformation is also a B system. We thus have illustrated a deterministic flow yielding measured values as random as a coin toss. We close this section by merely remarking that Sinai's hard sphere (or disk) gas is both a K system and a B system.

7. STATISTICAL DESCRIPTION OF CHAOTIC SYSTEMS

We have now demonstrated that deterministic systems can exhibit a wide spectrum of well-defined chaotic behavior. Moreover, for such chaotic systems, it is doubtful that obtaining an analytic solution would be either feasible or, in general, even useful. What we need is a scheme which, once we establish (or at least suspect) the chaotic category of the system, allows us to use straightforwardly statistical methods to predict system behavior. For a classical many-body problem, for example, if we can establish (or reasonably presume) that the system is ergodic (or mixing), we may use the well-known formulas of classical statistical mechanics to compute equilibrium properties. However, even there, the nonequilibrium problem is still open. In the following, we use the baker's transformation to illustrate even nonequilibrium statistical procedures that may be valid for more general systems.

Algebraically, the baker's transformation is specified by the equations

$$(11) \qquad (x_{n+1}, y_{n+1}) = \begin{cases} [2x_n, \frac{1}{2}y_n], & 0 \leq x_n < (\frac{1}{2}) \\ [(2x_n - 1), \frac{1}{2}(y_n + 1)], & \frac{1}{2} \leq x_n < 1. \end{cases}$$

Let us now define an initial probability density $f(x_0, y_0, 0)$ introduced, if for no other reason, because of limited accuracy in measuring the initial system state (x_0, y_0). We require only that

$$(12) \qquad \iint f(x_0, y_0, 0)\, dx_0\, dy_0 = 1,$$

where integration is over the unit square. Since this mapping is area-preserving, is invertible, and allows one and only one orbit to pass through each point, we have

$$(13) \qquad f(x_n, y_n, n) = f(x_0, y_0, 0),$$

where x_n and y_n are given by Eq. (11). Equation (13) merely states that the probability density initially at (x_0, y_0) is carried with this point as it "flows" to (x_n, y_n) under mapping iteration. Since this mapping is ergodic and mixing, the point values for any smooth initial $f(x_0, y_0)$ become uniformly mixed over the unit square. In particular, we have

$$(14) \qquad \lim_{n \to \infty} \iint g(x_n, y_n) f(x_n, y_n, n)\, dx_n\, dy_n = \iint g(x, y)\, dx\, dy$$

for any reasonable function $g(x, y)$. Thus time averages of any $g(x, y)$ may be computed just as if $f(x_n, y_n, n)$ tended everywhere to unity for large n. But because we are discussing a K system and a B system, we can prove even more.

By combining Eqs. (11) and (13), we may obtain

$$(15) \qquad f(x, y, n) = \begin{cases} f[\frac{1}{2}x, 2y, n - 1], & 0 \leq y < \frac{1}{2} \\ f[\frac{1}{2}(x + 1), (2y - 1), n - 1], & \frac{1}{2} \leq y < 1, \end{cases}$$

where x and y are the same on both sides of Eq. (15). Then, by direct integration of Eq. (15), we may show that the reduced probability density $W(x, n)$ given by

$$(16) \qquad W(x, n) = \int dy \, f(x, y, n)$$

satisfies the strictly irreversible rate equation

$$(17) \qquad W(x, n) = \tfrac{1}{2}[W(\tfrac{1}{2}x, n - 1) + W(\tfrac{1}{2}(x + 1), n - 1)].$$

From Eq. (17), it follows that $W(x, n)$ monotonically tends to unity as n becomes large and, because this is a C system, the relaxation to equilibrium is expected to be exponential. Finally, the random, B-system character of the baker's transformation is revealed by the stochastic Markov process nature of Eq. (17). Since the hard sphere (or disk) gas is now known to be a B system, one anticipates that similar results will eventually be derived for it in the future, although this derivation is expected to be highly nontrivial.

8. CLOSING REMARKS

In this brief chapter, we have described systems and procedures illustrating a possible relevance of contemporary ergodic theory to economics. An interested reader who feels that we have overly sacrificed clarity (or rigor) on the altar of brevity is encouraged to seek out the numerous longer (and sometimes simpler) review papers (in addition to Arnold and Avez [2], Scott et al. [28], Toda [31], Cukier et al. [4], Mazur and Montroil [21], Moser [24], Ford [9], Lebowitz and Penrose [17], and Billingsley [3], one might want to consult Farquhar [7], Zaslavsky and Chirikov [32], Saito et al. [27], and Galgani and Scotti [11]) that now exist in the literature.[1] But regardless of the accuracy with which this chapter has hit its intended mark, its aim has been to encourage information exchange and research collaboration between economists and other scientists, whatever their disciplinary stripe.

---

[1] A reader interested in reviewing the latest work in this and related areas might wish to subscribe to "Nonlinear Science Abstracts" by writing the present author at the address given. This free service provides a monthly or bimonthly abstract listing of current preprints and reprints giving author, title of paper, author's address, abstract, and proposed (or actual) publication journal. Both subscribers and abstract contributors working on dynamical systems and ergodic theory or in any other area of nonlinear science from astronomy to zoology are welcome.

REFERENCES

1. Arnold, V. I., *Russian Math. Surveys* **18**, 9 (1963).
2. Arnold, V. I., and Avez, A., "Ergodic Problems of Classical Mechanics," Appendix 26. Benjamin, New York, 1968.
3. Billingsley, P., "Ergodic Theory and Information." Wiley, New York, 1965.
4. Cukier, R. I., Shuler, K. E., and Weeks, J. D., *J. Statist. Phys.* **5**, 99 (1972).
5. Date, E., and Tanaka, S., *Progr. Theoret. Phys.* **55**, 457 (1976).
6. Dubrovin, B. A., Mateev, V. B., and Novikov, S. P., *Russian Math. Surveys* **31**, 59 (1976).
7. Farquhar, I. E., *in* "Irreversibility in the Mandy-Body Problem" (J. Biel and J. Rae, eds.). Plenum Press, New York, 1972.
8. Flaschka, H., *Phys. Rev. B* **9**, 1924 (1974).
9. Ford, J., *in* "Fundamental Problems in Statistical Mechanics" (E. D. G. Cohen, ed.), Vol. III, p. 215. North-Holland Publ., Amsterdam, 1975.
10. Ford, J., Stoddard, S. D., and Turner, J. S., *Progr. Theoret. Phys.* **50**, 1547 (1973).
11. Galgani, L., and Scotti, A., *Rev. Nuovo Cimento* **2**, 189 (1972).
12. Henon, M., *Phys. Rev. B* **9**, 1921 (1974).
13. Henon, M., *Commun. Math. Phys.* **50**, 69 (1976).
14. Henon, M., and Heiles, C., *Astron. J.* **69**, 73 (1964).
15. Kac, M., and van Moerveke, P., *Proc. Nat. Acad. Sci. USA* **72**, 2879 (1975).
16. Kolmogorov, A. N., *Proc. Internat. Congr. Math., Amsterdam* Vol. 1, p. 315. North-Holland Publ., Amsterdam, 1957.
17. Lebowitz, J. L., and Penrose, O., *Phys. Today* **26**, No. 2, 23 (1973).
18. Lorenz, E. N., *J. Atmos. Sci.* **20**, 130 (1963).
19. Manakov, S. V., *Sov. Phys.–JETP* **40**, 269 (1974).
20. May, R. M., *Nature (London)* **261**, 459 (1976), and the references listed therein.
21. Mazur, P., and Montroll, E., *J. Math. Phys.* **1**, 70 (1960).
22. Minorsky, N., "Introduction to Non-Linear Mechanics," Chapter 1. Edwards, Ann Arbor, Michigan, 1947.
23. Moser, J., *Nachr. Akad. Wiss. Gottingen II Math. Phys. K1* **1** (1962).
24. Moser, J., "Stable and Random Motions in Dynamical Systems." Princeton Univ. Press, Princeton, New Jersey, 1973.
25. Moser, J., *Adv. in Math.* **16**, 197 (1975).
26. Ruelle, D., and Takens, F., *Commun. Math. Phys.* **20**, 167 (1971); **23**, 343 (1971).
27. Saito, N. *et al.*, *Progr. Theoret. Phys. Suppl.* **45**, 209 (1970).
28. Scott, A. C., Chu, F. Y. F., and McLaughlin, D. W., *Proc. IEEE* **61**, 1443 (1973).
29. Sinai, Ya. G., *in* "Statistical Mechanics" (*Proc. IUPAP Meeting, Copenhagen, 1966*) (T. A. Bak, ed.). Benjamin, New York, 1967.
30. Sinai, Ya. G., *Russian Math. Surveys* **25**, No. 2, 137 (1970).
31. Toda, M., *Phys. Lett.* **18C**, No. 1 (1975).
32. Zaslavsky, G. M., and Chirikov, B. V., *Sov. Phys.–Usp.* **14**, 549 (1972).

SCHOOL OF PHYSICS
GEORGIA INSTITUTE OF TECHNOLOGY
ATLANTA, GEORGIA

Catastrophe Theory in Banking and Finance

Thomas Ho
Anthony Saunders

1. INTRODUCTION

Since the publication of Thom's book [25] on catastrophe theory there has been a wide debate as to its usefulness in the social and physical sciences. Some have argued, following Zeeman [35], that it can make quantitative and measurable predictions, while others, including Thom [27] himself, take a more conservative view. Indeed, Thom [27] believes that catastrophe theory provides a global qualitative viewpoint that generates valuable insights into a number of problems in the social and physical sciences not obtainable from many of the (more quantitative) models currently employed. In finance, for example, we have a particular penchant for linearization and the use of (linear) regression techniques; however, to paraphrase Golubitsky [6], the world may not be a cusp, but then it is probably not linear either.[1] Hence catastrophe theory allows us to escape the straitjacket of linearity to investigate the rich possibilities provided by its geometry.

The historical roots of catastrophe theory can be traced back to the works of Whitney [29] and Poincaré [18], and many of the technical theorems had been proved independently by Mather [11] prior to Thom's book. However, as Golubitsky [6] has pointed out, Thom's great contribution was to put the results into a coherent framework that allowed a precise statement, complete classification, and possible generalization of known results.[2]

---

[1] Golubitsky [6, p. 385].
[2] Golubitsky [6, p. 353].

Three ideas of particular importance emerge from Thom's work, which may well have a tremendous impact on future developments in economic and financial theory. These are the minimization of some potential (cost) function, the definition of a stable equilibrium, and the concept of structural stability. In particular, the idea of minimizing some potential (cost) function or its dual, the maximization of some profit or wealth function, is central to both economics and finance. Specifically, catastrophe theory may be applicable to the following classical problems in banking and finance.

A. Optimal Capital Structure

There has been considerable debate in the finance literature on the existence of an optimal capital structure that maximizes the value of a firm. The traditional view is that increases in the debt–equity ratio beyond some point will increase the firm's cost of debt and reduce its market value. Similarly, any decrease in the debt–equity ratio below some point, by debt retirement, for example, will increase the discount rate on the firm's cash flow and also reduce the value of the firm. Hence within Thom's framework the potential function is the cost-of-capital function, the minimization of which maximizes the market value of the firm. The minimization of this function is viewed as being in the best interests of both bondholders and stockholders. However, recent literature in the area has suggested that the assumption of bondholder and stockholder consensus may be unduly simplistic. In fact, the relationship between the two groups may depend on a number of system parameters, including corporate tax structure [5], bankruptcy costs [9, 10], personal income tax structure [14], and asymmetric information [20], the existence of which may lead to certain conflicts between the interests of these two groups [7]. Clearly, in financial theory we should seek to determine the optimal capital structure for each set of these parameter values. Of particular interest is how the optimal capital structure changes as these parameters change, whether changes in capital structure are continuous or discontinuous, and where any discontinuity (if any) occurs. Such questions are the essence of catastrophe theory.

B. Dividend Policy

In the past decade a number of theories have been put forward to explain why firms that supposedly maximize shareholders' wealth pay dividends. Since personal income taxes tend to be significantly higher than capital gains taxes, some have argued that no dividends should be paid at all [2]. Others have suggested that since bondholders do not have direct control over a firm's dividend policy, dividend payout may be a means of increasing shareholders' wealth at the expense of bondholders' [8], or that dividends will be made to provide informational value to the capital market [4]. In the framework of catastrophe theory the optimal dividend policy would involve maximizing shareholders' wealth (as the potential function), in a system of relationships involving stockholders and bondholders, for certain given parameters such as tax rates and the cost of information. Again a catastrophe model of dividend policy seeks to examine how the optimal dividend payout policy changes as the system parameters change, and whether or not these changes are continuous or discontinuous.

C. Bank Failure

There has been considerable debate in the banking literature (see Meltzer [13] for example) on the social costs of bank failure. It is generally believed that the social costs are greater than the private costs; hence there is a need to regulate banking. However, regulation may not be sufficient to prevent failure. Indeed, it can be shown that there are certain conditions under which the interactions of regulators, bank management, and depositors can result in catastrophic failure. In Section 3 we develop a model for analyzing catastrophic bank failure and assessing the policy implications of this model for "early-warning" systems. Initially, however, we will outline catastrophe theory in more detail [16, 24].

2. CATASTROPHE THEORY

Catastrophe theory investigates the qualitative aspects of discontinuity in natural phenomena. Thom's [25] classification theorem for stable universal unfoldings, the main result in catastrophe theory, provides a better understanding of causes and effects of catastrophic phenomena in many disciplines, including biology, physics, and engineering [26, 30–34].

The catastrophic phenomena we are interested in have the following three properties. The first is the property of divergence whereby small, continuous changes in initial conditions (or parameters) can lead to large, discontinuous (catastrophic) changes in state variables. This type of behavior contrasts with traditional, Hamiltonian, dynamic systems in which small changes in initial conditions result in only small changes in the state variable. The second is bifurcation (or asymmetries) in the behavior of a state variable x as certain parameters increase or decrease; bifurcation implies that there will be a discontinuous jump in x at some value of a control variable when it is increasing that is different from the behavior of x when the control variable is decreasing. As a result x will be multivalued over a certain range of the control variable. The third is the property of stability—the catastrophe condition is robust to marginal changes in the structural relationships underlying the system. Hence, although some relationships may (marginally) change, catastrophe will still occur, albeit at different values of the control variables in the system.

Before describing the theory, we should define the following four terms:

(1)   A system is a collection of qualities under investigation.

(2)   A state of a system is a set of maps from the system assigning to each quality a unique real number.

(3)   A process of the system is a selection of an actual state from possible states.

(4)   A parameter (i.e., an r-dimensional parameter) for a process is an r-tuple of real numbers on which the selection rule for determining the actual state of the process depends.

The phenomena under consideration may be thought of as being governed by a potential function of some form. In equilibrium, the states are determined such that the (potential) function is minimized. If the function has several minima, then more than one stable state may be possible. Changing the control parameters of the system may alter the form of the governing potential function in such a way as to change the states or even the number of local minima. Thus stable states may change in a discontinuous way as the control parameters change in a smooth fashion. These observed discontinuities have been labeled "catastrophes."

Elementary catastrophes are those generated by four or fewer control parameters. They are of particular interest because they occur in space–time in a structurally stable fashion. Thom's [25] classification theorem on elementary catastrophes is described below. Let Mv be the set of possible states such that the potential function is minimized or maximized. It can be shown that Mv is an r-dimensional submanifold in R^{n+r} (the control of parameter space). Let $x = (p, u)$ be a point in Mv. Then locally, around this minimal point, the potential function is equivalent to one of the seven universal unfoldings listed in Table 1.

TABLE 1

Seven Elementary Catastrophes

Name	Universal unfolding	Dimension of parameter space
The fold	$x^3 + ux$	1
The cusp	$x^4 + ux^2 + vx$	2
The swallowtail	$x^5 + ux^3 + vx^2 + wx$	3
The butterfly	$x^6 + ux^4 + vx^3 + wx^2 + tx$	4
The hyperbolic umbilic	$x^3 + y^3 + wxy + ux + vy$	3
The elliptic umbilic	$x^3 + 3xy^2 + w(x^2 + y^2) + ux + vy$	3
The parabolic umbilic	$x^2y + y^4 + wx^2 + ty^2 + ux + vy$	4

This classification theorem enables us to describe a catastrophic phenomenon, since for a certain potential function we can derive the catastrophe
set: The catastrophe set is the set of points in the parameter space in which
the location of the minima of the potential functions undergoes a sudden
change (i.e., a discontinuity) as the parameters vary. To determine the
catastrophe set, we recall that Mv is a submanifold of R^{n+r}. Let $\pi: R^{n+v} \to R^v$
be the natural projection such that $\pi(x, y) = y$. Then we let $Xv: Mv \to R^r$
be the map induced by the projection π, and we call Xv the catastrophe
map. Then the catastrophe set is simply the set of singular values of Xv.

It is illuminating to discuss an example of catastrophe assuming only two
control variables u and v and one state variable x. Let the potential function
be

$$(1) \qquad G(x, u, v) = \tfrac{1}{4}x^4 + \tfrac{1}{2}ux^2 + vx.$$

The catastrophe set of this potential function is a cusp. It can be derived as
follows. Consider

$$(2) \qquad \partial G/\partial x = x^3 + ux + v,$$

and then the two-dimensional manifold is given by

$$(3) \qquad M_G = \{(x, u, v)\,|\,x^3 + ux + v = 0\},$$

and the catastrophe map $X_G: M_G \to R^2$ is induced by the projection $R^{1+2} \to R^2$ into the parameter space. This is shown in Fig. 1.

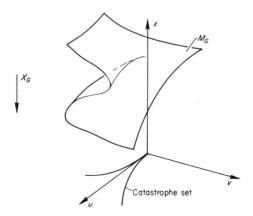

Fig. 1.   The cusp catastrophe.

3. CATASTROPHIC BANK FAILURE

In the model developed below we consider a system that consists of the following groups of economic agents: bank management, government regulators, and bank depositors. The state, or dependent variable, we seek to explain is the probability of bank failure F, which can be expected to be affected by a number of financial system parameters. To make the problem more concrete, we have assumed here that there are two parameters directly impacting on F for any bank[3]: the bank's capital–deposit ratio and its deposit risk class.

The bank is assumed to choose, through asset management, a desired depositor risk class, where risk class is defined by the variance of deposit flows facing the bank. At the same time it is also assumed to choose on the liability side of the balance sheet a desired level of bank capital (or capital–deposits ratio) which acts as an insurance fund for bank depositors. The bank is assumed to select these variables, hence an associated level of F, based on private profit-maximizing criteria. Obviously the higher the bank's risk class and the lower its capital, the greater the probability that the bank will fail.

To introduce the possibility of catastrophic failure we have to consider the behavior and preferences of bank regulators and depositors. The model developed below shows that there is a conflict between these two groups that can lead to catastrophe. It is assumed, quite reasonably, that regulators view the social costs of bank failure as being greater than the private costs, i.e., the cost to either individual bank managers (owners) or depositors. Consequently, regulators have a tendency to impose taxes in the form of reserve requirements and deposit insurance on banks in order to minimize the probability of failure, hence their social costs. While depositors prefer some regulation, to avoid the private risk of ruin, thereby receiving an implicit subsidy from regulatory intervention, it can be argued that the net benefit of regulatory intervention to depositors declines with the degree of regulatory intervention beyond some critical point. This is because part of the regulatory tax burden imposed on banks is passed on to depositors in the form of higher service charges and/or lower deposit interest rates. The greater the regulatory tax, the greater the burden passed on to depositors and the greater the private cost of regulation vis à vis its benefits. Clearly, a conflict will arise whenever the private costs of failure are significantly less than the social costs. Since regulators increase the tax burden to mini-mize the latter, there will be an inducement for depositors to withdraw their funds and find more attractive financial instruments in which to invest.

[3] Zeeman [35].

This conflict of interest between regulators and depositors, given a certain risk class and capital–deposit ratio of the bank, leads to a state that minimizes a cost function. The cost function can be viewed as the sum of social cost and private cost. However, we do not explicitly model this cost (potential) function here but rather derive a behavioral model that results in catastrophic bank failure.

Initially we define the following stochastic flow variables for a representative bank:

$\tilde{Y}$ = net cash inflows from asset interest and liquidations,

$\tilde{X}$ = net deposit inflows,

$\tilde{Z} = \tilde{X} + \tilde{Y}$ = net cash inflow.

Suppose that $\tilde{X}$ is sufficiently negative that

$$(4) \qquad \tilde{Z} = \tilde{X} + \tilde{Y} < 0.$$

That is, net deposit outflows are greater than the maximum cash inflow derivable from the bank's asset structure.[4] To prevent bankruptcy, the bank uses funds from its capital reserves K to offset or meet the net cash shortfall (see Votja [28]). Consequently, bankruptcy will occur only if

$$(5) \qquad \tilde{Z} = \tilde{X} + \tilde{Y} \leq -K.$$

In other words, bankruptcy occurs when negative net cash flow is greater than the bank's capital funds K, so that the latter are totally exhausted. Obviously for any Z, the smaller K, the higher the probability of bank failure. Dividing each term in Eq. (5) by the level of deposits, we find

$$(6) \qquad \tilde{Z}/D = \tilde{X}/D + \tilde{Y}/D \leq -K/D$$

or

$$(7) \qquad \tilde{z} = \tilde{x} + \tilde{y} \leq k,$$

where $k = -K/D$ and the lowercase letters show the above relationships in per-dollar terms. As defined above, the probability of bankruptcy or bank failure depends on the probability that $\tilde{x} + \tilde{y} \leq k$, i.e.,

$$(8) \qquad F = \text{probability of failure} = \text{prob}(\tilde{x} + \tilde{y} \leq k).$$

We assume that in determining the desired level of F, the bank has two control variables. The first is the risk class α it joins, and the second is the

---

[4] This relies on the implicit assumption that the bank cannot sell off all its assets at their market values. That is, it relies on the existence of some market imperfections, such as the non-existence of a secondary market for loans, to produce this result.

choice of a capital–deposits ratio.[5] With respect to the first variable, it is assumed that a bank by determining a particular type of assets portfolio policy (and hence $\bar{y}$) places itself in a certain risk class α and in turn attracts a certain depositor clientele. For simplicity, we identify the depositor clientele by the standard deviation σ of their deposit flows $\tilde{x}$. Hence, by altering its assets investment portfolio, a bank can indirectly influence its σ.[6,7] Moreover, we make the additional assumptions that, *ceteris paribus*, the higher the risk class α of the bank, the larger it is, and that in general we can associate high-α banks with large commercial banks and low-α banks with small commercial banks. The latter assumption seems reasonable given the special type of depositor clientele attracted by large banks.[8] The relationship between k and F is fairly obvious from Eq. (8); as k is increased (the capital–deposits ratio decreased), the probability of bank failure increases.

The relationship between our control variables and our state variable F can be written in general terms as

$$(9) \qquad \begin{aligned} F &= f(\alpha, k), \\ \partial f/\partial \alpha &> 0, \qquad \partial f/\partial k > 0. \end{aligned}$$

With the model developed so far, there is no possibility of catastrophic failure. To demonstrate this possibility, we consider the separate influences of bank regulators and of depositors' level of confidence on the shape of the equilibrium surface of the system. Our objective is to show one set of circumstances under which government policy and changes in depositors' confidence can actually induce catastrophic failure in the system.

The influence of government policy on the banking system has two main aspects. The first is at the microlevel, where bank regulators, such as the FDIC, attempt to maintain the soundness of the banking system through balance-sheet examinations, setting portfolio regulations and providing

---

[5] The choice of $k = -K/D$ instead of the actual capital–deposit ratio as the control variable is a mathematical convenience and has no substantive effect on the results.

[6] Assuming $\tilde{x} \sim N(0, \sigma^2)$.

[7] However, the bank does not have full control over σ, since it is assumed that σ is also affected by the levels of depositors' confidence in the bank, i.e., $\sigma = \sigma(\alpha, D)$, where D is the confidence level. This relationship is discussed more fully later in the text.

[8] A distinction has to be made between the variability and velocity of liabilities (Broadhaus [3], Morrison and Selden [15]). While small banks rely largely on demand (and passbook savings) deposits which tend to have a relatively high velocity (turnover) per unit of time, this velocity tends to be relatively stable over time, with low interperiod variability. However, larger banks have become increasingly reliant on borrowed funds and purchased liabilities, such as CDs, which tend to have a low velocity but high variability, as witnessed by the periods of disintermediation and reintermediation experienced by large commercial banks since 1969.

deposit insurance. The second is at the macrolevel: The Federal Reserve transmits changes in the money base and other monetary instruments through the banking system in an attempt to achieve certain macroeconomic goals. In our discussion we will only consider the effects of bank regulators on failure.

A number of motivations for regulatory intervention have been implied in the literature. Two are of particular importance for our model. The first is that intervention is positively related to a general or overall perception by regulators concerning the probability of a bank failing F,[9] while the second stresses the importance of asset quality and hence α, in determining regulator concern.[10] Consequently, it seems reasonable to assume that regulatory policy at the microlevel is functionally related to both α and F. That is, the higher the bank's risk class α for any perceived level of F, the greater the degree of regulatory intervention. Bank regulators are assumed to be more concerned with a large (high-α) bank failing than with a small (low-α) bank failing, given the same probability that each will fail. However, for any given α, the higher F is, the more likely it is that regulators will intervene. Let $G(\cdot)$ be the regulators' intervention function; then the probability of bank failure for any bank will depend partly on bank decision makers' preferences and partly on regulatory intervention, with regulatory intervention having two main effects on F. The first is to shift the whole surface downward, lowering the probability of failure for all banks (i.e., all α,k combinations). The second involves the slope of the equilibrium surface, since for any risk class the degree of intervention is likely to be positively related to the level of α. That is, as regulators tend to be more concerned with high-α banks than with low-α banks for any given F, this tends to flatten the equilibrium surface without changing the smooth and continuous nature of the adjustment path over time.

Dynamically, we can think of bank management selecting some k and α based on private return and cost considerations, with an associated probability of failure. The higher this probability of failure, the more likely it is that regulators will intervene to reduce F to some lower, more socially desirable level.[11] Thus new values of k and α, and hence F, will be arrived at through the interaction of bank management and regulators. The new equilibrium level of failure will depend on the precise functional forms of f and G in Eq. (10):

$$F = f(\alpha, k) - G(\alpha, F),$$
$$(10) \qquad \partial G/\partial \alpha > 0, \qquad \partial G/\partial F > 0.$$

---

[9] See Mayne [12].

[10] See Schweitzer [19].

[11] That is, the social costs of bank failure are greater than the private costs; see Meltzer [13].

We have assumed, for the purposes of simplicity, that the functions $f(\cdot)$ and $G(\cdot)$ are additive rather than multiplicative, the overall effect on bank failure being some linear combination of bank management preferences and regulatory intervention.

To introduce the possibility of catastrophic failure, we have to consider the effect of changes in depositor confidence on the probability of failure. The hypothesis is that, within any risk class, σ will also depend on depositor confidence as to the soundness of the banks in that class,[12] and that depositors are more likely to suffer a confidence crisis the higher the risk class of the bank. In a sense, by changing its assets portfolio, a bank not only chooses a new depositor clientele but also acquires certain attributes from that clientele, including some tendency for depositors to induce a collective crisis. While these crises may take the form of simultaneous demand deposit withdrawals, a failure to renew maturing CDs and other money market instruments, or both, a confidence crisis is hypothesized here as being more likely for higher-α banks than for low-α banks. We also make some reasonable assumptions about the likely effect of F on depositors' confidence. It is assumed here that the greater the depositors' perceptions that a bank is unsound (i.e., high F), the less confidence they have as a group in the bank's ability to survive and the more likely it is that some adverse depositors' reaction will be induced. Hence the depositors' crisis of confidence (deposit withdrawal) function D depends positively on both α and F as in

$$(11) \qquad \begin{aligned} D &= D(\alpha, F), \\ \partial D/\partial \alpha &> 0, \qquad \partial D/\partial F > 0. \end{aligned}$$

Assuming that the crisis of confidence effect is additive, we derive

$$(12) \qquad F = f(\alpha, k) - G(\alpha, F) + D(\alpha, F)$$

as the relationship among the three economic agents, the two control variables, α and k, and the probability of bank failure F.

The important question is: What are the precise conditions required to hold on the functional forms of G, D, and f necessary and sufficient to produce catastrophic failure for a bank? Thom [25] has shown that for catastrophe to occur, Eq. (12) has to be a cubic polynomial in F.[13]

---

[12] In general terms $\sigma = \sigma(\alpha, D)$, where D is a depositors' confidence index. Sinkey [22] has also analyzed the effects of adverse publicity on deposit flows to large banks that eventually failed.

[13] Strictly speaking, Thom's theorem applies to some neighborhood of the cusp point. Hence we assume the neighborhood is sufficiently large in our context, so that F is now only related to the probability of failure or bankruptcy. Therefore, we call F, a measure of bankruptcy, and without loss of generality we assume $F > 0$.

We make the assumption that[14]

(13) $G(\alpha, 0) = D(\alpha, 0) = \partial G/\partial F(\alpha, 0) = \partial D(\alpha, 0)/\partial F = 0.$

That is, when $F = 0$, a small increase in F will, *ceteris paribus*, have no effect on G and D. This seems a reasonable assumption to make and implies that the D and G functions pass through their respective origins as functions of F.

Now from the Malgrange preparation theorem we can express $G(\cdot)$ and $D(\cdot)$ as[15]

(14) $G(\alpha, F) = g_2(\alpha)F^2 + g_3(\alpha)F^3,$

(15) $D(\alpha, F) = d_2(\alpha)F^2 + d_3(\alpha)F^3.$

If we simplify Eqs. (14) and (15) by assuming that g_2, g_3, d_2, and d_3 are linear in α, then

(16) $G(\alpha, F) = g_2\alpha F^2 + g_3\alpha F^3,$

(17) $D(\alpha, F) = d_2\alpha F^2 + d_3\alpha F^3,$

where d_2, d_3, g_2, and g_3 are constants such that

$$g_2, g_3, d_2, d_3 > 0,$$

since we require $\partial G/\partial F$ and $\partial D/\partial F$ to be positive. Substituting Eqs. (16) and (17) into Eq. (12), we derive the cubic polynomial

(18) $0 = f(\alpha, k) - \alpha(g_3 - d_3)F^3 + \alpha(d_2 - g_2)F^2 - F.$

Condition. Now the cusp catastrophe will occur *if and only if* the following two conditions hold:

(19) $g_3 > d_3,$

(20) $d_2 > g_2.$

That is, when the second-order depositor reaction to F is greater than the second-order regulatory reaction, but the third-order regulatory reaction is greater than the third-order depositor reaction, catastrophe will occur. Figure 2 shows functional shapes for the G and D functions satisfying

---

[14] Strictly speaking, we mean $\lim_{F \to 0} G = D = \partial G/\partial F = \partial G/\partial D = 0.$

[15] The Malgrange preparation theorem implies that $G = g_2(\alpha)F^2 + g_3(\alpha)F^3 + g(\alpha, F)F^4$ and $D = d_2(\alpha)F^2 + d_3(\alpha)F^3 + d(\alpha, F)F^4$. But Thom's theorem implies that $g(\alpha, F) = d(\alpha, F)$. Hence here we only consider the relevant terms.

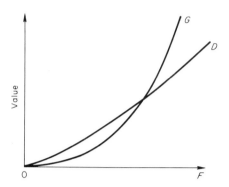

Fig. 2.   *G* and *D* functions.

conditions (13), (19), and (20) that are both necessary and sufficient to induce a cusp catastrophe.

The graphical relationship implies that depositors' confidence effects dominate at low levels of F, but the greater curvature of $G(g_3 > d_3)$ ensures that G will dominate D at higher levels of F. The real-world occurrence of the relationships shown in Fig. 2 certainly seems possible, since, in simple terms, they imply that regulators show relatively little concern for banks with a low probability of failure compared to the concern expressed by depositors. However, regulators become relatively more concerned with failure as the level of F rises. More importantly, this example shows that even if regulatory intervention is sufficient to outweigh a depositors' crisis of confidence at high F, catastrophic failure can still occur for the bank. Clearly, an important implication of the model for regulatory policy is that it is not regulation per se that will prevent catastrophic failure, but the power of regulatory intervention when compared to the confidence patterns exhibited by depositors over the whole range of F. Referring to Fig. 2 again, this implies that if G is always above D for all F and not just for high F, catastrophic failure cannot occur. The identification by regulatory agencies of banks with high F's and associated intervention may not in itself be sufficient to prevent failure of the type considered here.

We can make this example even more concrete by assuming that

(21) $d_3 = g_3 = 0,$

with conditions (13), (19), and (20) still holding. In this case

(22) $F = f(\alpha, k) - \alpha g F^3 + \alpha d F^2.$

Now we can explicitly analyze the properties of the catastrophe case. Rearranging Eq. (22),[16] we find that

$$(23) \quad \alpha g\left(F - \frac{d}{3g}\right)^3 + \left(1 - \frac{\alpha d^2}{3g}\right)\left(F - \frac{d}{3g}\right) = f(\alpha, k) - \frac{d}{3g} + \frac{2\alpha d^2}{27g^2}$$

$$= h(\alpha, k, g, d).$$

Since the right-hand side of Eq. (23) comprises constants d and g plus the control variables α and k, we can again rearrange Eq. (23) as

$$(24) \quad F_1^3 + \left(1 - \frac{\alpha d^2}{3g}\right)F_1 = \frac{h(\alpha, k)}{\alpha g} = p(\alpha, k)$$

after rewriting $F - (d/3g)$ as F_1 in Eq. (24).

Using the inverse function theorem, since $\partial f/\partial k > 0$ implies $\partial p/\partial k > 0$, we can view, without loss of generality, p and c as the relevant independent control variables, where c is defined as

$$(25) \quad c = -(1 - \alpha d^2)/\alpha g$$

so that Eq. (24) becomes

$$(26) \quad F_1^3 - cF_1 = p.$$

Differentiating Eq. (26), we get

$$(27) \quad 3F_1^2 - c = 0,$$

and hence

$$(28) \quad c = 3F_1^2.$$

Substituting Eq. (28) into Eq. (26) and solving for p, we find

$$(29) \quad p = -2F_1^3.$$

Using t as a dimensions parameter, we can derive a "cusp line":

$$(30) \quad (p, c) = (-2t^3, +3t^2),$$

with the origin of the cusp catastrophe line at $\alpha = 3g/d^2$. To ensure that the cusp catastrophe occurs at $F > 0$ and $\alpha > 0$, we require $d/3g > 0$, $d^2/3g > 0$ or, equivalently, $d, g > 0$. This proves that, in the general case, conditions (19) and (20) have to hold. Their relationships are shown in Fig. 3.

---

[16] Note that the control variables are defined in a neighborhood around the origin. This follows from condition [21].

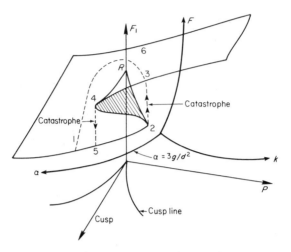

Fig. 3.   The cusp catastrophe for bank failure.

Note that in Fig. 3 the cusp has been determined by the interactions of the three economic agents described in this chapter.

Consider bank B, a high-risk-class (high-α) bank located at point 1 in Fig. 3. Suppose the bank proposes to keep its risk class constant but decides that its capital–deposits ratio is too high and chooses to lower its capital–deposits ratio (increase its k). Figure 3 indicates that although the bank could increase k without much of an increase in the probability of failure at the locality of point 1, a policy of continuously increasing k could lead to catastrophe, as the interactions among the three agents in the model are sufficient to create a discontinuity in the equilibrium relationship between k and F. It should now be clear, from our earlier examples, that if the bank allows k to increase as far as point 2 in Fig. 3, there will be a dramatic jump in the probability of the bank failing, increasing the probability of failure from a point at the bottom of the cliff (point 2) to a point at the top of the cliff (point 3). Hence this implies that for banks in this risk class, there is some cliff-edge value of k for which even a marginal fall below this level can push the bank into catastrophic failure.

However, Fig. 3 also indicates that the bank has an alternative, slower route to point 3. By changing both α and k, it could avoid the cusp and therefore any discontinuities on the equilibrium surface. This path is indicated by the dotted arrows in Fig. 3 and involves a path of small, continuous increases in F. It seems reasonably intuitive that while regulators' early-warning systems (see Altman [1], Sinkey [21, 23], Pettway and Sinkey [17]) may be able to identify as problem banks those banks that follow the slow, continuous path around the cusp, it is far more difficult for regulators to identify as problem banks those following the catastrophe path since, in the latter case, the increase in the probability of failure is so sudden. Indeed, it may prove impossible, as a practical matter, for regulators to prevent such failures unless they can identify, *ex ante*, the cliff-edge value of k for each risk class and impose minimum and enforcable k ratios below this value.

A further interesting implication of the model is the asymmetric relationship between k and F when k is increasing as opposed to decreasing. Suppose bank B reaches point 3 and then decides to reverse its policy and reduce k (increase its capital–deposits ratio). However, in this case there will be no sudden fall in F back to point 2; instead, there will be a gradual decline in F as k decreases until point 4 is reached, followed by a sudden drop in the probability of bank failure.

A logical explanation exists for such asymmetries within the model in that it takes time for depositors to regain their confidence in the soundness of a (former) problem bank. Moreover, the model implies that once this confidence is restored, there will be a dramatic decrease in the probability of the bank failing.

It is also worth adding that not all the banks in Fig. 3 are subject to the possibility of catastrophic failure. Consider a low-risk-class bank at point 6 on the equilibrium surface. If this bank maintains its risk class and increases its k, the path to increased probability of failure can only be slow and continuous, since the equilibrium path followed lies below the origin of the cusp. This result has the important implication that only high-risk-class banks are subject to the possibility of catastrophic failure. As we earlier identified high-risk-class banks as those heavily reliant on borrowed liabilities and money market deposits (see footnote 8), this suggests that large money market institutions, such as big New York City banks, are more prone to catastrophic failure than medium- or small-sized urban banks. This attempt at generalization does not of course totally preclude the possibility of catastrophic failure for small banks, especially those in small, rural communities where demand deposit flows tend to be highly variable. Banks of this latter type can also be classified as belonging to a high-risk-class group.

A final implication of the model is the circumstances under which a microcatastrophe can become a macrocatastrophe. So far we have been considering a representative bank in a certain risk class with a certain k. We have suggested that banks in high-risk classes can be identified as (large) money market institutions that appear to be more susceptible to catastrophic failure than small banks. To the extent that large money market banks compete in similar areas for similar types of deposits and draw their management from a similar pool of labor, we might reasonably expect them to adopt relatively homogeneous management policies toward k and asset selection over time. The more homogeneous the high-risk-class group of banks, the more likely it is that a microcatastrophe will also be a macrocatastrophe, since such banks would tend to follow similar policies toward k and α over time. If these banks were completely homogeneous, they would arrive simultaneously at the catastrophe point 2 in Fig. 3. Clearly, in this case the social costs of such a combined increase in the probability of bank failure could be enormous.

4. CONCLUSIONS AND SUMMARY

This chapter has discussed the principles of catastrophe theory, outlining some problems in banking and finance on which it might throw new light. At the same time we selected one of the problems to show the type of insights that catastrophe theory can provide. This involved developing a model for identifying possible conditions under which catastrophic bank failure might occur. Three economic agents were assumed to be involved in determining the overall probability of failure. It was shown that even if regulatory intervention were powerful in the case of banks perceived by regulators to have a high probability of failing, this might not be sufficient to prevent catastrophe. Indeed, one important implication of the model was that the cusp catastrophe condition depended on the scale of intervention by regulatory authorities over the whole range of F. In particular, it appears that the crucial relationship is a relative one, depending on the degree of regulatory intervention vis à vis the confidence of depositors in the bank's soundness at every level of F. If depositors' confidence is low, at reasonably low levels of F, this may be sufficient to induce a catastrophic failure before regulators can come to the aid of the bank. Under such circumstances early-warning systems based on *ex post* balance-sheet data may be of little use.

A further important implication of the model was to show that certain types of bank, namely, those in depositor high-risk classes, tend to be more susceptible to catastrophe than those in low-risk classes. Although this implication is qualitative, needing obvious empirical verification, it does suggest that there is a certain type of bank that might require increased regulatory attention. It certainly implies that regulators, if they are concerned with preventing catastrophe, should pay particular attention to banks that rely heavily on money market deposits and borrowed funds; especially as the unexpected failure of even a single billion-dollar bank could have enormous implications for the payments mechanism as a whole.

Clearly, further extensions of the model are possible, such as expanding the number of agents involved by including, for example, the Federal Reserve and monetary policy effects on bank failure. Also, experimentation might be made with the variables included in each agent's decision set in an attempt to discover other feasible circumstances under which catastrophe could occur. The fact that most problem banks have hitherto been *ex ante* identifiable by early-warning systems based on *ex post* data should not lull regulators into a sense of well-being. Catastrophic failure is a possibility, and appropriate regulatory action, such as the imposition of minimum capital–deposit ratios for each depositor risk class, should be actively considered.

REFERENCES

1. Altman, E. I., Predicting performance in the savings and loan industry, *Journal of Monetary Economics* **3**, 443–466 (1977).
2. Black, F., and Scholes, M., The effect of dividend yield and dividend policy on common stock prices and returns, *Journal of Financial Economics* **1**, 1–22 (1974).
3. Broadhaus, A., Linear programming: A new approach to bank portfolio management, *Federal Reserve Bank of Richmond Monthly Review* **58**, 3–11 (1972).
4. Elton, E. J., and Gruber, M. J., Marginal stockholders' tax rates and the clientele effect, *Review of Economics and Statistics* **52**, 68–74 (1970).
5. Fama, E. F., and Miller, M. H., "The Theory of Finance," Chapter 5. Holt, New York, 1972.
6. Golubitsky, M., An introduction to catastrophe theory and its applications, *SIAM Rev.* **20**, 352–387 (1978).
7. Jensen, M., and Meckling, W., Theory of the firm: Managerial behavior, agency costs and ownership structure, *Journal of Financial Economics* **3**, 305–360 (1976).
8. Kalay, A., Essays in Dividend Policy. Ph.D. Thesis, Univ. of Rochester (1978).
9. Kim, E. H., A mean variance theory of optimal capital structure and corporate debt capacity, *Journal of Finance* **33**, 45–64 (1978).
10. Kraus, A., and Litzenberger, R., A state-preference model of optimal financial leverage, *Journal of Finance* **28**, 911–922 (1973).
11. Mather, J., Notes on Right Equivalence. Unpublished papers.
12. Mayne, L., Importance of Federal Supervision on Bank Capital. Bull. No. 85–86, New York University, Graduate Business School (1972).
13. Meltzer, A. H., Major issues in the regulation of financial institutions, *Journal of Political Economy* **75**, 478–501 (1967).
14. Miller, E. H., Debt and taxes, *Journal of Finance* **32**, 261–275 (1977).
15. Morrison, G. R., and Selden, R. T., "Time Deposit Growth and the Employment of Bank Funds." Association of Reserve City Bankers, Chicago; Illinois, 1965.
16. Murphy, N. B., Disclosure of the problem bank lists: A test of the impact, *Journal of Bank Research* **9**, 88–96 (1979)..
17. Pettway, R. H., and Sinkey, J. H., Establishing On-Site Examination Priorities: An Early Warning System Using Accounting and Market Information. Unpublished Manuscript (1979).
18. Poincaré, H., "Sur Les propriété des fonctions défines pas les équations aux différentielles partielles." Gauthier-Villais, Paris, 1928.
19. Schweitzer, S. A., Bank loan losses: A fresh perspective, Federal Reserve Bank of Philadelphia, *Business Review*, 18–28 (1975).

20. Scott, J. H., Jr., A theory of optimal capital structure, *Bell Journal of Economics* **7**, 33–54 (1976).
21. Sinkey, J. F., A multi-variate statistical analysis of the characteristics of problem banks, *Journal of Finance* **30**, 21–35 (1975).
22. Sinkey, J. F., Adverse publicity and bank deposit flows: The cases of Franklin National Bank of New York and United States National Bank of San Diego, *Journal of Bank Research* **5**, 8–24 (1975).
23. Sinkey, J. F., Identifying large problem/failed banks: The case of Franklin National Bank of New York, *Journal of Financial and Quantitative Analysis* **12**, 779 (1977).
24. Sinkey, J. F., Identifying problem banks, *Journal of Money, Credit and Banking* **10**, 184–193 (1978).
25. Thom, R., "Stabilité Structurelle et Morphogenesè." Benjamin, New York, 1972.
26. Thom, R., Topological models in biology, *Topology* **8**, 313–335 (1969).
27. Thom, R., Structural stability, catastrophe theory and applied mathematics, *SIAM Review* **10**, 189–201 (1977).
28. Votja, G. J., "Bank Capital Adequacy." Citicorp, New York, 1973.
29. Whitney, H., On singularities of mappings of Euclidean spaces. I. Mappings of the plane into the plane, *Annals of Mathematics* **62**, 374–410 (1955).
30. Zeeman, E. C., Mathematics of the Brain. Mathematics Institute, Univ. of Warwick (1970).
31. Zeeman, E. C., The Geometry of Catastrophe. Mathematics Institute, Univ. of Warwick (1971).
32. Zeeman, E. C., A Catastrophe Machine. Mathematics Institute, Univ. of Warwick (1972).
33. Zeeman, E. C., Differential Equations for the Heartbeat and Nerve Impulse, Mathematics Institute, Univ. of Warwick (1972).
34. Zeeman, E. C., Catastrophe Theory in Brain Modelling, Mathematics Institute, Univ. of Warwick (1972).
35. Zeeman, E. C., Applications of Catastrophe Theory, Mathematics Institute, Univ. of Warwick (1973).

DEPARTMENT OF FINANCE
GRADUATE SCHOOL OF BUSINESS
NEW YORK UNIVERSITY
NEW YORK, NEW YORK

Order by Fluctuation and the Urban System

P. M. Allen

1. INTRODUCTION

A new paradigm has appeared concerning the evolution of complex systems. It unifies the hitherto divergent interpretations of the word "evolution" in the physical and human sciences. In the former, for example, this word has traditionally referred to a movement toward thermodynamic equilibrium, the elimination of nonuniformities, and an increase in disorder within the system, while in biology and sociology it has been associated with increasing complexity, specialization, and organization.

In a system containing innumerable atoms and molecules a physical description is made in terms of the average density of each component at a point in space and time. The evolution of such a system is then given by the partial differential equations governing the change in these densities resulting from chemical reactions, hydrodynamic flow, or diffusion. All such systems when isolated move toward thermodynamic equilibrium, toward molecular disorder. However, a system in contact with the external world can, under certain conditions, exhibit a quite different evolution, one corresponding to a decrease in entropy, to a self-organization.

A first condition for the observation of such behavior is that the system be subject to flows of energy or matter from the exterior, such that the internal entropy production (due to friction, chemical reactions, etc.) is more than compensated for. A second condition necessary for the occurrence

115

of self-organization is the existence of certain nonlinear interaction mechanisms between the microscopic elements of the system. In chemistry, for example, this corresponds to the presence of auto- or cross-catalytic reactions, and in hydrodynamics to nonlinear flow mechanisms. Structures that appear spontaneously are of an entirely different nature than those characterizing thermodynamic equilibrium, for example, crystals. They have been called dissipative structures in order to stress their total dependence on the dissipative flows and reactions taking place, which characterize the fact that the system is far from thermodynamic equilibrium [14].

A vital role in this phenomenon of self-organization is played by the fluctuations—deviations from the average values of variables, parameters, or behaviors inherently present in the system because of the statistical nature and perhaps the incompleteness of the description. This latter point concerns particularly the extension of these ideas to the evolution of variables representing populations of macroscopic objects, for example, in ecological, social, and economic systems. We shall return to this point later. Because of fluctuations, the evolution of a system containing nonlinear mechanisms is not necessarily determined uniquely by the equations governing the interacting variables.

The presence of fluctuations introduces a new element into the evolution of such a system—stability. A given state of the system will be stable if, when a fluctuation occurs that throws it off the trajectory dictated by the equations, it returns to this trajectory, damping out the fluctuation. However, this may perhaps not be the case; the fluctuation away from the path it was describing may be amplified, and the system will be driven toward some quite different branch of solution, perhaps reflecting a qualitative change in its characteristics. If this occurs, then it means that the original trajectory or solution was unstable and that the system will then evolve rapidly toward a new solution that is stable. This type of behavior is typical of a set of nonlinear differential equations whose variables are of a statistical nature and are hence subject to fluctuation. The nonlinear terms of the equations introduce the possibility of multiple steady-state solutions, some of which may be stable. The particular choice of a solution, how a given system actually evolves in time, depends on exactly which fluctuations occur, that is, on the history of the particular system. It is this process that underlies the formation of dissipative structures. It is similar in some ways to an adaptation and has been called order by fluctuation; as we see, it is a combination of deterministic and stochastic elements. In this way we see how the extension of physics to the description of systems far from equilibrium resolves the apparently divergent interpretations of evolution in the physical and human sciences. Elements of history and choice can arise for chemical and hydrodynamic dissipative structures.

However, order by fluctuation is a paradigm that can be applied equally well to the study of systems described in terms of basic units having themselves an internal structure and containing mechanisms governing their interaction with the environment and the other elements of the system. If these interactions are nonlinear, then once again density fluctuations can lead to the appearance of spatial structures entirely comparable to dissipative structures [16]. However, there exists a dramatic new freedom for such systems—the possibility of innovation.

In effect, there exists the possibility that the exact form of the basic elements of our description may not be completely stable and that following some internal crisis or event a new type of individual may appear. The impact of this on the whole system, which is made up of a great number of individuals or elements, is determined by the structural stability of the system to such an event [2]. In other words, if it occurs, will the interactions of the system lead to its amplification or will they on the contrary repress the new type of individual?

In a biological system in which the behavior of individuals is governed uniquely by their genetic makeup, the amplification of a new type of individual corresponds to Darwinian evolution by the natural selection of mutants appearing spontaneously in the system [1]. In the case of higher animals, however, we have the possibility of behavioral change and its adoption by imitation. It is of course this form of order by fluctuation that is particularly pertinent to the social system, since both new and important techniques characterized by enormously increased productivity as well as entirely frivolous fashions can both invade and conquer the system.

Summarizing this discussion, we see that the evolution of complex systems occurs through two, perhaps equally important, mechanisms: (1) movement along a stable trajectory determined by the equations of the variables, for which simple extrapolative predictions are possible, and (2) moments of instability when fluctuations in density or innovation drive the system off to some new, stable trajectory. These two processes succeed each other, giving a natural expression to the dual aspects of determinism and chance, of historical necessity and accident.

2. INTERURBAN DYNAMICS

The evolution of urban centers can be studied by formulating differential equations describing the population change at each point and by studying the effect of fluctuation on such equations.

When urban centers interact, the resulting evolution is rather complex. In some cases economic competition results in the growth of a particular center at the expense of those near it. However, in another case the growth of a center can be a stimulus for economic development of the region around it, including the appearance of flourishing industrial satellites and wealthy suburban dormitory communities. As populations increase, as economic innovations invade the system, and as transportation improves, hitherto independent towns and villages are gradually brought into interaction with each other; as a result, some grow and others decline. It has been observed by geographers that there exists a certain regularity in the relative sizes of the urban centers remaining in interaction within a region. This regularity is governed by what has been called the rank-size rule [5].

Considerable information has been amassed concerning this question, and a rather more complicated situation has been revealed. In particular, Berry [6] has studied the rank-size distributions of different countries and as a result has made the following classifications.

Thirteen out of the 38 urban centers he studied obeyed the simple rank-size rule known as Zipf's law [18]:

$$P_n = P_1/n^b,$$

where P_n is the population of the nth city, and b is some power. Fifteen others had a "primate" distribution, where the first or first few ranked cities were disproportionately large. Other intermediate situations exist, reflecting the play of historically different economic, social, and technological forces in the different regions. Any model purporting to describe the evolution of a system containing several interacting urban centers must be able to take into account the effects of historical circumstances as well as the operation of universal laws.

Another important characteristic of urban settlement is the relation between the average separation of centers and their size. Broadly speaking, large centers are separated by large distances, while small centers are on the average much closer to one another. The forces underlying such a distribution were clarified greatly by the work of Christaller [8], who introduced the concept of central places, broadly synonymous with towns, which serve as

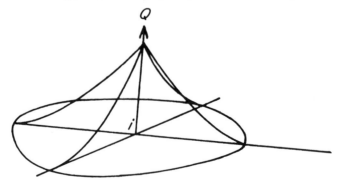

Fig. 2.1.   Cone of demand around point i.

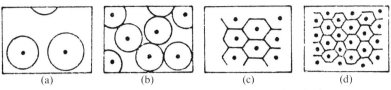

(a) (b) (c) (d)

Fig. 2.2.   Sequence of events leading to hexagonal territories.

centers for regional communities by supplying them with goods and services. Central places vary in importance, higher order centers offering a wider range of goods and services than lower order ones. In other words, the basic proposition of Christaller, which we shall adopt, is that the spatial and hierarchical relationships between urban centers reflect the play of economic forces, and that large centers are the seat of many economic functions while small centers possess only a few.

If we consider a center that supplies a certain good at price P, then assuming uniform transport costs, the area from which demand will come for the good will be circular, with the quantity demanded falling off from the center as illustrated in Fig. 2.1, giving rise to a demand cone.

The idea of Christaller was that the overlapping of these demand cones, constituting economic competition among centers, would give rise to a network of hexagonal territories, as depicted in the evolution shown in Fig. 2.2.

He then considered the superposition of different-size hexagonal lattices and suggested settlement patterns based on three different optimization criteria:

(a)   The distances traveled by consumers in order to obtain all possible goods and services are at a minimum, and for a population uniformly distributed give rise to the pattern shown in Fig. 2.3.

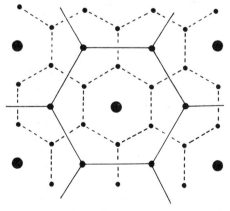

Fig. 2.3.   Christaller's central places, $K = 3$, corresponding to minimum distances.

(b) A traffic-optimizing case in which as many intermediate centers as possible lie on the important routes between large centers is shown in Fig. 2.4.

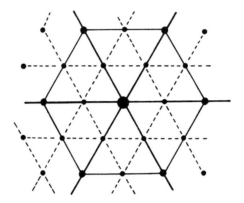

Fig. 2.4. Christaller's central places, $K = 4$.

(c) An optimization of an administrative nature whereby lower order centers are not shared by larger ones but fall clearly within a trading area is shown in Fig. 2.5.

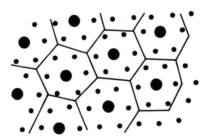

Fig. 2.5. Christaller's central places, $K = 7$.

It was Lösch [12], who later pointed out that these patterns corresponded also to functions having different market thresholds. For example, those requiring three basic population units as clientele tended to adopt a $K = 3$ network, those demanding four arranged themselves in a $K = 4$ network, and those requiring seven in a $K = 7$ network. Lösch suggested that human settlement was governed by superimposed lattices of different order, and that if one assumed the existence of a regional center offering all goods and services, then lower order centers would occur where rotation of the smaller-mesh lattices gave rise to the maximum coincidence of centers. In this case,

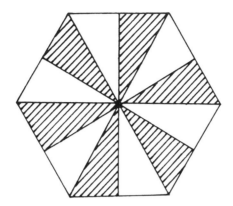

Fig. 2.6.   Loschian landscape with alternative city rich and city poor sectors.

he pointed out, one would find sectors radiating out from the regional center, and these sectors would be alternatively city rich and city poor, as shown in Fig. 2.6.

Many rather unrealistic assumptions underlie the work of Christaller and Lösch, however. For example, it is by no means clear how the multitude of individual decisions of entrepreneurs could lead to a spatial distribution that would optimize (minimize) globally the distances that must be traveled by consumers. In the first place, this would assume that consumers and entrepreneurs could be perfectly informed as to the distances and goods offered by other centers. Also, it is necessary to allow for the fact that the population ceases to be distributed uniformly once urban centers appear, and Isard [10] has refined the model to take into account the distortion of the size and form of the hexagons caused by the nonuniform population distribution.

A further severe limitation of such models is their static character. Consider, for example, what happens in a region of increasing population density. The market threshold of a particular good, which at some initial moment corresponds to four population units, will at some later time only require three. How can the settlement pattern change from a $K = 4$ network of hexagons to one corresponding to $K = 3$? Clearly, there is no dynamic mechanism by which this may occur. This type of model is an equilibrium description outside time. Despite this major drawback, however, the basic idea that it is economic forces that are behind the spatial and hierarchical relationships observed among urban centers in a region seems correct. Thus the "central place theory" has been developed to a considerable degree of mathematical sophistication and rightly occupies an important place in the study of urban hierarchies [4].

If geographers have tended to produce static models, economists have, on the other hand, developed dynamic models involving multiplier processes as, for example, the theories of Myrdal [13] and Perroux [15] where the differential growth of regions is supposed to be due to the existence of self-sustaining mechanisms of growth which can operate on initially small regional differences. From the point of view that we shall adopt here, this means that economic activity is autocatalytic: A local increase tends to produce a further increase, be it through the appearance of better local infrastructure, transport facilities, formation of a skilled labor force, etc. However, interregional economics, employing for example input/output techniques [11], although very useful for certain purposes, does not allow the internal spatial structure of a region to be studied. It is indeed a way of regarding a system as a "black box," whereas it is precisely our aim to study the effect of the urban structure on the economic functioning of the region and, for example, the full repercussions on the urban hierarchy and the regional economy of a new development in the transportation system. One may summarize the situation by saying that geographers have tended to produce spatial models that are outside time, while economists have produced dynamic models that are not truly spatial.

The model we shall develop in this section in order to describe interurban evolution is based on the idea of Christaller that the urban hierarchy is a result of the spatial distribution of economic functions. However, we shall introduce a dynamic mechanism whereby the economic functions are introduced into our system in a spatially random fashion but result nevertheless in spatial structuring of the population distribution into urban concentrations, which then become favored points for further growth as more economic activities are introduced into the system. We shall develop differential equations describing the evolution of population at each point in the system as economic activities grow and compete and local populations wax and wane.

A. The Mathematical Model

The urbanization of a region is viewed as being due to the successive integration of economic functions introduced at random places and times into the system, together with an evolution of the means of transport and communication, as the different centers grow and compete with one another and the population responds to the spatially inhomogeneous employment opportunities resulting from this.

Let us first consider the very simple equation for population growth first given by Verhulst:

$$dx/dt = bx(P - x) - dx$$

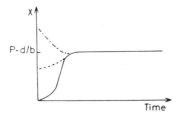

Fig. 2.7. Logistic growth for different initial conditions.

for the population x. The constants b and d are related to the birth and death rates, respectively, while P measures in some sense the natural richness of the environment. In Fig. 2.7 we see the trajectory of the population for different initial conditions.

If we wish to apply such an equation to the growth of a human population, then we must allow for the fact that the carrying capacity of a particular locality may be enhanced by the presence of an economic function at that point. It is this possibility of an agreement being reached among people that adds new dimensions to evolution, involving the division of labor and urbanization. Let us therefore represent our space by a lattice of points, each of which i has an equation for the change in its population:

$$(2.1) \qquad dx_i/dt = bx_i\left(P + \sum_k R^{(k)}S_i^{(k)} - x_i\right) - mx_i,$$

where b is related to the rate at which x_i can grow as a result of births and immigration from other points and m to the rate at which it can decrease as a result of natural mortality and emigration. The carrying capacity P for self-sufficient families is enhanced by a factor $R^{(k)}$ for each production unit of type k at point i. (See Fig. 2.8.)

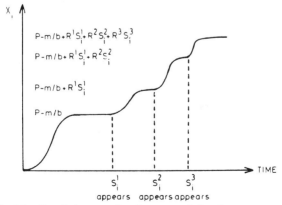

Fig. 2.8. Population growth at i as economic functions appear.

Having written down a simple equation describing how the population at a locality responds to the long-term employment capacity of that point, it is now necessary to develop an equation governing the evolution of this employment capacity as economic innovations are introduced, as different centers compete, and as transport networks develop. In order to do this, we write down an equation expressing the economic law governing the size of $S_i^{(k)}$, the number of production units of k situated at i, as it adjusts to the demand for the good or service attracted to i. This must be zero when the function does not exist at the point and grow at some rate to a ceiling determined by the market available, taking into account the competition coming from rival centers. We use the very simple form

(2.2) $dS_i^{(k)}/dt = \alpha S_i^{(k)}(\text{demand for } k \text{ at } i - \gamma^{(k)}S_i^{(k)})$.

Let us consider each term in detail. First, the parameter α is a measure of the time scale on which an entrepreneur reacts to possibilities of expansion or to the necessity of contraction. This is a function of the dynamism of local entrepreneurs, the availability of credit, the rewards in view, etc.

The demand for the good k that will be attracted to i (see Fig. 2.9) is written supposing that there exists some average reaction of the population relating the quantity an individual buys Q to the price demanded $P_i^{(k)}$.

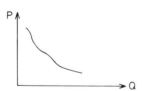

Fig. 2.9.   Schematic law of demand as a function of price.

We have supposed in the simulations that this relation has the form

(2.3) $Q = \varepsilon^{(k)}/P_i^{(k)e}$,

where e is some power. This inverse relation is particularly simple, but others may be used without changing the form of the results. If we allow for the cost of transportation between the consumer at point j and the producer at i, a distance $r_j - r_i$, then the price will be

(2.4) $P_{ij}^{(k)} = P_i^{(k)} + \phi^{(k)}(r_j - r_i)$,

where $\phi^{(k)}$ is some unit cost of transport for k. The quantity demanded by an individual situated at j is therefore, from Eq. (2.3),

(2.5) $\varepsilon^{(k)}/[P_i^{(k)} + \phi^{(k)}(r_j - r_i)]^e$, and the total demand coming from all the individuals situated at the different points j around i is, in the absence of competition,

(2.6) $$\sum_{j=1}^{n} x_j \varepsilon^{(k)} / [P_i^{(k)} + \phi^{(k)}(r_j - r_i)]^e.$$

It is necessary, however, to take into account the possibility that the consumers at j may be drawn away from i to a rival center. In order to do this, we must write a term that represents the relative attraction of the center i for the function k exercised on the population x_j at j, compared with the attraction of the other centers i' which also produce k. In order to deduce the form of such a function, we suppose, first, that the attraction of a center is all the greater if there are a number of other functions situated there. To some extent, then, a single trip can satisfy several needs. Thus if n is the number of functions situated at i, we shall suppose an attraction proportional to $1 + \rho n$, where ρ is some constant corresponding to this cooperativity. In addition, we shall suppose that the attraction is inversely proportional to the cost of buying the good there, giving a form

$$(1 + \rho n) / [P_i^{(k)} + \phi^{(k)}(r_j - r_i)].$$

In order to find the fraction of consumers drawn to center i from all the possible centers i', we have simply to write

(2.7)   Fraction attracted $= \dfrac{\{(1 + \rho n) / [P_i^{(k)} + \phi^{(k)}(r_j - r_i)]\}^I}{\sum_{i'} \{(1 + \rho n') / [P_{i'}^{(k)} + \phi^{(k)}(r_j - r_{i'})]\}^I}$,

where n' is the number of functions situated at point i'. The power I takes into account the sensitivity of the population to this relative attractivity—its discernment and its uniformity of response. It has the form of a factor of intervening opportunities well known to urban geographers [17]. For a very large value of I the least difference in attractivity is translated by a 100% response of the population at j, who all go to the most attractive center. As I decreases, the response becomes less clear-cut, and we then have a more realistic description in which the choices of center are distributed among the various possibilities, with probability proportional to the attractiveness of a particular center.

The theory of Christaller is based on $I \to \alpha$; that is, people have total information on the relative merits of centers, and all react in exactly the same way. Our model can thus deal with the more realistic situation in which the lack of information and the diversity of individuals produce an intermediate response. Also, the factor ρn plays a role in displacing the lines of consumer indifference further away from a center with many functions, corresponding to increased attraction. Also, if there exists a difference in price among centers because of economies of scale being realized by a large unit of production, then this is also reflected in its greater attractiveness to the surrounding clientele.

The term $\gamma^{(k)}S_i^{(k)}$ in Eq. (2.2) fixes the market threshold of the unit of production. Thus when $S_i^{(k)} = 1$, $\gamma^{(k)}$ is the figure that the economic demand for k at i must exceed if growth is to occur. It is supposed in our model that half of the turnover can be used for salaries, thus making $R^{(k)}$ of Eq. (2.1) equal to $\gamma^{(k)}/2$. Clearly, one can change the capital/labor intensity in time simply by changing the value of the fraction.

There now remains the economies of scale that can be inserted into the problem in the following manner. If the intrinsic price $P_i^{(k)}$ has the form

$$(2.8) \qquad P_i^{(k)} = \sigma^{(k)} + [\Delta^{(k)}/\gamma^{(k)}(aS_i^{(k)} - bS_i^{(k)^2})],$$

then it passes through a minimum at $S_i^{(k)} = a/2b$.

The installation of an exporting activity at a point will result in an increase in the domestic sector of the town's economy as the population at the point increases. This augmentation in the demand for local goods and services results in an increased employment capacity in the domestic sector, which in turn causes a further increase in the local population, and so on, increasing local demand and local population until a new steady state is attained. This state is marked by an increase in total population which is considerably greater than that initially introduced directly by introduction of the export activity. This amplifying mechanism is called the urban multiplier and appears quite naturally in play between the equation for the population [Eq. (2.1)] and equations for the domestic sector and for an export activity.

The second basic process present in our model is that as the system develops, and populations grow as a result of the installation of various functions, so new market thresholds are exceeded at these points, with the result that still more activities may appear where several are already concentrated. Let us now describe the simulations.

The domestic sector is represented by a function $S^{(1)}$ having $\varepsilon^{(1)} = 0.5$, $\gamma^{(1)} = 10$, $\phi^{(1)} = 1$, and $\Delta^{(1)} = 0$. With this first function the population passes from 50 to $66\frac{2}{3}$ at each point. It is then supposed that an innovation in the form of a new economic activity, which has a market threshold greater than the population at a single point, is characterized by a coefficient of transport permitting exportation of this good or service to other points and which appears first at some random point in the system. For values of the parameters $\gamma^{(2)} = 20$, $\varepsilon^{(2)} = 0.2$, and for $\phi^{(2)} = 0.1$, $\sigma^{(2)} = 0.8$, $\Delta^{(2)} = 4$, the function, when it appears at a point, can become established. At the point where this occurs, implantation of this export activity causes the population to increase and, through the effect of this on $S^{(1)}$, the urban multiplier to operate on the number of residents at this point.

The economic innovation, however, then appears at other random points at random moments, as other entrepreneurs imitate the first. Thus the lattice is gradually filled with centers providing function 2, and the effect of competition among rivals begins to be felt. In these simulations every point is tried as a center for this function, but only those that manage to obtain sufficient territory survive.

Figures 2.10–2.13 show a typical sequence of events. Function 2 was chosen with characteristic parameters such that it corresponds to that of a Christaller $K = 4$ lattice. Comparing our results with those of Christaller, however, we conclude that because entrepreneurs act as individuals in an unconcerted fashion, the symmetry of the Christaller pattern almost never occurs. It is only one of a great many possible *stable* final distributions of centers of function 2 and normally only occurs as a result of planning.

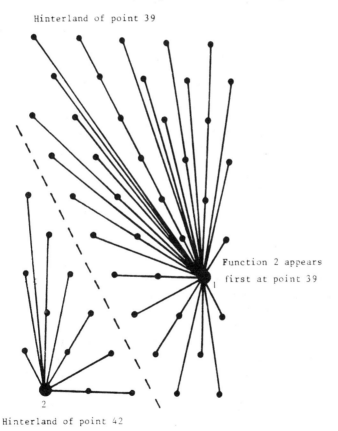

Fig. 2.10. Time evolution. Distribution at $t = 0.02$. $\gamma^{(1)} = 10$, $\varepsilon^{(1)} = 0.5$, $\phi^{(1)} = 1$, $\Delta^{(1)} = 2$, $\sigma^{(1)} = 0.8$, $\gamma^{(2)} = 20$, $\varepsilon^{(2)} = 0.2$, $\phi^{(2)} = 0.1$, $\Delta^{(2)} = 4$, $\sigma^{(2)} = 0.8$.

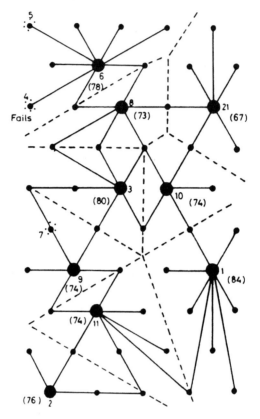

Fig. 2.11.   Distribution at $t = 0.5$.

Function 2 appears first at point 39 (Fig. 2.10), and the population at this point immediately starts to increase. Thus the domestic sector also expands, and the exportation "hinterland" of this initial point is the entire surface of the lattice. However, function 2 very quickly appears at point 42, and the lattice is then shared by these two points.

At a later time, $t = 0.15$, we see that there have been six attempts to imitate point 39. Five of these have been successful, but the imitation at point 1 fails very rapidly because of competition from points 11 and 4. As time goes on, more centers appear, and at the moment $t = 0.25$ we have the maximum number of centers that can simultaneously exist in a system of 50 points—nine in all. After this, there is a certain weeding out, and the number of centers drops to six by time $t = 1$. The point that first received the innovation, point 39, is still the largest, having had the longest continuous period of population growth. However, its hinterland has been cut down

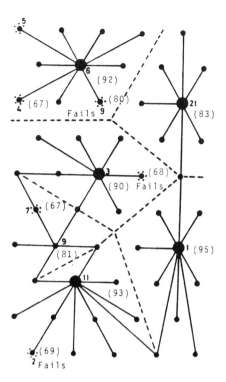

Fig. 2.12. Distribution at $t = 1$. At points 42, 27, 11, 15, and 22 the populations are still above 66.67, because activity 2 was situated at these points previously. Now there is unemployment at these centers following the failure of activity 2, and the populations relax slowly to 66.67.

from the whole lattice initially, to about eight surrounding points. As function 2 becomes fully integrated into the system and population growth ceases, the number of inhabitants at a particular point reflects the size of the hinterland it happens to possess at the end of the simulation. For example, by time $t = 5$, the initial point 39 is only the third largest center, having been overtaken by points 4 and 34.

From this first simulation we see that in the long run only six centers remain at the end. Since all 50 points were tried, at first sight it seems that 44 centers failed. This is not entirely true. In fact, six centers appeared, grew, and later were eliminated through competition, while the remaining 38 never exceeded the market threshold and never really existed. In some ways they correspond to a thought experiment on the part of an entrepreneur who, seeing that the conditions for the subsistence of a unit of production are not met at this point, dismisses the idea of starting an enterprise there. Of course, even if he persists in his attempt, the result will be the same.

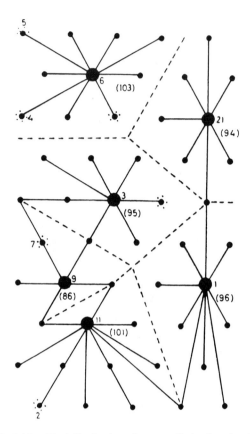

Fig. 2.13. Final distribution of centers offering function 2.

Coming back to Fig. 2.13, we see that overall, 12 centers have existed at different times, six of which remain, the rest having been eliminated; this type of figure showing the success and failure rates of the urbanization history of a region is not at all in disagreement with the results obtained by Berry for Iowa [17]. Neither is the evolution of the number of centers, which early on passes through a maximum and then as the centers interact declines to a lower level.

In Figs. 2.14–2.17 we see the final distribution resulting from simulations of the implantation of function 2, which has exactly the same values of the characteristic parameters and of the initial conditions, but where the random choice of the moments and points of implantation are different. That is to say, the history is different for each simulation. Because of this, the final distribution of centers is different in each case, although average values are roughly adhered to. For example, there are always between six and nine

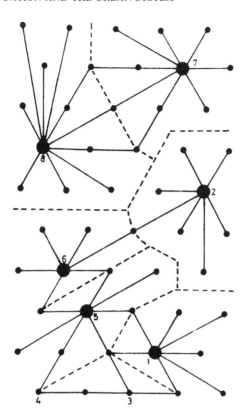

Fig. 2.14.   Final distribution of centers offering function 2. The values of the parameters are the same as for Figs. 2.10–2.13. The stochastic events, however, are different.

higher order centers on a lattice of 50 points, and the population of these centers is approximately 90 units but varies with the size of the territory each center finally controls.

In the next series of figures we study the effect of economies of scale which, by reducing the unit cost of production for the larger enterprise, gives a competitive advantage to earlycomers and also tends to lead to centers having larger populations and hinterlands. In Figs. 2.18–2.21 we present the final distributions corresponding to different degrees of economies of scale, that is, different values of $\Delta^{(k)}/\sigma^{(k)}$ in Eq. (2.8). We see that the sizes of the resulting centers and their territories increase with increasing effect of the economies of scale. Of course this also implies that there are fewer centers than without economies of scale, and so it is reasonable to conclude that as new techniques arise,

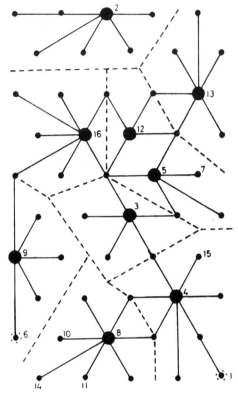

Fig. 2.15.   Final distribution of centers offering function 2. The values of the parameters for
this series of simulations (Figs. 2.14–2.17) are $\gamma^{(1)} = 10$, $\varepsilon^{(1)} = 0.5$, $\Delta^{(1)} = 0$, $\phi^{(1)} = 1$; $\gamma^{(2)} = 20$,
$\varepsilon^{(2)} = 0.1$, $\Delta^{(2)} = 0$, $\phi^{(2)} = 0.1$, $\rho = 0.2$.

which require larger units of production in order to be profitable, so their
implantation in the system will result in the growth of some centers
but also assuredly in the decline of others. In Fig. 2.22 we show that
the urban population supported by the system varies with the economies of
scale.

In the next series of figures we show the effect of launching further economic
innovations in a system that is already structured into centers offering
function 2. In this way we can study the evolution of an urban hierarchy as
new activities are integrated into the system. In Fig. 2.23 we show the state
of the system when function 2 has been introduced at all points at different
moments and where only seven centers remain in a stable configuration.
To this is added a third function, which has a large market threshold and
consequently establishes itself at only one point in the system. This point

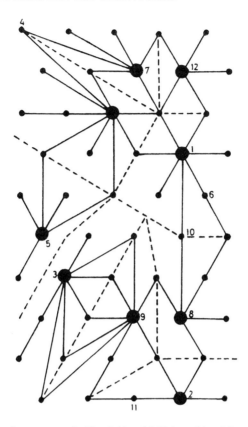

Fig. 2.16. Parameters as in Figs. 2.14 and 2.15, but with a different history.

is one at which function 2 is already established first, because there is a heavy concentration of population and hence of demand for function 3, and, second, because of the cooperativity that exists between functions. This effect occurs either because customers are able to fulfill two purposes in a single trip in the case of distributive activities, or because the transport facilities developed for function 2 can be used by activity 3 at very little extra cost. Thus in Eq. (2.7) the attraction of demand to a point having both functions 2 and 3 is greater than the sum of the attractions to two points, one with function 2 and the other with function 3. This point is allowed for when $\rho \neq 0$.

When function 3 is introduced, the result is as shown in Fig. 2.24. Centers having only function 2 that are too near the "capital," at point 18, are suppressed, while those that remain grow further. Thus the system structures into three levels, and the addition of a third function causes the difference

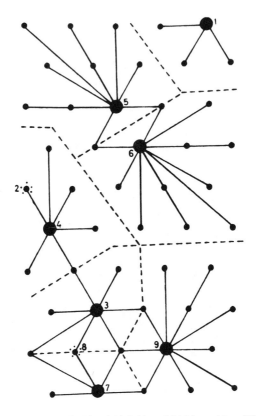

Fig. 2.17.   Parameters as in Figs. 2.14, 2.15, and 2.16 but with a different history.

between levels to increase. For Fig. 2.24 we have calculated the rank-size tule for a simple three-level hierarchy. We have supposed the law

$$P_2 = P_1/2^b, \qquad P_3 = P_1/3^b,$$

where P_1, P_2, and P_3 are the populations of the first, second, and third levels of the center, respectively. In this case, the capital has a population of 261, and the second-level centers offering function 2 have populations of 103, 100, and 99. These slight differences are purely the result of the random events leading to the capture of slightly different territories. We have therefore

$$b_{12} = [\log(P_1/P_2)]/\log 2 = 1.34$$

and

$$b_{13} = [\log(P_1/P_3)]/\log 3 = 1.24.$$

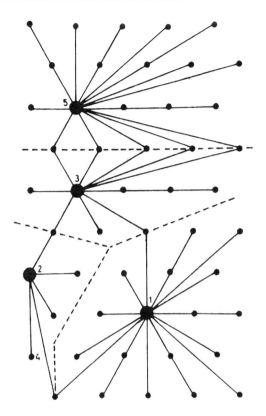

Fig. 2.18. Final distribution of function 2 with small economies of scale. The numbers indicate the order of appearance of a center, and the numbers in brackets its population. All parameters are as for the previous sequences, but $\Delta^{(1)} = 1$, $\sigma^{(1)} = 0.9$; $\Delta^{(2)} = 2$, $\sigma^{(2)} = 0.9$.

The fact that the value of b is almost constant shows that Zipf's law holds, although in the terms of Berry the distribution is slightly primate. This means that compared to the urban hierarchy which would give rise to a constant value of b, here the capital is a little too important.

In Figs. 2.25 and 2.26 we have the final distributions of two similar simulations on a lattice of 30 points. The introduction of the third function again causes the region to structure into three levels of centers. Again we may calculate the values of b relating to the rank-size rule for the region, and for Fig. 2.25 we find $P_1 = 265$; $P_2 = 110, 109, 102$; and $P_3 = 66.6$. This gives

$$b_{12} = 1.27, \qquad b_{13} = 1.26.$$

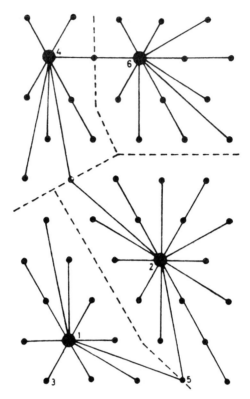

Fig. 2.19.   Final distribution of centers with economies of scale according to the coefficients $\Lambda^{(2)} = 10$ and $\sigma^{(2)} = 0.5$. It is for these values (see (4.16) and (4.18) as well) that the urban population is largest. This implies that the demand satisfied in the system is also a maximum.

We conclude that Zipf's law is a good approximation for the hierarchy. The figures for Fig. 2.26 are $P_1 = 327$; $P_2 = 136, 113$; $P_3 = 66.6$; and the values of b are

$$b_{12} = 1.39, \qquad b_{13} = 1.45.$$

Again the values of b are almost the same, showing that the relation $P_n = P_1/n^b$ is consistent, although a slightly different choice of parameters has led to a considerably higher level of urban population than in the preceding cases.

   In the following example (Fig. 2.27), on a lattice of 50 points we find a rather complex urban structure. In this case the values of b corresponding to the different levels are

$$b_{12} = 0.94, \qquad b_{13} = 0.89, \qquad b_{14} = 1.04.$$

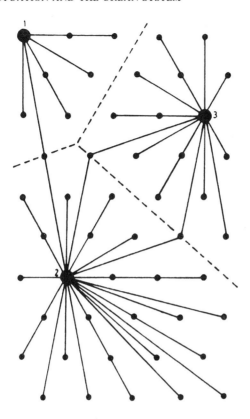

Fig. 2.20. Final distribution with economies of scale corresponding to $\Delta^{(2)} = 10$, $\sigma^{(2)} = 0.5$.

This rather uneven value reflects the difference in the spatial organization of the upper and lower halves of our diagram. In the lower half there is no center having both functions 2 and 3, and we may regard this as being an instance of the stochasticity vanquishing the interaction laws. The nonlinear action of the cooperativity between functions 2 and 3 was not sufficient to overcome the entirely haphazard implantation of these functions. It is interesting to note that if we compare the urban populations resulting directly from implantation of both functions at the point with those resulting from implantation at neighboring points, we find that the urban population due to functions 2 and 3 is 217, and that due to functions 2 and 3 at neighboring points is 162. This is obtained by studying the points 15, 35, and 36 of Fig. 2.27. The difference between 217 and 162 represents the difference in the effectiveness of the action of the urban multiplier on the same point, or the situation when the urban growth is split between two neighboring

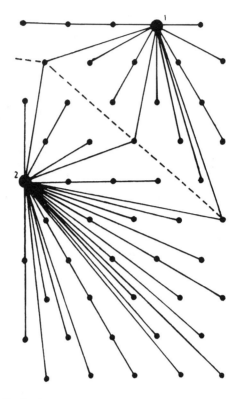

Fig. 2.21. Final distribution for function 2 which is characterized by very large economies of scale. $\Delta^{(2)} = 18$, $\sigma^{(2)} = 0.1$.

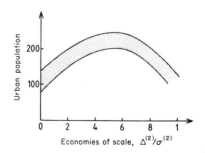

Fig. 2.22. The total urban population present in the final distribution as a function of the economies of scale.

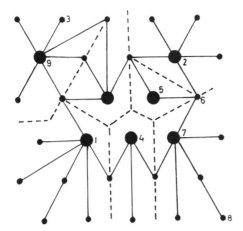

Fig. 2.23. Distribution of function 2 before the introduction of 3. Here $\gamma^{(2)} = 30$, $\varepsilon^{(2)} = 0.15$, $\phi^{(2)} = 0.1$, $\Delta^{(2)} = 0$, $\sigma^{(2)} = 1$; $\gamma^{(3)} = 50$, $\varepsilon^{(3)} = 0.1$, $\phi^{(3)} = 0.1$, $\Delta^{(3)} = 5$, $\sigma^{(3)} = 0.9$.

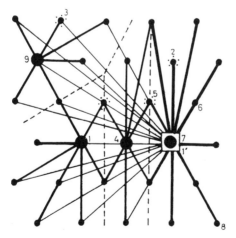

Fig. 2.24. Distribution of functions 2 and 3. Function 3 appears at point 18, where function 2 is already implanted. The combined attraction at this point causes the centers at 8, 15, and 17 to fail. The remaining centers of function 2 grow, and the system structures into a three-level urban hierarchy. Zipf's law applies with $b = 1.3$. ●, Center with function 2; ◙, center with functions 3 and 2.

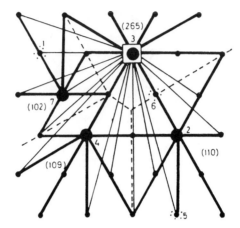

Fig. 2.25.   Final distribution of the centers offering functions 3 and 2 (point 6) and those exporting only function 2 (points 13, 14, and 18). It obeys the relationship $P_i = P_1/i^b$, $b = 1.26$.

points. In a certain sense the structure in the upper half is economically more effective than that in the lower.

In the final sequence of diagrams (Figs. 2.28–2.33), we show the evolution of the lattice of 30 points as functions 2, 3, and 4 are introduced. As seen, the choice of parameters corresponds to a regime that is highly centralizing, and as a result the final situation is one in which there has been a total

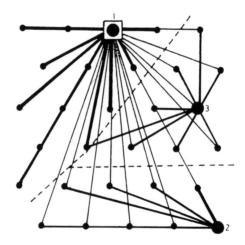

Fig. 2.26.   Final distribution of centers with functions 2 and 3 characterized by the parameters $\gamma^{(2)} = 30$, $\varepsilon^{(2)} = 0.15$, $\Delta^{(2)} = 10$, $\sigma^{(2)} = 0.7$; $\gamma^{(3)} = 50$, $\varepsilon^{(3)} = 0.1$, $\Delta^{(3)} = 15$, $\sigma^{(3)} = 0.7$. The value of b for the rank-size rule is 1.4. ●, Center with function 2; ■, center with functions 3 and 2.

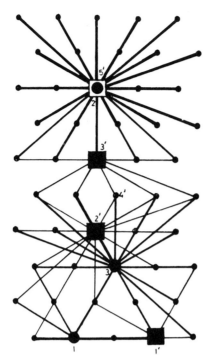

Fig. 2.27. Final distribution of centers after the launching of three functions. We have approximately a rank-size rule with $b \approx 1$. $\bullet$, Center with function 2; $\blacksquare$, center with function 3; $\boxed{\bullet}$, center with functions 2 and 3. Here $\gamma^{(2)} = 30$, $\varepsilon^{(2)} = 0.15$, $\Delta^{(2)} = 0$, $\sigma^{(2)} = 1$; $c^{(3)} = 50$, $\varepsilon^{(3)} = 0.15$, $\Delta^{(3)} = 10$, and $\sigma^{(3)} = 0.8$.

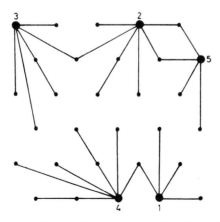

Fig. 2.28. Distribution of function 2 at time $t = 1$. Here $\gamma^{(2)} = 30$, $\varepsilon^{(2)} = 0.15$, $\Delta^{(2)} = 0$, $\sigma^{(2)} = 1$, $\rho = 0.2$.

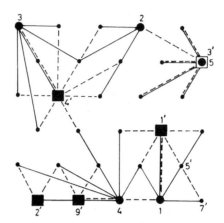

Fig. 2.29. Distribution during the implantation of functions 2 and 3 at $t = 1.3$. Here $\gamma^{(3)} = 30$, $\varepsilon^{(3)} = 0.1$, $\Delta^{(3)} = 3$, $\sigma^{(3)} = 0.9$.

collapse of all the economic functions onto a single point. The total urban population sustained by the activities increases constantly throughout the simulation, however, and is at a maximum in the final, collapsed state. It must be pointed out, however, that the real diseconomies of scale characterizing mammoth cities have not been put into our model. This insufficiency can very easily be remedied, and this is one of our immediate aims.

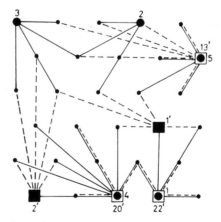

Fig. 2.30. Distribution at time $t = 1.4$. Function 3 has failed at point 12, where there is now, consequently, unemployment.

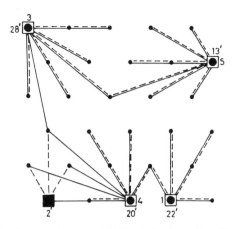

Fig. 2.31.   Distribution at time $t = 1.5$ after the implantation of functions 2 and 3.

All the simulations we have presented have supposed that the ease of transportation is uniform throughout the system. The values chosen for $\phi^{(k)}$ were in all cases

$$\phi^{(1)} = 1 \quad \text{and} \quad \phi^{(2)} = \phi^{(3)} = \phi^{(4)} = 0.1.$$

This corresponds to the reasonable supposition that the exported goods or services cost roughly 10% of their production cost to transport between neighboring points.

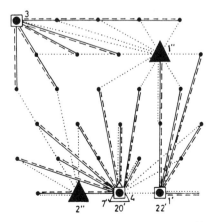

Fig. 2.32.   Distribution at time $t = 2$ after the implantation of function 4. Here $\gamma^{(4)} = 30$, $\varepsilon^{(4)} = 0.08$, $\Delta^{(4)} = 3$, $\sigma^{(4)} = \blacksquare$. $\boxed{\bullet}$, Center with functions 2 and 3; $\blacktriangle$, center with function 4; $\boxed{\!\blacktriangle\!\bullet}$, center with functions 2, 3, and 4.

Fig. 2.33. Distribution at the much later time $t = 8$. The point that possessed all four functions has "swallowed" all the economic activity of all other, lesser centers.

Let us now discuss briefly the significance of the results that have been obtained and the future studies that could be undertaken.

First, the general forms of the urban distributions resulting from our simulations are entirely reasonable, both in their spatial aspects and in their hierarchical size relations. This suggests that the basic form of our equations is correct, although further refinements can certainly be made. Our main aim in this work was to set up a method suitable for modeling the dynamic evolution of urban centers based on the concept of order by fluctuation, and in this we believe we have been successful. Now that we have laid the foundations, it is possible to move on to modeling more realistic situations. A particular urban hierarchy can, for example, be used to choose the parameters corresponding to the domestic and export functions present in the system, and having done this, it is then possible to study, among other things, the impact on this urban hierarchy of a modification in the interurban transportation system. This could perhaps be the introduction of a new ultrarapid means of transport or a sharp increase in the cost of fuel, etc.

Several possibilities suggest themselves for further study:

(a) The impact of a modification of the transport system on the regional or national structure;
(b) The effects of natural inhomogeneities in the intrinsic carrying capacity of different localities, e.g., mountain regions and marshes;
(c) The influence on urbanization of a nonhomogeneous initial distribution of the population and immigration pattern, such as occurred for the United States;

(d) The impact of the formation of a tariff-free zone involving two urban hierarchies;

(e) The relation between the spatial organization of a population and its global economic efficiency, and energy consumption;

(f) The effects on the system of specialized centers whose existence is directly linked to a local particularity, for instance, mining towns and tourist centers;

(g) The influence of external demand and external migration on the urban structures of the region.

This section has been devoted to a study of the evolution of the urban centers within a region, without making a distinction between the place of work and the place of residence of an individual. We have considered that on the scale involved, the distance separating these is almost negligible. Thus we describe simply the implantation of domestic and export functions at a point, as well as the residences of their agents, while neglecting the inevitable competition for space that will result in the internal structuring of each urban center. The formation and evolution of this internal structure are also amenable to study in terms of order by fluctuation, and this is the subject of Section B of this chapter. Intraurban evolution will be studied by magnifying the scale of our studies several times and concentrating on the evolution within a single point. This point will be the center of a hinterland which it supplies through its export activities, for example, point 6 in Fig. 2.25. However, when we study only the evolution of the internal structure of the point, the effect of the hinterland is simply represented by an external demand coming from an unspecified source. This external demand is then the stimulus for the growth of the particular town or city, requiring industrial premises, offices, and a city hall, as well as a population requiring housing, shops, and a variety of services. In Section B it is the evolution of the spatial disposition of these various elements, as the city grows, that will be studied.

B. Intraurban Model

Let us now turn to the internal evolution of an urban center where demand coming from the exterior provides the stimulus for growth and where residents and employers vie with each other for the available space. A full account of this work can be found elsewhere, and here it is only possible to give a brief description of the main points.

Two models have been studied to date: One is based on the scheme proposed by Beckmann [3] where employment is centrally located and individuals choose a place of residence around it. Here we study the evolution of the distribution of two different populations having different mobilities and spatial demands. The other describes the evolution of the distribution within the urban tissue of heavy industry, business and administrative offices, shops, and services, as well as the residential locations of our two populations of different socioeconomic classes.

Residential Location around a Central Point

We suppose that our space is represented by a lattice of 81 points, to each of which correspond two equations, describing the evolution of the two populations $P_i^{(1)}$ and $P_i^{(2)}$ at point i:

$$(2.9) \quad \begin{aligned} dP_i^{(1)}/dt &= (c^{(1)}F_i^{(1)} - P_i^{(1)}) \bigg/ \sum_{i'=1}^{81} F_{i'}^{(1)}, \\ dP_i^{(2)}/dt &= (c^{(2)}F_i^{(2)} - P_i^{(2)}) \bigg/ \sum_{i'=1}^{81} F_{i'}^{(2)}. \end{aligned}$$

The location function $F_i^{(k)}$ describes the attractiveness of point i for population $P_i^{(k)}$. It contains positive terms expressing the cooperative effects between the potential newcomer and the existing population at and around the point in terms of the proximity of urban infrastructure (electricity, water, sewers, medical care, etc.). It also includes negative effects arising from crowding when the density becomes high, or from being far from the center, which will involve the unpleasant task of commuting daily over a large distance. We have also allowed for the feeling of attraction or repulsion that may or may not assail an individual if the neighborhood is particularly full of his own, or the other, population type. By dividing the total net attraction by the sum of that for all the other points, we find what is really important for the change at point i, the relative attractivity of i.

At the initial time $t = 0$, the populations are all zero, and we then let the equations for each population at each point evolve, subject to the condition

$$(2.10) \quad dP^{(k)}/dt = \sum_i (dP_i^{(k)}/dt) = \sigma(D^{(k)} - P^{(k)}),$$

where $D^{(k)}$ is the external demand for work of type $k = 1, 2$, which has been taken as fixed during the simulation, thus limiting the total final population of the city.

Fluctuations, which play a vital role in the appearance of urban structure, are put into the computer simulation by perturbing the populations $P_i^{(k)}$ at intervals. We add or subtract a random quantity between, say, 0 and 10% of its value to each $P_i^{(k)}$. It is these fluctuations that being either amplified or repressed by the system, lead to the spatial organization of the urban center. As we have pointed out above, it is necessary to add these fluctuations artificially to the equations of interaction in order to explore the stability of solutions and to permit the distribution to structure; however, in any

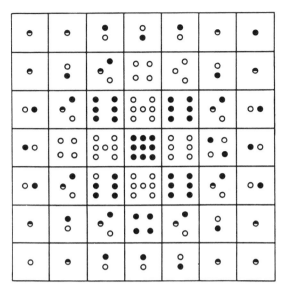

Fig. 2.34.   The final distribution of the poor and rich populations. ●, poor; ○, rich.

real system these fluctuations are always present, being inherent to the statistical nature of the description.

In Fig. 2.34 we show a typical distribution of the two populations resulting from such a simulation. In this case the final distribution of the total population obeys the relation

$$(2.11) \qquad P_r^{(1)} + P_r^{(2)} = Ae^{-br},$$

where r is the distance of the locality from the central point and A is the population at this central point. This is in agreement with many observed distributions.

By studying the distribution at different times of our simulation, it is possible to plot its evolution. A typical case is shown in Fig. 2.35.

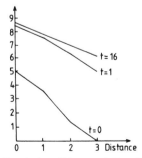

Fig. 2.35.   A typical case of evolution of the population distribution for a simulation.

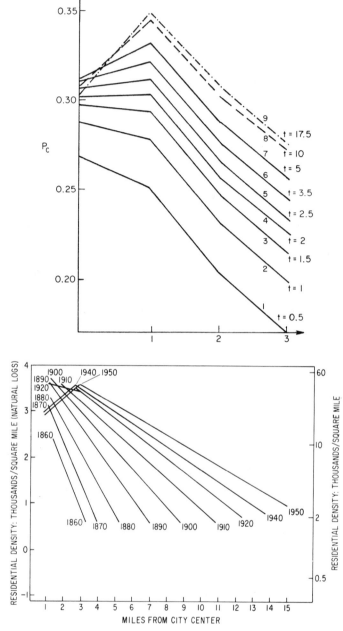

Fig. 2.36. Evolution of the population distribution for a simulation compared with that of Chicago. From Berry (1967).

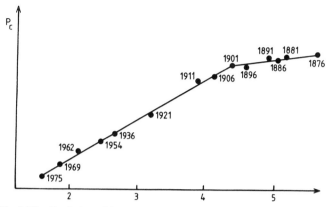

Fig. 2.37.   Evolution of the parameters A and B for Paris (after Buissiére).

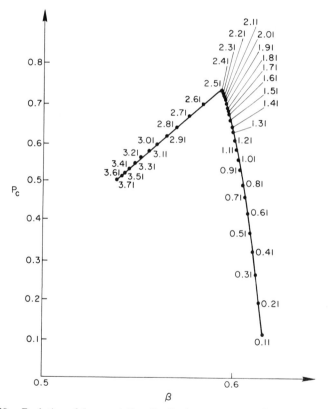

Fig. 2.38.   Evolution of the population distribution parameters when the transport system is suddenly improved.

In certain cases, particularly for very large cities, the competition for space in the center between residences and business premises leads to the formation of a "central crater" in the distribution of residences. By inserting into our equations a term representing such competition at the central point, evolution of the distribution is modified, and an evolution leading to the formation of such a crater is shown in Fig. 2.36. For comparison we show next to it the evolution of the residential distribution of Chicago.

Another interesting characteristic of many urban centers is the manner in which the distribution (Fig. 2.11) changes with time. Buissière has shown for numerous cities that the evolution of the parameters A and b for a given city follows a course like that shown in Fig. 2.37 for Paris. Following his suggestion, we have studied the effects of changing, during a simulation, the parameter corresponding to commuter mobility. Thus we have modeled the repercussions on the residential distribution of the introduction of a new transport system (trains, subways, etc.)

The evolution of our simulated system (Fig. 2.38) shows exactly the same movement along a straight line and suggests that the global repercussions of such innovations could be predicted by these methods.

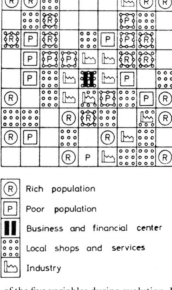

Fig. 2.39.   Distribution of the five variables during evolution. Different types of distribution are possible, and it is possible to find relations between the choice of the values of the various parameters of the differential equations and the resulting form of the distribution. It is of course then possible to study the global repercussions of changes in urban transportation and of different planning options for particular cases, and research is continuing into these possibilities.

Model of the Evolution of Economic and Residential Location within an Urban Center

The second model is considerably more complex and cannot be adequately described here. It simulates the evolution of five variables representing the intensity of economic activities and the number of residences at each point. We have exporting heavy industry, exporting services (administrative centers, etc.) rich and poor populations, and local shops and services. By writing down the equations describing the attraction of each point for these various functions, taking into account the effects of crowding, distance from place of employment, the working of economic multipliers, etc., it is possible to study the evolving spatial organization of the city as it grows. A typical distribution resulting is shown in Fig. 2.39, having a central business district, industrial zones, and roughly concentric rings of rich and poor residents.

3. CONCLUSION

Summarizing the main points of this chapter, we must first underline the generality of the idea of order by fluctuation in the universe. Instead of the view of an inevitable evolution toward disorder and uniformity, characteristic only of isolated systems, we see all around us processes of diversification, specialization, and increasing complexity, which result from the natural laws giverning open systems which are far from thermodynamic equilibrium. In terms of classical or quantum mechanics and equilibrium thermodynamics, most of our everyday experiences, indeed life itself, is inexplicable. It is the facts of nonequilibrium and of nonlinear mechanism, of dissipative structure and order by fluctuation, that underlie them.

In the new dynamics of such phenomena, we find that chance and determinism play conplementary roles. The particular state of a system cannot be explained uniquely in terms of a constant phenomenological law; it partly depends on its particular history, what actually occurred and where. Fluctuations occur at random moments and places, and the deterministic equations either repress or amplify them. We see that far from being unimportant, fluctuations and innovations play a decisive role in the evolution of such systems.

ACKNOWLEDGMENTS

This work was performed by an interdisciplinary group at Brussels University under the guidance of I. Prigogine. Its members are P. M. Allen, J. L. Deneubourg, M. Sanglier, F. Boon, A. de Palma, S. Pahaut, and I. Stengers. The group wishes to thank Professor I. Prigogine, whose ideas have inspired this work, for his constant interest and for many helpful discussions. This work has been made possible by financial support from Actions de Recherche Concertees

of the Belgian government, under convention No. 76/81 II.3, the Fonds National de Recherche
Scientifique, and the United States Department of Transportation, under contract No. T.S.C.
1185.

REFERENCES

1. Allen, P. M., *Bull. Math. Biol.* **37**, 389 (1975).
2. Allen, P. M., *Proc. Nat. Acad. Sci. USA* **73**, 665 (1976).
3. Beckmann, M., On the Distribution of Rent and Residential Density in Cities. Paper in
    Seminars on Mathematical Applications in the Social Sciences, Yale Univ. (1957).
4. Berry, B. J. L., "Geography of Market Centers and Retail Distribution," Prentice-Hall,
    Englewood Cliffs, New Jersey, 1967.
5. Berry, B. J. L., and Garrison, W. C., "Readings in Urban Geography" (H. M. Mayer and
    C. F. Kohn, eds.). Univ. of Chicago Press, Chicago, Illinois, 1959.
6. Berry, B. J. L., and Horton, F. E., "Geographic Perspectives on Urban Systems." Prentice-
    Hall, Englewood Cliffs, New Jersey, 1970.
7. Buissière, R., "London Papers in Regional Science." Vol. 3, Patterns and Processes in
    Urban and Regional Systems, pp. 83–113. Pion, London, 1973.
8. Christaller, W., "Die Zentralen Orte in Süddeutschland." Gustav Fischer, Jena, 1933
    [*English Trans.*: C. Baskin, Bureau of Population and Urban Research, Univ. of Virginia
    (1954)].
9. Glansdorff, P., and Prigogine, I., "Structure, Stability and Fluctuations." Wiley (Inter-
    science), London, 1971.
10. Isard, W., "Location and the Space Economy," Wiley, New York, 1956.
11. Leontieff, L., "Input/Output Analysis." Oxford Univ. Press, London and New York, 1967.
12. Lösch, A., "Die Raumliche Ordnung der Wirtschaft, " Fischer, Jena, 1939 [*English
    Trans.*: W. Woglan and W. Stopler, "Economics of Location." Yale Univ. Press, New
    Haven, Connecticut, 1954].
13. Myrdal, G. M., "Economic Theory and Underdeveloped Regions." London, 1957.
14. Nicolis, G., and Prigogine, I., "Self-organization in Non-Equilibrium Systems." Wiley,
    New York, 1977.
15. Perroux, F., "L'économie du XXiéme siècle," Part II, Poles de Croissance. Presses Univ.,
    Paris, 1961.
16. Prigogine, I., *in* "L'idée de Régulation dans les Sciences." Séminaires au Collège de France,
    Maloine and Doin, Paris, 1977 [*English transl.*: "Evolution and Conciousness" (E.
    Jantsch and C. Waddington, eds.). Addison-Wesley, Reading, Massachusetts, 1976].
17. Stouffer, S. A., Intervening opportunities: a theory relating mobility and distance, *Amer.
    Sociolog. Rev.* **5** (1940); Huff, D. L., Probability analysis of shopping centre trading areas,
    Land Econ. **53** (1963). Wilson, A. G., "Urban and Regional Models in Geography and
    Planning." Wiley, New York, 1974.
18. Zipf, G. K., "Human Behaviour and the Principle of Least Effort." Addison-Wesley,
    Reading, Massachusetts, 1949.

UNIVERSITÉ LIBRE DE BRUXELLES
BRUXELLES, BELGIUM

The Qualitative Analysis of Nonlinear Dynamic Economic Systems by Structural Methods

F. J. Evans
G. Fradellos

1. INTRODUCTION

In the modelling of truly physical engineering systems one can usually resort to some underlying principle in order to generate the descriptive equations. These principles are usually generally accepted, and therefore their validity goes unquestioned.

In economic and social systems, principles analogous to the central principles of motion in mechanics have been proposed and are more concerned with statics than dynamics. In macroeconomic dynamics one is often in the position of having no generally accepted theory in forming the framework of the mathematical model. Hence in these fields there often exists no proper understanding of the mechanism of operation. This often results in the most cherished of preconceived notions being built into the model a priori. Therefore the result is often a model that exhibits behavior that conforms to these preconceived ideas. There are further problems associated with establishing the nature of any existing nonlinearities in the system, for in the systems under discussion it is not possible to perform identification tests. Most of the methods used so far have usually fallen into the category of fitting past data by some form of time series. Models of this

153

nature suffer from the weakness that the final form exhibits no structural properties that can be associated with the structure of the system itself. The purpose of such models has largely determined their size, their variables, and the relationships among these variables, with often inadequate discussion of this aspect of model building. It is therefore not possible to relate any physical attributes to the system, and hence no understanding is obtained about the way the system actually works. Furthermore, such models provide a very poor basis on which to develop further refinements and, in the event that a sudden change takes place, either in the system or in the environment, it is not possible to make any intelligent modifications in the model. One can only return to a new set of data.

Apart from the general acceptance of nonlinearity it is possible that existing conditions of equilibrium have been much too closely associated with the idea of "stationarity." It is possible that the most general form of equilibrium is that associated with the existence of some form of nonlinear oscillation—a limit cycle. Clearly, one can never investigate a system that possesses this form of behavior from the basis of any linearized approximation. The argument that such systems have a behavior that is the aggregation of a large number of "forces," although basically true, does not mean that the related effect is not determined by a much smaller number of fundamental causes. This could mean that the problem of complexity is not, as is often claimed, completely, one of dimensionality but more of complexity of structure in the sense of gross nonlinearity.

From an engineering systems point of view one is only concerned with the "formal" aspect of economic theory, which is none other than the structural aspects of the observed economic phenomenon [6, 10]. The mathematical models used here will thus model only some of the dominant features of the problem and are many stages removed from policy applications. In analyzing the structural considerations of the behavior and operation of macroeconomic systems, we propose to use a technique already developed [1]. It involves mapping of the structural properties into a vector field, which allows the transient motion to be expressed as a resultant of gradient and rotational components. The aim is to examine the time behavior of a real system derived from basic properties of macroeconomics in a more qualitative way. In this way we may then be able to attribute to the system some type of basic structure that can be associated with a physical understanding of the underlying mechanisms that govern its motion.

Using this initial framework one can study the growth and propagation of economic activity in aggregated systems. This has led to a consideration of mutually coupled oscillators which can be important in the generation of business cycles and is much more realistic than existing attempts involving single economy systems. Entrainment is shown to be particularly relevant in the case of a national economy comprising a number of interacting regions and in a world model with its interacting national economies.

2. ASPECTS OF SYSTEMS STRUCTURE

The most usual form of descriptive equations adopted in modern dynamic systems analysis is the state space form of sets of first-order differential equations:

(2.1) $\qquad \dot{X}_i = f_i(X_1, X_2, \ldots, X_n) \qquad$ or $\qquad \dot{X} = AX.$

This can be interpreted by a vector field which, if continuous in a simply connected region and possessing first derivatives, can be resolved into an irrotational and a rotational component [1]. These components define a scalar field and a vector field, respectively:

(2.2) $\quad \dot{X}_i = \dot{X}_{i1} + \dot{X}_{i2} \qquad$ and $\qquad \dot{X} = -\nabla\Phi + \dot{X}_2 \qquad$ with $\qquad X'\dot{X}_2 = 0.$

This ordered form can under certain conditions be related to the algebraic property of any matrix A, which allows it to be expressed as the sum of symmetric and skew-symmetric components:

(2.3) $\qquad A = \frac{1}{2}(A + A') + \frac{1}{2}(A - A') = A_+ + A_-.$

Such a matrix relationship can then be related to the physical aspects associated with electrical networks in which the matrix A has a diagonal with elements formed of the resistive or dissipative elements of the networks. These elements do not normally appear in the off-diagonal positions, which are therefore only governed by the presence of energy storage within the system.

Electrical networks have the unique advantage over other classes of physical systems that their *actual* physical structure is isomorphic to the abstract mathematics structure, called the linear graph, that relates the "topology" or "connectivity" to the algebra of the physical variables. Thus, even if any other type of physical system is described by a set of equations that have not been derived from a linear graph directly, it is often possible to relate, by analogy, some degree of physical function to the elements of these equations. This will be demonstrated later in the case of certain economic problems.

To see how this is possible, a brief reference will be made to the differential equation forms representing the general electrical network. Such equations can only be obtained by selecting the correct set of independent variables (i.e., by choosing the correct tree of the linear graph; this is achieved by placing all capacitors and voltage sources in the tree, and all inductors and current sources in the links) [4].

The general form obtained is then

$$(2.4) \qquad \begin{bmatrix} \mathbf{L} & 0 \\ 0 & \mathbf{C} \end{bmatrix}\begin{bmatrix} \dot{\mathbf{i}}_L \\ \dot{\mathbf{v}}_C \end{bmatrix} = \begin{bmatrix} -\mathbf{R}_1 & -\mathbf{a} \\ \mathbf{a}^t & -\mathbf{R}_2^{-1} \end{bmatrix}\begin{bmatrix} \mathbf{i}_L \\ \mathbf{v}_C \end{bmatrix} + \mathbf{B}\begin{bmatrix} \mathbf{E} \\ \mathbf{I} \end{bmatrix},$$

where $\mathbf{L}$ and $\mathbf{C}$ are diagonal matrices composed of inductive and capacitive storage elements respectively, $\mathbf{R}_1$ and $\mathbf{R}_2$ resistive dissipative elements, $\mathbf{E}$ and $\mathbf{I}$ independent sources of voltage and current, and $\mathbf{i}$ and $\mathbf{v}$ currents and voltages, respectively, and the suffixes L and C give the distribution of these to inductors and capacitors, respectively.

Matrix $\mathbf{a}$ contains only ± 1 or 0 elements. These equations can now be expanded to

$$(2.5) \qquad \begin{bmatrix} \mathbf{L} & 0 \\ 0 & \mathbf{C} \end{bmatrix}\begin{bmatrix} \dot{\mathbf{i}}_L \\ \dot{\mathbf{v}}_C \end{bmatrix} = \begin{bmatrix} -\mathbf{R}_1 & 0 \\ 0 & -\mathbf{R}_2^{-1} \end{bmatrix}\begin{bmatrix} \mathbf{i}_L \\ \mathbf{v}_C \end{bmatrix} + \begin{bmatrix} 0 & -\mathbf{a} \\ \mathbf{a}^t & 0 \end{bmatrix}\begin{bmatrix} \mathbf{i}_L \\ \mathbf{v}_C \end{bmatrix} + \mathbf{B}\begin{bmatrix} \mathbf{E} \\ \mathbf{I} \end{bmatrix}$$

$$\equiv \mathbf{A}_+ \mathbf{x} + \mathbf{A}_- \mathbf{x},$$

where $\mathbf{B} = 0$ in the autonomous case, which can now be directly referred to the composition above.

Hence we see that Φ can thus be considered a dissipative (i.e., entropic) function and $\dot{\mathbf{X}}_2$ will be associated with energy storage (conservation) only. From a mathematical point of view, however, the convergence properties of the system will be governed by the gradient field, and the periodicity by the rotational component.

This approach can be particularly valuable in the study of systems that possess no "accepted" physics (as in economics) and of those for which the identification is hindered by the fact that the correlation between the nature of the input and the internal processes is completely unknown (as in biological systems).

It is also possible to synthesise highly nonlinear systems to fit known behavior and to decide nonlinear control strategy by shaping of the closed-loop vector fields.

It is now possible to extend the use of the $\nabla\Phi$ vector defined above by the further definition of new vectors and scalar functions. Referring to Fig. 1, we can write

$$F_\sigma = \text{resolved part of } \dot{\mathbf{x}} \text{ along } \mathbf{A}_+ \mathbf{x},$$

$$F_\tau = \text{resolved part of } \dot{\mathbf{x}} \text{ along } \mathbf{A}_- \mathbf{x}.$$

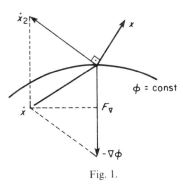

Fig. 1.

Then the following relations exist:

$$(2.6) \qquad F_\sigma = \left\langle \dot{\mathbf{x}}, \frac{-\nabla\Phi}{|\nabla\Phi|} \right\rangle \frac{-\nabla\Phi}{|\nabla\Phi|} = -\sigma \frac{\nabla\Phi}{|\nabla\Phi|^2},$$

$$(2.7) \qquad \sigma = \langle \dot{\mathbf{x}}, -\nabla\Phi \rangle = -F'_\sigma \cdot \nabla\Phi = \frac{\partial x}{\partial t}\frac{\partial \Phi}{\partial x} = -\frac{d\Phi}{dt},$$

$$(2.8) \qquad F_\tau = \left\langle \dot{\mathbf{x}}, \frac{\mathbf{A}_- \mathbf{x}}{|\mathbf{A}_- \mathbf{x}|} \right\rangle \frac{\mathbf{A}_- \mathbf{x}}{|\mathbf{A}_- \mathbf{x}|} = \tau \frac{\mathbf{A}_- \mathbf{x}}{|\mathbf{A}_- \mathbf{x}|^2},$$

$$(2.9) \qquad \tau = \langle \dot{\mathbf{x}}, \mathbf{A}_- \mathbf{x} \rangle = F'_\tau \mathbf{A}_- \mathbf{x},$$

$$(2.10) \qquad \sigma = \langle \dot{\mathbf{x}}, \mathbf{A}_+ \mathbf{x} \rangle = F'_\sigma \mathbf{A}_+ \mathbf{x}.$$

The Φ contours define stable and unstable regions if and only if they enclose "stable" and "unstable" points. The system will never remain in a $\sigma = 0$ contour, but a stationary point can exist on $\sigma = 0$ and will exist on *all* intersections $\tau = 0$, $\sigma = 0$. Contours of Φ and σ can be used for transient analysis of nonlinear problems—by computer-aided methods—but without explicit solution (i.e., integration). More details can be found in ref. (3).

It is also possible that the curvature of trajectories,

$$(2.11) \qquad |K| = |\dot{x} \times \ddot{x}|/|\dot{x}|^3,$$

where $x = x(t)$, can be a useful indicator of transient behavior.

3. THE NATURE OF NONLINEAR OSCILLATORY BEHAVIOR

It has been claimed [17] that there are two prototype equations that characterise the field of nonlinear differential equations; they are the classic oscillators of Van der Pol and Duffing, both of which are structurally stable perturbations of the classic harmonic oscillator. The first of these, which generates a self-sustaining (nonforced) oscillatory behavior, is of the form

(3.1) $\ddot{x} + \varepsilon(x^2 - 1)\dot{x} + x = 0,$ ε small constant $> 0,$

and the second is the simplest nonlinear forced damped oscillator and has the form

(3.2) $\ddot{x} + \varepsilon k\dot{x} + x + \varepsilon \alpha x^3 = \varepsilon F \cos \Omega t.$

They differ from a network or physical point of view in the fact that in the Van der Pol equation it is valid to consider the nonlinear properties as associated with the presence of a nonlinear dissipator or resistor, but in the Duffing equation the nonlinearity can be considered as residing in a "storage" or "spring"-like element. A variation of the Van der Pol equation is the so-called Rayleigh equation of the form

(3.3) $\ddot{x} + (\dot{x}^2 - 1)\dot{x} + x = 0,$

but this equation does not present different problems of analysis and in fact is transformable into the Van der Pol type.

It has been demonstrated [17] that both of the forms above can be related to the cusp catastrophe of Thom. For the purposes of this chapter it is the Van der Pol equation that is the most significant.

Writing it in state space matrix form we have, if $x = x_1$ (using the Rayleigh form),

(3.4) $\dot{x}_1 = x_2, \qquad \dot{x}_2 = -x_1 - (x_2^2 - 1)x_2,$

$$\begin{bmatrix} x_1 \\ x_2 \end{bmatrix} = \begin{bmatrix} 0 & 1 \\ -1 & -(x_2^2 - 1) \end{bmatrix} \begin{bmatrix} x_1 \\ x_2 \end{bmatrix}.$$

By reference to the previous section one can justify the simple network in Fig. 2 as being a physical realization of this equation.

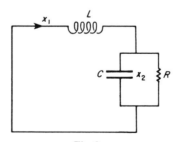

Fig. 2.

In this case $L = C = 1$ and $R = (x_2^2 - 1)^{-1}$; hence being a resistance its value of which is a function of its own voltage. Clearly, this resistor is not sign-definite and for small values of x_2 can possess negative values, which makes it indistinguishable from a generator. It is this latter property that permits the existence of self-maintained oscillations.

Rewriting Eq. (3.4) in separated form,

(3.5)

$$\begin{bmatrix} \dot{x}_1 \\ \dot{x}_2 \end{bmatrix} = \begin{bmatrix} 0 & 0 \\ 0 & -(x_2^2 - 1) \end{bmatrix} \begin{bmatrix} x_1 \\ x_2 \end{bmatrix} + \begin{bmatrix} 0 & 1 \\ -1 & 0 \end{bmatrix} \begin{bmatrix} x_1 \\ x_2 \end{bmatrix}$$

$$= -\nabla \phi + \dot{\mathbf{x}}_2,$$

$$-\nabla \phi = \begin{bmatrix} -\partial \phi / \partial x_1 \\ -\partial \phi / \partial x_2 \end{bmatrix} = \begin{bmatrix} 0 \\ -(x_2^2 - 1)x_2 \end{bmatrix},$$

$$\phi = \tfrac{1}{4}x_2^4 - \tfrac{1}{2}x_2^2 = \tfrac{1}{2}x_2^2[\tfrac{1}{2}x_2^2 - 1],$$

$$\sigma = -d\phi/dt = \langle \dot{\mathbf{x}}, -\nabla \phi \rangle = [x_2, -x_1 - x_2(x_2^2 - 1)] \begin{bmatrix} 0 \\ -(x_2^2 - 1)x_2 \end{bmatrix}$$

$$= x_1(x_2^2 - 1)x_2 + x_2^2(x_2^2 - 1)^2 = x_2(x_2^2 - 1)[x_1 + x_2(x_2^2 - 1)].$$

Van der Pol's equation has been subjected to the most detailed analysis [5], but it is proposed here that from the functions, as just generated above, a qualitative assessment can be usefully obtained.

In this simple case, the ϕ function and $\nabla \phi$ can be easily plotted, both being functions of a single variable. These are shown in Fig. 3. We consider, in addition, that the scalar product

(3.6) $$\langle \mathbf{x}, \dot{\mathbf{x}} \rangle = |\mathbf{r}|\dot{\mathbf{r}} = -x_2^2(x_2^2 - 1) = -\tfrac{1}{2}\phi,$$

where $\mathbf{r}$ is the radius vector for any state. Hence in the region where $\phi < 0$, we see that $\dot{\mathbf{r}} > 0$, and where $\phi > 0$ that $\dot{\mathbf{r}} < 0$. As the configuration is symmetric about the x_1 axis, one can see intuitively that there can exist a *closed* orbit which will traverse regions in which $\phi > 0$ and $\phi < 0$ such that around a whole cycle the net change in $\mathbf{r}$ is zero. It is the x_2 component in Eq. (3.5) that generates the periodicity.

For economic problems, and also for certain biological problems, the case of the driven Van der Pol (Rayleigh) system is probably of greater significance:

$$\ddot{x} + \varepsilon(\dot{x}^2 - 1)\dot{x} + x = A \cos \omega t.$$

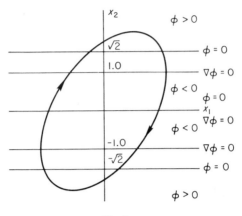

Fig. 3.

It is a general property of such systems that different frequencies can be generated within the system. As a result, modulation effects can occur in the amplitude of output variables, which can be interpreted as variations in the stored energy of the system. A further type of phenomenon may also appear, that of entrainment, in which the output frequency is identical to the forcing frequency and the output amplitudes can assume some constant value, after a transient period.

It may be nearer to reality in certain problems to consider, in addition, that the driving source is not in fact independent. We then have a system as shown in Fig. 4. Such a system, in an economic context, will be discussed later.

The behavior of composite systems of this type is still not fully understood, as they present great difficulties in analysis, but undoubtedly they possess

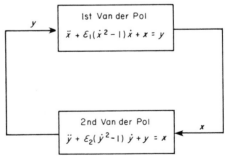

Fig. 4.

considerable importance in a wide variety of problems. These difficulties certainly arise, as stated earlier, from the fact that secondary frequencies are generated, and a modulation of amplitude must result, for under such conditions there can be no constancy of phase relationship, for phase has no meaning. Conversely, the existence of entrainment implies that, for reasons not yet understood, it is possible for a system to achieve a nonstationary equilibrium in which the rate of energy provided by the driving force is exactly equal to that dissipated within a certain narrow band of frequencies. Underlying all such behavior there must exist a conceptual mechanism akin to that of a power factor in alternating current electrical systems and usually expressed as a scalar product of two vectors:

$$\mathbf{x}, \mathbf{y} = |\mathbf{x}|\,|\mathbf{y}|\cos \measuredangle\, \mathbf{x}\mathbf{y}.$$

Equation (3.6) is a particular case of this:

$$\mathbf{x}, \dot{\mathbf{x}} = |\mathbf{r}|\,|\dot{\mathbf{r}}| = |\mathbf{x}|\,|\dot{\mathbf{x}}|\cos \measuredangle\, \mathbf{x}\dot{\mathbf{x}}.$$

Now clearly it is only if $\mathbf{x}$ and $\dot{\mathbf{x}}$ possess the same periodicity that the angle $\measuredangle\,\mathbf{x}\mathbf{x}$ has any meaning, although if their periodicities differ we can still attach some significance to $|\mathbf{r}|\,\dot{\mathbf{r}}$, and any change in sign will indicate a modulation.

In linear conservative systems the intimate relationship between natural frequency and the time averages of kinetic and potential energies was first expressed as Rayleigh's principle [15]. More recently other frequency-power formulas have been derived with reference to electrical systems [13], the most well known being those of Manley-Rowe [11].

4. ECONOMIC MODELS

There is a variety of models of various forms and scales [14]. Two principal groups of workers have contributed to the development of these models: researchers and practitioners. The distinction between them is perhaps rather arbitrary, since some economic theorists engage in controversial arguments as to what is relevant or rigorous, while others engage in a continuous exchange of ideas and expertise [8, 9]. Nevertheless, while some models have been constructed with a view to enhancing our understanding of behavioral patterns, others have been developed as a means of conveniently processing a large amount of data into a suitable form to enable estimates to be made of key quantities at a future date. It is to this former group of models that this chapter is directed.

The basic general model proposed is a closed system of two economies which, with the assignment of appropriate parameter values and the use of extra assumptions, becomes formally identical to the well-known simple models in the economic literature. It provides a platform for investigating coupled systems such as multimarket models with dynamic market interdependence, national economy models with interacting regions, economic community models, national economy models with distinct public and private sectors, and world models.

Consider a closed system of two national economies, N_1 and N_2. Their social or economic activity can be thought to be measured by their real economic activity, i.e., consumption, investment, production, and export–import activities.

Suppose, for example, that in economy N_1 a variation in income occurs. Then imports, which depend on income, also change, and this change means a change in the exports of economy N_2 to economy N_1. The change in exports in economy N_2 causes a change in income in that economy, and consequently economy N_2 imports from economy N_1 change. This means a change in economy N_1 exports and consequently in economy N_1 income, and so on.

The model is made up of the following equations:

$$Z_1 = C_1 + I_1 + E_1 - M_1, \qquad Z_2 = C_2 + I_2 + E_2 - M_2,$$

$$C_1 = c_1 Y_1, \qquad C_2 = c_2 Y_2,$$

$$Y_1 = \frac{1}{T_{01}D + 1} Z_1, \qquad Y_2 = \frac{1}{T_{02}D + 1} Z_2,$$

$$(4.1) \quad I_1 = \frac{1}{T_{11}D + 1} O_{D1}, \qquad I_2 = \frac{1}{T_{12}D + 1} O_{D2},$$

$$O_{D1} = f(\alpha_1 D Y_1), \qquad O_{D2} = f(\alpha_2 D Y_2),$$

$$E_1 = M_2 = \alpha_1 Y_1, \qquad M_2 = \frac{1}{T_{21}D + 1} E_2,$$

$$M_1 = \frac{1}{T_{11}D + 1} E_1, \qquad M_1 = E_2 = \alpha_2 Y_2,$$

$$D = d/dt.$$

The equations express, in order, the definitional identity for demand, the consumption function, that national product lags demand, that net investment flows lag investment decisions, that investment decisions are a function of the rate of change in income, the fact that the exports of one economy are the same as the imports of the other economy and the import functions, and that imports lag exports.

The following assumptions are made:

National product or output Y is related to capital stock K through the acceleration principle.
Net investment I is induced, and $I = dK/dt$.

It is assumed that the acceleration principle applies to induced investment (desired capital stock $= \alpha \times$ output; α is the acceleration coefficient or the inverse of the rate of return on capital) over some middle range, but that it passes to complete inflexibility at either extreme as shown in Fig. 5.

The lower limit is reached by scrapping at a rate $\dot{K}_2$ when the stock of capital K is in excess (desired capital $< K$, effectively limited to attrition from wear, from time, and from innovations), the middle linear part has a slope of α; the upper limit is reached by proceeding at capacity $\dot{K}_1$, when the stock of capital is insufficient (desired capital $> K$, entrepreneurial expectations provide resistance to it).

Consumption function is linear and unlagged.
Imports are related simply to the size of output.
Exports are similarly related.
The import–export flows include, for example, the migration of people, communication, technology, innovations, education, know-how, trade.
I represents the outlay for the total public and private investment.
Export–import lags and investment lags are identical for each economy.
Simple exponential lags were assumed for all processes.

The above assumptions secure the model "ideologically neutral" and are thus left open to various specific interpretations.

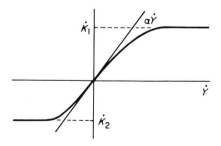

Fig. 5.

In reduced form the model is given by

$$(T_{01}D + 1)Y_1 = c_1 Y_1 + \frac{1}{T_{11}D + 1} f(\alpha_1 D Y_1) + \alpha_1 Y_1 - \frac{a_2 Y_2}{T_{11}D + 1},$$

$$(T_{02}D + 1)Y_2 = c_2 Y_2 + \frac{1}{T_{12}D + 1} f(\alpha_2 D Y_2) + a_2 Y_2 - \frac{\alpha_1 Y_1}{T_{11}D + 1},$$

(4.2)

$$D^2 Y_1 + \frac{T_{01} + T_{11} - c_1 T_{11} - \alpha_1 T_{11}}{T_{01} T_{11}} D Y_1 - \frac{1}{T_{01} T_{11}} f(\alpha_1 D Y_1)$$

$$- \frac{a_1 + c_1 - 1}{T_{01} T_{11}} Y_1 + \frac{a_2 Y_2}{T_{01} T_{11}} = 0,$$

$$D^2 Y_2 + \frac{T_{02} + T_{12} - c_2 T_{12} - \alpha_2 T_{12}}{T_{02} T_{12}} D Y_2 - \frac{1}{T_{02} T_{12}} f(\alpha_2 D Y_2)$$

$$- \frac{a_2 + c_2 - 1}{T_{02} T_{12}} Y_2 + \frac{a_1 Y_1}{T_{02} T_{12}} = 0.$$

In the usual notation

(4.3) $\ddot{y}_1 + \omega_1^2 y_1 = \varepsilon[\psi(\dot{y}_1) + K_1 y_2], \qquad \ddot{y}_2 + \omega_2^2 y_2 = \varepsilon[\psi(\dot{y}_2) + K_2 y_1],$

where

(4.4)

$$\omega_1^2 = \frac{1 - a_1 - c_1}{T_{01} T_{11}}, \qquad \varepsilon K_1 y_2 = - \frac{a_2}{T_{01} T_{11}} y_2,$$

$$\varepsilon \psi(\dot{y}_1) = \frac{-(T_{01} + T_{11} - c_1 T_{11} - \alpha_1 T_{11})}{T_{01} T_{11}} \dot{y}_1 + \frac{1}{T_{01} T_{11}} f(\alpha_1 \dot{y}_1).$$

For simulation purposes the nonlinear characteristic can be expressed by [9]

$$f(a\dot{y}) = \dot{K}_2 \left[\frac{\dot{K}_1 + \dot{K}_2}{\dot{K}_1 \exp{(-\alpha(\dot{K}_1 + \dot{K}_2)/\dot{K}_1 \dot{K}_2)\dot{y}} + \dot{K}_2} - 1 \right],$$

or alternatively $\psi(\dot{y})$ can be simulated by a cubic equation

(4.5) $\alpha \dot{y}_1^3 + \beta \dot{y}_1^2 + \gamma \dot{y}_1.$

We have thus arrived at a pair of coupled differential equations of the Rayleigh type. By a simple transformation of variables it is possible to express these equations in a Van der Pol form:

(4.6)
$$\ddot{y}_1 + \omega_1^2 y_1 = \varepsilon[\phi(y_1)\dot{y}_1 + K_1 y_2],$$
$$\ddot{y}_2 + \omega_2^2 y_2 = \varepsilon[\phi(y_2)\dot{y}_2 + K_2 y_1].$$

Thus let $\dot{y}_1 = \xi_1$, $\dot{y}_2 = \xi_2$.

By substitution in Eq. (4.3) and subsequent differentiation with respect to time we arrive at

(4.7)
$$\ddot{\xi}_1 + \omega_1^2 \xi_1 = \varepsilon[(3\alpha_1 \xi_1^2 + 2\beta_1 \xi_1 + \gamma_1)\dot{\xi} + K_1 \xi_2],$$
$$\ddot{\xi}_2 + \omega_2^2 \xi_2 = \varepsilon[(3\alpha_2 \xi_2^2 + 2\beta_2 \xi_2 + \gamma_2)\dot{\xi}_2 + K_2 \xi_1].$$

The state space variables are defined as

$$\dot{X}_1 = \varepsilon \int \phi_1(X_1)\,dX_1 + X_2, \qquad X_2 = -\omega_1^2 X_1 + \varepsilon K_1 X_3,$$

$$\dot{X}_3 = \varepsilon \int \phi_2(X_3)\,dX_3 + X_4, \qquad \dot{X}_4 = \varepsilon K_2 X_1 - \omega_2^2 X_3.$$

In matrix form:

(4.8)
$$\dot{\mathbf{X}} = \begin{vmatrix} \varepsilon\Phi_1(X_1) & 1 & 0 & 0 \\ -\omega_1^2 & 0 & \varepsilon K_1 & 0 \\ 0 & 0 & \varepsilon\Phi_2(X_3) & 1 \\ \varepsilon K_2 & 0 & -\omega_2^2 & 0 \end{vmatrix} \mathbf{X}.$$

A. The Goodwin Model

Goodwin [7] was perhaps the first to recognize the need for nonlinear structural relations as a basis for analyzing a wide range of phenomena in economics.

His most sophisticated model reduced to the Rayleigh form or, after a simple transformation, to the Van der Pol form. His assumptions have already been used in the formulation of the two-economy model, and it is thus possible to arrive at it using extra assumptions. Indeed in a "balance of payments" situation, $E - M = 0$, and the two economies decouple to two identical Goodwin models of the form

(4.9)
$$\dot{\mathbf{X}} = \begin{bmatrix} \varepsilon\Phi(X_1) & 1 \\ -\omega_1^2 & 0 \end{bmatrix} \mathbf{X},$$

where both ω_1 and $\Phi(X_1)$ are calculated with $a_1 = 0$.

The above form is particularly suitable for the application of the field method. Thus

(4.10)
$$\dot{\mathbf{X}} = \begin{bmatrix} \varepsilon\Phi(X_1) & 0 \\ 0 & 0 \end{bmatrix} \mathbf{X} + \begin{bmatrix} 0 & 1 \\ -\omega_1^2 & 0 \end{bmatrix} \mathbf{X}.$$

The rotational part of the system consists of an infinite number of concentric ellipses described in a clockwise sense in the phase space.

Alternatively,

$$(4.11) \qquad \dot{\mathbf{X}} = \tfrac{1}{2}\begin{bmatrix} 2\varepsilon\Phi(X_1) & 1 - \omega_1^2 \\ 1 - \omega_1^2 & 0 \end{bmatrix}\mathbf{X} + \tfrac{1}{2}\begin{bmatrix} 0 & 1 + \omega_1^2 \\ -1\omega_1^2 & 0 \end{bmatrix}\mathbf{X},$$

in which case the rotational part of the system consists of an infinite number of concentric circles described in a clockwise sense in the phase space. Both representations of the rotational part represent a stable, conservative system. The second form has the advantage of $\mathbf{X}'\mathbf{X}_2 = 0$. This component will not contribute to the stability of the system but only to its periodicity.

The scalar potential function associated with the irrotational component of Eq. (4.10) is given by

$$\phi = -\varepsilon \int \Phi(X_1)X_1 \, dX_1.$$

The particular quadratic form of Φ yields the following form for ϕ:

$$(4.12) \qquad \phi = -\varepsilon(\alpha_1 X_1^4/4 + \beta_1 X_1^3/3 + \gamma_1 X_1^2/2).$$

This indicates that the ϕ contours are lines parallel to the X_2 axis.

The importance of the field approach in the location and stability of limit cycles rests on the systematic way in which regions of opposite stability can be generated through the ϕ and σ contours.

The irrotational trajectories, shown by the arrows in Fig. 6, are moving globally toward the extrema of the ϕ function, indicating that the stationary

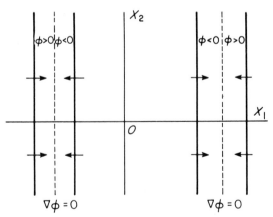

Fig. 6.

point of the system is unstable. The rotational trajectories are finitely closed, connecting the $\nabla\phi = 0$ contours, and thus there must be a stable region beyond $\nabla\phi = 0$ in which all the system trajectories are moving toward the origin. Since the origin is the only singularity and it is unstable, the Poincaré–Bendixson theorem [2] establishes the existance of a stable limit cycle.

From Eq. (4.10),

$$\dot{X}_1 = 0 \rightarrow \varepsilon\Phi(X_1)X_1 = X_2, \qquad \dot{X}_2 = 0 \rightarrow -\omega_1^2 X_1 = 0.$$

The first equation gives the curve in Fig. 7, while the second is a line coincident with the X_2 axis. Their intersection is the origin which is the only stationary point of the system. The limit cycle generated for such a system is shown by the curve linked by the broken lines in Fig. 7, and the stability properties clearly depend on the form of $\Phi(X_1)$ or, equivalently, on the variation of the gradient field. Having already observed that the ϕ contours are lines parallel to the X_2 axis, the irrotational component is thus parallel to the X_1 axis.

Since $\Phi(X_1)X_1 = -\nabla\phi$, the direction of the irrotational component changes only when this function changes sign.

From a geometric point of view it becomes apparent that a necessary and sufficient condition for Goodwin's model to exhibit limit cycle behavior is that the curve $\dot{X}_1 = 0$ intersects the X_1 axis $(2n + 1)$ times increasing in pairs away from the origin, where n is the number of limit cycles, which after all is only a generalization of the Poincaré–Bendixson theorem.

In terms of Goodwin's model, this means that, in general, the nonlinear accelerator must have n parts or progressively increasing steps and that the proportion of "saving or disinvestment" introduced in his dynamic multiplier must always be less than the acceleration coefficient α. Such a situation

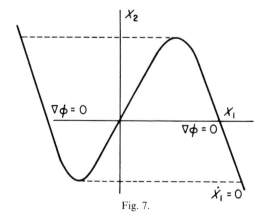

Fig. 7.

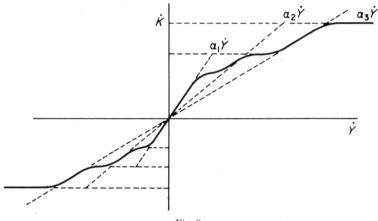

Fig. 8.

is depicted in Fig. 8. Speculative as it may appear, it seems that such behavior may be much nearer to reality than most. Further, such a structure brings both cycle and growth together and provides, in a schematic way, an explanation for their inseparable existence.

The small variations shown in Fig. 9, which seem to suggest the existence of subcycles, are in fact suppressed by the larger cycles—something that agrees with observation. This assertion is validated by the irrotational field portrait which indicates the narrow "rings" of insufficient stability enclosed within the limit cycles. Clearly, the cycles must alternate in stability. An appreciation of the roles played by each of the vector field components in the generation of the transient dynamics in economic systems can provide useful guidance for the design of control policies for such systems.

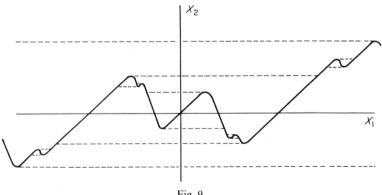

Fig. 9.

The following example is adapted from an economic model of Samuelson. Let K denote the capital and I the net investment in an economy. Thus I is the rate of change in K, or $I = \dot{K}$. Assume that there is an equilibrium level of capital denoted by $\bar{K}$ and that deceleration in the algebraic rate of investment and, conversely, a level of capital below this level leads to an increase in the rate of investment.

Thus let

$$k = K - \bar{K}.$$

Then

$$\dot{k} = \dot{K} = I, \qquad \dot{I} = -\lambda(K - \bar{K}) = -\lambda k.$$

Let

$$X_1 = k, \qquad X_2 = I.$$

Then

$$\dot{\mathbf{X}} = \begin{bmatrix} 0 & 1 \\ -\lambda & 0 \end{bmatrix} \mathbf{X},$$

which is a system consisting of a rotational part. Clearly, any coefficients of I and λ could consist of any positive definite function of I and k, respectively, without altering the fundamental oscillatory behavior of the system. Suppose that it is desired to prevent oscillations in the system, but for various political reasons the government desires to apply controls only in the form of subsidies. These subsidies U, constitute positive investment which is added to investment to give

$$\dot{k} = I + U.$$

Thus we have the modified system

$$\dot{\mathbf{X}} = \begin{bmatrix} 0 & 1 \\ -\lambda & 0 \end{bmatrix} \mathbf{X} + \begin{bmatrix} 1 \\ 0 \end{bmatrix} U.$$

The above system is clearly controllable, and thus the state of this system can be controlled to the origin by these subsidies.

Suppose now that investment lags excess capacity by a lag of unit length. Thus

$$I = -\lambda k/(D + 1) = -\lambda k - I.$$

The initial model thus becomes

$$\dot{\mathbf{X}} = \begin{bmatrix} 0 & 1 \\ -\lambda & -1 \end{bmatrix} \mathbf{X}$$

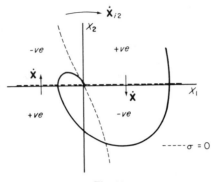

Fig. 10.

or

$$\mathbf{X} = \begin{bmatrix} 0 & 0 \\ 0 & -1 \end{bmatrix} \mathbf{X} + \begin{bmatrix} 0 & 1 \\ -\lambda & 0 \end{bmatrix} \mathbf{X};$$

i.e., it consists of an irrotational and a rotational part.

As an example consider $\lambda \alpha k^2$ and that the time constant is a:

(4.13) $\phi = \alpha X_2^2/2, \qquad \sigma = \alpha X_1^3 X_2 + \alpha^2 X_2^2.$

The ϕ contours are then parallel to the X_1 axis, and $\nabla \phi$ will be zero along the X_1 axis. The signs of the σ region are shown in Fig. 10, and we can conclude that the vector $\dot{\mathbf{X}}$ has the direction shown. Hence the system is asymptotically stable, as intuition suggests.

B. Coupled Oscillators

The power of the outlined approach is manifested in the analysis of higher order systems [1] where even simulation cannot provide conclusive answers. We thus return to Eq. (4.6) of the coupled oscillators.

Equilibrium points of Eq. (4.6) exist at $\dot{\mathbf{X}} = 0$. Thus

$$\varepsilon \Phi_1(X_1)X_1 + X_2 = 0, \qquad -\omega_1^2 X_1 + \varepsilon K_1 X_3 = 0,$$

$$\varepsilon \Phi_2(X_3)X_3 + X_4 = 0, \qquad \varepsilon K_2 X_1 - \omega_2^2 X_3 = 0.$$

From above it is evident that equilibrium points other than the origin are only possible if

$$\omega_1^2 \omega_2^2 = \varepsilon^2 K_1 K_2.$$

These are

$$X_1 = 0, \qquad \Phi_1(X_1) = 0, \qquad X_2 = 0,$$

$$X_3 = 0, \qquad \Phi_2(X_3) = 0, \qquad X_4 = 0.$$

In general $\omega_1^2\omega_2^2 \neq \varepsilon^2 K_1 K_2$, and the origin will be the only stationary point of the system.

It is important to be able to examine the dynamic behavior of Eq. (4.6) in view of the remarks on the equilibrium points made above.

They can be expressed in terms of components:

$$(4.14) \qquad \dot{\mathbf{X}} = \begin{bmatrix} \varepsilon\Phi_1(X_1)X_1 \\ 0 \\ \varepsilon\Phi_2(X_3)X_3 \\ 0 \end{bmatrix} + \begin{bmatrix} X_2 \\ -\omega_1^2 X_1 + \varepsilon K_1 X_3 \\ X_4 \\ \varepsilon K_2 X_1 - \omega_2^2 X_3 \end{bmatrix}.$$

The scalar potential function associated with the irrotational component above is given by

$$\phi = -\varepsilon \int \Phi_1(X_1)X_1\, dX_1 - \varepsilon \int \Phi_2(X_3)X_3\, dX_3.$$

The particular form of ϕ suggests that, in the four-space, the ϕ contours in the plane $X_1 X_3$ extend along the X_2, X_4 axis in a cylindrical form with cross sections either similar to the ones in Fig. 11, parallel to the $X_1 X_3$ plane, or cross sections orthogonal to the $X_1 X_3$ plane with the ϕ contours being planes parallel to the $X_2 X_4$ plane.

The stationary points of the irrotational components occur at

$$\Phi_1(X_1) = 0, \quad X_1 = 0 \quad \text{and} \quad \Phi_2(X_3) = 0, \quad X_3 = 0.$$

Assuming that $\beta_1^2 \neq 4\alpha_1\gamma_1$ and $\beta_2^2 \neq 4\alpha_2\gamma_2$ nine distinct singularity planes exist along and parallel to the $X_2 X_4$ plane. Figure 11 indicates that five of these singularity planes are unstable and that the four given by $\Phi_1(X_1) = 0$ and $\Phi_2(X_3) = 0$ are stable. Figure 11 indicates that beyond the contour $\phi = 0$ the gradient part of the system is globally moving toward the four stable planes and that the origin is an unstable equilibrium point.

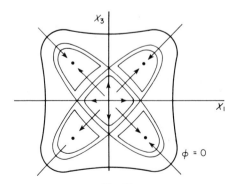

Fig. 11.

The nature of the rotational component can be investigated by examination of the rotational field on the principal planes.

This is conveniently done by examining the components of the rotational part in the two subspaces $X_1X_2X_4$ and $X_2X_3X_4$. It is thus noticed that the resulting subsystems possess the linear integral invariants $dX_2 + aX_4 = \mu$ and $cX_2 + bX_4 = \lambda$, respectively, where $a = \omega_1^2$, $b = \varepsilon K_1$, $c = \omega_2^2$, $d = \varepsilon K_2$, and these are the traces of the planes normal to the X_2X_4 plane on which the subsystem elliptical trajectories lie. The combination of these trajectories determines the motion of the rotational part of the system.

The behavior of such a motion is obviously critical to the stability properties of the system and can be ascertained by examining the roots of the linear differential equation

(4.15) $[D^4 + (a + c)D^2 + (ac - bd)]X_1 = 0.$

Thus if b and d, the coupling coefficients, are of the same sign, then the rotational part always has purely imaginary roots provided that

(4.16) $(c + a) > \sqrt{(c - a)^2 + 4bd}$

and the rotational trajectory is stable.

There are, of course, several other interesting cases, when b and d are of opposite sign, when Eq. (4.15) possesses a double imaginary root, and so on.

Having already ascertained the existence of two regions of stability as in Fig. 11, the Poincaré–Bendixson theorem indicates the existence of stable periodic motions.

The number of different limit cycles is clearly dependent on the relative positions of the integral invariant planes and the way in which the trajectories on these couple the four singularity planes, in exact analogy with the analysis of the Goodwin model.

Thus the sign and numerical values of the coefficients of Eq. (4.15) determine whether one, two, or no limit cycles occur.

In general it can be shown that, provided condition (4.16) holds, the system possesses at least one limit cycle.

If, however, b and d are of opposite sign and

$$(c - a)^2 + 4db < 0,$$

then the system possesses only one limit cycle.

Clearly, if $(c - a)^2 + 4db > 0$ and Eq. (4.16) does not hold, the system is totally unstable.

The above can be reinterpreted in terms of the parameters of the two economies and important insight gained.

In systems of coupled oscillators there may exist more than one stable state of synchronization, each one with its own frequency of oscillation. Thus after a disturbance the system may return to a limit cycle different from the one it was on before. There is little need to emphasize the importance of this in interacting economic systems, for the variety of causes of business cycles such as intraeconomy, intereconomy, noneconomic, and any combination of the above could be appropriately modelled and studied.

Mathematical analysis on its own has been found inadequate in dealing with such problems, and any qualitative information available together with simulation seems to be the only way of overcoming the difficulties. From the geometric point of view, it is clear that if the nonlinearity coefficient were made very small, then the overall stability would largely depend on the rotational component.

As nonconservative systems with limit cycles are in effect "isochronous," in the sense that for all initial conditions the system oscillates with the period of the limit cycle, it is only the nonlinearity that makes the existence of monofrequency oscillation possible.

The condition (4.16) postulated for the existence of imaginary roots and therefore distinct frequencies of the rotational component must hold for entrainment, so that the system can lock into the appropriate one with the action of the dissipative component.

As any conservative system (linear or nonlinear) is not structurally stable, [2], it is clear that it cannot support monofrequency oscillations of its own, and thus the value of the coupling is important, especially if sinusoidal oscillation is required. In the two coupled oscillators case entrainment requires that the outputs of both oscillators be of equal frequency, i.e., monofrequency oscillation. Simulation has shown that for a comparable entrainment condition of the absolute difference between the natural frequency and the driving frequency being a small number can intuitively be extended to the coupled oscillators case as the absolute difference of the output–input difference for each oscillator, being a small number, where the input is the appropriate coupling.

Such conditions can be reinterpreted in terms of the parameters of the system and valuable insight gained about the timing of the trade cycle, its effects on scarce resources, and the propagation of economic activity in general.

To illustrate the above the following numerical values for the parameters of this model were selected from the literature:

$$a_1 = 0.1 \qquad a_2 = 0.2$$
$$c_1 = 0.6 \qquad c_2 = 0.4$$
$$T_{11} = 1 \qquad T_{12} = 1.5$$
$$\alpha_1 = 2 \qquad \alpha_2 = 3$$
$$T_{01} = 0.5 \qquad T_{02} = 0.3.$$

The model then reduces to

(4.17)
$$\ddot{y}_1 + 0.6y_1 = 0.2[-8\dot{y}_1 + 10f(2\dot{y}_1) - 2y_2],$$
$$\ddot{y}_2 + 0.888y_2 = 0.2[-10\dot{y}_2 + 11.111f(3\dot{y}_2) - 1.111y_1].$$

or, after simulating $f(2\dot{y}_1)$ and $f(3\dot{y}_2)$ by cubic expressions,

$$\ddot{y}_1 + 0.6y_1 = 0.2(-0.3016\dot{y}_1^3 + 2.325\dot{y}_1^2 + 12\dot{y}_1 - 2y_2),$$
$$\ddot{y}_2 + 0.888y_2 = 0.2(-0.712\dot{y}_2^3 + 4.7869\dot{y}_2^2 + 21.111\dot{y}_2 - 1.111y_1).$$

The scalar potential function associated with the irrotational component is then given by

$$\phi = 0.01508x_1^4 - 0.155x_1^3 - 1.2x_1^2 + 0.0356x_2^4 - 0.3191x_2^3 - 2.111x_2^2$$

and is shown in Fig. 12. Its contours are shown in Fig. 13. Condition (4.16) is satisfied, and one trade cycle for both economies is obtained, i.e., an

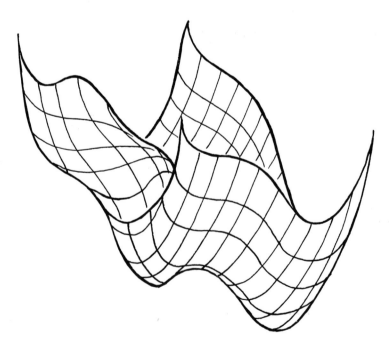

Fig. 12.

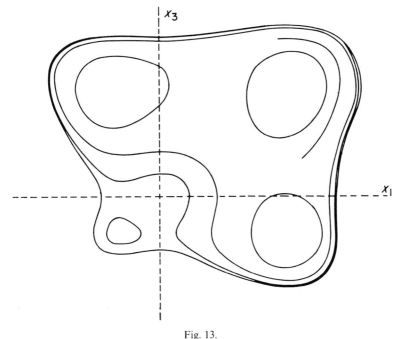

Fig. 13.

entrainment situation. The economic activity for each economy is shown in Fig. 14.

Economic systems of both the macro and micro type can be described by a set of nonlinear differential equations in state space form. In microeconomics Walrasian models formulate the price movement known as a tâtonnement process [16]; Marshallian models formulate the quantity movement [12].

The dynamic nature of such problems has recently attracted much interest, especially since it is not really known how price and quantity adjustment works.

Formulated in terms of excess demand and excess quantity, respectively, such models pose no fundamentally different stability problems for the well-known simple macroeconomic models.

In attempting to answer questions about the stability behavior of models of national economies, it is hoped that insight was gained into the operation of single markets. Further the issue of the need for multimarket models exhibiting dynamic market interdependence has often been raised, and in attempting to tackle the problem in macroeconomics it is hoped that we have progressed toward such a development.

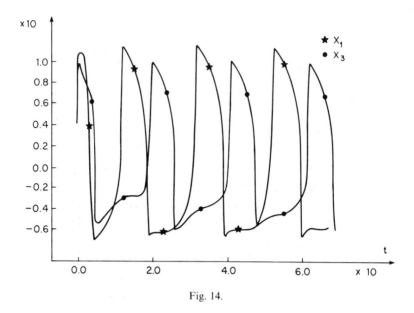

Fig. 14.

A simple model exhibiting the dynamics in a single market where both price and quantity change in response to disequilibrium will now be presented briefly.

Consider a simple dynamic system of price and quantity adjustment, combining the Walrasian and Marshallian approaches:

$$\dot{p} = f(p, q), \qquad \dot{q} = g(p, q),$$

where f and g are nonlinear, continuous, differentiable functions defined for all $p, q \geqslant 0$, representing the demand and supply curves, respectively.

The intersection of

$$f = 0 \qquad \text{and} \qquad g = 0$$

determines the equilibrium points of the system.

A number of conditions on f and g are required to make them "economically" meaningful as, for instance, that price will rise when there is excess demand, and fall when there is excess supply, with a speed that will increase as the "error" between supply and demand increases, and that the total expenditure for this product is bounded. Also, output will rise when price exceeds cost and fall when cost exceeds price with a speed that will increase as the "error" between price and cost is increased, and that for a sufficiently high price a positive quantity will be supplied and that beyond a sufficiently large quantity the cost has a positive lower bound.

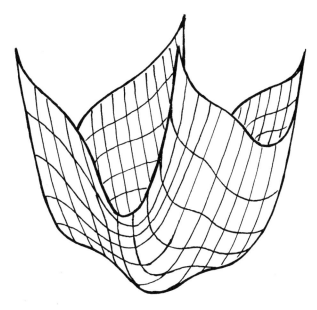

Fig. 15.

This is illustrated using a particular model from Beckmann and Ryder [3]. Thus consider the system with a linear demand curve of negative slope:

$$q = (-1 + \varepsilon)p_d, \qquad 1 > \varepsilon > 0$$

and a cubic supply curve

$$p_s = \delta q^3 - q, \qquad \delta > 0$$

given by

$$\dot{p} = (-1 + \varepsilon)p - q, \qquad \dot{q} = p + (1 - \delta q^2)q,$$

or in matrix form

$$\begin{bmatrix} \dot{p} \\ \dot{q} \end{bmatrix} = \begin{bmatrix} -1 + \varepsilon & -1 \\ 1 & 1 - \delta q^2 \end{bmatrix} \begin{bmatrix} p \\ q \end{bmatrix} = \begin{bmatrix} -1 + \varepsilon & 0 \\ 0 & 1 - \delta q^2 \end{bmatrix} \begin{bmatrix} p \\ q \end{bmatrix} + \begin{bmatrix} 0 & -1 \\ 1 & 0 \end{bmatrix} \begin{bmatrix} p \\ q \end{bmatrix},$$

$$\phi = [(1 - \varepsilon)/2]p^2 - (q^2/2) + (\delta q^4/4),$$

$$\sigma = (-1 + \varepsilon)^2 p^2 + (2 - \varepsilon)pq - \delta pq^3 + q^2 + \delta^2 q^6 - 2\delta q^4.$$

The ϕ and σ functions are shown in Figs. 15 and 16.

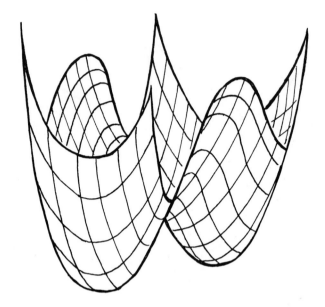

Fig. 16.

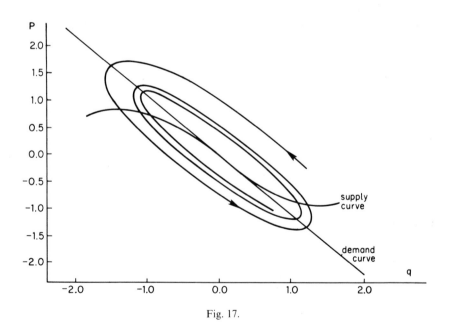

Fig. 17.

For the case $\delta = \varepsilon = 0.1$, the limit cycle as well as the demand and supply curves are shown in Fig. 17.
Thus persistent cycles may occur in the market.

REFERENCES

1. Abd-Ali, A. H., Fradellos, G., and Evans, F. J., *Intern. J. Control* **22**, 481 (1975).
2. Andronov, A. A., Vitt, A. A., and Khaikan, S. E., "Theory of Oscillators." Pergamon, Oxford,
3. Beckamnn, M. J., and Ryder, H. E., *Econometrica* **37**, 3 (1969).
4. Bryant, P. R., IEE Monograph 414E, London (November 1960).
5. Cartwright, M. L., and Littlewood, J. E., *J. London Math. Soc.* **20**, 180-89 (1945); *Ann. Math.* **48**(2), 472-494 (1947).
6. Forrester, J. W., *Simulation* **25** (4), 125 (1975).
7. Goodwin, R. M., *Econometrica* **19** (1), 1 (1951).
8. Gordon, R. A., *Amer. Ec. Rev.* **66** (1), 1 (1976).
9. Hollis, M., and Nell, E., Rational Economic Man, Cambridge V. P. (1975).
10. Hummon, P. N., Doreian, P., and Tenter, K., *Amer. Soc. Rev.* **40**, 813 (1975).
11. Manley, J. M., and Rowe, H. E., *Proc. IEEE* **44**, 904-913 (1956).
12. Marshall, A., "Principles of Economics." London, 1890.
13. Penfield, P., "Frequency Power Relations." MIT, Cambridge, Massachusetts and Wiley, New York, 1960.
14. Runyan, H. M., *IEEE Trans.* **SMC-1** (1), 8 (1971).
15. Temple, G., and Bickley, W. G., "Rayleigh's Principle." Dover, New York, 1956.
16. Walras, L., "Elements of Pure Economics," Allan and Unwin, London, 1954.
17. Zeeman, E. C., *Bull. Inst. Math. Appl.* (GB) (July 1976).

DEPARTMENT OF ELECTRICAL AND ELECTRONIC ENGINEERING
QUEEN MARY COLLEGE
UNIVERSITY OF LONDON
LONDON, ENGLAND

Part III

A REAPPRAISAL OF ESTABLISHED METHODS

Optimal Consumption Plans – A Dynamic Programming Approach

Martin J. Beckmann*

In discussing the uses of dynamic programming in economic theory, it seems best to consider some well-understood economic problems and utilize the approach completely. The first of the problems I propose to consider is that of consumption planning over time. It is best to visualize not a household with its life cycle and other biological complexities, but a foundation that can look forward to an indefinite life. Applications to a firm that must allocate its profits to dividends and investment are also immediate.

1. CONSUMPTION PLANNING UNDER CERTAINTY

The problem of consumption planning over time will be approached through the following simple model, variants of which have appeared in the literature [1–3, 6, 7].

Let the initial assets be y. The assets bear interest at the annual rate i. The utility of consumption $u(x)$ is the same in all periods and is additive, where x is the consumption expenditure. Future utility is discounted at the discount rate ρ.

How should the owner of wealth y, planning for an infinite future, allocate his or her wealth to consumption and savings? Is it ever optimal to accumulate or decumulate forever? Is there a target level of wealth to be striven for?

* This work was supported in part by NSF Grant SES 79 19376.

183

What is the present value of the utility of an optimal consumption plan and has it any economic significance?

2

To study these and related questions it is useful to consider first a specific utility function that is sometimes proposed in development planning:

(1) $$u(x) = x^\alpha, \qquad 0 < \alpha \leq 1.$$

(Any factor of proportionality has been suppressed as irrelevant.) The restriction of α to positive values not exceeding one reflects the law of diminishing marginal utility. The case of proportional utility requires special treatment. A limiting case of Eq. (1) is the logarithmic function

(2) $$u(x) = \log x,$$

which was used by Radner [7].

3

Through the principle of optimality in dynamic programming the infinite sequence of consumption–savings decisions can be reduced to one present decision. A prerequisite for this is the introduction of a value function representing the value achieved under an optimal policy. This value may be conditional on properties of the present state, that is, on state variables. To discover the relevant state variables is part of the problem of setting up the right model. In the consumption–savings problem, economic theory or economic intuition will usually suggest the economic variables on which a rational decision maker's strategy should depend. Clearly, wealth is one such variable in the present case. Whether it is the only one can be determined by trying a model involving it as the only state variable. Certainly, more complex situations are conceivable and could be cast into models in which other variables affect the consumption decision as well. These might be age as it affects life expectancy, economic forecasts, or the assets structure of wealth. However, at this stage it is not our aim to be complicated but to be as simple as possible. Additional state variables will be needed as the analysis unfolds in the case of uncertainty.

Let $v_n(y)$ be proposed tentatively as the maximal present value of utility, conditional on present wealth y and a decision horizon n. The basic observation is that the decision problem repeats itself after one period with horizon $(n - 1)$ and a wealth level and state variable that depend on the present decision. If consumption is chosen to be x, then next year's wealth is $(1 + i)$

$(y - x)$ and the present value of maximal consumption starting the next period is

$$v_{n-1}[(1 + i)(y - x)].$$

Total utility at present is the sum of utility of consumption in the first period $u(x)$ and the discounted value of the utility of subsequent consumption:

$$u(x) + \rho v_{n-1}[(1 + i)(y - x)].$$

The object is to maximize this value by choosing a current consumption x. Upon maximization we obtain the maximal present value of utility $v_n(y)$:

(3) $$v_n(y) = \underset{x}{\text{Max}}\{u(x) + \rho v_{n-1}[(1 + i)(y - x)]\}.$$

The value function $v_n(y)$ may be said to represent the consumer's attainable level of satisfaction, his or her welfare. Observe that, while u is a flow concept, v_n represents a stock.

A consumption level exceeding current wealth y is not admissible, for it might open the door to unlimited borrowing with repayment indefinitely deferred. Thus the constraint for $0 \leq x \leq y$ will be added when needed. The principle of optimality is then

(4) $$v_n(y) = \underset{0 \leq x \leq y}{\text{Max}}\{u(x) + \rho v_{n-1}[(1 + i)(y - x)]\}$$

with an initial condition $v_0(y) = 0$ or, equivalently,

(5) $$v_1(y) = u(y).$$

The first observation is that the optimal consumption x depends on wealth y. It depends on income in the current period by virtue of the fact that this income was added to previous wealth. The marginal propensity to consume out of income is therefore the same as the marginal propensity to consume out of wealth.

4

In principle the system (4), (5) can be solved by successive substitutions starting with $n = 1$. A question that naturally arises is whether a value function exists in the limiting case $n = \infty$ and whether it satisfies the limiting form of Eq. (4) and is determined uniquely by it.

Rather than answer these questions in general by applying the mathematical principles of dynamic programming, we propose to examine the wealth function and the consumption (or savings) strategy for the special utility function (1).

Substitution in Eq. (4) for $n = 2$ yields

$$v_2(y) = \text{Max}_x[x^\alpha + \rho\gamma^\alpha(y - x)^\alpha],$$

where we have set $1 + i = \gamma$.

Now the maximizing x is readily found to be

$$\hat{x}_2 = y/[1 + (\rho\gamma^\alpha)^{1/(1-\alpha)}]$$

and

$$v_2(y) = [1 + (\rho\gamma^\alpha)^{1/(1-\alpha)}]^{1-\alpha}y^\alpha.$$

This suggests the trial solution

(6) $$v_n(y) = b_n y^\alpha,$$

which will now be verified by substitution in Eq. (3):

(7) $$b_n y^\alpha = \text{Max}_x[x^\alpha + \rho\gamma^\alpha b_{n-1}(y - x)^\alpha].$$

Setting the derivative with respect to x equal to zero we have

$$\alpha x_n^{\alpha-1} - \alpha\rho\gamma^\alpha b_{n-1}(y - x_n)^{\alpha-1} = 0$$

and for the maximizer x_n,

$$x_n = (\rho\gamma^\alpha b_{n-1})^{1/(\alpha-1)}(y - x_n)$$

or

(8) $$x_n/y = 1/[1 + (\rho\gamma^\alpha b_{n-1})^{(1/1-\alpha)}].$$

Observe that the second term in the denominator is positive, so that the proportion of wealth consumed is between zero and one:

(9) $$0 < x_n/y < 1.$$

Write

(10) $$\beta_n = b_n^{1/(1-\alpha)},$$

(11) $$\omega = (\rho\gamma^\alpha)^{1/(1-\alpha)}.$$

Substituting Eq. (8) into Eq. (7),

$$b_n y^\alpha = y^\alpha/(1 + \omega\beta_n)^\alpha + \rho\gamma^\alpha b_{n-1}[\omega\beta_n/(1 + \omega\beta_n)]^\alpha y^\alpha,$$

$$b_n = [1 + \omega^{1-\alpha}\beta_{n-1}^{1-\alpha}(\omega\beta_{n-1})^\alpha]/(1 + \omega\beta_{n-1})^\alpha$$

$$= (1 + \omega\beta_{n-1})^{1-\alpha},$$

or

(12) $$\beta_n = 1 + \omega\beta_{n-1}.$$

Recall that $\beta_1 = 1$. Thus

(13) $$\beta_n = \sum_{k=0}^{n-1} \omega^k,$$

where

(14) $$\omega = (\rho\gamma^\alpha)^{1/(1-\alpha)}.$$

The results may be summarized in the following theorem.

Theorem. *Let* $u = x^\alpha$. *Then the value function for the* n*-period problem in Eq. (3) is*

(15) $$v_n(y) = b_n y^\alpha,$$

where

(15') $$b_n = \left[\sum_{k=0}^{n-1} (\rho^{1/(1-\alpha)}\gamma^{\alpha/(1-\alpha)})^k \right]^{1-\alpha}$$

is a generalized n*th-order mean value of* $\rho\gamma^\alpha$. *The optimal consumption is*

(16) $$\hat{x} = \left(1 \Big/ \sum_{k=0}^{n-1} \omega^k \right) y = \frac{y}{\beta_n}.$$

This last statement is proved by substituting Eq. (15) into Eq. (8).

Notice that b_n, hence v_n, is an increasing function of the horizon n: The utility of wealth increases with the length of time available for its investment and consumption. In the special case that $\rho\gamma = 1$,

$$\omega = \rho^{1-\alpha}, \qquad b_n = \left(\sum_{k=0}^{n-1} \rho^k \right)^{1/(1-\alpha)},$$

and

$$\beta_n = \sum_0^{n-1} \rho^k = \frac{1 - \rho^n}{1 - \rho}.$$

We shall now examine how the value of the optimal consumption plan and the level of consumption depend on the problem data n, ρ, γ, and α.

(1) The value increases with n at a decreasing rate. Consumption decreases with y at a decreasing rate, the rates depending on

$$\omega^n = (\rho\gamma^\alpha)^{n/(1-\alpha)}.$$

(2) Since ω is an increasing function of both ρ and γ, it follows that the value increases and consumption falls with both ρ and γ. Thus saving is

higher the higher the growth rate of assets and the smaller the interest rate in discounting future consumption. Consider

$$\frac{\partial}{\partial \alpha} \beta_n = \sum_{k=0}^{n-1} k\omega^{k-1} \cdot \omega \log \gamma = \frac{1}{\omega} \sum_0^{n-1} k\omega^k \cdot \log \gamma > 0.$$

Consumption increases with α. The dependence of the value function on α is more complicated. In the special case $\rho\gamma = 1$ we have

$$b_n = \left(\sum_0^{n-1} \rho^k\right)^{1-\alpha} = \left(\frac{1-\rho^n}{1-\rho}\right)^{1-\alpha},$$

$$\frac{dv_n}{d\alpha} = v_n\left[\log y - \log \frac{1-\rho^n}{1-\rho}\right],$$

so that v_n is increasing or decreasing with respect to α according as y exceeds or is less than $\beta_n = (1 - \rho^n)/(1 - \rho)$.

5

With increasing horizon, the value function approaches a finite limit provided

(17) $$\rho\gamma^\alpha < 1.$$

It is easily verified that the limit function

(18) $$v(y) = \frac{y^\alpha}{1 - \rho^{1/(1-\alpha)}\gamma^{\alpha/(1-\alpha)}} = \frac{y^\alpha}{1 - \omega}$$

satisfies the principle of optimality and that the optimal consumption ratio is

(19) $$\frac{x}{y} = \frac{1}{1 + [(\rho\gamma^\alpha)^{1/(1-\alpha)}/(1 - \rho^{1/(1-\alpha)}\gamma^{\alpha/(1-\alpha)})]} = \frac{1}{1 + 1/[(\rho\gamma^\alpha)^{1/(\alpha-1)} - 1]}$$

$$= 1 - (\rho\gamma^\alpha)^{1/(1-\alpha)} = 1 - \omega.$$

In other words, the optimum savings rate is

(19′) $$s = (\rho\gamma^\alpha)^{1/(1-\alpha)} = \omega.$$

For the existence of an infinite horizon consumption plan condition (17) has the following meaning: The growth rate of assets may be larger than the inverse discount rate but not larger than $1/\rho^\alpha$.

The optimal savings strategy can be summarized simply: Always save a proportion of your wealth. This proportion depends on the three parameters of the problem, ρ, γ, and α. Equation (19') shows that $\alpha = 1$ and $\rho\gamma^\alpha = 1$ are exceptional cases: The savings rate will always be 1, and no consumption will ever take place. This is clearly not an optimum strategy.

6

What does a constant consumption rate imply about the behavior of wealth over time? From Eq. (16) one has

(20)
$$y_{n-1} = \gamma(y_n - x_n) = \gamma[(1/b_n)^{1/(1-\alpha)} - 1]y_n,$$

$$y_{n-1}/y_n = \gamma \sum_{k=1}^{n-1} \omega^k \bigg/ \sum_{k=0}^{n-1} \omega^k$$

$$= (\gamma\rho)^{1/(1-\alpha)} \sum_{0}^{n-2} \omega^k \bigg/ \sum_{k=0}^{n-1} \omega^k$$

$$= (\gamma\rho)^{1/(1-\alpha)}\beta_{n-1}/\beta_n = (\gamma\rho b_{n-1}/b_n)^{1/(1-\alpha)}.$$

For $\gamma\rho \le 1$, one sees that y_n is clearly decreasing as the horizon shrinks, since b_n is increasing with n.

For infinite horizon problems $b_{n-1}/b_n \to 1$ and Eq. (20) shows that wealth accumulates, stays constant, or is used up according as $\gamma\rho \gtreqless 1$. This may also be seen directly from Eq. (19). Let next year's wealth be

(21)
$$\tilde{y} = \gamma(y - x)(y) = \gamma(\rho\gamma^\alpha)^{1/(1-\alpha)}y$$

$$= (\gamma\rho)^{1/(1-\alpha)}y.$$

Thus $\tilde{y} \gtreqless y$ according as $\rho\gamma \gtreqless 1$. This must be true also for sufficiently long but finite horizons. Notice that the exponent α does not enter this criterion at all.

7

We shall now generalize the proposition that accumulation (decumulation) is optimal if and only if the rate of return on assets exceeds (falls short of) the implied interest rate for postponed consumption, to arbitrary concave monotone differentiable value functions.

Suppose that the utility function $u(x)$ has infinitely many derivatives and is concave and monotone. It may be shown by induction that the value function $v(x)$ is then also concave, monotone, and differentiable.

Proposition 1. *Optimal consumption* $\hat{x}_n$ *is a decreasing function of the discount factor* ρ.

Proof. Since u and v are concave, so is the right-hand side of Eq. (3). The optimal consumption x_n is the unique solution of

$$(22) \qquad u'(x_n) - \rho\gamma v'_{n-1}[\gamma(y - x_n)] = 0.$$

We first show by induction that

$$0 < \partial x_n/\partial y < 1;$$

the marginal propensity to consume lies between zero and one. Denote the left-hand side of Eq. (22) by $\Phi(x_n, y)$. Taking the implicit derivative

$$\frac{dx_n}{dy} = -\frac{\Phi_y}{\Phi_{x_n}} = -\frac{-\rho\gamma^2 v''_{n-1}[\gamma(y - x_n)]}{u'' + \rho\gamma^2 v''_{n-1}[\gamma(y - x_n)]},$$

since both $u'' < 0$ and $v''_{n-1} < 0$, the assertion follows. Next

$$\frac{\partial^2 v_n}{\partial y\,\partial\rho} = \frac{\partial}{\partial y}\left(u'\frac{\partial x_n}{\partial\rho} + v_{n-1} + \rho\frac{\partial v_{n-1}}{\partial\rho} - \rho\gamma v'_{n-1}\frac{\partial x_n}{\partial\rho}\right)$$

$$= \frac{\partial v_{n-1}}{\partial y}\gamma\left(1 - \frac{\partial x_n}{\partial y}\right) + \gamma\rho\frac{\partial^2 v_{n-1}}{\partial y\,\partial\rho}\left(1 - \frac{\partial x_n}{\partial y}\right) > 0$$

by an induction hypothesis.

Finally from Eq. (22)

$$\frac{dx_n}{\partial\rho} = -\frac{\Phi_\rho}{\Phi_{x_n}} = -\frac{-\gamma(\partial v_{n-1}/\partial y) - \rho\gamma(\partial^2 v_{n-1}/\partial y\,\partial\rho)}{\Phi_{xx}} < 0$$

since the numerator is positive and the denominator negative by the condition for a maximum in x.   Q.E.D.

Proposition 2.   *Let* $\rho\gamma = 1$. *Then the optimal consumption rate* $\hat{x}$ *in an infinite horizon problem is the annual interest* $yi/(1 + i)$ *on discounted assets so that the initial wealth* y *is preserved forever.*

Proof. To verify this we show that an annual consumption of $x = yi/(1 + i)$ satisfies the principle of optimality in Eq. (3). Optimality of this solution follows from the general principles of dynamic programming (Beckmann [1, 2]).

A stream of constant consumption

$$x = (1 - \rho)y = [1 - 1/(1 + i)]y = [i/(1 + i)]y$$

implies a value function

$$(23) \qquad v(y) = \sum_{n=0}^{\infty} \rho^n u[(1 - \rho)y] = \frac{u[(1 - \rho)y]}{(1 - \rho)}.$$

Substitution in the right-hand side of Eq. (3) for $n = \infty$ and maximization yield

$$\operatorname{Max}_{x}\left\{u(x) + \rho v\left[\frac{1}{\rho}(y - x)\right]\right\} = \operatorname{Max}_{x}\left\{u(x) + \frac{\rho}{1 - \rho}u\left[\frac{1 - \rho}{\rho}(y - x)\right]\right\},$$

$$(24) \qquad u'(x) = u'\left[\frac{1 - \rho}{\rho}(y - x)\right].$$

Since u' is a monotone decreasing function (in view of concavity), the arguments of u' must be equal:

$$x = [(1 - \rho)/\rho](y - x) = (1 - \rho)y.$$

Substituting in Eq. (24), we have

$$u[(1 - \rho)y] + \rho\,\frac{u\{(1 - \rho)[y - (1 - \rho)y]\}/\rho}{1 - \rho}$$

$$= u[(1 - \rho)y] + \frac{\rho}{1 - \rho}u[(1 - \rho)y] = \frac{u[(1 - \rho)y]}{1 - \rho} = v(y),$$

so that Eq. (23), $v(y) = u[(1 - \rho)y]/(1 - \rho)$, and Eq. (22), $x = (1 - \rho)y$, satisfy the principle of optimality in Eq. (3).   Q.E.D.

Proposition 3. *Since cξnsumption preserves wealth when $\rho\gamma = 1$, and consumption is a decreasing function of ρ, it follows that in an infinite horizon problem*

$$\text{wealth is}\begin{cases}\text{accumulated}\\\text{preserved}\\\text{expended}\end{cases}\text{according as } \rho\gamma\begin{cases}>\\=\\<\end{cases}1.$$

We show next that for finite horizon problems, when $\rho\gamma = 1$, consumption is equalized over all periods. This includes the proposition of a constant level of wealth for infinite horizon problems when it is observed that optimal consumption is a constant fraction of wealth.

We calculate first the initial wealth y_n needed to sustain a rate of consumption $\bar{x}$ over n periods. Subtracting consumption $\bar{x}$ from this wealth y_n we have the discounted wealth in an $(n - 1)$-period problem:

$$(25) \qquad y_n = \bar{x} = \rho y_{n-1},$$

since $\rho\gamma = 1$ by assumption. The initial condition of this difference equation is

$$(26) \qquad y_1 = \bar{x}.$$

The solution of Eqs. (25) and (26) is readily seen to be

$$(27) \qquad y_n = \bar{x}(1 - \rho^n)/(1 - \rho).$$

It follows in turn that the consumption rate $\bar{x}_n$ that can be sustained over n periods with initial wealth y is

$$(28) \qquad \bar{x}_n = y(1 - \rho)/(1 - \rho^n).$$

The verification that

$$(29) \qquad v_n(y) = \sum_{i=0}^{n-1} \rho^i u\left(y \frac{1 - \rho}{1 - \rho^n}\right) = \frac{1 - \rho^n}{1 - \rho} u\left(y \frac{1 - \rho}{1 - \rho^n}\right)$$

and Eq. (26) satisfy the principle of optimality is now straightforward. Substituting in the right-hand side of Eq. (3),

$$\underset{x}{\text{Max}}\{u(x) + \rho v_{n-1}[(1/\rho)(y - x)]\}$$

$$= \underset{x}{\text{Max}}\left\{u(x) + \rho \frac{1 - \rho^{n-1}}{1 - \rho} u\left[\frac{1}{\rho}(y - x)\frac{1 - \rho}{1 - \rho^{n-1}}\right]\right.$$

$$\times u'(x) - u'\left[\frac{1}{\rho}\frac{1 - \rho}{1 - \rho^{n-1}}(y - x)\right]\right\} = 0,$$

from which

$$\bar{x}_n = \frac{[(1 - \rho)/(\rho - \rho^n)]y}{1 + (1 - \rho)/(\rho - \rho^n)} = \frac{1 - \rho}{\rho - \rho^n + 1 - \rho} y = \frac{1 - \rho}{1 - \rho^n} y. \qquad \text{Q.E.D.}$$

Using Proposition 1 we arrive at the following.

Proposition 4. *In a finite horizon problem*

$$\text{consumption}\begin{Bmatrix} \text{increases} \\ \text{is constant} \\ \text{decreases} \end{Bmatrix} \text{over time according as } \rho\gamma \begin{Bmatrix} > \\ = \\ < \end{Bmatrix} 1.$$

In particular, when the rate of return on assets is zero (the pure consumption case investigated by Bellman), consumption always decreases as the horizon shrinks as shown by Hotelling [4], and when consumption is not discounted, it always increases. When $\rho\gamma = 1$, it is seen that consumption

$$\bar{x} = [(1 - \rho)/(1 - \rho^n)]y$$

is smaller the longer the horizon. It is easily seen that, when $\rho\gamma = 1$, wealth decreases with time since

$$y_{n-1} = (1/\rho)[1 - (1 - \rho)/(1 - \rho^n)]y_n$$

or

$$y_{n-1}/y_n = (1 - \rho^{n-1})/(1 - \rho^n) < 1.$$

This remains true when $\rho\gamma < 1$, but with $\rho\gamma > 1$ wealth may increase initially as shown above for the special utility function $u = x^\alpha$.

8

In concluding this chapter let us briefly discuss some alternatives not treated in our analysis.

First, the utility function $u = -x^\alpha$, $\alpha < 0$, is increasing, concave, and bounded from above. The value function then is

$$v_n = -b_n y^\alpha,$$

where b_n is given by Eq. (15′) as before. Observe that $\omega = \rho\gamma^\alpha < 1$ for all $\rho \le 1$, $\gamma > 1$, so that the condition (17) is no restriction: The series (13) always converges, and an infinite horizon consumption plan exists. The logarithmic utility function

(30) $$u = \log x$$

generates a value function

(31) $$v(y) = b_n \log y + c_n,$$

where b_n is given by the same formula [Eq. (15)] as in the power function case with $\alpha = 0$. The optimal consumption ratio is

$$\hat{x}/y = 1/b_n, \qquad b_n = \beta_n = \sum_0^{n-1} \rho^k,$$

hence it also fits the power case with $\alpha = 0$. Then b_n converges for $\rho < 1$. It can be shown that power functions and logarithms are the only utility functions (with infinitely many derivatives) for which optimal consumption is always proportional to wealth.

Second, let $0 < \alpha < 1$, but $\rho\gamma^\alpha > 1$. Then for finite horizon problems all results apply. However, b_n grows indefinitely with increasing n, and $\hat{x}_n/y$ approaches zero. The problem for an infinite horizon is ill-defined. The principle of optimality has no finite solution. There exists no optimal policy. Zero consumption is dominated by any finite horizon consumption plan. The optimal consumption plan for horizon $(n + 1)$ dominates the optimal consumption plan for horizon n.

Third, let $\alpha = 1$. Then for finite horizon problems

$$x_n = y \qquad \text{for} \quad \rho\gamma < 1,$$

$$\bar{x}_n \text{ arbitrary}, \bar{x}_1 = y \qquad \text{for} \quad \rho\gamma = 1,$$

$$x_n = 0, \quad n > 1, \qquad \bar{x}_1 = y \qquad \text{for} \quad \rho\gamma > 1.$$

In the first two cases the value function is $v_n(y) = y$, and in the last case $v_n(y) = (\rho\gamma)^n y$. An infinite horizon optimal consumption plan exists only in the first two cases, and it is not unique in the second case.

Fourth, let $\alpha > 1$. Then the utility function x^α is convex and so is $v_n(y)$, as may be shown by recursive induction. The optimal consumption plan is

$$\hat{x}_n = y \qquad \text{for} \quad \rho\gamma^\alpha < 1,$$

$$\hat{x}_m = y, \quad m \text{ arbitrary}, \qquad \text{for} \quad \rho\gamma^\alpha = 1,$$

$$\hat{x}_n = 0, \quad n > 1, \qquad \hat{x}_1 = y \qquad \text{for} \quad \rho\gamma > 1.$$

An optimal consumption plan for an infinite horizon problem exists only in the first two cases, and it is not unique in the second case.

9. RISK

So far the annual rate of return i has been assumed constant and known. To explore the implication of stochastic returns, we assume again a utility function (1) $u = x^\alpha$. Let $P(\gamma)$ be the distribution of $\gamma = 1 + i$. The principle of optimality assumes the form

$$(32) \qquad v_n(y) = \operatorname*{Max}_{0 \le x \le y} \left\{ u(x) + \rho \int v_{n-1}\left[\gamma(y - x) \right] dP(\gamma) \right\}.$$

For the utility function (1) we postulate again that the value function is also a power function with the same exponent:

$$(33) \qquad v_n(y) = \tilde{b}_n y^\alpha.$$

Substituting in Eq. (32),

$$(34) \qquad \tilde{b}_n y^\alpha = \operatorname*{Max}_x \left[x^\alpha + \rho\tilde{b}_{n-1}(y - x)^\alpha \int \gamma^\alpha \, dP(\gamma) \right].$$

We write

$$(35) \qquad \tilde{\gamma} = \left[\int \gamma^\alpha \, dP(\gamma) \right]^{1/\alpha}.$$

Equation (34) is then identical to Eq. (7) provided we substitute $\tilde{b}_n$ and $\tilde{\gamma}$ for b_n and γ. We conclude that the optimal consumption policy is

$$(36) \qquad \tilde{x}_n = (1/\tilde{b}_n)^{1/(1-\alpha)} y = \left(1 \left/ \sum_{k=0}^{n-1} \omega^k \right. \right) y,$$

where

$$(37) \qquad \tilde{\omega} = \left[\rho \int \gamma^\alpha \, dP(\gamma) \right]^{1/(1-\alpha)},$$

and that the value function is

$$(38) \qquad v_n(y) = \tilde{b}_n y^\alpha = y \left\{ \sum_{k=0}^{n-1} \left[\int \rho \gamma^\alpha \, dP(\gamma) \right]^{k/(1-\alpha)} \right\}^{1-\alpha}.$$

Thus the pattern of proportional consumption is optimal also under risk with this special utility function. In general, however, when the rate of return cannot be factored out of the utility function (or summed out as in the case of logarithmic utility), the optimal consumption depends in a more complicated way on current wealth.

It follows in the same way that an infinite horizon optimal consumption plan exists provided $\rho \tilde{\gamma}^\alpha < 1$. The expected value of consumption and of wealth is increasing, constant, or decreasing according as $\rho \tilde{\gamma} \gtreqless 1$, where $\tilde{\gamma}$ is the expected value of γ. But this conclusion is restricted to the special utility functions (1) and (2).

10

So far we have assumed that γ is identically and independently distributed in every period. Suppose next that there is a linear relationship between the expected value of γ, $\bar{\gamma}_t$ and the previous value of γ, γ_{t-1}:

$$(39) \qquad \bar{\gamma}_t = a + c\gamma_{t-1} + \varepsilon_t,$$

and that the errors ε_t are independently and identically distributed. The principle of optimality has the form

$$(40) \quad \tilde{b}_n(\gamma_{t-1})y^\alpha = \underset{x}{\mathrm{Max}} \left[x^\alpha + \rho \int \tilde{b}_{n-1}(\gamma)\gamma^\alpha (y-x)^\alpha \, dP(\gamma - a - c\gamma_{t-1}) \right],$$

from which we obtain in the same way as above

$$x_n(g, y) = \hat{x} = \hat{x}_n(g, y)$$

$$(41) \qquad = y \left/ \left\{ 1 + \left[\rho \int b_{n-1}(\gamma)\gamma^\alpha \, dP(\gamma - a - cg) \right]^{1/(1-\alpha)} \right\} \right.,$$

$$\hat{x}_n(g, y) = [1/b_n(g)^{1/(1-\alpha)}]y,$$

where $b_n(g)$ are given by the recursive relationship in $b_n(g)$:

$$(42) \qquad b_n(g) = \left\{ 1 + \left[\int \rho \gamma^\alpha b_{n-1}(\gamma) \, dP(\gamma - a - cg) \right]^{1/(1-\alpha)} \right\}^{1-\alpha},$$

where g denotes the rate of return in the previous period. For the problem with infinite horizon we have the nonlinear integral equation in $b(g)^{1/(1-\alpha)} = \beta(g)$, say,

$$(43) \qquad \beta(g) = 1 + \left[\int \rho \gamma^\alpha \beta(\gamma)^{1-\alpha} \, dP(\gamma - a - cg) \right]^{1/(1-\alpha)}.$$

If the predicted mean of the distribution of γ depends on the realized γ values in several past periods, we have a more general relationship:

$$(44) \quad \beta(g_1, g_2, \ldots, g_m) = 1 + \left[\left[\int \rho \gamma^\alpha \beta(\gamma), g_1, g_2, \ldots, g_{m-1} \right]^{1-\alpha} \right. $$
$$\left. \times dP\left(\gamma - a - \sum_i c_i g_i \right) \right)^{1/(1-\alpha)}.$$

Of particular interest is the case of a "geometrically distributed lag":

$$\bar{\gamma} = (1 - \lambda)(g_1 + \lambda g_2 + \lambda^2 g_3 + \cdots + \lambda^{n-1} g_n + \cdots), \quad -1 < \lambda < 1,$$

where the constant term is absent and the weights are geometrically decreasing and add to one. In this case it is useful to define the sufficient statistic

$$g = (1 - \lambda) \sum_{i=0}^{\infty} g_i \lambda^i.$$

Notice that the observation γ of this year's rate of return generates a next value of g equal to

$$g' = (1 - \lambda)\gamma + \lambda g.$$

Thus the integral equation for β has the form

$$(45) \quad \beta(g) = 1 + \left\{ \int \rho \gamma^\alpha \beta[(1 - \lambda)\gamma + \lambda g]^{1-\alpha} \, dP(\gamma - g) \right\}^{1/(1-\alpha)}.$$

The special case $\lambda = 0$, where next year's expected rate of return equals this year's realized return, corresponds to a martingale.

In the finite horizon case we have an equation system

$$(46) \quad \beta_n(g) = 1 + \left\{ \int \rho \gamma^\alpha \beta_{n-1}[(1 - \lambda)\gamma + \lambda g]^{1-\alpha} \, dP(\gamma - g) \right\}^{1/(1-\alpha)},$$
$$\beta_0(g) \equiv 0$$

or

$$\beta_1(g) \equiv 1, \quad \text{i.e.,} \quad b_1(g) \equiv 1.$$

Observe that in every case

$$\hat{x}_n = (1/\beta_n)y.$$

A high rate of return in the last period now has an income and a substitution effect. The income effect stems from the larger value of wealth y, and the substitution effect from the induced expectation of higher returns γ in the future. Which of the two effects is larger can be stated only when the function β has been determined.

11

The exponentially distributed lag is a special Markov process. In a more general Markov process, the probability distribution of next year's yield γ is then a function of only this year's yield g:

$$\text{pr}(\gamma) = p(\gamma \,|\, g).$$

Substituting in the principle of optimality one shows that the optimal consumption strategy is again of the form

(47) $\hat{x}_n = [1/\beta_n(g)]y,$

where $\beta_n(g)$ is determined recursively by

(48) $\beta_n(g) = 1 + \left[\int \rho \gamma^\alpha \beta_{n-1}^{1-\alpha}(\gamma) p(\gamma \,|\, g) \, d\gamma \right]^{1/(1-\alpha)}.$

Let M_n be the maximum of $\beta_n(g)$ on the finite interval $0 \leq g \leq c$. It may be shown by induction that $\beta_n(g)$ is continuous, so that the maximum exists. Substituting in Eq. (48) we have the inequality

(49) $M_n \leqq 1 + M_{n-1} \underset{g}{\text{Max}} \int \rho \gamma^\alpha p(\gamma \,|\, g) \, d\gamma \leq 1 + aM_{n-1},$

where

$$a = \underset{g}{\text{Max}} \int \rho \gamma^\alpha p(\gamma \,|\, g) \, d\gamma.$$

Through successive substitution

$$M_n \leq (1 + a + a^2 + \cdots + a^{n-2} + a^{n-1})M_1,$$

but $M_1 = \beta_1 \equiv 1$. Thus $\beta_n(g) \leqq 1/(1-a)$ provided $|a| < 1$. An infinite horizon consumption plan exists, therefore, provided

(50) $\int \rho \gamma^\alpha p(\gamma(g)) \leq 1 - \varepsilon < 1$ for all g.

This condition generalizes the previous condition (17).

REFERENCES

1. Beckmann, M., A Dynamic Programming Model of the Consumption Function, Cowles Commission Discussion Paper 69, March, 1959.
2. Beckmann, M., "Dynamic Programming of Economic Decisions." Springer, Heidelberg and New York, 1968.

3. Bellman, R., "Dynamic Programming." Princeton University Press, Princeton, New Jersey, 1957.
4. Hotelling, H., The economics of exhaustible resources, *Journal of Political Economy* 137–175 (1939).
5. National Bureau of Standards, "Handbook of Mathematical Functions." Washington, D.C., 1965.
6. Phelps, E., The accumulation of risky capital: A sequential utility analysis, *Econometrica* **30**(4), 729–743 (1962).
7. Radner, R., Notes on the Theory of Economic Planning. Center for Economic Research, Athens, 1963.

DEPARTMENT OF ECONOMICS
BROWN UNIVERSITY
PROVIDENCE, RHODE ISLAND
    AND
INSTITUTE OF STATISTICS
TECHNICAL UNIVERSITY
MUNICH, WEST GERMANY

Generalized Separation Property for Dynamic Portfolio Models

Piera Mazzoleni

1. INTRODUCTION

The capital asset pricing model was first proposed by Markowitz and Sharpe in a single-period framework. Although various considerations in favor of its realism have been made by later authors, Merton has shown in a number of examples that portfolio behavior is significantly different for an intertemporal maximizer and that the two contexts are not equivalent. Therefore the importance of dynamic decisions describing the portfolio choice at different times must be emphasized.

The model we describe is based on consumption–investment behavior. A first-step decision subdivides the resources between consumption and investments according to a suitable utility function; a second step individuates the optimal portfolio of investments.

This economic problem is formulated as a control model: Wealth and instantaneous return on any asset are the state variables; consumption and the amount invested in each asset are the control variables. Denote by $W(t)$ the investor wealth in money units and by $x_0(t)$ the instantaneous consumption flow. The aim of the investor is to calculate the fraction of his wealth invested in the ith asset, $x_i(t)$, for $i = 1, \ldots, n$, and the fraction devoted to consumption in order to maximize the expected value of utility flow:

$$(1.1) \qquad E_0\left\{ \int_0^T U[x_0(t), t]\, dt + B[W(T), T] \right\},$$

199

where E_0 is the expectation operator, conditional on the current state of the system at time $t = 0$; U the utility function, which is bounded, infinitely differentiable, and strictly concave in x_0; and B the "terminal wealth" function, which describes the behavior of the investor with respect to the terminal level of wealth and is assumed to be bounded, infinitely differentiable, and strictly concave. The evolution equation for wealth takes the form

$$(1.2) \qquad dW = \boldsymbol{\alpha}^T \mathbf{x} W \, dt - x_0 \, dt + (d\boldsymbol{\gamma})^T \mathbf{x} W,$$

with the initial condition $W(0) = W^0$.

Along these general lines, in Section 2 we present a revised version of the Merton model and emphasize its economic meaning. In Section 3 we prove a complete separation theorem with respect to intrinsic risk, exchange, and inflation risk. Such a model is then extended in order to include any number of risks. In this way it is possible to see how diversification can be interpreted as an insurance process. Finally, in the appendix we present a brief outline of stochastic control.

2. REVISED MERTON MODEL

Denote by $K(t)$ the amount of capital employed by a firm at time t, measured in physical units, with $P_k(t)$ its unit price and β the rate of its physical depreciation. The number of shares $N(t)$ of the firm and the price per share $P(t)$ can now be defined by the difference equations

$$(2.1) \qquad P(t + h) = A(t)/N(t), \qquad\qquad P(0) = P^0,$$

$$(2.2) \qquad N(t + h) = N(t) + B(t)/P(t), \qquad N(0) = N^0,$$

where $A(t) = D(t) + (1 - \beta)P_k(t + h)K(t)$ represents the sum of cash flow $D(t)$ plus the value of undepreciated capital and

$$B(t) = P_k(t + h)[K(t + h) - (1 - \beta)K(t)] - D(t)$$

is equal to the value of gross new investment in excess of cash flow. In this framework $[P(t + h) - P(t)]/P(t)$ is the rate of return on the asset over the time interval $[t, t + h]$ in units of consumption goods.

Beyond the assumptions of the classical asset pricing model, the hypothesis of continuous trading is the fundamental one, and it allows the returns and the changes in the opportunity set to be described by continuous-time stochastic processes. Continuous trading is an abstraction from physical reality. However, the continuous-trading solution is a reasonable approximation to the discrete-trading one, not only for economic phenomena referred to very short time intervals but also for models linked to longer periods of time. Indeed, Merton [3] effectively proves that the continuous-trading solution provides a uniformly valid approximation to the discrete-trading solution under nonrestrictive economic assumptions.

With reference to the limit process introduced in the appendix to define Itô integrals, the behavior of the expected return on assets is described here for discrete-trading intervals of length h, and the limit is taken as $h \to 0$.

Let the random variable

$$(2.3) \qquad \varepsilon(t) = P(t) - P(t-1) - E_{t-1}[P(t) - P(t-1)]$$

represent the unanticipated price change in the asset between $t - 1$ and t, conditional on being at time $t - 1$ when there are no "rare events." The mathematical assumption that the partial sums $\sum_{t=1}^{n} \varepsilon(t)$ form a martingale is very useful for the analytical results and nonrestrictive from the economic point of view. Suppose the uncertainty associated with $\varepsilon(t)$ is neither eliminated nor dominant and is significant in all trading periods. If for all assets with a finite price the expected rate of return per unit time over the trading horizon is finite, then the sample paths for prices are continuous over time, but almost nowhere differentiable. Thus we must refer to stochastic differential calculus (see the appendix).

This being stated, we define for each asset the expected rate of return and variance per unit time as

$$(2.4) \qquad \alpha \equiv E_t \left[\frac{P(t+h) - P(t)}{P(t)} \right] / h,$$

$$(2.5) \qquad \sigma^2 \equiv E_t \left[\left(\frac{P(t+h) - P(t)}{P(t)} - \alpha h \right)^2 \right] / h, \qquad \sigma^2 > 0,$$

and let α, σ^2 be finite and continuous functions of h. Then the return dynamic between t and $t + h$ is

$$(2.6) \qquad \frac{P(t+h) - P(t)}{P(t)} = \alpha h + \sigma \zeta(t) \sqrt{h},$$

and the realized return over the trading interval will be completely dominated by its unanticipated component $\sigma \zeta(t) \sqrt{h}$.

Because of the properties of a martingale, we can take the limit and obtain the stochastic differential equation

$$(2.7) \qquad dP_i / P_i = \alpha_i \, dt + \sigma_i \, dz_i$$

for each asset $i = 1, \ldots, n$. Thus far we have placed no relevant restrictions on dz_i. Now we are led to the usual assumption that the stochastic process is a time-homogeneous Markov process leading to a Wiener process $z(t)$. The opportunity set can be characterized by parameters $\{\alpha_i, \sigma_i, \sigma_{ij}\}$ for i,

$j = 1, \ldots, n$, where n is the number of firms and σ_{ij} the instantaneous covariance coefficient between z_i and z_j. Moreover, when the opportunity set varies with time, α_i and σ_i describe a stochastic process and the Markov system

$$(2.8) \qquad d\alpha_i(t) = a_i\, dt + b_i\, dv_i, \qquad d\sigma_i(t) = f_i\, dt + g_i\, dw_i$$

is added to the model.

This being stated, we can derive the accumulation equation for wealth. Referring to the consumption flow over the time interval $[t, t + h]$, we have

$$(2.9) \quad -x_0(t + h)h = [\mathbf{N}(t + h) - \mathbf{N}(t)]^{\mathrm{T}}\mathbf{P}(t + h)$$
$$= [\mathbf{N}(t + h) - \mathbf{N}(t)]^{\mathrm{T}}[\mathbf{P}(t + h) - \mathbf{P}(t)] + [\mathbf{N}(t + h)$$
$$- \mathbf{N}(t)]^{\mathrm{T}}\mathbf{P}(t).$$

If we divide by h and take the limit as $h \to 0$, we obtain the consumption in terms of the number and the price of shares:

$$(2.10) \qquad -x_0(t) = [d\mathbf{N}(t)^{\mathrm{T}}/dt][d\mathbf{P}(t) + \mathbf{P}(t)].$$

Thus by applying the Itô lemma, the change in the capital invested in shares $W(t) = \mathbf{N}(t)^{\mathrm{T}}\mathbf{P}(t)$ can be described as the effect of variations in the unit price of shares:

$$(2.11) \qquad dW = \mathbf{N}^{\mathrm{T}}\, d\mathbf{P} + d\mathbf{N}^{\mathrm{T}}(d\mathbf{P} + \mathbf{P}).$$

Denote by $x_i(t) = N_i(t)P_i(t)/W(t)$ the fraction of wealth invested in the ith asset as a function of the number of shares of the ith asset and set $N_i = x_i W/P_i$ in (2.11).

By comparing Eqs. (2.10) and (2.11) and taking into account the differential equations for prices $dP_i/P_i = \alpha_i\, dt + \sigma_i\, dz_i$, $i = 1, \ldots, n$, we finally obtain the evolution equation for wealth:

$$(2.12)$$
$$dW = \boldsymbol{\alpha}^{\mathrm{T}}\mathbf{x}W\, dt - x_0\, dt + (d\boldsymbol{\gamma})^{\mathrm{T}}\mathbf{x}W, \quad \text{with} \quad d\boldsymbol{\gamma} = [\sigma_1\, dz_1, \ldots, \sigma_n\, dz_n]^{\mathrm{T}}.$$

The variance–covariance matrix for processes dz_i, dz_j, $\Sigma = [\sigma_{ij}]$ is supposed to be nonsingular. Thus the problem faced by the investor is to maximize the expected value of utility flow,

$$(2.13) \qquad \max E_0\left\{\int_0^{\mathrm{T}} U[x_0(t), t]\, dt + B[W(T), T]\right\},$$

under the accumulation equation (2.12) and the budget constraint $\mathbf{e}^{\mathrm{T}}\mathbf{x}(t) = 1$, where $\mathbf{e}$ is the vector of ones.

The theory we briefly describe in the appendix leads to a solution to the new problem

$$(2.14) \qquad 0 = \max_{e^T x(t) = 1} \{U[x_0(t), t] + \mathscr{D}(J) \stackrel{\text{def}}{=} \Phi(\hat{x}, \hat{y}, t)\},$$

where $\mathscr{D}$ denotes the differential operator on variables

$$\tilde{y} = [W, P_1, \ldots, P_n] = [y_0, \mathbf{y}]$$

for a given state vector

$$(2.15) \qquad \begin{aligned} \tilde{\mathbf{x}} &= [x_0, x_1, \ldots, x_n], \\ \mathscr{D}(J) &= J'_t + (\boldsymbol{\alpha}^T \mathbf{x} y_0 - x_0)J'_{y_0} + \tfrac{1}{2}\mathbf{x}^T \Sigma \mathbf{x} y_0^2 J''_{y_0} + \mathbf{f}^T J'_{\mathbf{y}} \\ &\quad + \tfrac{1}{2}\mathbf{g}^T A \mathbf{g} + (\mathbf{g} J''_{\mathbf{y}, y_0})^T H(\boldsymbol{\sigma}\mathbf{x}) y_0; \end{aligned}$$

$\mathbf{f}$ and $\mathbf{g}$ are assigned in (2.8); ξ_{ij} denotes the instantaneous correlation coefficient between dv_i, dz_j; ν_{ij} denotes the one between dv_i, dv_j; and we set

$$A = [J''_{y_i, y_j} \nu_{ij}], \qquad H = [\xi_{ij}],$$

$$\boldsymbol{\sigma}\mathbf{x} = \sum_{i=1}^{n} \sigma_i x_i, \qquad \mathbf{g} J''_{\mathbf{y}, y_0} = \sum_{i=1}^{n} g_i J''_{y_i, y_0}.$$

In order to derive optimal controls $x_0^*, x_1^*, \ldots, x_n^*$, we introduce a Lagrange function

$$(2.16) \qquad L = \Phi + \lambda(1 - \mathbf{e}^T \mathbf{x})$$

and obtain the first-order conditions

$$(2.17a) \qquad U'_{x_0}(x_0, t) - J'_{y_0} = 0,$$

$$(2.17b) \qquad 1 - \mathbf{e}^T \mathbf{x} = 0,$$

$$(2.17c) \qquad -\lambda \mathbf{e} + \boldsymbol{\alpha} y_0 J'_{y_0} + \Sigma \mathbf{x} y_0^2 J''_{y_0} + \boldsymbol{\eta}^1 = 0,$$

for $\boldsymbol{\eta}^1 = H(\mathbf{g} J''_{\mathbf{y}, y_0})\boldsymbol{\sigma} y_0$ and with the condition $J[y_0(T), T] = B[W(T), T]$.
The second-order conditions are satisfied. Indeed the Hessian matrix for L is given by

$$(2.18) \qquad H_L = L''_{\tilde{\mathbf{x}}} = y_0^2 J''_{y_0} \begin{bmatrix} U''_{x_0}/y_0^2 J''_{y_0} & \cdots & \mathbf{0}^T \\ \vdots & \ddots & \vdots \\ \mathbf{0} & \cdots & \Sigma \end{bmatrix},$$

and we assume $J''_{y_0} < 0$ and Σ to be positive definite.

Equation (2.17a) individuates the optimal consumption as a function of J'_{y_0}; the linear system in $\mathbf{x}$, λ [Eqs. (2.17b)–(2.17c)] gives the following expression for fractions of wealth invested in assets:

$$(2.19) \qquad \mathbf{x}^* = \frac{\Sigma^{-1}}{\mathbf{e}^T\Sigma^{-1}\mathbf{e}}\left(\frac{J'_{y_0}}{J''_{y_0 y_0}}\Omega\boldsymbol{\alpha} - \mathbf{e}\right) + \frac{1}{J''_{y_0 y_0}}\frac{\Sigma^{-1}}{\mathbf{e}^T\Sigma^{-1}\mathbf{e}}\Omega\boldsymbol{\eta}^1,$$

with $\Omega = \mathbf{e}^T\Sigma^{-1}\mathbf{e}I - \mathbf{e}\mathbf{e}^T\Sigma^{-1}$ in terms of parameters $\tilde{\mathbf{y}}, t, J'_{y_0}, J''_{y_0}, J''_{y_j, y_0}$. Thus in this case, referring to the mutual fund theorem derived by Merton, a third term appears, which represents a hedge against variations in the opportunity set.

Assume now that $n - 1$ assets have a random unit price, the nth one instantaneously riskless so that $\sigma_n = 0$ and $\alpha_n = r(t)$, but $b_n \neq 0$. In this situation the constraint on control variables $x_1, \ldots, x_n$ can be ignored, because x_n can always be chosen in order to fulfil condition $\mathbf{e}^T\mathbf{x} = 1$.

Then, for

$$(2.20) \quad \mathcal{D}(J) = J'_t + \{[(\hat{\boldsymbol{\alpha}} - r\hat{\mathbf{e}})^T\mathbf{x} + r]y_0 - x_0\}J'_{y_0}$$
$$+ \tfrac{1}{2}\mathbf{x}^T\hat{\Sigma}\mathbf{x}y_0^2 J''_{y_0} + \hat{\mathbf{f}}^T J'_{\mathbf{y}} + \tfrac{1}{2}\hat{\mathbf{g}}^T\hat{A}\hat{\mathbf{g}} + (\hat{\mathbf{g}}J'_{\mathbf{y}, y_0})^T\hat{H}(\hat{\sigma}\mathbf{x})y_0,$$

where the caret $\hat{}$ refers to $n - 1$ risky investments, the first-order conditions in $\mathbf{x}$,

$$(2.21) \qquad\qquad 0 = (\hat{\boldsymbol{\alpha}} - r\hat{\mathbf{e}})y_0 J'_{y_0} + \hat{\Sigma}\mathbf{x}y_0^2 J''_{y_0} + \hat{\boldsymbol{\eta}}^1,$$

give the optimal solution

$$(2.22) \qquad\qquad \hat{\mathbf{x}}^* = -\frac{J'_{y_0}}{J''_{y_0 y_0}}\hat{\Sigma}^{-1}(\hat{\boldsymbol{\alpha}} - r\hat{\mathbf{e}}) - \frac{1}{J''_{y_0 y_0}}\hat{\Sigma}^{-1}\hat{\boldsymbol{\eta}}^1,$$

and one fund is represented by the instantaneously riskless asset.

A further simplification is a constant-investment opportunity set in which the corresponding parameters $\boldsymbol{\alpha}$, r, and $\Sigma = [\sigma_{ij}]$ do not vary with time. In this case the distribution of unit price P_i is lognormal:

$$(2.23) \qquad\qquad d\log P_i = (\alpha_i - \sigma_i^2/2)\,dt + \sigma_i\,dz_i,$$

and the solutions to (2.19)–(2.22) become, respectively,

$$(2.24) \qquad \mathbf{x}^* = (\Sigma^{-1}/\mathbf{e}^T\Sigma^{-1}\mathbf{e})[-(J'_{y_0}/J''_{y_0}y_0)\Omega\boldsymbol{\alpha} - \mathbf{e}],$$

$$(2.25) \qquad\qquad \hat{\mathbf{x}}^* = -(J'_{y_0}/J''_{y_0}y_0)\Sigma^{-1}(\hat{\boldsymbol{\alpha}} - r\hat{\mathbf{e}}).$$

Such a result is economically equivalent to the one obtained in the deterministic one-period analysis.

3. A COMPLETE SEPARATION THEOREM FOR ALTERNATIVE RISKS

When an investor makes arrangements for investing an amount of money, he also seeks to reduce the probability of suffering losses. Thus he may decide to cede a fraction of his investments to another investor having the role of an insurance company. This transaction can be carried out in a certain way when the aim of the investor is to obtain a complete separation of risks.

Let us first consider a reduced portfolio problem. Contracts linked to the price level would provide a useful device for reducing the effects of unanticipated inflation. Correspondingly, issuance of an indexed bond would introduce an asset protecting portfolio holders against a risk that they could not otherwise completely avoid.

Another aspect worth taking into account is the rapid growth of international investments. A fundamental dimension of this international market is the existence of exchange risk and mechanisms providing protection to investors unwilling to carry this kind of risk. Together with the standard assumptions of market perfection, we assume that there are no constraints on international capital flow, investors' consumption is limited to their home country, and the opportunity set does not vary with time. But there is no universal risk-free asset, and the presence of exchange risk alters the characteristics of the same investment in different countries. Let us consider an investor who can choose from four different investments:

An asset in a foreign currency;
A bond in a foreign currency, depending on a price index;
A risk-free asset in a foreign country;
A risk-free asset in his own country.

In this range we can recognize three different kinds of risks: the particular risk linked to the structure of the asset chosen by the investor, inflation, and exchange risk.

Define a reference price index I which changes stochastically with time and represent the dynamic of the inflation rate as

$$(3.1) \qquad dI/I = p\,dt + s\,dz.$$

Therefore, for p and s constant with time, I follows a lognormal distribution.

Denote by f the exchange rate between the foreign and domestic currencies involved. Under the assumption

$$(3.2) \qquad df/f = \phi\,dt + \psi\,dq,$$

ϕ is the expected change in parity and ψ its standard deviation.

Assume that we can individuate the effect of inflation on the return dynamic of the risky asset being examined. Let us express such a return in the domestic currency as $\tilde{R}_1 = fIR$ and suppose that the dynamic of the proper risk is $dR/R = a_1\,dt + \sigma_R\,dz_R$. Then by applying the Itô lemma (see the appendix) we can write the dynamic of the return as

$$(3.3) \qquad d\tilde{R}_1/\tilde{R}_1 = d(fIR)/(fIR)$$

$$= (\phi + p + a_1)\,dt + \psi\,dq + s\,dz + \sigma_R\,dz_R.$$

From now on, covariances a_{ij} between the Wiener processes introduced will be assumed to be negligible in order to obtain the subsequent analytical results.[1] Assume that the foreign bond pays a return $\tilde{R}_2$ linked to the realized rate of inflation. Then the instantaneous return expressed in the domestic currency, $\tilde{R}_2 = fIB_1$, varies according to

$$(3.4) \quad d\tilde{R}_2/\tilde{R}_2 = d(fIB_1)/(fIB_1) = [\phi + (a_2 + p)]\,dt + s\,dz + \psi\,dq.$$

Finally, the portfolio contains a foreign risk-free asset, which has to be converted to the investor's domestic currency:

$$(3.5) \qquad d\tilde{R}_3/\tilde{R}_3 = d(fB_2)/(fB_2) = (\phi + a_3)\,dt + \psi\,dq.$$

The investor is supposed to maximize his expected utility, given his current wealth, the state variables of the investment opportunity set, and the distribution of his wage income.

This problem can be formalized as

$$(3.6) \qquad \max E_0\left\{\int_0^T U(x_0, \tau)\,d\tau + B[W(T), T]\right\}$$

under the accumulation equation

$$(3.7) \quad dW = \{x_1\,d\tilde{R}_1/\tilde{R}_1 + x_2\,d\tilde{R}_2/\tilde{R}_2 + x_3\,d\tilde{R}_3/\tilde{R}_3 + x_4\,dR_4/R_4\}W$$

$$+ (v - x_0)\,dt,$$

where v denotes the wage income of the investor, x_0 the instantaneous consumption flow, R_4 the instantaneous return on a domestic risk-free asset, and $x_i, i = 1, \ldots, 4$, the proportion of wealth invested in the different forms.

A suitable change of variables,

$$(3.8) \qquad \begin{array}{l} u_1 = x_1 \\ u_2 = x_1 + x_2 \\ u_3 = x_1 + x_2 + x_3 \end{array} \qquad \text{i.e.,} \quad \mathbf{u} = \begin{bmatrix} 1 & 0 & 0 \\ 1 & 1 & 0 \\ 1 & 1 & 1 \end{bmatrix}\mathbf{x},$$

---

[1] This is possible because the exchange rate can be linked to the price index of the other country and inflation rates can be assumed to be uncorrelated.

leads us to the new fractions

$$
(3.9) \quad
\begin{array}{l}
x_1 = u_1, \\
x_2 = u_2 - u_1, \\
x_3 = u_3 - u_2,
\end{array}
\quad \text{i.e.,} \quad
\mathbf{x} =
\begin{bmatrix}
1 & 0 & 0 \\
-1 & 1 & 0 \\
0 & -1 & 1
\end{bmatrix}
\mathbf{u}
$$

$$
= \left(
\begin{bmatrix}
1 & 0 & 0 \\
0 & 1 & 0 \\
0 & 0 & 1
\end{bmatrix}
-
\begin{bmatrix}
0 & 0 & 0 \\
1 & 0 & 0 \\
0 & 1 & 0
\end{bmatrix}
\right) \mathbf{u},
$$

showing a very interesting property. Indeed the return on the risky portfolio can be written in terms of the new variables as

$$
(3.10) \quad \tilde{R}_1 x_1 + \tilde{R}_2 x_2 + \tilde{R}_3 x_3 = (\tilde{R}_1 - \tilde{R}_2) u_1 + (\tilde{R}_2 - \tilde{R}_3) u_2 + \tilde{R}_3 u_3.
$$

Let us examine the right-hand side: The first term $(\tilde{R}_1 - \tilde{R}_2) u_1$ shows that an investment $\tilde{R}_1 u_1$ in the foreign country is hedged against risks due to exchange and inflation by a loan in the form of a foreign indexed bond. Thus $(\tilde{R}_1 - \tilde{R}_2) u_1$ contains only the proper risk of the investment.

The second term $(\tilde{R}_2 - \tilde{R}_3) u_2$ denotes an investment $\tilde{R}_2 u_2$ in the foreign indexed bond, which is hedged against inflation risk by a loan made in the form of a foreign risk-free asset.

Finally $\tilde{R}_3 u_3$ represents only the exchange risk.

Relation (3.10) can also be written as

$$
(3.11) \quad \tilde{R}_1 x_1 + \tilde{R}_2 x_2 + \tilde{R}_3 x_3 = (\tilde{R}_1 u_1 + \tilde{R}_2 u_2 + \tilde{R}_3 u_3)
$$
$$
- (\tilde{R}_2 u_1 + \tilde{R}_3 u_2) = \tilde{R}\mathbf{u} - S\mathbf{u},
$$

so that we can distinguish a fraction of risk accepted by the investor leading to the return $\tilde{R}\mathbf{u}$ and a fraction transferred to other investors, with $S\mathbf{u}$ corresponding to a certain form of insurance.

The budget constraint $\sum_{i=1}^{4} x_i = 1$ becomes

$$
(3.12) \quad u_1 + (u_2 - u_1) + (u_3 - u_2) + x_4 = u_3 + x_4 = 1,
$$

leading to the last change $x_4 = 1 - u_3$.

Making the suitable substitutions, the accumulation equation for wealth becomes

$$
(3.13) \quad dW = (\{(a_1 - a_2)u_1 + [(a_2 - a_3) + p]u_2 + [(a_3 - r) + \phi]u_3 + r\}W
$$
$$
+ (v - x_0)) \, dt + u_1 W \sigma_R \, dz_R + u_2 W s \, dz
$$
$$
+ u_3 W \psi \, dq.
$$

The necessary optimality conditions for an investor who acts according to (3.6)–(3.13) in choosing his consumption and investment program are

$$(3.14) \quad 0 = \max\{U(x_0, t) + J'_t + (W\{(a_1 - a_2)u_1 + [(a_2 - a_3) + p]u_2$$
$$+ [(a_3 - r) + \phi]u_3 + r\} + (v - x_0))J'_W + \tfrac{1}{2}\mathbf{u}^{\mathrm{T}}\Sigma\mathbf{u}J''_{WW}W^2\},$$

where Σ is the variance matrix of the Wiener processes.

Necessary conditions for (3.14) are

$$(3.15a) \qquad\qquad\qquad U'_{x_0} - J'_W = 0,$$

$$(3.15b) \qquad\qquad J'_W(a_1 - a_2) + J''_{WW}W\sigma_R^2 u_1 = 0,$$

$$(3.15c) \qquad\qquad J'_W[(a_2 - a_3) + p] + J''_{WW}W\sigma_I^2 u_2 = 0,$$

$$(3.15d) \qquad\qquad J'_W[(a_3 - r) + \phi] + J''_{WW}W\sigma_f^2 u_3 = 0.$$

Let $b = -J'_W/J''_{WW}W$. Then the solution is given by[2]

$$(3.16a) \qquad\qquad u_1^* = b(a_1 - a_2)/\sigma_R^2,$$

$$(3.16b) \qquad\qquad u_2^* = b[(a_2 - a_3) + p]/\sigma_I^2,$$

$$(3.16c) \qquad\qquad u_3^* = b[(a_3 - r) + \phi]/\sigma_f^2,$$

$$(3.16d) \qquad\qquad x_4^* = 1 - u_3^*,$$

and we have been able to separate completely all the different risks.

A Four-Fund Theorem. All risk-averse investors who maximize the actual flow of utility are indifferent in choosing between portfolios from among all the original assets or from four funds, three associated with only one pure form of risk and the fourth risk-free.

The case just examined is characterized by $n - 1$ alternative investments, with the nth risk-free and $m = n - 1$ forms of risk. Correspondingly we notice that the linear transformation $\mathbf{x} = Q\mathbf{u}$ can be split into $\mathbf{x} = (Q_1 - Q_2)\mathbf{u}$, where Q_1 is the $m \times m$ identity matrix and Q_2 has a subdiagonal of ones.

Let us now add two risky investments in which we can recognize three different forms of risk, a proper risk for one of them and a common variability linked with two different price indexes. Thus we are led to case $m > n - 1$.

The return on the risky portfolio can be written in terms of the new variables as

$$\sum_{i=1}^{5} \tilde{R}_i x_i = (\tilde{R}_1 - \tilde{R}_2)u_1 + (\tilde{R}_2 - \tilde{R}_3)u_2 + \tilde{R}_3 u_3 + (\tilde{R}_4 - \tilde{R}_5)u_4 + \tilde{R}_5 u_5$$
$$= (Q_1 - Q_2)\mathbf{u},$$

but $\tilde{R}_5 u_5$ contains two kinds of risks.

[2] For the sufficiency conditions see the appendix.

If the investor wants to separate completely the different forms of risks, he will require the issuance of an insurance contract giving a return S_1 so that a component u_6 is added to vector $\mathbf{u}$. The complete transformation becomes

$$\sum_{i=1}^{5} \tilde{R}_i x_i = (\tilde{R}_1 - \tilde{R}_2)u_1 + (\tilde{R}_2 - \tilde{R}_3)u_2 + \tilde{R}_3 u_3 + (\tilde{R}_4 - \tilde{R}_5)u_4$$

$$+ (\tilde{R}_5 - S_1)u_5 + S_1 u_6$$

$$= (\hat{Q}_1 - \hat{Q}_2)\hat{\mathbf{u}}.$$

Thus each term on the right-hand side is associated with only one form of risk, and again we can see how the decision maker lends a fraction of his investments as a form of insurance.

Finally, we consider a number of risks $m < n - 1$.

Let us consider an investor who can choose from four indexed bonds and a risk-free asset in a foreign country. The only two risks due to inflation and exchange can be easily separated if we set

$$\sum_{i=1}^{5} R_i x_i = \left(\sum_{i=1}^{4} R_i - R_5 \right)u_1 + R_5 u_2.$$

Thus the portfolio is represented in terms of two pure risks. The procedure can obviously be extended to other different forms of risk, provided that the market is able to give alternative investments to hedge the investor against them.

Assume there are n investments in the market including a risk-free asset and that it is possible to recognize m different risks. By means of a suitable linear transformation, $\mathbf{x} = Q\mathbf{u}$, where Q is an $n \times m$ matrix which can be split into $Q = Q_1 - Q_2$, we can associate with each new variable only one risk and the initial return $R\mathbf{x}$ becomes $R\mathbf{x} = RQ\mathbf{u} = RQ_1\mathbf{u} - RQ_2\mathbf{u}$, which is the return of some investments and some loans. Thus we can recognize an insurance process.

This being stated, operator (2.20) becomes

(3.17) $$\mathscr{D}(J) = J_t' + \{[(Q\mathbf{u})^T(\hat{\boldsymbol{\alpha}} - r\hat{\mathbf{e}}) + r]y_0 - x_0\}J_{y_0}'$$

$$+ \tfrac{1}{2}(Q\mathbf{u})^T\hat{\Sigma}(Q\mathbf{u})J_{y_0}''y_0^2 + \hat{\mathbf{f}}^T J_{y_0}' + \tfrac{1}{2}\hat{\mathbf{g}}^T Q\hat{\mathbf{g}}$$

$$+ (\hat{\mathbf{g}}J_{y, y_0}')^T H(\hat{\sigma}Q\mathbf{u})y_0.$$

The first-order conditions in $\mathbf{u}$,

(3.18) $$Q^T(\hat{\boldsymbol{\alpha}} - r\hat{\mathbf{e}})y_0 J_{y_0}' + Q^T\hat{\Sigma}Q\mathbf{u}J_{y_0}''y_0^2 + \hat{\boldsymbol{\eta}}^1 = 0,$$

give the optimal solution for a nonsingular $m \times m$ matrix $Q^T\hat{\Sigma}Q$

$$(3.19) \quad \mathbf{u}^* = -\frac{J'_{y_0}}{J''_{y_0}y_0}(Q^T\hat{\Sigma}Q)^{-1}Q^T(\hat{\alpha}-r\hat{\mathbf{e}}) - \frac{1}{J''_{y_0}y_0}(Q^T\hat{\Sigma}Q)^{-1}\hat{\boldsymbol{\eta}}^1,$$

which for a constant-investment opportunity set is simplified to

$$(3.20) \quad \mathbf{u}^* = -(J'_{y_0}/J''_{y_0}y_0)(Q^T\hat{\Sigma}Q)^{-1}Q^T(\hat{\alpha}-r\hat{\mathbf{e}}).$$

The budget constraint $\hat{\mathbf{e}}^T\mathbf{x} + x_{n+1} = \hat{\mathbf{e}}^TQ\mathbf{u} + x_{n+1} = 1$ allows one to determine the fraction invested in the risk-free asset $x^*_{n+1} = 1 - \hat{\mathbf{e}}^TQ\mathbf{u}^*$.

Thus we can conclude with a complete separation theorem.

A Mutual-Fund Theorem. All risk-averse investors who maximize the actual flow of utility are indifferent in choosing between portfolios from among all the original assets or from m funds each associated with only one risk and one risk-free asset.

APPENDIX. A BRIEF OUTLINE OF STOCHASTIC CONTROL

Let $(S, \mathscr{S}, \mu)$ be a probability space, where S is a nonempty set, $\mathscr{S}$ a σ algebra of subsets in S, and $\mu\colon \mathscr{S} \to [0, 1]$ a σ-additive function with $\mu(\varnothing) = 0$, $\mu(S) = 1$. The elements of $\mathscr{S}$ are the events.

A *random variable* is a map $x\colon S \to R$, $\mathscr{S}$-measurable, such that condition $B \in \mathscr{B}_R$ implies $\{s \in S\colon x(s) \in B\} = \{x \in B\} \in \mathscr{S}$, where $\mathscr{B}_R$ denotes the Borel σ algebra on R.

A *stochastic process* is a map associating a random variable x_t with each time $t \geq 0$. If we write $x_t(s) = x(t, s)$ for any $s \in S$, function $x(\cdot, s)$ is a path of process $x = \{x_t\colon t \geq 0\}$.

A real *Wiener process* or *Brownian motion* z is a real stochastic process satisfying the following conditions:

$$(A.1) \quad z_0 = 0,$$

$$(A.2) \quad t_1 < t_2 \quad \text{implies} \quad z_{t_2} - z_{t_1}$$

is a normal random variable with mean 0 and variance $t_2 - t_1$,

$$(A.3) \quad z \quad \text{has independent increments.}$$

A Wiener process is a martingale and a Markov process.

Denote $\mathscr{F}_t^z$ the σ algebra generated by $\{z_\tau\colon 0 \leq \tau \leq t\}$, where z is a Wiener process, and introduce an increasing family $\mathscr{G} = \{\mathscr{G}_t\colon t \geq 0\}$ of σ algebras in $\mathscr{S}$, nonanticipative with respect to z. Let f be a stochastic process defined on $[0, T]$, adapted to $\mathscr{G}$, and $\mathscr{B}_{[0, T]} \times \mathscr{S}$-measurable.

The *Itô integral* on the class $C(0, T)$ of stepwise processes

(A.4) $f(t) = \sum_{i=1}^{n} f(t_{i-1}) x_{[t_{i-1}, t_i)}$, $f(t_i)$ being $\mathcal{G}_{t_i}$-measurable,

is defined as

(A.5) $I(f) = \int_0^T f(t) \, dz_t = \sum_{i=1}^{n} f(t_{i-1})(z_{t_i} - z_{t_{i-1}})$.

Any process belonging to class $L_z^2(0, T)$ of stochastic processes defined in $[0, T]$ and satisfying condition

(A.6) $\mu\left[\int_0^T |f(t)|^2 \, dt < +\infty\right] = 1$

can be approximated by a sequence in $C(0, T)$. Then the following definition can be assigned.

(A.7) Definition. The Itô integral in $L_z^2(0, T)$ is the limit in probability of a sequence of Itô integrals in $C(0, T)$,

(A.8) $I(f) = \int_0^T f(t) \, dz_t = \lim_{n \to \infty} \int_0^T f_n(t) \, dz_t$, $\{f_n(t)\} \subset C(0, T)$,

and the following theorem can be stated.

(A.9) Theorem. Let f be continuous and $\Delta = \{0 = t_0 < t_1 < \cdots < t_n\}$ be any decomposition of $[0, T]$ with $l_\Delta = \max_i |t_{i+1} - t_i|$. Then the limit relation holds:

(A.10) $I(f) = \lim_{l_\Delta \to 0} \sum_{i=1}^{n} f(t_{i-1})(z_{t_i} - z_{t_{i-1}})$ in probability.

The Itô integral can be defined in R^n for vector-valued functions and n-dimensional Wiener processes $\mathbf{z}(t) = [z_1(t), \ldots, z_n(t)]$.

A stochastic process $\mathbf{y}(t)$ belongs to class $L_z^2[0, T, \mathcal{L}(R^n)]$ if the elements of matrix y_{ij} belong to $L_z^2(0, T)$ and we set

$$\left(\int_0^T \mathbf{y}(t) \, d\mathbf{z}(t)\right)_j = \sum_{i=1}^{n} \int_0^T y_{ij}(t) \, dz_j.$$

(A.11) Definition. The vector $\mathbf{y}$ has a stochastic differential

(A.12) $d\mathbf{y} = \boldsymbol{\alpha}(t) \, dt + \sigma(t) \, d\mathbf{z}(t)$

if the following relation holds:

$$(A.13) \qquad \mathbf{y}(t) = \mathbf{y}(0) + \int_0^t \boldsymbol{\alpha}(s) \, ds + \int_0^t \sigma(s) \, d\mathbf{z}_s$$

for $\boldsymbol{\alpha} \in L_z^1(0, T, R^n)$, $\sigma \in L_z^2[0, T, \mathscr{L}(R^n)]$, and $\mathbf{z}(t)$ a standard Wiener process.

A more general form of (A.12) can be obtained:

$$(A.14) \quad dy/y = f[x(t), y(t), t] \, dt + g[x(t), y(t), t] \, dz(t), \qquad y(0) = y^0$$

for $f, g: X^n \times X^m \times [0, T] \to X^n$, X^n the space of control variables, X^m the space of state variables, and $X = (S, \mathscr{S}, \mu)$ a probability space. From now on we shall assume that convenient assumptions are fulfilled so that Eqs. (A.12)–(A.14) admit a solution.

We can now conclude with the classical Itô theorem.

(A.15) Theorem. Assume $Y = F(t, x_1, \ldots, x_n): [0, T] \times R^n \to R$ be continuous with its partial derivatives $F_t, F_{x_i}, F_{x_i, x_j}, i, j = 1, \ldots, n$ and let dy be as in (A.12). Then the following relationship holds:

$$(A.16) \qquad dF(t, \mathbf{x}) = (F_t + \mathscr{D}F) \, dt + \sum_{i, j=1}^n \sigma_{ij} F_{x_i}(t, \mathbf{x}) \, dz_j,$$

with operator $\mathscr{D}$ given by

$$(A.17) \qquad \mathscr{D}F = \sum F_{x_i}(t, \mathbf{x})\alpha_i(t) + \tfrac{1}{2} \sum_{i, j, h=1}^n \sigma_{ih} \sigma_{jh} F_{x_i, x_j}(t, \mathbf{x}).$$

The particular case $Y = x_1 x_2 \cdots x_n$ leads to the very simple relation

$$(A.18) \qquad \frac{dY}{Y} = \sum_i \frac{dx_i}{x_i} + \tfrac{1}{2} \sum_{i, j=1}^n \sigma_{ij} \frac{dx_i}{x_i} \frac{dx_j}{x_j}.$$

Let us introduce the control problem

$$(A.19) \qquad \max_{x(t) \in \hat{X} \subset X^n} E\left\{ \int_0^T F(\mathbf{x}, y, t) \, dt + B[y(T), T] \right\}$$

with an evolution equation for the state variables of the form (A.14). Define the optimal performance functional

$$(A.20) \qquad J[y(t), t] = \max_{x(t) \in \hat{X}} E\left\{ \int_t^T F(\mathbf{x}, y, s) \, ds + B[y(T), T] \right\},$$

referred to time t and state y with the final condition $J[y(T), T] = B[y(T), T]$. According to the recurrence relationship of dynamic programming,

$$(A.21) \qquad J[y(t), t] = \max_{x(t) \in \hat{X}} E\{F(\mathbf{x}, y, t)h + J(y + k, t + h)\},$$

application of the Taylor theorem and the mean-value theorem for integrals
lead to

(A.22) $$0 = \max_{\mathbf{x}(t) \in \hat{X}} E\left\{F(\mathbf{x}, y, t) + J_t' + J_y' \frac{k}{h} + \tfrac{1}{2}J_{yy}'' \frac{k^2}{h} + \cdots\right\}.$$

Taking the limit as $h \to 0$ yields the continuous-time version of the Bellman–
Dreyfus recurrence equation:

(A.23) $$0 = \max_{\mathbf{x}(t) \in \hat{X}} \{F(\mathbf{x}, y, t) + \mathcal{D}J\}.$$

Carrying out the maximization over $\mathbf{x}$ and thereby eliminating $\mathbf{x}$, we obtain
a nonlinear partial differential equation in y. Under suitable assumptions an
analytical solution can be obtained.

Assume f and g to be linear and to depend only on control variables x_0,
$x_1, \ldots, x_n$; the only state variable explicitly considered, y, changes according
to n Wiener processes $dz_1, \ldots, dz_n$, and the evolution equation is

(A.24) $$dy = -\alpha_0 x_0\, dt + \boldsymbol{\alpha}^{\mathrm{T}}\mathbf{x}y\, dt + (d\boldsymbol{\gamma})^{\mathrm{T}}\mathbf{x}y$$

for $d\boldsymbol{\gamma} = [\sigma_1\, dz_1, \ldots, \sigma_n\, dz_n]^{\mathrm{T}}$.

Maximization of the expected value of the utility requires solution of the
Bellman–Dreyfus equation,

(A.25) $$0 = \max_{x_0, \mathbf{x}} \{U(x_0) + J_t + [-\alpha_0 x_0 + \boldsymbol{\alpha}^{\mathrm{T}}\mathbf{x}y]J_y' + \tfrac{1}{2}\mathbf{x}^{\mathrm{T}}\Sigma \mathbf{x}y^2 J_{yy}''\},$$

where Σ is the variance–covariance matrix of the Wiener processes. Different
forms of the utility index have been suggested by various authors, leading
to an analytical solution. Here we refer to the simple form $U(x_0) = x_0^\delta/\delta$ for
$0 < \delta < 1$.

The first-order conditions for a regular interior maximum are

(A.26a) $$0 = x_0^\delta/\delta + J_t' + [-\alpha_0 x_0 + \boldsymbol{\alpha}^{\mathrm{T}}\mathbf{x}y]J_y' + \tfrac{1}{2}\mathbf{x}^{\mathrm{T}}\Sigma \mathbf{x}y^2 J_{yy}'',$$

(A.26b) $$0 = x_0^{\delta-1} - \alpha_0 J_y',$$

(A.26c) $$0 = \boldsymbol{\alpha}^{\mathrm{T}}yJ_y' + \tfrac{1}{2}\mathbf{x}^{\mathrm{T}}\Sigma y^2 J_{yy}'',$$

subject to the boundary condition

(A.26d) $$J[y(T), T] = \hat{c}y(T)^\delta/\delta.$$

From Eqs. (A.26b)–(A.26c) we have

(A.27) $$x_0 = (\alpha_0 J_y')^{1/(\delta-1)}, \qquad \mathbf{x} = -(J_y'/yJ_{yy}'')\Sigma^{-1}\boldsymbol{\alpha},$$

which when substituted into (A.26a) gives a nonlinear partial differential
equation

(A.28) $$0 = [(1-\delta)/\delta](\alpha_0 J_y')^{\delta/(\delta-1)} + J_t' - \tfrac{1}{2}\boldsymbol{\alpha}^{\mathrm{T}}\Sigma_T^{-1}\boldsymbol{\alpha}[(J_y')^2/J_{yy}''].$$

The introduction of a trial solution $J[y(t), t] = c(t)y(t)^{\delta}/\delta$ transforms (A.28) into an ordinary differential equation:

$$(A.29) \quad c(t) - \tfrac{1}{2}[\delta/(\delta - 1)]\boldsymbol{\alpha}^{\mathrm{T}}\Sigma_{\mathrm{T}}^{-1}\boldsymbol{\alpha}c(t) + (1 - \delta)[\alpha_0 c(t)]^{\delta/(\delta - 1)} = 0$$

to which the known solution methods can be applied.

REFERENCES

1. Breeden, D. T., On the intertemporal asset pricing model with stochastic consumption and investment opportunities, *Journal of Financial Economics* **7**, 265–296 (1979).
2. Kushner, H., "Introduction to Stochastic Control." Holt, New York, 1971.
3. Merton, R. C., On the mathematics and economic assumptions of continuous time models, M.I.T. Working paper No. 981, (March) 1978.

INSTITUTE OF MATHEMATICS
UNIVERSITY OF VENICE
VENICE, ITALY

Hierarchical Control and Coordination in Dynamical Systems

Krzysztof Malinowski

1. INTRODUCTION

In recent years it has become important to consider methods for on-line control and management of large-scale systems. The most important stimuli for this are perhaps the increasing pressures of resource constraints. The limited amount of water resources, for example has made it necessary to develop (in some regions at least) complex water management systems directed towards efficient exploitation of these resources in order to satisfy the increasing demand for water. The nature of the systems arising creates a need for the elaboration of new hierarchical and decentralized control structures different from those, for example, developed for process control in the chemical industry.

It should be noted that complex problems of decision making have been considered by many economists and nonlinear programming specialists in the past. This has given rise to the development of methods for hierarchical decision making (e.g., Geoffrion [5], Lasdon [6]). Among these methods, those involving price mechanisms can be distinguished as the most important. Yet it is clear that hierarchical decision making (mostly hierarchical optimization) can form only part of the on-line control structure of the complex systems, which must use properly the available on-line data (measurements) and must adjust current decisions in order to compensate for modeling errors and real-life uncertainties.

In this chapter we shall describe briefly the price coordination mechanism for hierarchical decision making and show (Section 3) how the results of coordination may be useful in determining where structural changes—if possible—should be made in the dynamic system in order to achieve better performance. Then we shall demonstrate (Section 4) that, by properly adapting the price mechanism, we can develop a two-level structure for complex systems with inventories. In this structure hierarchical optimization is used periodically at the higher level, and lower-level controllers track the model optimal inventory level with reasonable accuracy based on on-line measurements.

2. HIERARCHICAL OPTIMIZATION BY PRICE COORDINATION

In this section we present a brief description of the interaction balance method (IBM)—the basic hierarchical optimization algorithm in which price coordination is used.

Consider the following optimization problem (OP):

OP: $\min_{m, u} Q(m, u)$ subject to

(1) $$y_i = F_i(m_i, u_i), \qquad i \in \overline{1, N},$$

(2) $$P(u, y) = \sum_{i=1}^{N} P_i(u_i, y_i) = 0,$$

(3) $$(m_i, u_i) \in MU_i, \qquad i \in \overline{1, N},$$

where $m = (m_1, \ldots, m_N); u = (u_1, \ldots, u_N); y = (y_1, \ldots, y_N); m_i \in \mathcal{M}_i; u_i \in \mathcal{U}_i; y_i \in \mathcal{Y}_i;$ and $\mathcal{M}_i, \mathcal{U}_i, \mathcal{Y}_i$ are real Hilbert spaces.

We assume that

(4) $$Q(m, u) = \sum_{i=1}^{N} Q_i(m_i, u_i), \qquad Q_i: \mathcal{M}_i \times \mathcal{U}_i \to \mathbb{R}$$

is the performance function and that it has an additively separable form. Equations (1) denote the *subsystem equations* $F_i: \mathcal{M}_i \times \mathcal{U}_i \to \mathcal{Y}_i$; Eq. (2) denotes the *system couplings*, $P_i: \mathcal{U}_i \times \mathcal{Y}_i \to \mathcal{P}$ (where $\mathcal{P}$ is a real Hilbert space); and Eqs. (3) denote the *local constraints* $MU_i \in \mathcal{M}_i \times \mathcal{U}_i$. The terms F_i and Q_i may depend also on an external disturbance input which is fixed for optimization and therefore not explicitly shown in the above formulation.

In order to introduce the IBM we define the Lagrangian

(5) $$L(m, u, p) = Q(m, u) + \langle p, P[u, F(m, u)] \rangle,$$

where $F(m, u) = [F_1(m_1, u_1), \ldots, F_N(m_N, u_N)]$ and $\langle \cdot, \cdot \rangle$ denotes a scalar product. It is clear that L is additively separable in (m_i, u_i); that is,

$$(6) \qquad L(\dot{m}, u, p) = \sum_{i=1}^{N} L_i(m_i, u_i, p).$$

Now we can formulate the infimal (lower-level) problem (IP) of the IBM:

IP: for given $p \in \mathscr{P}$, find $\hat{m}(p)$, $\hat{u}(p)$ such that

$$L[\hat{m}(p), \hat{u}(p), p] = \min_{(m, u) \in MU} L(m, u, p),$$

where $MU = MU_1 \times \cdots \times MU_N$.

The IP can be solved as N *independent* local problems (LP$_i$):

LP$_i$:   for given $p \in \mathscr{P}$ find $\hat{m}_i(p)$, $\hat{u}_i(p)$ such that

$$L_i[\hat{m}_i(p), \hat{u}_i(p), p] = \min_{(m_i, u_i) \in MU_i} L_i(m_i, u_i, p).$$

Denote the set of solutions of IP for given p by $\overline{MU}(p) = \overline{MU}_1(p) \times \cdots \times \overline{MU}_N(p)$.

The coordinator problem (CP) of the IBM may now be defined:

CP: find $\hat{p} \in \mathscr{P}$ such that the set $\overline{MU}(\hat{p})$ is nonempty and *for every* $(m, u) \in \overline{MU}(\hat{p})$ we have $P[u, F(m, u)] = 0$.

The formulation of the IBM originates from mathematical programming (Lasdon [6]). It was introduced in a slightly different form for system optimization by Mesarovic, Macko, and Takahara [11]; the above formulation was given in Malinowski [7].

The following proposition is essential for application of the IBM (the proof is elementary):

Proposition. If there exists $\hat{p}$—a solution of the CP—then *every* $[\hat{m}(\hat{p}), \hat{u}(\hat{p})] \in \overline{MU}(\hat{p})$ is a solution of the OP.

Therefore the first crucial question concerning the method considered is connected with the existence of $\hat{p}$—a solution of the CP and many conditions are known that guarantee its existence (see, e.g., Lasdon [6], Mesarowic *et al.* [11], Malinowski [7]). It has been shown (e.g., Malinowski [8]) that in many cases the IBM can even be applied successfully to nonconvex problems.

If the IBM is applicable to the OP, to find $\hat{p}$ we must have appropriate algorithms (coordination strategies). Let us make the assumption that the solution of the IP is unique $\forall p \in \mathcal{P}_0 \subset \mathcal{P}$. Then the dual function $\phi(\cdot)$ defined as

$$(7) \qquad \phi(p) = L(\hat{m}(p), \hat{u}(p), p]$$

is Gateau-differentiable on $\mathcal{P}_0$ and

$$(8) \qquad \nabla\phi(p) = -W(p) = P[\hat{u}(p), F(\hat{m}(p), \hat{u}(p)].$$

Therefore we can use gradient numerical optimization procedures for solving the CP; e.g., steepest ascent or conjugate gradient algorithms for unconstrained optimization may be applied. However, in some situations we shall want to use the coordination algorithms not only for solving the CP but also as *on-line* coordination strategy (see Findeisen *et al.* [3]) in various control structures. In these cases we want the coordination algorithm to solve the modified equation

$$(9) \qquad T(p) = 0,$$

where

$$T(p) = W(p) + s(p), \qquad s: \mathcal{P} \to \mathcal{P},$$

instead of solving the equation

$$(10) \qquad W(p) = 0.$$

Also, in some cases we want the value of an appropriate norm of $W(p^{(n)})$ [or $T(p^{(n)})$] to be decreased for each subsequent value of $p^{(n)}$ as generated by the coordination algorithm (see Section 4).

Because of the above reasons we have to develop a suitable contracting algorithm for solving Eq. (10) [or—more generally—for solving Eq. (9)]. We may consider the following algorithm, which generates a sequence $\{p^{(n)}\}$ of the coordination variable p.

Algorithm A

$$(11) \qquad p^{(n+1)} = p^{(n)} - \varepsilon_n A T(p^{(n)}),$$

where $\varepsilon_n > 0$ and $A: \mathcal{P} \to \mathcal{P}$ is a linear continuous operator. Algorithm A can be used for solving eq. (10); then we take $s(p) \equiv 0$. The following results specify sufficient conditions guaranteeing the desired contraction property and the convergence of Algorithm A.

Theorem 1. (contraction property).   Assume that
1. $\forall p, p + h \in \mathcal{P}_1 \subset \mathcal{P}_0$ the following conditions are satisfied:

(i) $\|W(p+h) - W(p)\| \le \sigma_1 \|h\|$,
(ii) $\langle W(p+h) + W(p), h \rangle \ge \sigma \|h\|^2, \sigma > 0$,
(iii) $\|s(p+h) - s(p)\| \le \sigma_{II} \|h\|$.

2. Operator A in (11) is self-conjugated and $\forall p \in \mathscr{P}$

$$\mu_1 \|p\|^2 \leq \langle p, Ap \rangle \leq \mu_2 \|p\|^2, \qquad \mu_1 > 0.$$

3. $\sigma \mu_1 > \sigma_{\mathrm{II}} \mu_2$ [this assumption is always satisfied when $s(p) \equiv 0$].

Let us define a new norm $\| \cdot \|_A$ in $\mathscr{P}$:

$$\|p\|_A \triangleq \sqrt{\langle p, Ap \rangle}.$$

Then there exists a nonempty set $[q_0, 1) \subset \mathbb{R}_+$ such that $\forall q \in [q_0, 1)$, there exists a set $[\varepsilon'_q, \varepsilon''_q] \subset \mathbb{R}_+$ such that, if $\varepsilon_n \in [\varepsilon'_q, \varepsilon''_q]$ and $p^{(n)}, p^{(n+1)}$ [given by (11)] belong to $\mathscr{P}_1$, then

(12) $$\| T(p^{(n+1)}) \|_A \leq q \| T(p^{(n)}) \|_A. \quad \blacksquare$$

Theorem 2. (convergence of Algorithm A). Suppose that the assumptions of Theorem 1 are fulfilled and that the starting point $p^{(0)}$ for Algorithm A has been chosen in such a way that for some $q \in [q_0, 1)$ we have

$$\overline{\mathscr{B}}_1 = \left\{ p \in \mathscr{P}: \|p - p^{(0)}\| \leq \varepsilon''_q \mu_2 \frac{1}{1-q} \| T(p^{(0)}) \| \right\} \subset \mathscr{P}_1.$$

Then the sequence $\{p^{(n)}\}_{n=0}^{\infty}$ generated by algorithm A belongs to $\overline{\mathscr{B}}_1$ and converges (in norm topology) to $\bar{p} \in \mathscr{P}_1$, where $\bar{p}$ is a (unique in $\mathscr{P}_1$) solution of Eq. (9). $\quad \blacksquare$

The proofs of the above theorems are given in Malinowski [9] and Findeisen *et al.* [4] together with some other results and the conditions that guarantee the fulfillment of the crucial assumptions 1(i) and 1(ii) of Theorem 1. It should be noted that the differentiability of $\hat{m}(\cdot), \hat{u}(\cdot)$ on $\mathscr{P}_1$ is *not required* to prove the convergence of Algorithm A.

3. PRICE COORDINATION AND OPTIMIZATION OF COMPLEX SYSTEMS WITH INVENTORY COUPLINGS

Usually the system coupling constraint (2) is assumed to have the form

(13) $$u - Hy = 0$$

or

(14) $$u_i = \sum_{j=1}^{N} H_{ij} y_j = H_{iy}, \qquad i \in \overline{1, N},$$

where H_{ij} are linear operators (mainly matrices with zero or one entries).

In this section—since we are interested in the analysis of changes in system structure—we shall examine what can be achieved if we modify the rigid structure of Eq. (13) into the form

(15) $$P_0(u - Hy) = 0,$$

where P_0 is a particular form of operator P in (2); in addition we assume P_0 to be linear and continuous.

For such a modification we can give a clear physical interpretation. Assume that u, y are vectors of time functions on some interval $[t_0, t_f]$ and assume that y_{jk} (the kth output of subprocess j) is connected to u_{il} (the lth interconnection input to subprocess i) by a rigid relation [see Eq. (14)]:

(16) $$u_{il}(t) = y_{jk}(t) \qquad \text{for a.e.} \quad t \in [t_0, t_f].$$

Let us now suppose that $y_{ik}(t)$ is a stream flow of some material produced by subprocess j and used by subprocess i, and that it is possible to put an inventory between subprocesses such that Eq. (16) can be replaced by

(17) $$\int_{t_0}^{t_f} [u_{il}(t) - y_{jk}(t)] \, dt = 0$$

(where we assume that u_{il}, y_{jk} are integrable), which has the form of coupling constraint (15). It is possible of course to consider such a simple inventory model only if we can assume that the physical constraints

$$w_1 \leq \int_{t_0}^{t} [y_{jk}(\tau) - u_{il}(\tau) \, d\tau] \leq w_2$$

are either nonexistent or nonbinding.

Now we can formulate two optimization problems:

    I. OPS: $\min_{m,u} Q(m, u)$ subject to Eqs. (1), (3), and

$$u - Hy = 0.$$

    II. OPI: $\min_{m,u} Q(m, u)$ subject to Eqs. (1), (3), and

$$P_0(u - Hy) = 0.$$

We shall now discuss an application of price coordination to OPS and OPI. The constraints (15) can be formulated as

(18) $$[u - HF(m, u)] \in N(P_0) = U \subset \mathcal{U},$$

where the null space of P_0, $N(P_0) = U$, is a closed subspace of $\mathcal{U}$. Then the dual function $\phi(\cdot)$ as defined for OPS can be taken the same for OPI on the set $U^{\perp}$.

Under appropriate uniqueness assumptions (see Section 2) the CP of the IBM is equivalent to the following OP:

(19)   1. Find $\hat{p}_S = \arg \max_{p \in \mathcal{U}} \phi(p)$ for OPS,

(20)   2. Find $\hat{p}_I = \arg \max_{p \in U^I} \phi(p)$ for OPI,

where $U^\perp$ is an orthogonal subspace of U and $U^\perp \oplus U = \mathcal{U}$.

Let us assume that $\hat{p}_S$, $\hat{p}_I$ exist and that they are uniquely specified by (19) and (20).

Under these assumptions the following corollary is true.

Corollary

$$\hat{Q}_I = \phi(\hat{p}_I) < \phi(\hat{p}_S) = \hat{Q}_S \Leftrightarrow \hat{p}_I \neq \hat{p}_S \notin U^\perp,$$

where by $\hat{Q}_S$, $\hat{Q}_I$ we denote the optimal performance values for OPS and OPI.

This means that we can deduce the possibilities of the improvement of Q based on the knowledge of $\hat{p}_S$. That is, $\|\tilde{p}_S\|$, where $\tilde{p}_S$ is an orthogonal projection of $\hat{p}_S$ on U, can be taken as a measure of the possibility of improving Q by introducing the inventories. If constraint (18) can be decomposed into the form

$$[u_i - H_i F(m, u)] \in U_i \subset \mathcal{U}_i, \qquad i \in \overline{1, N},$$

where U_i is a closed subspace of $\mathcal{U}_i$ (i.e., when separated inventories at each interconnection are considered), then $U^\perp$ can be represented as

$$U^\perp = U_1^\perp \times \cdots \times U_N^\perp.$$

So we can use the above corollary to determine the most advantageous placement of inventories in the system. In particular, based on the knowledge of the ith coordinate of the price vector $\hat{p}_S$, we can deduce to a certain extent whether the location of an inventory at the ith interconnection is suitable.

Example.   Consider a dynamic system composed of three subsystems described by linear equations:

1. $\dot{x}_1(t) = m_1(t) + 0.5u_1(t), \qquad x_1(0) = 0, \qquad y_1(t) = x_1(t);$
2. $\dot{x}_2(t) = x_2(t) + m_2(t) + u_2(t), \qquad x_2(0) = 0, \qquad y_2(t) = x_2(t) + m_2(t);$
3. $\dot{x}_3(t) = m_3(t) + u_3(t), \qquad x_3(0) = 0, \qquad y_3(t) = x_3(t).$

Constraints (14) have the form

(14a) $u_1(t) = y_3(t), \qquad u_2(t) = y_1(t), \qquad u_3(t) = y_2(t).$

We assume that $m_i \in L^2[0, 1]$, $u_i \in L^2[0, 1]$ and that performance index Q is given in an additive form:

$$Q(m, u) = \sum_{i=1}^{3} Q_i(m_i, u_i),$$

where $Q_i(m_i, u_i) = \int_0^1 [m_i^2(t) + D_i[u_i(t) - B_i]^2] \, dt$ and $D_1 = 4$, $D_2 = D_3 = 1$, $B_1 = 2$, $B_2 = B_3 = 0.5$. It has been assumed that constraints (14a) can be replaced by integral constraints

(14b) $$\int_0^1 [u_1(t) - y_3(t)] \, dt = 0, \qquad \text{etc.}$$

The IBM was used to solve the OPS for the system described. Time functions $p_1(t)$, $p_2(t)$, $p_3(t)$ were discretized in interval $[0, 1]$; $p_i(t)$ was taken as constant in every interval Δ_j, $j = 1, \dots, k$, where $\Delta_j = [(j - 1)/k, \, j/k]$ and $k = 10$.

After solving the OPS it appeared that the projection of $\hat{p}_{S1}$ on $U_1(U_1 = \{u_1 \in L^2[0, 1]: \int_0^1 u_1(t) \, dt = 0\})$ had a much larger norm than the projections of $\hat{p}_{S2}$, $\hat{p}_{S3}$, respectively, on U_2, U_3 ($\hat{p}_{S1}$ had the greatest variation). Therefore we then considered the two cases:

OPI (1)   optimization problem with one inventory I1 replacing the first rigid interconnection in (14a).

OPI (3)   optimization problem with three inventory constraints replacing (14a).

The following results were obtained:

1. $\hat{Q}_S = 5.7487 = 1\hat{Q}_S$ for OPS;
2. $\hat{Q}_{I1} = 4.3584 = 0.75\hat{Q}_S$ for OPI(1);
3. $\hat{Q}_{I3} = 3.9882 = 0.69\hat{Q}_S$ for OPI (3).

From these results it can be seen that—as predicted—the major improvement of the performance value was achieved after introducing an inventory between the third and the first subsystems.

More results related to the optimization of systems with inventory couplings (including the costs of inventories) can be found in Malinowski and Terlikowski [10].

4. TWO-LEVEL CONTROL STRUCTURE WITH PRICE COORDINATION FOR SYSTEMS WITH INVENTORY COUPLINGS

In this section we show that price coordination can be used to develop an on-line control mechanism for a complex system. To introduce one such mechanism we consider a case of practical interest in which the system elements are static although time-varying and the system couplings have exclusively the form described by Eq. (17); i.e.,

$$(21) \qquad \int_{t_0}^{t_f} [\bar{H}_1 u(t) - \bar{H}_2 y(t)] \, dt = 0,$$

where $\bar{H}_1, \bar{H}_2$ are matrices of appropriate dimensions and are composed of zero and one entries.

When describing the system elements we must introduce explicitly the dependence of subsystem output on process disturbances. It should be noted that these are the disturbances or unknown process parameters that create a necessity for introducing the on-line control actions based on current measurements and do not permit the control design problem to be reduced to a standard OP.

Therefore we assume the subsystems to be described by

$$(22) \qquad y_i(t) = f_i[m_i(t), u_i(t), z_i(t)], \qquad i \in \overline{1, N},$$

where $z_i(t)$ is the disturbance (or parameter) vector. The performance function is defined for any time interval $\Delta_{12} = [t_1, t_2]$ as

$$(23) \qquad Q = \sum_{i=1}^{N} \int_{\Delta_{12}} q_i[m_i(t), u_i(t), z_i(t)] \, dt.$$

We assume also that the controls $m_i(t), u_i(t)$ are constrained and that $[m_i(t), u_i(t)] \in MU_i^0 \subset \mathbb{R}^{n_{mi}} \times \mathbb{R}^{n_{ui}} \, \forall t$.

Let us now make some preliminary assumptions concerning the control structure and the information pattern. Suppose that the local decision unit is placed in each of the subsystems and that it possesses all the *a priori* information concerning its performance function and subsystem equations. Suppose also that, because of measurements taken, the local decision units can independently update at times t_{j_k} the predicted values $\bar{z}_i(t)$ of the disturbance vectors $z_i(t)$ at a future time $t \geq t_{j_k}$. In addition, we assume that at time t_j measurements of the current inventory level $w(t)$ are available, where

$$(24) \qquad w^r(t) = \int_{t_0}^{t} [\bar{H}_2 y^r(t) - \bar{H}_1 u(t)] \, dt$$

and

$$(25) \qquad \begin{aligned} y(t) &= (y_1^r(t), \ldots, y_N^r(t)], \\ y_i^r(t) &= f_i[m_i(t), u_i(t), z_i^r(t)], \end{aligned}$$

where $z_i^r(t)$ is the real disturbance value.

Based on the above assumptions it is possible to develop the following two-level control structure.

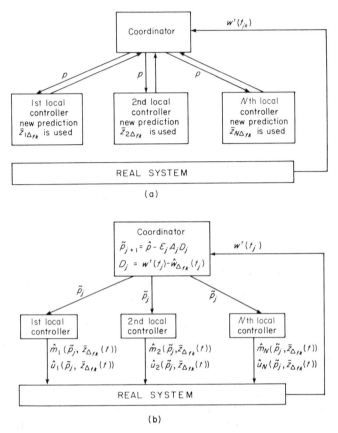

Fig. 1. (a) Operation of the control structure at times t_{j_k}. Hierarchical optimization by the IBM over Δ_{f_k}. After the iterative decision making process is terminated the coordinator gathers information about the values of $\hat{w}_{\Delta_{f_k}}(t_j)(j_k \leqslant j < j_{k+1})$. (b) Operation of the control structure at time t_j (inventory level control). The correction is made using the available on-line measurements and formula (38).

Control Structure[1]

(i) At times t_{j_k} the global optimization over time interval $\Delta_{f_k} = [t_{j_k}, t_f]$ is solved for an updated prediction of disturbances $\bar{z}_{\Delta_{f_k}}$ and the real value of inventory levels at $t = t_{j_k}$. To avoid sending model and disturbance data to one decision unit we can use the price coordination (the IBM) that requires introduction of the coordinating controller—yet this controller does not have to possess all the *a priori* information and does not have to know the

---

[1] See Fig. 1.

on-line measurements of the disturbances. After the local controllers know the coordinating price vector $\hat{p}$ (constant over Δ_{fk}), they can compute optimal control trajectories $\hat{m}_{\Delta_{fk}}$, $\hat{u}_{\Delta_{fk}}$ and the optimal trajectory of the inventory level—inventory policy—defined as

$$(26) \quad w_{\Delta_{fk}}(t) = w^r(t_{j_k}) + \int_{t_{j_k}}^{t} [\overline{H}_2 f[\hat{m}_{\Delta_{fk}}(t), \hat{u}_{\Delta_{fk}}(t), \overline{z}_{\Delta_{fk}}(t)] - \overline{H}_1 \hat{u}_{\Delta_{fk}}(t)] \, dt.$$

(ii)   The task of the control mechanism used at times t_j, located between times t_{j_k}, consists of causing $w^r(t_j)$, the real inventory level at $t = t_j$, to follow the desired level $\hat{w}_{\Delta_{fk}}(t_j)$ [Eq. (26)]. This can be achieved to some extent by updating the price vector p at times t_j. Indeed, if we apply the IBM for solving the system optimization problem, then in the present case of non-dynamic elements the solutions of the IP (see Section 2) will be $\hat{m}[p, \overline{z}_{\Delta_{fk}}(t)]$ and $\hat{u}[p, \overline{z}_{\Delta_{fk}}(t)]$, which will result from the following static problem:

ISP: minimize $\mathscr{L}[m(t), u(t), p, \overline{z}_{\Delta_{fk}}(t)]$, $[m(t), u(t)] \in MU^0$,

where $MU^0 = MU_1^0 \times \cdots \times MU_N^0$ and

$$\mathscr{L}[m(t), u(t), p, \overline{z}_{\Delta_{fk}}(t)] = \sum_{i=1}^{N} q_i[m_i(t), u_i(t), \overline{z}_{i\Delta_{fk}}(t)]$$
$$+ \langle p, \overline{H}_1 u(t) - \overline{H}_2 f[m(t), u(t), \overline{z}_{\Delta_{fk}}(t)] \rangle.$$

Therefore, at $t = t_j$, if p is adjusted to the level $p = \tilde{p}_j$, then the real inventory level at $t = t_{j+1}$ will be

$$w^r(t_{j+1}) = w^r(t_j) + \int_{t_j}^{t_{j+1}} (\overline{H}_2 f\{\hat{m}[\tilde{p}_j, \overline{z}_{\Delta_{fk}}(t)], \hat{u}[\tilde{p}_j, \overline{z}_{\Delta_{fk}}(t)], z^r(t)\}$$
$$(27) \qquad\qquad - \overline{H}_1 \hat{u}[\tilde{p}_j, \overline{z}_{\Delta_{fk}}(t)]) \, dt.$$

Control of Inventory Level

We now describe and analyze the control interventions made at times t_j. We can propose that the task of the "high-frequency" control mechanism [step (ii) above] should consist of generating at each time t_j the price $\tilde{p}_j$ such that the following condition will be satisfied:

$$(28) \qquad\qquad w^r(t_{j+1}) = \hat{w}_{\Delta_{fk}}(t_{j+1}).$$

This means that we would like to follow up—at each consecutive $t = t_j$— exactly the model—optimal inventory levels as determined by the "low-frequency" (upper-layer) controller [step (i) above]. Since the model and the real system descriptions are different $[\overline{z}_{\Delta_{fk}}(t) \neq z^r(t)]$, strict fulfillment of condition (28) cannot be achieved and we have to set a more realistic goal.

Let us consider the possibility of developing an on-line control strategy for solving the following (high-frequency) control problem:

OCP: over a sequence $\{[t_j, t_{j+1}]\}(j_k \le j < j_{k+1})$ of time intervals, adjust (during the system operation—at times t_j) the prices $\tilde{p}_j$ so as to satisfy the following condition at each $t = t_j$:

$$(29) \qquad \qquad \|w^r(t_j) - \hat{w}_{\Delta_{fk}}(t_j)\| \le C_0,$$

where C_0 is a given positive number.

We would like to make C_0 as small as possible, but we expect also that some compromise should be made between the value of C_0 and the simplicity of control strategy. It is also clear that we cannot expect C_0 to be arbitrarily small.

To make further considerations easier to read we now introduce

$$(30) \qquad \qquad D_j = w^r(t_j) - \hat{w}_{\Delta_{fk}}(t_j),$$

which means that D_j is the deviation of the real inventory level from the model optimal level at the beginning of the jth time interval (D_{j_k} would be zero);

$$(31) \quad G_j(p) = w^r(t_j) + \int_{t_j}^{t_{j+1}} (\bar{H}_2 f\{\hat{m}[p, \bar{z}_{\Delta_{fk}}(t)], \hat{u}[p, \bar{z}_{\Delta_{fk}}(t)], \bar{z}_{\Delta_{fk}}(t)\}$$
$$- \bar{H}_1 \hat{u}[p, \bar{z}_{\Delta_{fk}}(t)]) \, dt - \hat{w}_{\Delta_{fk}}(t_{j+1}).$$

Thus $G_j(p)$ is the value of deviation D_{j+1} predicted at the beginning of $\Delta_j = [t_j, t_{j+1}]$ on the basis of the known deviation D_j and assuming the price over Δ_j is p. From (30) the real deviation D_{j+1} is

$$(32) \qquad \qquad D_{j+1} = G_j(p) + \int_{t_j}^{t_{j+1}} r[p, \bar{z}_{\Delta_{fk}}(t), z^r(t)] \, dt,$$

where

$$(33) \quad r(p, \bar{z}_{\Delta_{fk}}(t), z^r(t)) = \bar{H}_2 f\{\hat{m}[p, \bar{z}_{\Delta_{fk}}(t)], \hat{u}[p, \bar{z}_{\Delta_{fk}}(t)], z^r(t)\}$$
$$- \bar{H}_2 f\{\hat{m}[p, \bar{z}_{\Delta_{fk}}(t)], \hat{u}[p, \bar{z}_{\Delta_{fk}}(t)], \bar{z}_{\Delta_{fk}}(t)\}.$$

Suppose now that at time t_j we measure D_j and choose $\tilde{p}_j$ such as to obtain

$$(34) \qquad \qquad G_j(\tilde{p}_j) = 0.$$

This can obviously be done by using the models and solving the global OP with (34) as a constraint using, for example, the IBM method. In such a case the coordinator must receive from the local units information concerning the value of $G_j(p)$ and must transmit p to these local units until condition (34) is satisfied. If (34) is satisfied, the bound on D_{j+1} is given by

$$(35) \qquad \int_{t_j}^{t_{j+1}} \| r(\tilde{p}_j, \bar{z}_{\Delta_{fk}}(t), z^{\tau}(t)) \| \, dt.$$

Therefore, if the following condition is fulfilled: $\forall t$, $\forall [m(t), u(t)] \in MU^0$,

$$(36) \qquad \| \bar{H}_2 \{ f[m(t), u(t) \, \bar{z}_{\Delta_{fk}}(t)] - f[m(t), u(t), z^{\tau}(t)] \} \| \le \beta;$$

then from (32), (34,) and (35) we obtain

$$\| D_{j+1} \| \le \beta |\Delta_j| \qquad \forall j.$$

Condition (36) can be easily satisfied if set MU^0 is bounded.

The choice of $\tilde{p}_j$ as proposed by (34) provides the solution of the OCP if $C_0 \ge \beta |\Delta_j|$ [see (29)]. However, this strategy requires the short horizon system OP to be solved at the beginning of each time interval Δ_j in order to find $\tilde{p}_j$. The computational effort, amount of information exchanged between the coordinator and the local decision units, etc., can render this approach either impossible or highly uneconomical. It seems therefore that a more realistic compromise between the degree of complication of the on-line control strategy and the reduction of D_{j+1} should be proposed. A possibility is offered by Algorithm A [see Eq. (11)] and its contraction property. We can apply this algorithm in solving Eq. (34) at the supremal level; the price vector values are adjusted using the formula

$$(37) \qquad p_j^{(n+1)} = p_j^{(n)} - \varepsilon_j A_j G_j(p_j^{(n)}),$$

where $\varepsilon_j > 0$ and A_j is a self-adjoint, positively defined matrix. Under proper assumptions the above algorithm has the contraction property (see Section 2), that is,

$$\exists \, \delta_j < 1 \qquad \forall n \colon \| G_j(p_j^{(n+1)}) \|_{A_j} \le \delta_j \| G_j(p_j^{(n)}) \|_{A_j}.$$

Since we have $G_j(\hat{p}) = D_j$, the simplest control strategy using the above algorithm can be based on the following decision rule (DR):

DR: adjust the values of p according to (37) (with $p_j^{(1)} = \hat{p}$) until $(\delta_j)^{n_j} \sqrt{\mu_2^j / \mu_1^j} \le \delta < 1$ (μ_1^j, μ_2^j are, respectively, the smallest and the largest eigenvalues of A_j); then take $\tilde{p}_j = p_j^{(n_j+1)}$) and apply it in the system over Δ_j.

If algorithm (37) provides a contraction in norm in a single step, then we may also use the following price correction:

$$(38) \qquad \tilde{p}_j = \hat{p}_j - \varepsilon_j A_j D_j.$$

The algorithm (38) can be used if we are sure that $\forall_j ; \delta_j \leq \delta < 1$. When applying it we have to exchange the information between the coordinator and the local units only once.

In both cases we can estimate the norm of deviation D_{j+1} as

$$\|D_{j+1}\| \leq \delta \|D_j\| + \beta a,$$

where condition (36) is assumed to hold and $\forall j; |\Delta_j| \leq a$. Therefore

$$(39) \qquad \forall j : \|D_{j+1}\| \leq \beta a \sum_{s=j_k}^{j-1} (\delta)^{s-j_k} \leq \frac{1}{1-\delta} \beta a \qquad (D_{j_k} = 0).$$

Thus the proposed approach results in the solution of the OCP [see (29)] with $C_0 = \beta a [1/(1 - \delta)]$. More details about the described control scheme are given in Findeisen and Malinowski [2], where it is also demonstrated with a numerical example how this control mechanism can operate.

REFERENCES

1. Findeisen, W., "Multilevel Control System." PWN, Warsaw, (1975) (in Polish).
2. Findeisen, W., and Malinowski, K., Two level control and coordination for dynamical systems, *Arch. Autom. Telemech.* **24**(1), (1979).
3. Findeisen, W., Brdyś, M., Malinowski, K., Tatjewski, P., and Woźniak, A., On line hierarchical control for steady-state systems, *IEEE Trans. Aut. Control* **AC-23**, (1978).
4. Findeisen, W., Bailey, F. N., Brdyś, M., Malinowski, K., Tatjewski, P., and Woźniak, A., "Control and Coordination in Hierarchical Systems." Wiley, New York, 1980.
5. Geoffrion, A. M., Elements of large scale mathematical programming, *Management Sci.* **16** (1970).
6. Lasdon, L. S., "Optimization Theory for Large Systems." Macmillan, New York, 1970.
7. Malinowski, K., Properties of two balance methods of coordination, *Bull. Pol. Acad. Sci.* **23**(9) (1975).
8. Malinowski, K., Application of the Lagrange multiplier method to the optimization of quadratic Systems, *IEEE Trans. Automat. Control* **AC-22** (4), (1977).
9. Malinowski, K., Multilayer-multiechelon control structures for dynamical systems in "Elektronika 38." Editions of the Technical University of Warsaw, Warsaw.
10. Malinowski, K., and Terlikowski, T., Problems in optimization of complex systems with inventory couplings, *Ricerche di Automatica*, **8**(1) (1977).
11. Mesarowic, M. D., Macko, D., and Takahara, Y., "Theory of Hierarchical, Multi-level Systems." Academic Press, New York, 1970.

INSTITUTE OF AUTOMATIC CONTROL
TECHNICAL UNIVERSITY OF WARSAW
WARSAW, POLAND

Discontinuous Solutions
in *n*-Person Games*

G. P. Szegö
G. Gambarelli

1. INTRODUCTION

One of the basic concepts of the theory of *n*-person games is the so-called Shapley value [21] which allows the power of each player to be defined, taking into account the payoff of all possible coalitions that can be joined by the player. The Shapley value has a number of practical applications, for instance in voting schemes, ranging from the case of political parties to that of shareholders of companies.

The drawback of the original formulation of the Shapley value is the complexity of its computation which is based on set-theoretical operations; thus only in certain cases have suitable numerical algorithms [11] been developed.

Only recently was Gambarelli able to produce a simpie geometric rule [3, 7] and a corresponding algorithm [5] for computation of the Shapley value for all possible games. The application of this formula to a variety of problems led to some interesting results, especially if one includes in the game the actual "buying" and "selling" operations performed by a player in order to increase its value, which, as we shall see, induce a set of discontinuities in the Shapley value.

* Research sponsored by the GNAFA of the Consiglio Nazionale delle Ricerche.

Not all authors, however, agree on the significance and the weight of the Shapley value in describing cooperative games, and other solutions have therefore been proposed. Among these we recall the recent results of Banzhaf [1], Maschler, Peleg, and Shapley [13], Pressacco [17], Lemaire [9], Harsanìy [8], and Myerson [15]. For further information see Papayano-poulos [16] and Lucas [10].

Common to all these new "solutions" is the concept of the "set of minimal winning coalitions," i.e., winning coalitions that become losing coalitions when any one of the participants abandons it.

During this investigation we shall, however, prove that the weight distributions carrying a constant decisional power are in general the same for all players regardless of the definition of this decisional power.

2. WEIGHTED MAJORITY GAMES

Throughout this chapter we shall use the following simplified definition of a weighted majority game.[1] A weighted majority game is defined by an n-dimensional column vector $w \in R^n$ such that

$$(2.1) \qquad\qquad e'w = W, \qquad w \geq 0,$$

where e is the n-dimensional column unit vector and e' its transpose.

The set of all vectors w satisfying (2.1) forms an n simplex S in an n-dimensional Euclidean space.

The characteristic function v of the game, i.e., the function that associates with each particular coalition G a certain normalized payoff, is defined by the relationships

$$(2.2) \qquad \begin{aligned} v(w, G) &= 1 \qquad \text{if } \sum_{i \in G} w_i > W/2, \\ v(w, G) &= 0 \qquad \text{if } \sum_{i \in G} w_i \leq W/2. \end{aligned}$$

Thus the normalized payoff has the value one for each winning coalition and the value zero for each losing one.

---

[1] A classical more general definition of a weighted majority game can be found, for instance, in von Neumann and Morgenstern [24] where relationships (2.2) take the more general form

$$\begin{aligned} v(w, G) &= 1 \qquad \text{if } \sum_{i \in G} w_i \geq q, \\ v(w, G) &= 0 \qquad \text{if } \sum_{i \in G} w_i < q, \end{aligned} \qquad q > W/2.$$

The simplifying assumption that we have made [$G = W/2 + \varepsilon$] is justified by the applications in which we shall use our theory, all of which are connected with situations in which the majority is defined by $> 50\%$ of the votes.

Consider then the attribution, i.e., the payoff relative to each player according to all possible coalitions in which he can take part, relative to the characteristic function v. This attribution is an n-dimensional column vector $\alpha \in R^n$ such that

(2.3) $$e'\alpha = 1, \qquad \alpha_i \geq v(w, i), \qquad i = 1, \ldots, n.$$

Thus the attribution associates with each player i a payoff α_i which is at least as large as the one the player can achieve by not joining any coalition. On the other hand, α_i must be such that the sum of the attributions of all players coincides with the value of the game, which is the most the players can obtain by forming one "grand" coalition in which all take part.

The set of all possible attributions identifies a simplex $S^\alpha(w)$ of the space R^n. The problem of identifying among the various imputations a unique imputation that satisfies all players has been solved by different authors under different assumptions. Among the different solutions that have been proposed, we recall the Shapley value [21], the value of Maschler *et al.* [13], the Pressacco value [18], the Lemaire value [9], the Harsaniy value [8], the Myerson value [15], and the Banzhaf value [1].

In the following discussion we shall make some more general assumptions concerning the game. These assumptions will enable us to use not only the Shapley value but also other possible solutions. This generalization is based on the concept of a power function which will be presented in the following.

(2.4) Definition. Given a simplex $w \in S$, we call a "generalized power function" each single-valued function

$$\Omega: S \to S_\phi^\alpha(w)$$

which associates with each game $w \in S$ a vector $\Phi \in S^\alpha$, which will be called "power," such that the following properties are satisfied:

(a) If $w_i = w_j$, then $\Phi_i = \Phi_j$.
(b) If $w_i > w_j$, then $\Phi_i \geq \Phi_j$.
(c) If at two distinct points $w, v \in S$ we have

(2.5) $$\Phi_i(w) < \Phi_i(v),$$

then there exists at least one coalition G for which

(2.6) $$v(w, G) = 0 \quad \text{and} \quad v(v, G) = 1.$$

From conditions (a) and (b) it follows that equal power is associated with players with equal weight, while if player i has a weight that is larger than the weight associated with player j, his power cannot be less that the power of player j.

Note that from this definition it follows that if

(2.7) $\Phi_i < \Phi_j,$ then $w_i < w_j,$

i.e., different weights must correspond to different powers.

Condition (c) says that if the power of a player changes in two different games, there exists at least one coalition that is the winning one in one game and the losing one in the other.

It is easy to show that the Shapley value [21], the Harsaniy value [8], the Banzhaf value [1], the Lemaire value [9], and the value of Maschler *et al.* [13] have all the previously mentioned properties. The same properties are also satisfied by the Myerson value [15] on a completely connected graph or in the case of bipolar imputations (see Pressacco [18]) and in general in the kernel of the game.

The Pressacco value [17] does not satisfy the previous hypothesis (a)–(c), since it is not defined on all points of S.

3. THE CASE OF THREE-PERSON GAMES

We shall begin our discussion by presenting the special case of a majority game with three players. From this particular case we shall derive some basic considerations that can be applied to the general case of n players.

Consider for the case $n = 3$ the three-dimensional vector w defined in (2.1) as

$$w_1 + w_2 + w_3 = W, \qquad w_i \geq 0, \quad i = 1, 2, 3.$$

This vector takes values on the points of the triangle ABC as shown in Fig. 1. At each point of this triangle in which player 1 has a weight $w_1 > W/2$, this player wins the game, since his characteristic function takes the value $v = 1$ [see Eq. (2.2)].

Now since Φ is an attribution from (2.3), it follows that

$$\Phi_1 = 1, \qquad \Phi_2 = \Phi_3 = 0.$$

For the triangle ADE (see Fig. 2), with the exception of the segment DE, we have

$$\Phi = (1, 0, 0).$$

If we apply the same kind of argument to the other players, we find that (see again Fig. 2) $\Phi = (0, 1, 0)$ at all points of the triangle BEF with the exception of those belonging to the segment EF, while

$$\Phi = (0, 0, 1)$$

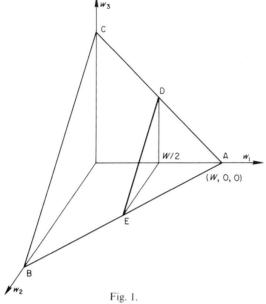

Fig. 1.

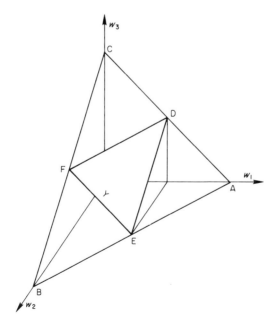

Fig. 2.

at all points of the triangle BEF with the exception of those belonging to the segment DF.

At all interior points of the triangle DEF (for instance at the point $(49/100)W$, $(49/100)W$, $(2/100)W$), each player has exactly the same power, since any player playing alone always loses against a coalition of the other two. This fact implies that any player has the possibility of being determinant in the formation of two winning coalitions. We have therefore that

$$\Phi = (\tfrac{1}{3}, \tfrac{1}{3}, \tfrac{1}{3})$$

at all interior points of the triangle DEF. Concerning the boundary of the triangle DEF, Shapley [19] suggests the following powers:

$$\Phi = (\tfrac{2}{3}, \tfrac{1}{6}, \tfrac{1}{6}), \qquad \Phi = (\tfrac{1}{6}, \tfrac{2}{3}, \tfrac{1}{6}), \qquad \Phi = (\tfrac{1}{6}, \tfrac{1}{6}, \tfrac{2}{3})$$

for the points belonging to the segments DE, EF, and DF, respectively. (Other authors associate these points with different power values or even do not define them.) We have defined in this way regions with which a constant power Φ can be associated. These regions are formed by triangles and line segments. From our previous consideration it follows that

(a)   there are regions in which, even if each player has some nonzero weight, the corresponding power is zero; and

(b)   there are regions in which the power of each player is the same, while the respective weights might be quite different.

This implies *a different* (and discontinuous) *power per unit of weight* for each player based on the whole structure of the game.

Under certain circumstances each player can attempt to increase his own power per unit of weight by buying weight from or selling weight to other players.

In order to investigate this modification of the original weight distribution of the game, we shall first consider a particular case and assume that player 2 sells to player 1 an amount of weight s. The location of the game will therefore move (see Fig. 3) from the point

$$w = (w_1, w_2, w_3)$$

to the point

$$v = (w_1 + s, w_2 - s, w_3).$$

Note that in this particular example we have

$$w_3 = v_3,$$

since player 3 is not involved in the transaction and his weight remains therefore unchanged.

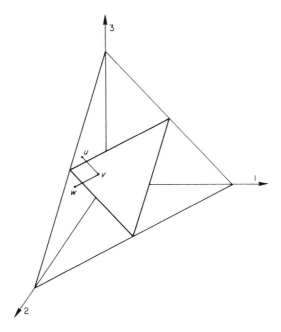

Fig. 3.

In order to decide the selling price, player 2 must know the new value of this power.

In this particular example (see Fig. 3) we have

$$\Phi_2(w) = 1, \quad \text{while} \quad \Phi_1(w) = \Phi_3(w) = 0.$$

In the new location v we have

$$\Phi_2(v) = \tfrac{1}{3}, \quad \text{while} \quad \Phi_1(v) = \Phi_3(v) = \tfrac{1}{3}.$$

We therefore have

$$\Delta\Phi_2 = \Phi_2(w) - \Phi_2(v) = \tfrac{2}{3}.$$

The variation in the power of the second player associated with the particular sale is therefore $\tfrac{2}{3}$.

We must assume that the selling price of the weight s when sold by player 2 to player 1 must be at least $\tfrac{2}{3}$. We can assume for the time being that it is exactly $\tfrac{2}{3}$.

After the sale from player 2 to player 1 it is, however, possible that player 1 will sell the weight s to player 3 (possibly at a price higher than $\tfrac{2}{3}$). As shown in Fig. 3, in our particular example the game will be characterized by the vector

$$u = (w_1, w_2 - s, w_3 + s)$$

and

$$\Phi_2(u) = 0.$$

Clearly, the original sale from player 1 to player 2, which with the outside payment of $\frac{2}{3}$ transformed the game from the weight w to the weight v, was not convenient for player 2, who at the end of the sale (the state u) finds himself with the power 0.

Player 2, in order to prevent the worst possible new situation for himself, must fix the selling price of s as if he were selling this amount of weight to the player capable of inflicting on him the greatest damage. So the price for which s is sold by player 2 to player 1 must be

$$\Phi_2(w) - \Phi_2(v) = 1.$$

Note that this value does not depend on s as long as s is such that the new distribution of the game is characterized (see Fig. 3) by a power distribution different from the original.

In this sense the function Φ_2 that defines the transfer of weight from player 2 to player 3 is a step function that is monotonically nonincreasing as the quantity of weight sold increases (see Fig. 4). Its point of discontinuity

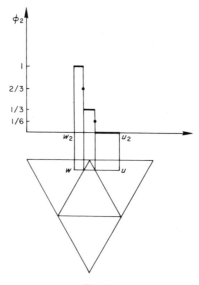

Fig. 4.

corresponds to the intersections with the boundaries of the region of constant powers.

4. CONSTANT-POWER SETS

Let b be an n-dimensional vector whose elements can have only the value 0 or 1 and consider the set of all vectors $x \in S$ such that

$$(4.1) \qquad x'b = W/2.$$

If we denote by $|b|$ the number of components of the vector b that have value 1, from (2.1) it immediately follows that

$$(4.2) \qquad 0 < |b| < n.$$

Equation (4.1) identifies $(2^{n-1} - 1)$ distinct b simplexes. Indeed it is the number of dispositions with a repetition of two elements of class n, with the exception[2] of 0 and e.

Note that for all integers h and k such that $0 < h < k < n$, all h simplexes S^h belong to the k simplexes S^k.

Now the set of the $(n - 1)$ simplexes (4.1) divides S into 2^{n-1} disjoint open simplexes S^n with vertexes given by

$$(4.3) \qquad x'b = W/2, \qquad x'e = W, \qquad |b| = 1.$$

The simplexes S^h have the following property.

(4.4) Theorem. The power Φ is constant in each simplex S^h.

Proof. Assume that there exist two points v, $w \in S^h$ with $\Phi(v) \neq \Phi(w)$. Then at least for player i we have

$$(4.5) \qquad \Phi_i(v) < \Phi_i(w).$$

Now from condition (c) of Definition (2.4), because of property (2.2), it follows that there exists at least one coalition G such that

$$(4.6) \qquad \sum_{i \in G} v_i < W/2, \qquad \sum_{i \in G} w_i > W/2.$$

Since $w \in S^h$ cannot belong to the boundary, it then follows that

$$(4.7) \qquad \sum_{i \in G} w_i \neq W/2.$$

---

[2] The number of such dispositions is $(2^n - 2)/2$. The division for two is down to the dual simplexes.

Then there exists a vector b with the properties given above such that

(4.8) $v'b < W/2, \qquad w'b > W/2.$

Now since both v and w belong to the open simplex S^h, each convex linear combination of them also belongs to S^h. On the other hand, if we consider the convex linear combination of v and w given by

(4.9) $x = \lambda v + (1 - \lambda)w \qquad (0 \leq \lambda \leq 1),$

we can compute a value of λ such that

(4.10) $x'b = W/2,$

i.e., such that x does not belong to S^h.

In order to do that, let [see Eq. (4.8)]

(4.11)
$$v'b = (W/2) - r \qquad (0 < r < W/2)$$
$$w'b = (W/2) + s \qquad (0 < s < W/2).$$

Then, if we let

(4.12) $\lambda = s/(s + r) \qquad (\lambda < 1),$

(4.10) follows. This contradiction proves the theorem.   Q.E.D.

Having identified for the case of a game with n players the regions characterized by a constant power, we shall proceed to identify the selling price for the weights allocated to each player, generalizing the results obtained in Section 3.

5. SHARE TRADING

Consider the case in which, starting from an initial situation w, player j sells s shares to various buyers; then the game moves from w to w^1, and the power of player j changes from $\Phi_j(w)$ to $\Phi_j(w^1)$.

Subsequent purchases of the s shares by other stockholders can then take the game to the final state w^*. Given s, in order to identify the selling price it is necessary to take into account, from among all possible final points w^*, the one for which the allocation $\Phi_j(w^*)$ is minimal. If next we change the number of shares that have been traded, there exists in correspondence with each value of s a final point $w^*(s)$ for which the allocation function $\Phi_j(w^*(s))$ is minimal. The function $\Phi_j(w^*(s))$ is a discontinuous function which is monotonic and not increasing, with points of discontinuity on the boundary of the regions of constant power.

The increment $\Phi_j(w^*(s)) - \Phi_j(w)$ identifies unequivocally the price of the shares.

We shall prove that if the initial point w is an interior point of a region of discontinuity, the final point $w^*(s)$ corresponds to the sale of all s shares to the player with the maximum number of shares. If, instead, the initial point is an interior point of a region with constant power, we must identify among all possible sale directions the one that represents the shortest distance to a discontinuity region. From the point of discontinuity identified in this fashion, we shall proceed as in the former case. Indeed, in this case the general rule connecting the sale direction with the location of the shareholder who can cause the maximum damage (see the following Theorem 5.13) does not apply.

Assume that the jth player sells an amount s of his original weight to the kth player. From the original weight distribution w we move to the weight distribution

$$(5.1) \qquad (w_1, \ldots, w_j - s, \ldots, w_k + s, \ldots, w_n).$$

As s changes within the constraints

$$(5.2) \qquad 0 \le s \le w_j,$$

the game will correspondingly change along the straight line

$$(5.3) \qquad x_i = w_i, \qquad x'e = W \qquad (i = 1, \ldots, n; \quad i \ne j \ne k).$$

Now the values of $\Phi_j(s)$ remain constant on the open intervals of the straight line (5.3) whose extremals are the intercepts between (5.3) and the boundaries of the simplexes S^h. Hence these intercepts fully describe the behavior of the function $\Phi_j(s)$ relative to the seller j.

The sequence of intercept points as s varies on (5.2) is given by the following theorem.

(5.4) Theorem. The sequence of the discontinuity points of $\Phi_j(s)$ as s (the number of weights sold by j to k) varies according to (5.2), has the following components:

$$(5.5) \qquad x_j = (W/2) - \sum_{\substack{i=1 \\ i \ne j \ne k}}^{n} b_i w_i.$$

Proof. Let us represent the straight line (5.3) in the form

$$(5.6) \qquad \sum_{\substack{i=1 \\ i \ne j \ne k}}^{n} w_i + x_j + x_k = W.$$

We consider next the equations of the hyperplanes that are the boundaries of the simplexes S^h. Clearly, in order to have an interception with (5.6), the coefficients of the terms x_j and x_k of these hyperplanes cannot have zero for both values or one for both values. Indeed, if this situation were to arise, then either these planes would be parallel to (5.6) or (5.6) would be contained in such planes. This would imply that the power of the players could not be altered by the sale of weights.

If we eliminate these pathological cases from the possible situations, we can consider the following equations of the boundary hyperplanes:

$$(5.7) \qquad x_j + \sum_{\substack{i=1 \\ i \neq j \neq k}}^{n} b_i x_i = W/2$$

and

$$(5.8) \qquad x_k + \sum_{\substack{i=1 \\ i \neq j \neq k}}^{n} b_i x_i = W/2.$$

Because of (5.6), (5.8) becomes

$$(5.9) \qquad x_j = (W/2) + \sum_{\substack{i=1 \\ i \neq j \neq k}}^{n} w_i(b_i - 1).$$

If we let

$$(5.10) \qquad a_i = 1 - b_i,$$

(5.9) takes the form

$$(5.11) \qquad x_j = (W/2) - \sum_{\substack{i=1 \\ i \neq j \neq k}}^{n} a_i w_i,$$

where a_i has the same form as b_i (it can be either 0 or 1). Thus both acceptable solutions, (5.7) and (5.11), are equivalent to (5.5).   Q.E.D.

As the $(n - 2)$ free components of the vector b vary $(b_j = b_k = 0$ are fixed), the expression (5.5) identifies the coordinates of all discontinuity points of the step function Φ_j. These coordinates are obtained by the positive solutions of (5.5), since because of (2.3) possible solutions with negative values must be discarded. Thus the step function Φ_i relative to the seller j can be fully identified as a sequence of segments connecting the initial point with the closest discontinuity hypersurface and then in sequence each point thus identified with the next on each discontinuity hypersurface.

With a similar procedure it is possible to obtain the function relative to buyer k.

This procedure, which allows identification of the most damaging path for the seller, i.e., the buyer who could damage the seller most with respect to a decrease in the power Φ, is rather cumbersome. We shall next develop a faster procedure. In order to do that, we shall first order the players with increasing indexes corresponding to the weights originally attributed to them. Thus

$$(5.12) \qquad 1 < m \qquad \text{if and only if} \quad w_1 \leq w_m.$$

We then have the following theorem.

(5.13) Theorem. Having identified among the possible initial sale directions the one that takes the nearest discontinuity point, the successive sales of weights will produce maximum damage to the seller if the buyer is the player with the greatest weight among all the other players.

Proof. Assume that player j, instead of selling to player k, sells to player p, with

$$(5.14) \qquad 0 < p < k.$$

Then relationship (5.5) becomes

$$(5.15) \qquad x_j = (W/2) - \sum_{\substack{i=1 \\ i \neq j \neq p}}^{n} b_i w_i.$$

Comparing (5.5) with (5.15), we can see that the transaction straight line (5.3) in (5.5) will cross the discontinuity hyperplane at a distance that is shorter than or equal to the distance in (5.15). Thus the step function Φ_j relative to the sale to player p is not better than the one relative to the sale to player k. From the first discontinuity point, the most damaging point is the one with the greatest weight. Q.E.D.

6. THE GENERATING ALGORITHM

In order to identify the sale price, we shall proceed in two steps. In the first step by means of equation (5.5) we must identify player k for which x_j is minimal.

After computing the power corresponding to the new point, we shall then generate the sequence of the successive points x_j following the result of Theorem (5.3). This implies the construction of all 2^{n-2} vectors b with dimension $(n - 2)$, i.e., all vectors whose elements can have either the value zero or the value one for a given dimension. This is clearly the sequence of all integer numbers expressed in binary form with $(n - 2)$ digits.

Once this sequence has been generated, we must then compute the value of Φ_i at a point in each region with constant power. We shall need then at most

$$2 \cdot 2^{n-2} = 2^{n-1}$$

evaluations of Φ_i in order to compute the complete sequence.

7. FURTHER OUTSTANDING PROBLEMS

Having dealt so far with the trading of a single company's shares, a natural extension would be to consider more companies. This problem could be inserted in a framework of portfolio selection theory [12, 22, 23]. In other words, one might establish a theory whereby an investor allocates his wealth to n risky investments, maximizing his objective function which might include, besides the expected returns and risks, the sum of decisional powers obtained by the control shares (this is the innovative point). A particular approach to this problem has been proposed by Ragazzi [19] in the case of a company with only one "strong player," the others having negligible weight.

An extension of these results could suggested through "large games" [14, 20], where there are many strong players. Finally, we suggest that algorithms be established to generate automatically the values of Φ, given the sequence of discontinuity points. For instance, in the case of the Shapley value, one could adapt the method provided in Mann et al. [11].

8. CONCLUSIONS

The results we have presented in this chapter stress the existence of discontinuities in the power functions, discontinuities that affect the form of the selling price for each player. For practical application of this theory, for instance in the case of the stock market where shares of companies are traded, we must extend this result by including two additional important aspects: an intrinsic value of the weight[3] and the presence of market forces which, if based on the only intrinsic value, act in opposition to the seller by reducing the price when more shares become available. The market forces therefore have the effect of reducing the discontinuities induced by the consideration of power functions. As shown by the preceding theory, discontinuities predominate when large blocks of shares are traded, while continuous phenomena prevail when a smaller number of shares are traded. From this point

---

[3] To the weight of each player, which is the number of shares held, there corresponds not only a power in the game-theoretical sense but also an intrinsic value. Both components comprise the correct selling price.

of view the contribution presented here may constitute yet another example of the economics of discontinuities, which is becoming of ever increasing relevance in the interpretation of economic reality.

REFERENCES

1. Banzhaf, J. F., Weighted voting doesn't work: A mathematical analysis, *Rutgers Law Review*, **19**, 317–343 (1965).
2. Gambarelli, G., Evaluation of political elections in Europe by the Shapley value of a game, *Proceedings of Convegno Internazionale su Programmazione Matematica e sue Applicazioni Economiche, Venezia, Ca' Foscari* **6**, 12–16 (1978).
3. Gambarelli, Geometrical considerations on the Shapley value of a game, *Proc. of 1° Convegno AMASES* pp. 183–196. Giappichelli, Torino, 1979.
4. Gambarelli, G., Sulla determinazione del prezzo delle azioni con riferimento ai possibili accordi per il controllo di una compagnia, *Atti del 3° Convegno AMASES, Napoli, Istituto Navale* (1979) (forthcoming).
5. Gambarelli, G., Algorithm for the numerical computation of the Shapley value of a game, in *Rivista di Statistica Applicata* (forthcoming).
6. Gambarelli, G., Algorithm for the automatic generation of the winning coalitions in weighted majority games, *Rivista di Statistica Applicata* (forthcoming).
7. Gambarelli, G., and Zambruno, Analytical reformulation of the Shapley value of a game, *Proc. of 1° Convegno AMASES* pp. 197–211. Giappichilli, Torino, 1979.
8. Harsaniy, J., A bargaining model for *n*-person game, "Contributions to the Theory of Games" (W. Kuhn and W. Tucker, eds.), Vol. IV, Annals of Math. Studies 40). Princeton Univ. Press, Princeton New Jersey, 1959.
9. Lemaire, J., A new value for games without transferable utilities, *International Journal of Game Theory* **3**(4), 205–213 (1974).
10. Lucas, W. F., Measuring power in weighted voting systems, "Cases Studies in Applied Mathematics" (M. Thompson, ed.). Mathematical Association of America, Washington, D.C., 1976.
11. Mann, I., and Shapley, L. S., Values of Large Games, VI: Evaluating the Electoral College Exactly, Memorandum RM-3158-PR-May. Rand Corporation, Santa Monica, California (1962).
12. Markowitz, H., "Portfolio Selection." Wiley, New York, 1959.
13. Maschler, M., Peleg, B., and Shapley, L. S., Geometric Properties of the Kernel, Nucleolus, and Related Solution Concepts, P-6027. The Rand Corporation, Santa Monica, California (October 1977).
14. Milnor, J. W., and Shapley, L. S., Values of large games, II: Oceanic games, *Mathematics of Operations Research* **3**, No. 4, 290–307 (1978).
15. Myerson, R. B., Graphs and cooperation in games, *Mathematics of Operations Research* **2**, No. 3, 225–229 (1977).
16. Papayanopoulos, L., Democratic representation and appointment: Quantitative methods, measures and criteria, *Annals of New York Academy of Science* **219** (1973).
17. Pressacco, F., Arbitraggi bilanciati per giochi omogenei di maggioranza ponderata, *Rivista matematica di Science Economiche e Sociali, Milano*, No. 1 (1978).
18. Pressacco, F., Su una nuova interpretazione del valore di Shapley per giochi di n persone a somma costante. Università degli Studi di Trieste-Facoltà di Economia e Commercio, Istituto di Mateamatica Finanziaria, Pubbl. No. 28 (1979).

19. Ragazzi, G., On the relation between ownership dispersion and the firm's market value, *Journal of Banking and Finance* **5** (1981).
20. Shapiro, N. Z., and Shapley, L. S., Values of large games, I: A limit theorem, *Mathematics of Operations Res.* **3** No. 1, 1–9 (1978).
21. Shapley, L. S., A value for n-person game, "Contributions to the Theory of Games" (W. Kuhn and W. Tucker, eds), Annals of Math. Studies 39, Vol. II, pp. 307–317. Princeton Univ. Press, Princeton New Jersey, 1953.
22. Sharpe, W., Capital asset prices: A theory of market equilibrium under conditions of risk *Journal of Finance* **19**, 625–642 (1969).
23. Szegö, G. P., "Portfolio Theory with Application to Bank Asset Management." Academic Press, New York, 1980.
24. von Neumann, J., and Morgenstern, O., "Theory of Games and Economic Behavior," 3rd ed. Princeton Univ. Press, Princeton New Jersey, 1953.

DEPARTMENT OF MATHEMATICS AND STATISTICS
UNIVERSITY OF BERGAMO
BERGAMO, ITALY

Part IV

SPECIAL PROBLEMS

Elementary Properties of Nonnegative Matrices

Giulio Cesare Barozzi

In this chapter I shall try to illustrate in a simple manner those properties of nonnegative matrices that are relevant to economic applications. The main results will be stated without proof; the interested reader can refer to such classical references as Gantmacher [4] and Bellman [1]. Other results can be found in Seneta [6]. It must be noted that the subject is still actively pursued: See the papers covered by *Math. Rev.* under MOS Classification Number 14A48. For economic applications one can consult Pasinetti [5] and the literature quoted therein.

Let us begin with a few definitions. A square matrix $A = [a_{ij}]$ is *nonnegative* if $a_{ij} \geq 0$ for every couple (i, j). If A and B are square matrices of the same order, $A \leq B$ means that $a_{ij} \leq b_{ij}$ and $A < B$ means that $a_{ij} < b_{ij}$ for every couple (i, j). Some authors write $A \leq B$ instead of $A \leq B$, the latter notation meaning that $a_{ij} < b_{ij}$ for at least one couple (i, j). Analogous notations are adopted for vectors of R^n: $x \leq y$ means that $x_i \leq y_i$ and $x < y$ means that $x_i < y_i$ for each i. If 0 denotes the null vector, the set of nonnegative vectors $x \geq 0$ is, by definition, the nonnegative cone of R^n.

Clearly a nonnegative matrix A maps the nonnegative cone into itself: $x \geq 0$ implies $Ax \geq 0$. The first question is: Does the nonnegative cone of R^n contain an eigenvector of A? In other words, we look for a vector $x \geq 0$, $x \neq 0$, such that

$$Ax = \lambda x;$$

in such a case λ must obviously be nonnegative: $\lambda \geq 0$. Since eigenvectors are defined up to a scalar factor, we can restrict our search to a set having at least one point in common with every half-line stemming from the origin of R^n and belonging to the nonnegative cone. The simplest choice is the set of nonnegative points belonging to the plane $x_1 + x_2 + \cdots + x_n = 1$; i.e.,

$$S = \left\{ x \in R^n \,|\, x_i \geq 0, \sum_i x_i = 1 \right\}.$$

Incidentally, we observe that the vectors of S may be interpreted as probability vectors. The identity

$$x = x_1 e_1 + x_2 e_2 + \cdots + x_n e_n,$$

where $x = (x_1, x_2, \ldots, x_n)$ and $e_1, e_2, \ldots, e_n$ are the vectors of the canonical base of R^n, shows that the vectors of S are precisely those that can be obtained as linear convex combinations of the vectors e_j.

We can therefore rephrase the previous problem in the following way: to find x in S such that $Ax = \lambda x$, where λ is necessarily ≥ 0. A first result in this connection, limited to positive matrices, was achieved by the German mathematician Oskar Perron in 1907.

Theorem (Perron). *Let $A = [a_{ij}]$ be a positive matrix, $a_{ij} > 0$; then there exists a unique nonnegative eigenvector $v_1 \in S$. This eigenvector is in fact positive, $v_1 > 0$, the corresponding eigenvalue λ_1 being positive, simple, and strictly dominating the remaining eigenvalues:*

$$|\lambda_j| < \lambda_1, \qquad j = 2, 3, \ldots, n.$$

When we say that λ_1 is simple, we refer to its multiplicity as a root of the characteristic equation. Perron's theorem states that the spectral radius of A, $r(A)$ is actually an eigenvalue

$$r(A) = \lambda_1,$$

while the remaining eigenvalues are inside the circle with center at the origin and radius λ_1.

One of the many possible proofs of the theorem goes along the following lines. If A is positive, it maps vectors of S into positive vectors:

$$x \in S \qquad \text{implies} \qquad Ax > 0.$$

(It is sufficient to consider that the vector e_j of the canonical base is mapped into the jth column of A). With each vector x of S we can associate a scalar $\lambda(x)$, defined as the largest nonnegative number such that

$$\lambda(x)x \leq Ax$$

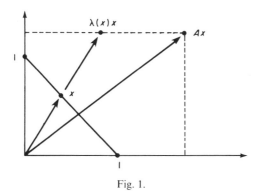

Fig. 1.

(see Fig. 1). Since $Ax > 0$, $\lambda(x) > 0$. The function $x \to \lambda(x)$ can be shown to be continuous on S, and this, by virtue of Weierstrass' theorem, implies that the maximum

$$\lambda_1 = \max\{\lambda(x) \,|\, x \in S\}$$

exists and is positive. Let $v_1 \in S$ be a vector such that $\lambda(v_1) = \lambda_1$; we have

$$\lambda_1 v_1 \leqslant A v_1.$$

If one of the components of $\lambda_1 v_1$ is strictly less than the corresponding component of $A v_1$, then a vector $w \in S$ can be found such that $\lambda(w) > \lambda(v_1)$ $= \lambda_1$, contrary to our assumptions.

The hypothesis that A is a strictly positive matrix is too narrow for many applications, so we are interested in extensions of Perron's result, or part of it, to larger classes of matrices. We can first observe that Perron's theorem is valid if A is a *primitive* matrix, i.e., a nonnegative matrix with a positive power:

$$A \geq 0, \qquad A^k > 0 \qquad \text{for some} \quad k > 0.$$

For instance, a tridiagonal matrix such as

$$A = \begin{bmatrix} a_{11} & a_{12} & & & 0 \\ a_{21} & a_{22} & a_{23} & & \\ & & \ddots & & \\ 0 & & & a_{n,n-1} & a_{nn} \end{bmatrix}, \qquad a_{ij} > 0 \quad \text{for} \quad |i - j| < 2$$

is primitive since $A^n > 0$. The validity of Perron's theorem for primitive matrices is connected with the fact that the eigenvalues of A^k are those of A to the kth power.

A further significant extension is achieved considering nonnegative *irreducible* matrices. Let us give the relevant definition. A square matrix A of order ≥ 2 is reducible if it can be decomposed in the following manner:

$$(*) \qquad\qquad A = \begin{bmatrix} A_{11} & A_{12} \\ 0 & A_{22} \end{bmatrix},$$

where A_{11} is square and of order n_1, A_{22} is square and of order n_2, and 0 stands for the $n_2 \times n_1$ zero matrix. For such a matrix one easily obtains

$$\det(A - \lambda I) = \det(A_{11} - \lambda I_{n_1})\det(A_{22} - \lambda I_{n_2}),$$

so that the search for the eigenvalues of A is "reduced" to the analogous problem for A_{11} and A_{22} separately. More generally, A is reducible if and only if it can be brought to the form $(*)$ by a suitable permutation of its rows and the *same* permutation of its columns. In other words, A is reducible if and only if a permutation matrix P exists such that PAP^T is of type $(*)$.

Concerning the geometrical meaning of reducibility, the following remarks can be made. Let A be of type $(*)$; let us decompose every $x \in R^n, n = n_1 + n_2$, in a similar manner:

$$x = \begin{bmatrix} x^{(1)} \\ x^{(2)} \end{bmatrix}, \qquad x^{(1)} \in R^{n_1}, \qquad x^{(2)} \in R^{n_2}.$$

We obtain

$$Ax = \begin{bmatrix} A_{11} & A_{12} \\ 0 & A_{22} \end{bmatrix} \begin{bmatrix} x^{(1)} \\ x^{(2)} \end{bmatrix} = \begin{bmatrix} A_{11}x^{(1)} + A_{12}x^{(2)} \\ A_{22}x^{(2)} \end{bmatrix}.$$

If $x^{(2)} = 0$ (i.e., the last n_2 components of x are vanishing), the same holds for the transformed vector Ax. Equivalently, we find that the coordinate subspace

$$V = \{x \in R^n \,|\, x_{n_1+1} = \cdots = x_n = 0\}$$

is invariant under premultiplication by A. If PAP^T is of type $(*)$, the same will be true for the subspace

$$P^T(V) = \{\hat{x} \in R^n \,|\, \hat{x} = Px, x \in V\}.$$

This geometrical interpretation of reducibility, despite its simplicity, is not of much help in deciding whether a particular matrix is reducible. We shall go back to this problem at the end of the chapter, and we shall see that an alternative interpretation, in terms of graph theory, will provide an efficient algorithm for solving the problem of reducibility.

Let us consider the class of nonnegative irreducible matrices. Since powers of reducible matrices are still reducible, primitive matrices are irreducible. Actually the class of irreducible matrices is larger than the class of primitive matrices. For instance, the matrix

$$A = \begin{bmatrix} 0 & a \\ a & 0 \end{bmatrix}, \qquad a > 0$$

is clearly irreducible, since the unique (nonidentical) permutation on two elements leaves A invariant:

$$PAP^{\mathrm{T}} = A, \qquad P = \begin{bmatrix} 0 & 1 \\ 1 & 0 \end{bmatrix}.$$

But no power of A is strictly positive. The eigenvalues of A are

$$\lambda_1 = a, \qquad \lambda_2 = -a,$$

and this simple example shows that $r(A)$ is still an eigenvalue, but it does not strictly dominate the other eigenvalue.

This means that change must be made in the formulation of Perron's theorem in order to obtain an analogous result for nonnegative irreducible matrices. The German mathematician Georg Frobenius, in a series of papers published between 1908 and 1912, obtained the following result.

Theorem (Frobenius). *Let A be a nonnegative irreducible matrix. Then there exists a unique nonnegative eigenvector $v_1 \in S$; this eigenvector is in fact positive, $v_1 > 0$, the corresponding eigenvalue λ_1 being positive, simple, and dominating the other eigenvalues of A:*

$$|\lambda_j| \le \lambda_1, \qquad j = 2, 3, \ldots, n.$$

The eigenvalue λ_1 is a continuous and increasing function of A; i.e., if B is a matrix with the same properties of A and $A \le B$, then $\lambda_1(A) \le \lambda_1(B)$. Finally, if

$$r_i = \sum_j a_{ij}, \qquad c_j = \sum_i a_{ij},$$

then

$$\min_i r_i \le \lambda_1 \le \max_i r_i, \qquad \min_j c_j \le \lambda_1 \le \max_j c_j.$$

The last double inequality implies that any *stochastic* matrix A ($A \ge 0$, $\sum_i a_{ij} = 1$) has the number 1 as the first eigenvalue. If $r_i < 1$ for any i (or $c_j < 1$ for any j), then

$$r(A) < 1,$$

and consequently $(I - A)^{-1}$ exists, is nonnegative, and is given by $\sum_{k=0}^{\infty} A^k$. A closer analysis would show that $(I - A)^{-1}$ is actually positive under the hypothesis $r_i \le 1$ for any i and $r_i < 1$ for at least one i (the same conclusion holds for c_j in place of r_i).

If we drop the hypothesis of irreducibility, we obtain the existence of $\lambda_1 \geq 0$ dominating the remaining eigenvalues, but we cannot guarantee either the simplicity of λ_1 or the positivity of the corresponding eigenvector. Examples can easily be constructed by considering diagonal or, more generally, triangular matrices.

So we are left with the problem of deciding whether a given nonnegative matrix is reducible. We first observe that the actual value of each term a_{ij} does not matter: The only important thing is the condition $a_{ij} \neq 0$. Second, we note that the diagonal terms a_{ii} of A do not enter the definition of irreducibility. During the transformation from A to PAP^T, with P a permutation matrix, the diagonal terms do not leave the diagonal and consequently their nullity (or nonnullity) is irrelevant to our question.

This means that we can associate with A a matrix $M = [m_{ij}]$ defined as

$$m_{ii} = 0, \qquad i = 1, 2, \ldots, n$$

$$m_{ij} = \begin{cases} 1 & \text{if } a_{ij} \neq 0, \\ 0 & \text{otherwise,} \end{cases} \quad i \neq j.$$

The matrix A is reducible if and only if M is reducible. Now M can be thought of as the *adjacency matrix* of a *directed graph* G, having n vertices and without *loops*. The irreducibility of M is equivalent to the *strong connectivity* of G, i.e., to the fact that for any two distinct vertices $x_i \neq x_j$ there is at least one path from x_i to x_j. So we decide whether or not A is reducible by constructing the *reachability matrix* $R = [r_{ij}]$ of G defined as

$$r_{ij} = \begin{cases} 1 & \text{if vertex } x_j \text{ is reachable from vertex } x_i \\ 0 & \text{otherwise.} \end{cases}$$

By "reachable" we mean of course that at least one path exists from vertex x_i to vertex x_j (see, for example, Christophides [2]).

The following algorithm (see Floyd [3]) will replace *in situ* the adjacency matrix M by the reachability matrix R.

Algorithm. The adjacency matrix $M = [m_{ij}]$, $i, j = 1, 2, \ldots, n$, of a directed graph G with n vertices is replaced by the reachability matrix of the same graph.

1. For $i = 1, 2, \ldots, n$

   1. For $j = 1, 2, \ldots, n$

      1. If $m_{ji} = 1$, then: 1. For $k = 1, 2, \ldots, n$

                           1. If $m_{ik} = 1$, then $m_{jk} \leftarrow 1$.

ble if and only if at the end of the algorithm $m_{ij} = 1$ for $i \neq j$.

REFERENCES

1. Bellman, R., "Introduction to Matrix Analysis." McGraw-Hill, New York, 1970.
2. Christophides, N., "Graph Theory: An Algorithmic Approach." Academic Press, New York, 1975.
3. Floyd, R. W., Algorithm 96 ANCESTOR, CACM 5 (1962).
4. Gantmacher, F. R., "The Theory of Matrices." Chelsea, New York, 1959.
5. Pasinetti, L., "Lezioni di Teoria della Produzione." Il Mulino, Bologna, 1975.
6. Seneta, E., "Nonnegative Matrices." Halstead Press, New York, 1973.

INSTITUTE OF APPLIED MATHEMATICS
UNIVERSITY OF BOLOGNA
BOLOGNA, ITALY

Optimal Control of Econometric Models: Some Experimental Results for the Italian Monetary Sector

Corrado Corradi

1. INTRODUCTION

Macroeconometric models have been used for several years, mostly for simulation or forecast purposes and to a limited extent as aids in policy making. The availability of computational algorithms for the efficient solution of simultaneous difference equations has made the computer simulation of econometric models a useful way to determine and compare the dynamic effects of different policies. However, simulation does not provide a direct means of obtaining a policy that is "optimal" with respect to a given objective.

The past decade has seen the publication of numerous contributions concerning the application of optimal control in the econometric area, thus extending the range of problems solvable by a policy maker. Control theory has been applied to about 100 different macroeconomic models containing from 1 to 300 equations, including models of the United States, Canada, the United Kingdom, West Germany, France, Belgium, Australia, and The Netherlands (cf. [8]), using a wide range of control theory methods. Deterministic methods for both linear quadratic and general nonlinear models have been used. Uncertainty has been introduced into the equations in the form of additive noise and in the form of uncertainty about parameters. The models have been solved either with closed loop control policies and/or

255

open loop optimal feedback policies. Recently, adaptive control procedures and a few applications of decentralized control techniques and of differential games have begun to be used on the smaller models.

This chapter reviews some results obtained during the last 2 yr by a research team formed by econometricians, engineers, and mathematicians within the Economy and Systems Theory Group (GES) of the National Research Council [2, 3]. The authors focused on the monetary sector of the quarterly LINK Project model developed at the University of Bologna [6], in which some fundamental instruments for the policy maker are present. The basic framework of the analysis is analogous to that of the classic paper by Pindyck and Roberts [11]. The problem involves tracking nominal output and nominal policy trajectories subject to a quadratic cost functional and the constraint of a linear model, ignoring the stochastic properties of the model or making simplifying assumptions about them that allow "certainty equivalence" [13] to be invoked in obtaining a solution. Several points should be discussed about the choice of the deterministic linear quadratic scheme, mostly because numerous recent works try to remove the above restrictions: (i) the quadratic cost functional, (ii) the linearity of the model, and (iii) the deterministic approach. Let us examine these three items separately.

(i) The quadratic cost functional has become familiar in economic optimization problems and is usually considered a reasonable way to model the costs of the deviations for several objectives [14]. It may be remarked that this specification has been extended by working with a cost functional that is piecewise quadratic [7].

(ii) A linear model can be a more serious restriction than the quadratic cost functional. Most econometric models are quasi-linear, but sometimes the more interesting aspects of their dynamic behavior arise from nonlinearities. Recently much effort has been expended to make nonlinear optimal control problems numerically treatable on a computer, despite the large core and time requirements [5]. However, a fundamental question can be raised: Is the nonlinear optimization worth the added computational expense that it entails? [9]. It is still perhaps an open question whether the results obtained with a nonlinear model are significantly better than those obtained using a linearized version of the model with the same cost functional. In fact, when dealing with nonlinear models it is all the more difficult to obtain an analytical understanding of the dynamics of the optimal policy and to assess the degree of suboptimality involved in a linearization of the model. In addition, although certain nonlinear equations can be handled statistically, nonlinearities in general create problems for the econometrician; furthermore, equations whose coefficients are time varying present statistical difficulties even worse than those presented by nonlinearities. Therefore the choice of linear time-invariant systems can be regarded as a reflection of the present state of the art of describing the real world using econometric models.

(iii) Some of the remarks raised above partially apply also to the choice between a deterministic and a stochastic approach to finding optimal policies. The econometric model is indeed a stochastic system, and three sources of uncertainty can be included: additive noise in the reduced form of the macro-econometric model, additive noise in the observation vectors, and uncertainty about the parameter values. A large number of applications of the stochastic approach (mostly involving only the first source of uncertainty, namely, additive system noise) are available in the literature: A detailed list is given in [8]. However, justification for a deterministic treatment, at least in a preliminary stage of the research, can be twofold. First, a complete analysis of the autocorrelation of the additive disturbances as well as the stochastic properties of the coefficients of the model would make its application difficult, if not impossible. Second, the uncertainty about the economy is reflected mostly in the fact that the researcher is free to choose among alternative specifications of the model, so that to gain a deeper understanding of this problem it would perhaps be more fruitful to study the dynamics of the deterministic optimization solutions for several alternative model specifications. For further comments on these points see [10].

In the next section we shall describe briefly the monetary model used for the experiments and outline the computational scheme for solving the tracking problem, while in the last section we shall present some examples of the results obtained.

2. THE COMPUTATIONAL SCHEME

Since the monetary model described in [6] is nonlinear, two alternative procedures can be employed, namely, linearization using Taylor series expansions, as suggested by Theil [14], or reestimation of a linear version of the same model. The former has been used in [2]; here we shall refer basically to the experiments described in [3], where the latter has been employed. We shall give only a general idea of the model, whose structure is sketched in the appendix; a complete list of the estimated equations can be found in [3].

The model considers the market and the total bank deposits D for which the supply from financial institutions and the demand by the public are in equilibrium at a given level of the interest rate RLTB. A first behavioral assumption is that economic agents have in mind "desired" relations between the stocks and the level of interest rates consistent with the maximization of the net worth. A second assumption is that from period to period the deviations of the actual stocks held by the banks and the public from the desired stock are proportional to the difference between the desired and the actual values themselves. We note that "potential" deposits appear in the interest rate equations, which account for those parts of the total reserves of the banks that are always equal to the required reserves according to the rules imposed by the Central Bank. Through the monetary base (UBAS) not borrowed by the banks and the discount rate (RB) the Central Bank can influence the level of total deposits, determining the desired level of liquidity of the system. The model described in the appendix can be written compactly as

$$(1) \qquad y_t = \sum_{i=0}^{L} A_i y_{t-i} + \sum_{i=0}^{L} B_i u_{t-i} + b,$$

where y_t is the p vector of the endogenous variables, u_t the m vector of the exogenous variables (instruments and nonmanipulated variables), b a constant vector, A_i and B_i properly sized matrices of the estimated coefficients, and L the greatest lag in the model. Equation (1) can be rewritten using polynomial matrices in the unit-time forward shift operator, i.e., $zy_t = z_{t+1}$, as

$$(2) \qquad P(z)y_t = \left[\sum_{i=1}^{L} Q_i z^{L-i}, \sum_{i=1}^{L} S_i z^{L-i} \right] \begin{bmatrix} u_t \\ c \end{bmatrix} + P(z)[E, I] \begin{bmatrix} u_t \\ c \end{bmatrix}$$

by defining $S_i = (I - A_0)^{-1} A_i, c = (I - A_0)^{-1} b$,

$$(3) \qquad P(z) = Iz^L - \sum_{i=1}^{L} S_i z^{L-i}, \qquad E = (I - A_0)^{-1} B_0;$$

the $p \times m$ matrices $Q_1, \ldots, Q_L$ are such that

$$P(z)y_t = \sum_{i=1}^{L} Q_i z^{L-i} u_t + P(z)Eu_t + z^L c.$$

The above formulation permits separation of the purely dynamic part of the model [given by the first term on the right-hand side of (2)] and the input–output instantaneous effect. Now before optimization experiments can be performed the model must be put in the state variable form [12]

$$(4) \qquad x_{t+1} = Ax_t + G_1 u_t + G_2 c, \qquad y_t = Hx_t + Eu_t + c.$$

This can be achieved using an extension of results for linear dynamic system canonical representations given in [1] and [15], to which the reader can refer for technical details. As a result of this procedure the state vector x_t can be expressed as a linear combination of the measurable input–output variables

Some gain in computational efficiency can be achieved by observing that the transformation (4) need not be performed on the complete model (2). In fact, let us partition the model into two submodels, say M_1 and M_2, defined as follows: (i) The dynamics of M_1 influence but are not influenced by those of M_2; (ii) M_2 is not autoregressive; (iii) the set of output vectors of M_1 contains all endogenous variables appearing in the objective functional (see below). This decomposition can be easily performed by checking the null columns having the same position in the matrices S_i defined in (3), and by a suitable reordering. In the present case the above partition yields (see the appendix for the symbols used)

$$M_1 = \{CIR, DR, DRCR, RLTB, RCR, DCC, DCCR, D, DPOT, RR\},$$

$$M_2 = \{RES, UR, DPD\}.$$

The final step is to separate the exogenous variables into two subvectors, i.e., instruments s_t, and variables w_t that cannot be considered by the policy maker. This leads to

$$
(5) \qquad
\begin{aligned}
x_{t+1} &= Ax_t + Bs_t + [C_1, G_2 c]z_t, \\
y_t &= Hx_t + Ds_t + [D_1, c]z_t,
\end{aligned}
$$

where $G_1 = [B, C_1]$, $E = [D, D_1]$, $z_t = [w'_t, 1]'$.

Now, given the dynamic constraint (5), the initial state $x_0 = \xi$, and the quadratic cost functional

$$
(6) \qquad \frac{1}{2}\left\{ \sum_{t=1}^{N} (y_t - \hat{y}_t)'Q(y_t - \hat{y}_t) + \sum_{t=0}^{N} (s_t - \hat{s}_t)'R(s_t - \hat{s}_t) \right\},
$$

where $\hat{s}_t$ and $\hat{y}_t$ are nominal input and output values, Q and R positive semi-definite and definite weighting matrices, and N the finite planning horizon, by writing the necessary conditions for the minimum of (6) over $s_t, t = 0, \ldots, N$, we obtain, after rather cumbersome algebra,

$$K_N = H'QPH,$$

$$g_N = H'Q[P(Fz_N - \hat{y}_N) + D\hat{R}^{-1}R\hat{s}_N],$$

$$K_t = NK_{t+1}E_{t+1}^{-1}N' + H'QPH,$$

$$
\begin{aligned}
g_t &= Ng_{t+1} + NK_{t+1}E_{t+1}^{-1}\{Cz_t - B\hat{R}^{-1}[D'Q(Fz_t - \hat{y}_t) + B'g_{t+1} - R\hat{s}_t]\} \\
&\quad + H'Q[P(Fz_t - \hat{y}_t) + D\hat{R}^{-1}R\hat{s}_t], \qquad t = 1, \ldots, N-1;
\end{aligned}
$$

$$x_0 = \xi,$$

$$x_1 = E_1^{-1}[Ax_0 - B(R^{-1}B'g_1 - \hat{s}_0) + Cz_0],$$

$$
\begin{aligned}
x_{t+1} &= E_{t+1}^{-1}\{N'x_t - B\hat{R}^{-1}[D'Q(Fz_t - \hat{y}_t) + B'g_{t+1} - R\hat{s}_t] \\
&\quad + Cz_t\}, \qquad t = 1, \ldots, N-1;
\end{aligned}
$$

$$s_0 = -R^{-1}B'(K_1x_1 + g_1) + \hat{s}_0,$$

$$
\begin{aligned}
s_t &= -\hat{R}^{-1}[D'Q(Hx_t + Fz_t - \hat{y}_t) + B'(K_{t+1}x_{t+1} + g_{t+1}) \\
&\quad - R\hat{s}_t], \qquad t = 1, \ldots, N-1,
\end{aligned}
$$

$$s_N = -\hat{R}^{-1}[D'Q(Hx_N + Fz_N - \hat{y}_N) - R\hat{s}_N].$$

In the above expressions we have denoted $C = [C_1, G_2 c]$, $F = [D_1, c]$, $P = I - D\hat{R}^{-1}D'Q$, $\hat{R} = R + D'QD$, $M = A' - H'QDR^{-1}B'$, $N = A' - H'QD\hat{R}^{-1}B$, $E_1 = I + BR^{-1}B'K_1$, $E_{t+1} = I + B\hat{R}^{-1}B'K_{t+1}$, $t = 1, \ldots, N - 1$.

It is readily seen that the solution of the problem under study requires a large number of matrix operations, but from the numerical standpoint the main problem is the inversion of a positive definite matrix, for which well-known stable algorithms are available. It may be remarked that the above formulas are similar but not identical to those given in [9] owing to the presence of the instantaneous input–output relation mentioned. A formulation analogous to the above is reported in [4].

3. EXPERIMENTAL RESULTS

Space does not allow the reproduction of even a small fraction of the results obtained by past control experiments. The objective of this section is just to give an illustrative example of the kind of practical experiments that can be done within the framework of optimal control.

In the previous section we mentioned that the Central Bank may as part of its objectives try to reach targets for both total deposits D and the interest rate RLTB. This may be impossible even in a deterministic world, so it can be interesting to draw trade-off curves: A single trade-off curve is obtained by performing several optimization runs in which different weights are

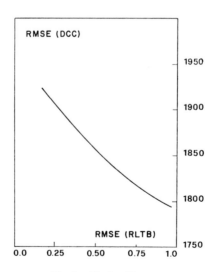

Fig. 1.   Trade-off curve.

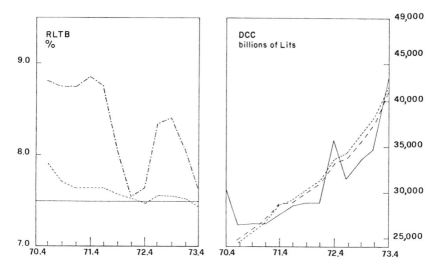

Fig. 2.   Optimal trajectories: (——) nominal; (– –) optimal (minimum RMSE); (–·–) optimal (maximum RMSE).

placed in the Q matrix coefficients for the deposit variables, fixing the RLTB coefficient at a high value and setting all the other coefficients at zero. For the instruments, a very high cost is associated with the discount rate RB, while almost no cost is attached to the level of the UBAS, so allowing the monetary base to move freely. A point on the trade-off curve is obtained by calculating the root mean square error RMSE of the nominal path from the optimal path over the whole control period (1971.1–1973.4). The nominal trajectories are chosen to reflect the achievement of a "neutral" monetary policy, with interest rates held constant, while assuming a fixed ratio between the stocks and the level of the gross national product in current values (GNPP). The trade-off curve for this experiment is shown in Fig. 1. The curve is parametrized by the Q coefficients of DCC and DCCR, assuming values from 50 to 500. The optimal trajectories for the target variables are shown in Fig. 2. By examining the reported results it seems possible to state that the interest rate has a more critical sensitivity to the preference weights than the stock variables have. In fact, when a high cost is attached to the money stock, the optimal trajectory for the interest rate strongly deviates from the nominal path. The above result seems to be an indicator that, within the context of the model used, it might be preferable for the monetary authority to focus attention on the interest rate rather than on the money stock. Therefore, if interest rates are the intermediate targets of the monetary authority, precise control is easier to obtain. The important question could be raised whether intermediate target strategies are desirable in the first place. This could be studied by considering the monetary market as a subsector of the complete macroeconometric model and then performing optimization experiments in which the targets are macro variables such as GNP, unemployment, and prices.

APPENDIX

Behavioral Equations

CIR $\quad = $ CIR (CIR$_{-1}$, RCR, RCR$_{-1}$, RCR$_{-2}$, GNPP, GNPP$_{-1}$, GNPP$_{-2}$)

DR $\quad = $ DR (DR$_{-1}$, GNPP$_{-1}$, GNPP$_{-2}$, RCR$_{-1}$, RCR$_{-2}$, RCR$_{-3}$, RLTB, RLTB$_{-1}$, RLTB$_{-2}$, Q1, Q2, Q3)

DRCR $\quad = $ DRCR (DRCR$_{-1}$, GNPP$_{-1}$, GNPP$_{-2}$, RCR$_{-1}$, RCR$_{-2}$, RCR$_{-3}$, RLTB, RLTB$_{-1}$, RLTB$_{-2}$, Q1, Q2, Q3)

RLTB $\quad = $ RLTB (RLTB$_{-1}$, RLTB$_{-2}$, RLTB$_{-3}$, RB, RB$_{-1}$, RB$_{-2}$, DPD, DPD$_{-1}$, DPD$_{-2}$)

RCR $\quad = $ RCR (RB, RB$_{-1}$, RB$_{-2}$, RB$_{-3}$, DPD, DPD$_{-1}$, DPD$_{-2}$, DPD$_{-3}$)

RES $\quad = $ RES (DCC, DCC$_{-1}$)

DCC $\quad = $ DCC (DCC$_{-1}$, GQT2, GQT2$_{-1}$, GQT2$_{-2}$, GQT2$_{-3}$, (RLTB − RCR), (RLTB − RCR)$_{-1}$, (RLTB − RCR)$_{-2}$, Q1, Q2, Q3)

DCCCR $ = $ DCCCR (DCCCR$_{-1}$, GQT2, GQT2$_{-1}$, GQT2$_{-2}$, GQT2$_{-3}$, (RLTB − RCR), (RLTB − RCR)$_{-1}$, (RLTB − RCR)$_{-2}$, Q1, Q2, Q3),

where GQT2 $=$ GNPP $-$ (10QT $-$ QT^2/10,000).

Definition Equations

UR $\quad = $ UBAS $-$ CIR

D $\quad = $ DCC $+$ DR

DPOT $= $ DCC $+$ 1/0.225 (UR $-$ RR)

RR $\quad = $ RR$_{-1}$ $+$ 0.225(DCC $-$ DCC$_{-1}$ $-$ DCCCR $+$ DCCCR$_{-1}$) $+$ RES $+$ 0.1(DCCCR $-$ DCCCR$_{-1}$)

DPD $\quad = $ (DPOT $-$ D)/1000

Endogenous Variables

CIR   = currency outside banks
DR   = time deposits with commercial banks
DRCR = savings deposits with Casse di Risparmio
RLTB = interest rate on long-term bonds
RCR   = interest rate on demand deposits
RES   = residual required reserves
DCC   = demand deposits with commercial banks
DCCCR = demand deposits with Casse di Risparmio
UR   = unborrowed reserves
D   = total deposits
DPOT = potential deposits
RR   = required reserves of commercial banks
DPD   = difference between potential and total deposits

Exogenous Variables

GNPP, inflated gross national product at market price
RB, discount rate
UBAS, unborrowed monetary base
Qi, seasonal dummy for the ith quarter
QT, dummy for time

REFERENCES

1. Bonivento, C., Guidorzi, R., and Marro, G., Irreducible canonical realization from external data sequences, *Internat. J. Control* **17**, 553–563 (1973).
2. Bonivento, C., Capitani, G., Corradi, C., Gambetta, G., and Scarani, C., Esperimenti di controllo ottimale con un modello monetario, *in* "Teoria dei Sistemi ed Economia" (Secretary of the G.E.S., ed.). Il Mulino, Bologna, 1976.
3. Bonivento, C., Capitani, G., Corradi, C., Gambetta, G., Scarani, C., and Tonielli, A., A contribution to the modelling and control of the Italian monetary system, *Proc. IFAC Internat. Conf. Dynamic Modelling and Control of Nat. Economics, 2nd, Vienna, January 1977.* "Models and Decision Making in National Economies," J. M. L. Janssen, L. F. Pau, A. Straszak (eds.) © North-Holland Publishing Company, 1979. North Holland Publ., Amsterdam, 1979, pp. 179–186.
4. Bray, J., Optimal control of a noisy economy with the U.K. as an example, *J. Roy. Statist. Soc. Ser. A* **138**, 339–373 (1975).
5. Craine, R., Havenner, A., and Tinsley, P., Optimal control of large nonlinear stochastic econometric models, *Proc. Summer Computer Simulation Conf., San Francisco, 1975.*

6. D'Adda, C., de Antoni, E., Gambetta, G., Onofri, P., and Stagni, A., "Il Modello Econo-
    metrico dell' Universita' di Bologna: Struttura e Simulazioni." Il Mulino, Bologna, 1976.
7. Friedman, B. M., Methods in optimization for economic stabilization policy, Ph.D.
    Thesis (Economics), Harvard University, 1971.
8. Kendrick, D., Applications of control theory to macroeconomics, *Annals of Economic and
    Social Measurement* **5**, 171–185 (1976).
9. Pindyck, R. S., Optimal stabilization policies via deterministic control, *Annals of Economic
    and Social Measurement* **1**, 385–390 (1972).
10. Pindyck, R. S., An application of the linear-quadratic tracking problem to economic
    stabilization policy, *IEEE Trans. Automat. Control* **AC-17**, 287–300 (1972).
11. Pindyck, R. S., Roberts, S. M., Optimal policies for monetary control, *Annals of Economic
    and Social Measurement* **3**, 207–238 (1974).
12. Preston, A. J., and Wall, K. D., Some aspect of the use of state-space models in econo-
    metrics, Discussion paper no. 5, Programme of research into econometric methods,
    Queen Mary College and Imperial College, University of London, 1973.
13. Theil, H., A note on certainty equivalence in dynamic planning, *Econometrica* **25**, 346–349
    (1957).
14. Theil, H., "Optimal Decision Rules for Government and Industry." North-Holland,
    Amsterdam, 1964.
15. Wolovich, W. A., The determination of state-space representations for linear multi-
    variable systems, *Automatica* **9**, 97–106 (1973).

INSTITUTE OF ECONOMIC SCIENCE
   AND
INSTITUTE OF APPLIED MATHEMATICS
UNIVERSITY OF BOLOGNA
BOLOGNA, ITALY

Stability and Instability in a Two-Dimensional Dynamical System: A Mathematical Approach to Kaldor's Theory of the Trade Cycle

Franco Cugno
Luigi Montrucchio

1

The purpose of this chapter is to contribute to the mathematical theory of economic fluctuations related to Kaldor's 1940 model (see [3, 5-8, 11]).

By using the conceptual framework of the traditional Keynesian model, we obtain the differential system

$$\mu\dot{x}/x = f(x, z) - F(x, z),$$

$$\dot{z}/z = c_0 - f(x, z),$$

where x is the production of consumption goods to capital ratio, z the autonomous investment to capital ratio, f the capital growth rate, F the savings to capital ratio, c_0 the autonomous investment growth rate, $1/\mu$ the velocity of the reaction of x to discrepancies between this variable and the demand for consumption goods to capital ratio.

We shall discuss the qualitative behavior of the system under very general assumptions about the functions f and F. In particular, we shall discuss the Lagrange stability, the Liapunov stability, and the existence of cyclical solutions. The critical role played by the parameter μ will be stressed.

265

As far as cyclical solutions are concerned, we shall not consider the possibility of applying Hopf's theorem on bifurcations arising from a weak focus (see [10]). Otherwise, we should assume a greater smoothness for the functions (at least of the C^4 class, as Ruelle and Takens showed) and conditions on the third-order derivatives (the vague attraction condition) whose economic meaning is not easily defined.

Also, considering the influence of the parameter c_0 on the qualitative behavior of the system, we shall develop a generic bifurcation diagram on the (μ, c_0) plane. In addition, the structural stability (in a weaker meaning than Peixoto's) of the system will be investigated.

2

Let us assume a closed economy without public intervention and without technical progress. Let us assume further that prices, wages, and interest rates are constant in the Keynesian unemployment area, to which we restrict our analysis. Therefore we can analyze the behavior of the economy by the fixed-prices method (see [4]).

Part of the investment is considered autonomous and growing at the rate c_0. On the other hand, the nonautonomous investment is considered an increasing function of income and a decreasing function of the available capital. Then we can write

(1) $$I = I(Y, K) + A,$$

(2) $$\dot{A}/A = c_0,$$

where I is the global investment, Y the income, K the capital, A the autonomous investment, and $I_1' > 0, I_2' < 0$.

Further, let us assume that capital goods, once they are made, last forever, and let us assume that the equilibrium condition $I = I^0$, where I^0 is the production of investment goods, always holds. Then

(3) $$I = I^\circ = \dot{K}.$$

If we assume that I is homogeneous in the first degree in Y and K, since by definition

(4) $$Y = I^0 + C^0,$$

where C^0 is the production of consumption goods, and since by assumption I_1' is always smaller than unity, we can write

(5) $$I/K = f(C^0/K, A/K),$$

where $f_1' > 0, f_2' > 0$.

Let savings be an increasing function of Y and a decreasing function of K (which in this case represents the net wealth); i.e.,

(6) $$S = S(Y, K),$$

where S is savings and $S'_1 > 0, S'_2 < 0$.

Assuming that S is homogeneous in the first degree in Y and K and taking into account Eqs. (3), (4), and (6), we obtain

(7) $$S/K = F(C^0/K, A/K),$$

where $F'_1 > 0, F'_2 > 0$.

As far as consumption goods are concerned, we do not assume that the equilibrium condition $C = C^0$, where C is the demand for consumption goods, always holds, but we assume that, if C/K is greater (smaller) than C^0/K, then C^0/K will increase (decrease) over time. This assumption can be formalized as

(8) $$\mu(\dot{C}^0/C^0 - \dot{K}/K) = C/K - C^0/K,$$

where μ is a positive parameter.

Since

(9) $$C = Y - S,$$

by taking into account Eqs. (3), (4), and (8), we obtain

(10) $$\mu(\dot{C}^0/C^0 - \dot{K}/K) = I/K - S/K.$$

Therefore, we can write the following differential system:

$$(\sigma) \quad \begin{aligned} \mu(\dot{C}^0/C^0 - \dot{K}/K) &= f(C^0/K, A/K) - F(C^0/K, A/K), \\ \dot{A}/A - \dot{K}/K &= c_0 - f(C^0/K, A/K). \end{aligned}$$

3

Let us begin the qualitative analysis of the differential system (σ). If we write

$$C^0/K = x, \qquad A/K = z,$$

the system (σ) becomes

$$(\Sigma) \quad \begin{aligned} \mu\dot{x}/x &= f(x, z) - F(x, z), \\ \dot{z}/z &= c_0 - f(x, z). \end{aligned}$$

For the functions f and F we present the following hypotheses:

(H_1) f and F are defined and continuous on $Q = \{(x, z) | x \geq 0$ and $z \geq 0\}$.

(H_2) f and F are C^1 functions on $Q^+ = \{(x, z) | x > 0$ and $z > 0\}$, with partial derivatives having the following signs: $f'_x > 0$, $f'_z > 0$, $F'_x > 0$. For $F(x, z) = S[x + f(x, z), 1]$, the condition $F'_z > 0$ holds, but we shall drop this condition in order to generalize the model.

(H_3) For any $z > 0$ we can find a number $\varepsilon > 0$ and a number $E > 0$ such that for any couple (x_1, z_1) for which $|z - z_1| < \varepsilon$ and $x_1 > E$ we have

$$F(x_1, z_1) - f(x_1, z_1) > 0.$$

Moreover, for any $z \geq 0$ we can find a number $x_2 > 0$ such that we have

$$F(x, z) - f(x, z) < 0 \qquad \text{for any} \quad 0 \leq x \leq x_2.$$

In other terms, for any value of z, the capital growth rate is lower (higher) than the savings to capital ratio if the x level is adequately high (low). These assumptions are similar to Kaldor's hypotheses about the form of the investment and savings functions (see [6]).

(H_4) There exists only one couple $(x_0, z_0) \in Q^+$ warranting the steady state, i.e., such that

$$f(x_0, z_0) = F(x_0, z_0) = c_0.$$

Furthermore, at the point $P_0 \equiv (x_0, z_0)$ we have

$$f'_x(x_0, z_0) > F'_x(x_0, z_0),$$

$$F'_z(x_0, z_0)f'_x(x_0, z_0) - f'_z(x_0, z_0)F'_x(x_0, z_0) < 0.$$

The assumption that at the steady state point the capital growth rate is more sensitive than the savings/capital ratio to a change in x is similar to the fundamental Kaldorian hypothesis (see [6]).

Note that the last inequality is surely satisfied if $F(x, z) = S[x + f(x, z), 1]$. In fact, in this case $F'_z f'_x - f'_z F'_x = -S'_1 f'_z < 0$.

By the assumptions $H_1 - H_2 - H_4$, it follows that the set

$$\gamma = \{(x, z) \in Q^+ | f(x, z) = c_0\}$$

is a nonempty connected subvariety of Q^+. Moreover, γ is the graph of a C^1-differentiable function $x = \gamma(z)$ strictly decreasing.

(H_5) If $0 \in \bar{J}$, where J is the domain of $x = \gamma(z)$, then

$$\lim_{z \to 0^+} \gamma(z) = +\infty.$$

In such a way, we formalize the obvious condition that the equality between c_0 (the autonomous investment growth rate) and f (the capital growth rate) can hold only if z (the autonomous investment to capital ratio) is strictly positive.

(H_6) If the J interval is unbounded, then there must exist a number z^* sufficiently great that

$$\inf_{z \geqslant z^*} \inf_{0 \leqslant x \leqslant \gamma(z)} [f(x, z) - F(x, z)] \geqslant \eta > 0.$$

3.1. Proposition. The set $\{(x, z) \mid F(x, z) = c_0\}$ is a subvariety δ, which is the graph of a C^1-differentiable function $x = \delta(z)$. If we let I be the domain of $x = \delta(z)$, then $I \supseteq J$, and further,

$$\delta(z) < \gamma(z) \quad \text{for} \quad z < z_0 \quad \text{and} \quad z \in I \cap J,$$

$$\delta(z) > \gamma(z) \quad \text{for} \quad z > z_0 \quad \text{and} \quad z \in I \cap J.$$

3.2. Lemma. Let $P(t) = [x(t), z(t)]$ be a solution of system (Σ) which, at time $t = 0$, belongs to the region

$$\mathscr{D} = \{(x, z) \in Q^+ \mid z \geqslant z_0 \text{ and } x < \gamma(z)\}.$$

At a finite time $t > 0$, the orbit reaches γ at the point $P_2 \equiv [\gamma(z_2), z_2]$, where $z_2 > z(0) \geqslant z_0$.

Proof First, the solution $P(t)$ cannot reach in a finite time the half-line $x = 0$. In fact, by H_3 and H_6, there exists a number $L > 0$ such that $f - F \geqslant -L$ for any $(x, z) \in \mathscr{D}$. If we, *per absurdum*, let $\tau > 0$ be the time of the first intersection with $x = 0$, then we have

$$\dot{x}/x \geqslant -L/\mu \quad \text{for any} \quad t \in [0, \tau[.$$

Therefore, we should have

$$x(t) \geqslant x(0)e^{-(L/\mu)t} \geqslant x(0)e^{-(L/\mu)\tau},$$

which is manifestly absurd.

Let us assume therefore that $P(t) = [x(t), z(t)]$ belongs to $\mathscr{D}$ for any $t \geqslant 0$. Since $\dot{z}$ is always positive in $\mathscr{D}$, $z(t)$ is a strictly increasing function, so that there exists its (finite or infinite) limit

$$\lim_{t \to +\infty} z(t) = m > 0, \quad m \leqslant +\infty.$$

If we now consider the function

$$V(x, z) = \log x^\mu z,$$

we have

$$\dot{V}(t) = dV[x(t), z(t)]/dt = c_0 - F[x(t), z(t)] > 0$$

and also

$$\lim_{t \to +\infty} V(t) = M, \qquad M \le +\infty.$$

Let us assume now that $m < +\infty$ (and this must be the case if J is a bounded interval). Since $x(t)$ is bounded, there exists the finite limit

$$\lim_{t \to +\infty} \log x(t).$$

Therefore there exists also the finite limit $\lim_{t \to +\infty} x(t)$. So we can state that, as $t \to +\infty$, the trajectory approaches the only singular point $P_0 \equiv (x_0, z_0)$. But this cannot be true, since $z(t)$ is a strictly increasing function.

Let us assume now that $m = +\infty$, from which $M = +\infty$ and $\lim_{t \to +\infty} z(t) = +\infty$. Since $z(t)$ is monotonic, we can assume $z(t) > z^*$ for any $t \ge t_0$ (see H_6). So we have

$$0 \le x(t) \le \gamma[z(t)] \le \gamma(z^*).$$

By H_6 we obtain

$$\inf_{t \ge t_0} \{ f[x(t), z(t)] - F[x(t), z(t)] \} \ge \eta.$$

From the above statement, we obtain

$$\mu \dot{x}(t) \ge \eta x(t),$$

i.e.,

$$x(t) \ge x(t_0) \exp(\eta/\mu)(t - t_0).$$

But this conclusion is manifestly absurd, because the set of $x(t)$ for $t > 0$ is bounded.

This absurd result derives from having assumed that the positive semi-trajectory is contained in $\mathscr{D}$. Therefore the trajectory must reach γ at the point P_2 in a finite time (Fig. 1).　　Q.E.D.

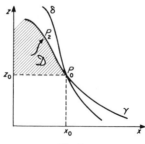

Fig. 1.

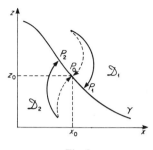

Fig. 2.

3.3. Theorem. Let $\mathscr{D}_1$ and $\mathscr{D}_2$ be the domains (Fig. 2)

$$\mathscr{D}_1 = \{(x, z) \in Q^+ \,|\, z > \gamma^{-1}(x)\},$$

$$\mathscr{D}_2 = Q^+ \backslash \mathscr{D}_1.$$

The positive semitrajectory through a point $P \in \mathscr{D}_1$ either approaches the singular point P_0 or intersect $x = \gamma(z)$ at the point $P_1 \equiv (x_1, z_1)$, where $x_1 > x_0$, within a finite time.
Similarly, the positive semitrajectory through a point $P \in \mathscr{D}_2$ either approaches the singular point P_0 or intersect $x = \gamma(z)$ at the point P_2 $\equiv (x_2, z_2)$, where $x_2 < x_0$.

Proof Let us assume, *per absurdum*, that, for any $t \geqslant 0$, $P(t) =$ $[x(t), z(t)]$ is contained in $\mathscr{D}_1$ and that $P(t)$ does not approach P_0.
By the usual arguments, since $\dot{z} < 0$ in $\mathscr{D}_1$, there exists the limit

$$\lim_{t \to +\infty} z(t) = m.$$

Then, by H_3, it is easy to find that $x(t)$ is bounded for $t \geqslant 0$. Therefore the ω-limit set of the trajectory is not empty.
The Poincaré–Bendixson theorem states that, for the two-dimensional dynamical system, there exist only three types of bounded ω-limit sets: singular points, closed orbits, and trajectories between two singular points (see [9]). Since all these cases are impossible, we find that the trajectory reaches γ.
The proof for the second part of this theorem is similar to the proof for Lemma 3.2.   Q.E.D.

3.4. Theorem.   The dynamical system (Σ) is positively Lagrange-stable in Q^+.

If the system does not admit closed orbits, then the singular point P_0 is a global attractor; that is, P_0 is a ω-limit for any point in Q^+. If $\mu < \mu_0$, where

$$\mu_0 = x_0[f'_x(x_0, z_0) - F'_x(x_0, z_0)]/z_0 f'_z(x_0, z_0),$$

then the system admits a nonstationary periodic solution.

Proof   By H_3 there exists a strip $OPML$ (Fig. 3) such that, for any couple (x, z) of the strip, we have

$$f(x, z) - F(x, z) \geqslant \eta > 0.$$

Let Γ be the trajectory through the point M. By Lemma 3.2, we know that Γ reaches γ at the point T. Because of H_3, there exists a segment QS parallel to the z-axis, where $F - f > 0$ holds. The domain $UMTQS$ (shaded in Fig. 3) is, by construction, positively invariant. Further, by Theorem 3.3, it follows that any positive semitrajectory through any point in Q^+ reaches the above-mentioned domain within a finite time. In other terms, the shaded domain is a global attractor for the system (Σ) (see [2]).

Let us now write the characteristic equation of the singular point P_0:

$$\mu\rho^2 + \rho\{\mu z_0 f'_z(P_0) - x_0[f'_x(P_0) - F'_x(P_0)]\} + z_0 x_0[f'_z(P_0)F'_x(P_0)$$
$$- f'_x(P_0)F'_z(P_0)] = 0.$$

By H_4, P_0 is always a singular nondegenerate point; i.e., its characteristic roots are not null.

Considering the signs of the roots, it follows that the singular point is locally asymptotically unstable (stable) if μ is smaller (greater) than μ_0.

The Poincaré–Bendixson theorem easily provides the other statements.

Q.E.D.

By Theorem 3.4 we can affirm that, under the assumptions H_1–H_2–H_3–H_4–H_5–H_6 and if $\mu < \mu_0$ (i.e., if the reaction velocity of x to the discrepancies between f and F is sufficiently high), x (the production of consumption goods

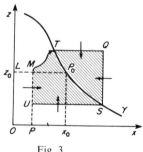

Fig. 3.

to capital ratio), z (the autonomous investment to capital ratio), f (the capital growth rate), and F (the savings/capital ratio) do not approach the steady-state, but they approach the oscillatory state.

In fact, the singular point of the system (Σ) is unstable, and further, any (Σ) orbit either is a closed orbit or it approaches a closed orbit.

4

Let us consider the role of the parameter c_0 and of the functions f and F in the system

$$(\Sigma(c, f, F)) \qquad \begin{aligned} \mu \dot{x}/x &= f(x, z) - F(x, z), \\ \dot{z}/z &= c - f(x, z), \end{aligned}$$

where $c \in I$ and $I \subseteq \mathbb{R}$ is a relatively compact interval containing c_0.

Let us assume that the functions f and F satisfy the assumptions $H_1 - H_2 - H_3 - H_4$ and that

(H_5') there exist a number $\varepsilon > 0$ and a number $N > 0$ such that

$$\inf_{x \geqslant N} \inf_{0 \leqslant z \leqslant \varepsilon} [c_0 - f(x, z)] > 0$$

(note that H_5' implies H_5);

(H_6') there exists a number z^* sufficiently great that

$$\inf_{c \in I} \inf_{z \geqslant z^*} \inf_{0 \leqslant x \leqslant \gamma_c(z)} [f(x, z) - F(x, z)] \geqslant \eta > 0,$$

where γ_c is the subvariety

$$\gamma_c = \{(x, z) \in Q^+ \mid f(x, z) = c\}.$$

Let us consider the perturbation space for the functions f and F.

Let K be a relatively compact open such that

$$P_0(x_0, z_0) \in K \qquad \text{and} \qquad \bar{K} \subset Q^+.$$

Let $\mathscr{P}$ be the vectorial space of the couples of the C^1 functions (ϕ, Φ) defined on Q^+ and with compact support contained in K.

Let us assign over $\mathscr{P}$ the C^1 topology, for example, with the norm

$$\|(\phi, \Phi)\| = \sup_{(x, z) \in Q^+} [|\phi| + |\Phi| + |\phi_x'| + |\Phi_x'| + |\phi_z'| + |\Phi_z'|].$$

In this way, the functional set

$$\mathscr{T}_K^1(f, F) = (f, F) + \mathscr{P}$$

becomes a Banach (linear) variety.

Since, for any μ, the set of systems $(\Sigma(c, \hat{f}, \hat{F}))$ has a one-to-one relationship with the triplet $(c, \hat{f}, \hat{F})$, we can topologize the set $(\Sigma(c, \hat{f}, \hat{F}))$ by identifying it with the product space

$$I \times \mathcal{T}^1_K(f, F).$$

4.1. Theorem. If the pair of functions (f, F) satisfies the assumptions H_1–H_2–H_3–H_4–H'_5–H'_6, then there exists a neighborhood of (c_0, f, F) in $I \times \mathcal{T}^1_K(f, F)$ such that, for any $(\hat{c}, \hat{f}, \hat{F})$ belonging to it, the same hypotheses hold.

Proof The proof is clear as far as the assumptions H_1–H_2–H_3–H'_5–H'_6 are concerned.

Let us show now that H_4 is stable. Let $\rho: I \times \mathcal{T} \to C^1(Q^+, \mathbb{R}^2)$ be the C^1 representation having the evaluation map

$$ev_\rho: I \times \mathcal{T} \times Q^+ \to \mathbb{R}^2,$$

defined by (see [1])

$$(c, \hat{f}, \hat{F}, x, z) \mapsto [\hat{f}(x, z) - \hat{F}(x, z), \hat{f}(x, z) - c].$$

Let W be the subvariety: $\{(0, 0)\} \subseteq \mathbb{R}^2$. If

$$\rho_{(c, \hat{f}, \hat{F})}(x, z) \in W, \quad \text{i.e.,} \quad \hat{f}(x, z) = \hat{F}(x, z) = c,$$

it follows that

$$\rho_{(c, \hat{f}, \hat{F})} \pitchfork_{(x, z)} W$$

if and only if

$$\hat{F}'_z(x, z)\hat{f}'_x(x, z) - \hat{f}'_z(x, z)\hat{F}'_x(x, z) \neq 0.$$

Therefore, since assumption H_4 holds for (f, F), it follows by the transversal intersection openness theorem (see [1]) that the set

$$\mathcal{A}_M = \{(c, \hat{f}, \hat{F}) \in I \times \mathcal{T} \mid \rho_{(c, \hat{f}, \hat{F})} \pitchfork_{(x, z)} W, \forall(x, z) \in M\},$$

where M is a compact contained in Q^+ and is open and nonempty.

By H'_6 it follows that the set of (x, z) solutions of

$$\begin{aligned}\hat{F}(x, z) &= c, \\ \hat{f}(x, z) &= c,\end{aligned} \quad c \in I \quad \text{and} \quad (\hat{f}, \hat{F}) \in \mathcal{T}^1_K(f, F)$$

are contained in a compact $M \subset Q^+$.

Therefore the set

$$\mathcal{A} = \{(c, f, F) \in I \times \mathcal{T}^1 \mid \rho_{(c, \hat{f}, \hat{F})} \pitchfork W\}$$

is an open set.

Utilizing the transversal intersection isotopy property (see [1]) and further considering a smaller neighborhood, it follows that, for any $(c, \hat{f}, \hat{F}) \in \mathscr{A}$, the system $(\Sigma(c, \hat{f}, \hat{F}))$ has only a singular point in Q^+. Besides, the dependence of the singular point $P(c, \hat{f}, \hat{F})$ on $(c, \hat{f}, \hat{F})$ is C^1-differentiable.

By the latter property, it is easy to show that the following inequality also holds:

$$\hat{f}'_x(P) > \hat{F}'_x(P). \qquad \text{Q.E.D.}$$

Theorem 4.1 states a certain "structural stability" for the model.

Let us consider now the instability points (bifurcations) of the model. Let us add the simplifying hypotheses:

(H$_7$) $\qquad F'_z(x, z)f'_x(x, z) - f'_z(x, z)F'_x(x, z) < 0 \qquad \forall (x, z) \in Q^+.$

4.2. Lemma. Under the assumptions H_1–H_2–H_3–H_4–H'_5–H'_6–H_7, there exists an open neighborhood Ω of (f, F) in $\mathscr{T}^1_K(f, F)$ such that, for any $(\hat{f}, \hat{F}) \in \Omega$, the above assumptions hold.

Further, for any term $(c, \hat{f}, \hat{F}) \in I \times \Omega$ the system $(\Sigma(c, \hat{f}, \hat{F}))$ has only one singular point $P[x(c, \hat{f}, \hat{F}), z(c, \hat{f}, \hat{F})]$ differentiably depending on $(c, \hat{f}, \hat{F})$.

Proof See the proof of Theorem 4.1.

4.3. Lemma. If, in addition to the assumptions of Lemma 4.2, f and F are of the C^2 class and if we let $\mathscr{T}^2_K(f, F)$ be the C^2-perturbations space with compact support contained in K and if $K \supseteq M$ (see Theorem 4.1), then there exists a subset $\hat{\Omega}$ that is open and dense in Ω, with the property

$$(x, z) \in M \qquad \text{and} \qquad \hat{f}(x, z) - \hat{F}(x, z) = 0$$

and

$$\hat{f}'_x(x, z) - \hat{F}'_x(x, z) = 0 \Rightarrow \hat{f}''_{xx}(x, z) - \hat{F}''_{xx}(x, z) \neq 0 \qquad \forall (\hat{f}, \hat{F}) \in \hat{\Omega}.$$

Proof Let ρ be the C^1 representation with the evaluation map

$$ev_\rho: \mathscr{T}^2_K(f, F) \times K \to \mathbb{R}^2$$

defined by

$$(\hat{f}, \hat{F}, x, z) \mapsto [\hat{f}(x, z) - \hat{F}(x, z), \hat{f}'_x(x, z) - \hat{F}'_x(x, z)].$$

Since ev_ρ is a submersion, it follows that $ev_\rho \pitchfork W$, where $W \equiv \{(0, 0)\} \subseteq \mathbb{R}^2$.

Therefore, by the transversal density theorem (see [1]), the set

$$\mathscr{A} = \{(\hat{f}, \hat{F}) \in \mathscr{T}^2 \mid \rho_{(\hat{f}, \hat{F})} \pitchfork W\}$$

is residual in $\mathscr{T}^2_K(f, F)$.

Therefore, for the open set

$$\mathcal{B} = \{(\hat{f}, \hat{F}) \in \mathcal{T}^2 \,|\, \rho_{(\hat{f}, \hat{F})} \pitchfork_{(x, z)} W, \forall (x, z) \in M\},$$

we have the inclusion $\mathcal{B} \supseteq \mathcal{A}$, and therefore $\mathcal{B}$ is also dense in $\mathcal{T}^2$.
Considering now the transversality condition

$$\rho_{(\hat{f}, \hat{F})} \pitchfork_{(x, z)} W,$$

we can state

$$(\hat{f}'_z - \hat{F}'_z)(\hat{f}''_{xx} - \hat{F}''_{xx}) \neq 0$$

if

$$(\hat{f}, \hat{F}) \in \mathcal{B}$$

and

$$\hat{f}(x, z) - \hat{F}(x, z) = \hat{f}'_x(x, z) - \hat{F}'_x(x, z) = 0. \qquad \text{Q.E.D.}$$

4.4. Theorem.   Under the assumptions of Lemmas 4.2 and 4.3, for any $(\hat{f}, \hat{F}) \in \hat{\Omega}$, the set of the points $c \in I$ for which

$$\hat{f}'_x[x(c), z(c)] = \hat{F}'_x[x(c), z(c)],$$

where $P(c) = [x(c), z(c)]$ is the only singular point of the system $(\Sigma(c, \hat{f}, \hat{F}))$, is a discrete set in I.

If we let $(\ldots, \hat{c}_{-1}, \hat{c}_1, \hat{c}_2, \ldots)$ be the above discrete set (where $\hat{c}_{-1} < c_0 < \hat{c}_1$), the sign of $\hat{f}'_x[x(c), z(c)] - \hat{F}'_x[x(c), z(c)]$ is constant on any interval $[\hat{c}_i, \hat{c}_{i+1}]$ and further is different on contiguous intervals.

Proof   Let θ be the C^1 mapping

$$\theta: I \to \mathbb{R}, \qquad c \mapsto \hat{f}'_x[x(c), z(c)] - \hat{F}'_x[x(c), z(c)].$$

Let us write the condition $\theta \pitchfork \{0\}$. Then $d\theta/dc \neq 0$ for any c for which $\theta(c) = 0$.
Since

$$d\theta/dc = (\hat{f}''_{xx} - \hat{F}''_{xx}) \, dx/dc + (\hat{f}''_{xz} - \hat{F}''_{xz}) \, dz/dc,$$

where

$$dz/dc = -(\hat{f}'_x - \hat{F}'_x)/(\hat{f}'_z \hat{F}'_x - \hat{f}'_x \hat{F}'_z),$$
$$dx/dc = (\hat{f}'_z - \hat{F}'_z)/(\hat{f}'_z \hat{F}'_x - \hat{f}'_x \hat{F}'_z),$$

then

$$d\theta/dc = (\hat{f}''_{xx} - \hat{F}''_{xx}) \, dx/dc$$

for any c for which $\theta(c) = 0$.

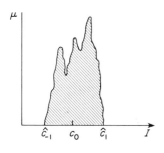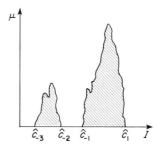

Fig. 4.

By Lemma 4.3, we have that $d\theta/dc \neq 0$ for any $(\hat{f}, \hat{F}) \in \hat{\Omega}$. Further, by $\theta \pitchfork \{0\}$, it follows that the subset $\theta^{-1}(0) \subset I$ is a one-codimensional sub-variety of I. The zero existence theorem provides, if applied to the θ map, the remaining conclusions.   Q.E.D.

Theorem 4.4 allows us to draw on the (μ, c) plane a qualitative bifurcation diagram for the singular point of a "typical" system.

If $(\hat{f}, \hat{F}) \in \hat{\Omega}$ (the residual set of Lemmas 4.2 and 4.3) and if we let $P(c) = [x(c), z(c)]$ be the singular point, the characteristic equation of $P(c)$ is

$$\mu\rho^2 + \rho[\mu z(c)\hat{f}_z' - x(c)(\hat{f}_x' - \hat{F}_x')] + x(c)z(c)(\hat{f}_z'\hat{F}_x' - \hat{f}_x'\hat{F}_z') = 0.$$

If we let μ_0 be the number

$$\mu_0 = x(c)\{\hat{f}_x'[x(c), z(c)] - \hat{F}_x'[x(c), z(c)]\}/z(c)\hat{f}_z'[x(c), z(c)],$$

the singular point $P(c)$ is locally stable for $\mu > \mathrm{Max}(0, \mu_0)$ and locally unstable for $\mu < \mathrm{Max}(0, \mu_0)$.

By Theorem 4.4, we can draw a diagram (Fig. 4) where the shaded areas represent the set of the unstable states.

5. SUMMARY

We saw that, under more general conditions than Chang and Smyth's (see [3]), the Kaldorian model presents the following characteristics:

(1) Lagrange stability, which is an essential requisite for an economic model.

(2) The existence of periodic nonconstant solutions if the velocity of reaction of C°/K to the discrepancies between f and F is high enough.

(3) "Structural stability," which is an essential requisite for a theoretical model.

In addition, we observed the system behavior by varying the autonomous investment growth rate. The result we obtained is necessarily vague, because of the extreme generality of the functions f and F. Such a generality does not even allow us to obtain simple results either about the global stability or about the number of periodic solutions and their stability. What we can surely affirm is that, given μ and c, the Kupka–Smale theorem allows the possibility of shifting the former system slightly so that it admits a finite number of periodic orbits, stable and unstable in turn. The most difficult part, which we did not face, is the study of orbit variations when μ and c vary, in other words, analysis of the system bifurcation points.

REFERENCES

1. Abraham, R., and Robbin, J., "Transversal Mapping and Flows." Benjamin, New York, 1967.
2. Bhatia, N. P., and Szegö, G. P., "Dynamical Systems: Stability Theory and Applications." Springer-Verlag, Berlin and New York, 1967.
3. Chang, W. W., and Smyth, D. J., The existence of cycles in a non-linear model: Kaldor's 1940 model reexamined, *Review of Economic Studies* 38, 37–44 (1971).
4. Hicks, R., "Capital and Growth." Oxford University Press, London and New York, 1965.
5. Ichimura, S., Toward a general non-linear macroeconomic theory of economic fluctuations, *in* "Post-Keynesian Economics" (K. K. Kurihara, ed.). Rutgers University Press, New Brunswick, New Jersey, 1955.
6. Kaldor, N., A model of the trade cycles, *Economic Journal* 50, 78–92 (1940).
7. Klein, L. R., and Preston, R. S., Stochastic non-linear models, *Econometrica* 37, 96–106 (1969).
8. Kosobud, R. S., and O'Neill, W. D., Stochastic implications of orbital asymptotic stability of a non-linear trade cycle model, *Econometrica* 40, 69–86 (1972).
9. Sansone, G., and Conti, R., "Non-Linear Differential Equations." Pergamon, Oxford, 1964.
10. Torre, V., Existence of limit cycles and control in complete Keynesian systems by theory of bifurcations, *Econometrica* 45, 1457–1466 (1977).
11. Yasui, T., Self-excited oscillations and business cycles, Cowles Commission Discussion Paper, no. 2056, 1953.

Franco Cugno
COGNETTI DE MARTIIS LABORATORY
  OF POLITICAL ECONOMY
UNIVERSITY OF TURIN
TURIN, ITALY

Luigi Montrucchio
MATHEMATICS INSTITUTE
TURIN POLYTECHNIC
TURIN, ITALY

Competitive Equilibrium and Indivisible Commodities

Aldo Montesano

1. INTRODUCTION

The usual demonstrations of the existence of a competitive equilibrium require, by assumption, the divisibility of commodities. This assumption is needed to ensure that the choice of economic agents be continuous, as required by the fixed-point theorems on which these demonstrations are based. Since the perfect divisibility for all commodities seems to be a convenient assumption for the analysis, though not necessary or realistic, we must verify whether the presence of indivisible commodities significantly alters the results at which the economic analysis obtains through the assumption of perfect divisibility. For this purpose, the problem of the existence of a competitive equilibrium is certainly of great relevance. In other words, we must verify whether the perfect divisibility of commodities is only a convenient assumption for the existence of a competitive equilibrium or a determining one.

The problem of the existence of a competitive equilibrium in economies with indivisible commodities has been examined by Henry [7], Dierker [4], Broome [2], and Mas-Colell [9].[1] Henry has demonstrated that a competitive

---

[1] The last article was published after the Bressanone conference, but before the final version of this chapter was ready.

equilibrium exists if there are two commodities, only one of which is indivisible, and $m \geq 2$ agents. He has also shown that a competitive equilibrium does not necessarily exist if there are more than two commodities, of which at least one is indivisible. Dierker, Broome, and Mas-Colell have demonstrated, with different assumptions, that when the number of agents is very large, an equilibrium can be defined with a price vector that determines agents' choices not feasible by an amount that is negligible with regard to the size of the economy. These demonstrations require assumptions that are not completely satisfactory, mainly because some fundamental features of economies with indivisible commodities are disregarded. The principal one, from a realistic point of view, is that the number of indivisible commodities is not constant (as the demonstrations assume) and that the amount of each indivisible commodity does not necessarily increase when the number of agents increases. In fact, many indivisible commodities are similar to masters' paintings: If the paintings of a master are considered units of an indivisible commodity and the paintings of different masters different commodities, then, when the size of the economy increases, the total amount of each commodity remains constant while the number of commodities increases (if the number of masters increases). Moreover, Broome and Mas-Colell[2] assume the presence, along with the indivisible commodities, of a divisible commodity that is so strongly preferred to the indivisible ones by the agents that a "sufficient gain in the divisible commodity will make up for any other loss."[3] Let us emphasize the importance given to this divisible commodity in economies characterized by the presence of indivisible commodities. On the contrary, as shown later, if fundamental indivisibilities prevail, not only may a competitive equilibrium not exist, but there may be no tendency toward equilibrium either when the size of the economy increases.

A preliminary methodology question, which is not so evident in the analysis of an economy with divisible commodities (though existing there, too), involves a definition of the homogeneity of commodities. First, the test for establishing the economic homogeneity of commodities cannot be merely a physical one, because an agent can evaluate two physically identical commodities as not necessarily being identical. Consequently, based on this agent's preferences, such commodities would not be considered homogeneous. Furthermore, a psychological test is not sufficient either. In other words, it is not sufficient that two commodities be considered identical by all agents for them to be economically homogeneous: in fact, in a competitive economy they might also have different prices. This aspect does not seem to be con-

[2] Mas-Colell [9] also considers agents a continuum, an assumption that seems incompatible with the presence of indivisible commodities.

[3] Broome [2, p. 228 (assumption 2.5)] and Mas-Colell [9, p. 445 (assumption 2)].

sidered in the economics literature, where the economic homogeneity of commodities is based on a physical and/or psychological test,[4] on the implicit assumption that physical and/or psychological homogeneity necessarily implies the existence of a unique price for each of the commodity units. On the contrary, as we shall later demonstrate in Example C, commodities considered perfect substitutes by all agents can have different prices. Furthermore, this condition can be essential to the existence of a competitive equilibrium. The methodological consequence of this argument is that an economy with indivisible commodities must be generally analyzed by considering them all unique, i.e., commodities of which there is only one unit, while in the economics literature dealing with equilibrium in economies with indivisible commodities, the case of unique commodities is not considered at all.

In the first part of this chapter, it is demonstrated by an example that a pure exchange economy with unique commodities does not necessarily allow a competitive equilibrium, both in economies with unique commodities only and in those having divisible ones also. In addition, it is shown that a competitive equilibrium does not necessarily represent a Pareto optimum and that a Pareto optimum does not necessarily correspond to a competitive equilibrium. In the second part of this chapter, we shall demonstrate that there is a competitive pseudoequilibrium that is defined, for an economy with unique commodities, by making the economy convex and closing it in a certain way. After defining the degree of disequilibrium occurring in the case of a competitive pseudoequilibrium, we must analyze whether it decreases when the economy grows. (Should this happen, the competitive pseudo-equilibrium would give us a good approximation of a large-dimension competitive economy with indivisible commodities). Two examples are given where the degree of disequilibrium remains constant: the first with two agents and an increasing number of unique commodities, and the second with an increasing number of agents and commodities.

2. THE PROBLEM OF THE EXISTENCE OF A COMPETITIVE EQUILIBRIUM IN AN ECONOMY WITH UNIQUE (OR INDIVISIBLE) COMMODITIES

We consider, for the sake of simplicity, a pure exchange economy, i.e., one without the production of commodities.[5] First we shall examine the case

---

[4] For Debreu [3, p. 30] for instance, this test is merely physical: "A commodity is . . . defined by a specification of all its physical characteristics, of its availability date, and of its availability location. As soon as one of these three factors changes, a different commodity results."

[5] The problems created by the presence of indivisible commodities in the production theory are analyzed by Frank [5].

in which all commodities are unique. Each agent owns, before the exchange, some unique commodities. These commodities can be reallocated among the agents if they benefit, i.e., if each of them obtains a commodity bundle preferable to the initial one. A stochastic allocation process leading to a Pareto optimum, also in the case of indivisible commodities, is described by Hurwicz, Radner, and Reiter.[6] The problem considered here concerns the existence of a competitive equilibrium, chiefly the existence of a system of equilibrium prices. Of course, since we are considering an economy with only unique commodities, the ratio between two prices does not indicate a direct exchange ratio between the two commodities, but an indirect one. In fact, the unique unit of a commodity is not necessarily exchanged for the unique unit of another commodity (therefore with an exchange ratio necessarily equal to one), but we can have complex exchanges among the agents for which the price ratios are not unity.

In slightly formal terms the problem appears in the following way, with n unique commodities and m agents.

The commodity set is represented by the subset B^n of R^n and is composed of 2^n vectors with n elements, each equal to zero or one. In other words, having defined the set B of numbers 0 and 1, i.e., $B = \{0, 1\}$, the set B^n is the Cartesian product of n sets B. Therefore, the set B^n is composed of 2^n isolated points (in this way, it is not connected and, consequently, convex). The preferences of the ith agent (with $i = 1, \ldots, m$) at the points $\mathbf{x}$ of the set B^n are assumed to be such that there is a complete and transitive preference ordering. More precisely, we assume that for any pair of vectors $\mathbf{x}, \mathbf{y} \in B^n$, we have $\mathbf{x} \gtrsim_i \mathbf{y}$ or $\mathbf{y} \gtrsim_i \mathbf{x}$ (complete ordering) and that for any triplet of vectors $\mathbf{x}, \mathbf{y}, \mathbf{z} \in B^n$ with $\mathbf{x} \gtrsim_i \mathbf{y}$ and $\mathbf{y} \gtrsim_i \mathbf{z}$, we have $\mathbf{x} \gtrsim_i \mathbf{z}$ (transitive ordering). (The symbol $\gtrsim_i$ indicates a weak preference, i.e., $\mathbf{x} \gtrsim_i \mathbf{y}$ means that the ith agent considers bundle $\mathbf{x}$ no less better than bundle $\mathbf{y}$. In addition, the symbol $\succ_i$ is used to indicate a strong preference, i.e, $\mathbf{x} \succ_i \mathbf{y}$ means that $\mathbf{x} \gtrsim_i \mathbf{y}$ holds and $\mathbf{y} \gtrsim_i \mathbf{x}$ does not; and the symbol $\sim_i$ is used to indicate indifference, i.e., $\mathbf{x} \sim_i \mathbf{y}$ means that both $\mathbf{x} \gtrsim_i \mathbf{y}$ and $\mathbf{y} \gtrsim_i \mathbf{x}$ hold).

Let the initial commodity bundle of the ith agent (with $i = 1, \ldots, m$) be represented by the vector $\bar{\mathbf{x}}_i \in B^n$. Since we are examining a pure exchange economy, we have

$$\sum_{i=1}^{m} \bar{\mathbf{x}}_i = \mathbf{e},$$

where $\mathbf{e}$ is the vector whose elements are all equal to one, i.e., the totality of commodities of the economy. A price vector $\mathbf{p}$ is defined as a semipositive

---

[6] Hurwicz et al. [8, especially pp. 203–205].

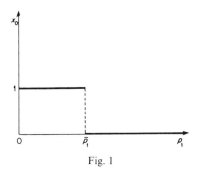

Fig. 1

vector with n elements (i.e., a vector whose elements are all nonnegative and at least one is positive).

In a competitive economy, the choice of the ith agent is represented, for any vector $\mathbf{p}$, by one or more vectors $\hat{\mathbf{x}}_i \in B^n$ for which the budget constraint is satisfied, i.e.,

$$\mathbf{p}'(\hat{\mathbf{x}}_i - \bar{\mathbf{x}}_i) \leq 0,$$

which are, moreover, preferred to all the other vectors that satisfy the budget constraint, i.e., we have $\hat{\mathbf{x}}_i \succsim_i \mathbf{y}$ with respect to all vectors $\mathbf{y} \in B^n$ for which $\mathbf{p}'(\mathbf{y} - \bar{\mathbf{x}}_i) \leq 0$. (If two or more of the vectors $\hat{\mathbf{x}}_i$ correspond to the same vector $\mathbf{p}$, these vectors are indifferent to the ith agent). The set of vectors $\hat{\mathbf{x}}_i$ associated in this way with vector $\mathbf{p}$ represents the choice of the ith agent, which can be indicated formally as the mapping $\phi_i(\mathbf{p})$, where

$$\phi_i(\mathbf{p}) = \{\hat{\mathbf{x}}_i | \hat{\mathbf{x}}_i \in B^n, \mathbf{p}'(\hat{\mathbf{x}}_i - \bar{\mathbf{x}}_i) \leq 0; \mathbf{p}'(\mathbf{y} - \bar{\mathbf{x}}_i) \leq 0 \Rightarrow \hat{\mathbf{x}}_i \succsim_i \mathbf{y} \ \forall \ \mathbf{y} \in B^n\}.$$

We note that the point-to-set mapping $\phi_i(\mathbf{p})$ (which is generally a multivalued function that becomes a single-valued function if only one vector $\hat{\mathbf{x}}_i$ is associated with each vector $\mathbf{p}$) is not necessarily continuous and not even upper semicontinuous (or closed).[7] In fact, it is sufficient that the choice $\hat{\mathbf{x}}_i$ is not the same for all vectors $\mathbf{p}$ to have a discontinuity; it is sufficient that there is only one vector $\hat{\mathbf{x}}_i$ corresponding to a vector $\mathbf{p}$ where the image set $\phi_i(\mathbf{p})$ is not connected in order for the mapping $\phi_i(\mathbf{p})$ not to be upper semicontinuous. A possible section of the mapping $\phi_i(\mathbf{p})$ in the plane with axes p_1, x_1 is represented in Fig. 1, which shows a mapping that is not upper semicontinuous at $\bar{p}_1$ if $\hat{x}_1 = 1$ corresponds to $\bar{p}_1$ but $\hat{x}_1 = 0$ does not.

---

[7] Nikaido [10, pp. 65–66] distinguishes between upper semicontinuous and closed mappings. On the other hand, Arrow and Hahn [1, p. 423] call upper semicontinuous those mappings that Nikaido calls closed. A mapping $\phi(x)$ is called upper semicontinuous (closed, following Nikaido) at x if for any sequences $\{x^v\}$ and $\{y^v\}$ the conditions $x^v \to x$, $y^v \to y$, and $y^v \in \phi(x^v)$ for all v imply $y \in \phi(x)$. An equivalent definition requires, for every real number α, that the set $\{x | x \in X, \phi(x) \geq \alpha\}$ be closed.

Considering all agents, we can define a mapping $\phi(\mathbf{p})$, which expresses the collective choice:

$$\phi(\mathbf{p}) = \sum_{i=1}^{m} \phi_i(\mathbf{p}),$$

i.e., for each $\mathbf{p}$, the image set $\phi(\mathbf{p})$ is composed of all the vectors obtained by summing the vectors of the image sets $\phi_i(\mathbf{p})$.

A competitive equilibrium requires that there exist at least one pair of vectors $\mathbf{p}^*$ and $\mathbf{x}^*$ with

$$\mathbf{p}^* \geqslant \mathbf{0}, \qquad \mathbf{x}^* \in \phi(\mathbf{p}^*), \qquad \mathbf{x}^* \leq \mathbf{e}, \qquad \mathbf{p}^{*\prime}(\mathbf{x}^* - \mathbf{e}) = 0.$$

(This condition means that there is, among the choices that correspond to the equilibrium prices $\mathbf{p}^*$, a choice that requires a unitary quantity of the commodities whose prices are positive and a null or unitary quantity of the commodities whose prices are zero.) For $\mathbf{p}^* > \mathbf{0}$, the equilibrium condition is $\mathbf{e} \in \phi(\mathbf{p}^*)$.

Example A. It will now be shown by a numerical example that a competitive equilibrium might not exist in an economy such as the one previously described. Let us consider an economy with two agents and four commodities, i.e., with $m = 2$ and $n = 4$. The initial bundles are

$$\overline{\mathbf{x}}_1 = \begin{bmatrix} 1 \\ 1 \\ 0 \\ 0 \end{bmatrix}, \qquad \overline{\mathbf{x}}_2 = \begin{bmatrix} 0 \\ 0 \\ 1 \\ 1 \end{bmatrix}.$$

The preferences of both agents are such that for any pair of vectors $\mathbf{x}, \mathbf{y} \in B^4$, if $\mathbf{e}'(\mathbf{x} - \mathbf{y}) > 0$, then $\mathbf{x} \succ_i \mathbf{y}$ (with $i = 1,2$); if $\mathbf{e}'\mathbf{x} = \mathbf{e}'\mathbf{y} = 3$ or 1, then $\mathbf{x} \sim_i \mathbf{y}$. Furthermore, having defined the vectors

$$\mathbf{a}_1 = \begin{bmatrix} 1 \\ 1 \\ 0 \\ 0 \end{bmatrix}, \quad \mathbf{a}_2 = \begin{bmatrix} 0 \\ 0 \\ 1 \\ 1 \end{bmatrix}, \quad \mathbf{a}_3 = \begin{bmatrix} 1 \\ 0 \\ 1 \\ 0 \end{bmatrix}, \quad \mathbf{a}_4 = \begin{bmatrix} 1 \\ 0 \\ 0 \\ 1 \end{bmatrix}, \quad \mathbf{a}_5 = \begin{bmatrix} 0 \\ 1 \\ 1 \\ 0 \end{bmatrix}, \quad \mathbf{a}_6 = \begin{bmatrix} 0 \\ 1 \\ 0 \\ 1 \end{bmatrix},$$

the preferences of the two agents are, respectively,

$$\mathbf{a}_3 \sim_1 \mathbf{a}_6 \succ_1 \mathbf{a}_1 \succ_1 \mathbf{a}_2 \succ_1 \mathbf{a}_4 \sim_1 \mathbf{a}_5$$

and

$$\mathbf{a}_4 \sim_2 \mathbf{a}_5 \succ_2 \mathbf{a}_2 \succ_2 \mathbf{a}_1 \succ_2 \mathbf{a}_3 \sim_2 \mathbf{a}_6.$$

Since each agent can retain the initial commodity bundle (no matter what the prices are), we examine, in order to look for a competitive equilibrium, only the commodity bundles $x \in B^4$ with $e'x \geq 2$ and, for $e'x = 2$, only those bundles for which $x \gtrsim_i \bar{x}_i$.

The equilibrium condition requires (since we must have for an equilibrium, with the previously assumed preferences, no commodity whose price is zero) that there be a pair of vectors $x_1 \gtrsim_1 \bar{x}_1$ and $x_2 \gtrsim_2 \bar{x}_2$ such that

$$x_1 + x_2 = \bar{x}_1 + \bar{x}_2 = e.$$

This equality is satisfied only in one case, when $x_1 = a_1$ and $x_2 = a_2$, i.e., if both agents retain their initial bundles. However, in order for this allocation to be competitive equilibrium, prices must be such that neither of the two agents can obtain a commodity bundle that is preferred, respectively, to a_1 or a_2. In other words, for the first agent, since he prefers bundles a_3 and a_6 to bundle a_1— the prices must be such that

$$p'(a_3 - \bar{x}_1) > 0, \qquad p'(a_6 - \bar{x}_1) > 0,$$

i.e.,

$$p_3 > p_2, \qquad p_4 > p_1.$$

Similarly for the second agent, since he prefers bundles a_4 and a_5 to bundle a_2, the prices must be such that

$$p'(a_4 - \bar{x}_2) > 0, \qquad p'(a_5 - \bar{x}_2) > 0,$$

i.e.,

$$p_1 > p_3, \qquad p_2 > p_4.$$

These conditions, however, are contradictory, since they require prices that must be

$$p_3 + p_4 > p_1 + p_2$$

to make the first agent choose bundle a_1, and

$$p_1 + p_2 > p_3 + p_4$$

to make the second agent choose bundle a_2.

Therefore, we have shown that a competitive equilibrium does not exist for Example A. Moreover, the allocation $x_1 = \bar{x}_1$ and $x_2 = \bar{x}_2$ is a Pareto optimum. Consequently, we have a Pareto optimum that is not a competitive equilibrium.

The nonexistence of a competitive equilibrium depends directly on the indivisibility of the commodities. In fact, if we consider an example that differs from Example A only in this feature, we find that there exists a competitive equilibrium. Let us assume that the two agents have preferences described by the utility functions

$$U_1 = 3x_{11}x_{13} + 3x_{12}x_{14} + 2x_{11}x_{12} + x_{13}x_{14} - x_{11}x_{12}(x_{13} + x_{14})$$
$$- \tfrac{11}{2}(x_{11}^2 + x_{12}^2 + x_{13}^3 + x_{14}^2) + 10(x_{11} + x_{12} + x_{13} + x_{14}),$$

$$U_2 = 3x_{22}x_{23} + 3x_{21}x_{24} + 2x_{23}x_{24} + x_{21}x_{22} - x_{23}x_{24}(x_{21} + x_{22})$$
$$- \tfrac{11}{2}(x_{21}^2 + x_{22}^2 + x_{23}^2 + x_{24}^2) + 10(x_{21} + x_{22} + x_{23} + x_{24}),$$

where $0 \le x_{ij} \le 1$ indicates the quantity of the jth commodity relative to the ith agent (with $i = 1, 2$ and $j = 1, \ldots, 4$). These utility functions represent a preference ordering which is, for $\mathbf{x} \in B^4$, the same as that assumed in the example with unique commodities. However, we find that there exists a unique competitive equilibrium with

$$p_1^* = p_2^* = p_3^* = p_4^* > 0,$$
$$x_{11}^* = x_{12}^* = x_{23}^* = x_{24}^* = (27 - \sqrt{573})/6,$$
$$x_{21}^* = x_{22}^* = x_{13}^* = x_{14}^* = (-21 + \sqrt{573})/6.$$

Not even the presence of divisible commodities, together with indivisible ones, necessarily determines the existence of a competitive equilibrium. In fact, we can obtain from example A an example without a competitive equilibrium, although there are divisible commodities.

Example B. In this example there are two agents, four unique commodities, and one perfectly divisible commodity. The initial commodity bundles are

$$\overline{\mathbf{x}}_1 = \begin{bmatrix} \mathbf{a}_1 \\ \hline \overline{m}_1 \end{bmatrix}, \qquad \overline{\mathbf{x}}_2 = \begin{bmatrix} \mathbf{a}_2 \\ \hline \overline{m}_2 \end{bmatrix},$$

where the subvectors $\mathbf{a}_1$ and $\mathbf{a}_2$ have been defined previously in Example A and the elements $\overline{m}_1$ and $\overline{m}_2$ indicate the quantities of the divisible commodity owned by the two agents before the exchange. The preferences of the agents are such that for every agent

$$\begin{bmatrix} \mathbf{a}_k \\ \hline m_k \end{bmatrix} \succ_i \begin{bmatrix} \mathbf{a}_j \\ \hline m_j \end{bmatrix}, \qquad i = 1, 2,$$

if $\mathbf{e}'\mathbf{a}_k > \mathbf{e}'\mathbf{a}_j$ or if $\mathbf{e}'\mathbf{a}_k = \mathbf{e}'\mathbf{a}_j$ and $m_k > m_j$. Then we have for the first agent

$$\begin{bmatrix} \mathbf{a}_3 \\ \hline m_1 \end{bmatrix} \sim_1 \begin{bmatrix} \mathbf{a}_6 \\ \hline m_1 \end{bmatrix} \succ_1 \begin{bmatrix} \mathbf{a}_1 \\ \hline m_1 \end{bmatrix} \succ_1 \begin{bmatrix} \mathbf{a}_2 \\ \hline m_1 \end{bmatrix} \succ_1 \begin{bmatrix} \mathbf{a}_4 \\ \hline m_1 \end{bmatrix} \sim_1 \begin{bmatrix} \mathbf{a}_5 \\ \hline m_1 \end{bmatrix}$$

and for the second agent

$$\begin{bmatrix} \mathbf{a}_4 \\ \hline m_2 \end{bmatrix} \sim_2 \begin{bmatrix} \mathbf{a}_5 \\ \hline m_2 \end{bmatrix} \succ_2 \begin{bmatrix} \mathbf{a}_2 \\ \hline m_2 \end{bmatrix} \succ_2 \begin{bmatrix} \mathbf{a}_1 \\ \hline m_2 \end{bmatrix} \succ_2 \begin{bmatrix} \mathbf{a}_3 \\ \hline m_2 \end{bmatrix} \sim_2 \begin{bmatrix} \mathbf{a}_6 \\ \hline m_2 \end{bmatrix}.$$

As in the example without divisible commodities (Example A), the unique pair of vectors $\mathbf{x}_1 \succsim_1 \bar{\mathbf{x}}_1$ and $\mathbf{x}_2 \succsim_2 \bar{\mathbf{x}}_2$, with

$$\mathbf{x}_1 + \mathbf{x}_2 = \bar{\mathbf{x}}_1 + \bar{\mathbf{x}}_2,$$

results to be $\mathbf{x}_1 = \bar{\mathbf{x}}_1$ and $\mathbf{x}_2 = \bar{\mathbf{x}}_2$. But, in order for this allocation to represent a competitive equilibrium, the prices must be such that neither of the two agents can obtain a preferred commodity bundle. In other words, for the first agent the prices must be such that

$$\mathbf{p}'\left[\left(\frac{\mathbf{a}_3}{m_1}\right) - \bar{\mathbf{x}}_1\right] > 0, \qquad \mathbf{p}'\left[\left(\frac{\mathbf{a}_6}{m_1}\right) - \bar{\mathbf{x}}_1\right] > 0,$$

i.e.,

$$p_3 > p_2, \qquad p_4 > p_1,$$

and for the second agent

$$\mathbf{p}'\left[\left(\frac{\mathbf{a}_4}{m_2}\right) - \bar{\mathbf{x}}_2\right] > 0, \qquad \mathbf{p}'\left[\left(\frac{\mathbf{a}_5}{m_2}\right) - \bar{\mathbf{x}}_2\right] > 0,$$

i.e.,

$$p_2 > p_4, \qquad p_1 > p_3.$$

These conditions are contradictory, and consequently they exclude the existence, in this example, of a competitive equilibrium.

Example C. Before considering the competitive equilibrium of an economy with unique commodities with respect to Pareto optimality, let us consider another example. This example will show that the assumption by which commodities that are physically and psychologically homogeneous have the same price can exclude the existence of a competitive equilibrium which, on the contrary, exists if this assumption is not admitted.

We consider an economy with two agents and two commodities. There are two indivisible units of each commodity. The two units of the first commodity are owned initially by the first agent, and the two units of the second commodity by the second agent, i.e.,

$$\bar{\mathbf{x}}_1 = \begin{bmatrix} 2 \\ 0 \end{bmatrix}, \qquad \bar{\mathbf{x}}_2 = \begin{bmatrix} 0 \\ 2 \end{bmatrix}.$$

The preferences of the first agent are represented by the relationships

$$\begin{bmatrix} 2 \\ 2 \end{bmatrix} \succ_1 \begin{bmatrix} 1 \\ 2 \end{bmatrix} \succ_1 \begin{bmatrix} 2 \\ 1 \end{bmatrix} \succ_1 \begin{bmatrix} 0 \\ 2 \end{bmatrix} \succ_1 \begin{bmatrix} 1 \\ 1 \end{bmatrix} \succ_1 \begin{bmatrix} 2 \\ 0 \end{bmatrix} \succ_1 \begin{bmatrix} 0 \\ 1 \end{bmatrix} \succ_1 \begin{bmatrix} 1 \\ 0 \end{bmatrix} \succ_1 \begin{bmatrix} 0 \\ 0 \end{bmatrix},$$

and those of the second agent by the relationships

$$\begin{bmatrix} 2 \\ 2 \end{bmatrix} \succ_2 \begin{bmatrix} 1 \\ 2 \end{bmatrix} \succ_2 \begin{bmatrix} 2 \\ 1 \end{bmatrix} \succ_2 \begin{bmatrix} 1 \\ 1 \end{bmatrix} \succ_2 \begin{bmatrix} 0 \\ 2 \end{bmatrix} \succ_2 \begin{bmatrix} 2 \\ 0 \end{bmatrix} \succ_2 \begin{bmatrix} 0 \\ 1 \end{bmatrix} \succ_2 \begin{bmatrix} 1 \\ 0 \end{bmatrix} \succ_2 \begin{bmatrix} 0 \\ 0 \end{bmatrix}.$$

There is no competitive equilibrium, since, by considering bundles $\mathbf{x}_i \gtrsim_i \bar{\mathbf{x}}_i$ (with $i = 1, 2$), we get

$$\mathbf{x}_1 + \mathbf{x}_2 = \bar{\mathbf{x}}_1 + \bar{\mathbf{x}}_2$$

only in two cases: if

$$\mathbf{x}_1^a = \begin{bmatrix} 1 \\ 1 \end{bmatrix}, \qquad \mathbf{x}_2^a = \begin{bmatrix} 1 \\ 1 \end{bmatrix}$$

or if

$$\mathbf{x}_1^b = \begin{bmatrix} 2 \\ 0 \end{bmatrix}, \qquad \mathbf{x}_2^b = \begin{bmatrix} 0 \\ 2 \end{bmatrix}.$$

In order for case a to represent a competitive equilibrium, prices must be such that

$$\mathbf{p}'(\mathbf{x}_1^a - \bar{\mathbf{x}}_1) \le 0, \qquad \mathbf{p}'\left[\begin{pmatrix} 0 \\ 2 \end{pmatrix} - \bar{\mathbf{x}}_1 \right] > 0,$$

i.e.,

$$p_1 + p_2 \le 2p_1, \qquad 2p_2 > 2p_1;$$

but these conditions are contradictory. In order for case b to represent a competitive equilibrium, prices must be such that

$$\mathbf{p}'\left[\begin{pmatrix} 1 \\ 1 \end{pmatrix} - \bar{\mathbf{x}}_1 \right] > 0, \qquad \mathbf{p}'\left[\begin{pmatrix} 1 \\ 1 \end{pmatrix} - \bar{\mathbf{x}}_2 \right] > 0,$$

i.e.,

$$p_1 + p_2 > 2p_1, \qquad p_1 + p_2 > 2p_2;$$

but these conditions are contradictory.

This example is represented in the Edgeworth diagram (Fig. 2), where at each point with integer coordinates the preferences of the two agents are indicated by utility indexes, the first of which is referred to the first agent and the second to the second agent. The initial allocation is represented by point A.

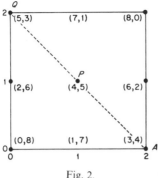

Fig. 2.

The prices that lead to point P, which is the only one preferred by both agents to point A, are such that the first agent chooses the commodity bundle of point Q while the second agent chooses the bundle of point P; therefore there is no equilibrium. Moreover, all other straight lines passing through point A (i.e., all other prices) are such that one of the two agents can obtain the commodity bundle represented by point P. Therefore, since he prefers the bundle represented by point P to that of point A, point A does not represent a competitive equilibrium.

On the contrary, if we do not accept the assumption that commodities that are perfect substitutes must have the same price, we find for this example that competitive equilibria exist. In fact, when the four commodity units are considered four unique commodities, the problem appears in the following way. The initial allocation is

$$\bar{\mathbf{x}}_1 = \begin{bmatrix} 1 \\ 1 \\ 0 \\ 0 \end{bmatrix}, \qquad \bar{\mathbf{x}}_2 = \begin{bmatrix} 0 \\ 0 \\ 1 \\ 1 \end{bmatrix}.$$

For vectors $\mathbf{x} \in B^4$, with $\mathbf{x} \succsim_i \bar{\mathbf{x}}_i$ (the only ones relevant for a competitive equilibrium, since each agent, if he prefers, can retain the initial bundle for any price), the preferences of the first agent are described by the relationships

$$\begin{bmatrix} 1 \\ 1 \\ 1 \\ 1 \end{bmatrix} \succ_1 \begin{bmatrix} 1 \\ 0 \\ 1 \\ 1 \end{bmatrix} \sim_1 \begin{bmatrix} 0 \\ 1 \\ 1 \\ 1 \end{bmatrix} \succ_1 \begin{bmatrix} 1 \\ 1 \\ 1 \\ 0 \end{bmatrix} \sim_1 \begin{bmatrix} 1 \\ 1 \\ 0 \\ 1 \end{bmatrix} \succ_1 \begin{bmatrix} 0 \\ 0 \\ 1 \\ 1 \end{bmatrix} \succ_1 \begin{bmatrix} 1 \\ 0 \\ 1 \\ 0 \end{bmatrix} \sim_1 \begin{bmatrix} 1 \\ 0 \\ 0 \\ 1 \end{bmatrix} \sim_1 \begin{bmatrix} 0 \\ 1 \\ 1 \\ 0 \end{bmatrix}$$

$$\sim_1 \begin{bmatrix} 0 \\ 1 \\ 0 \\ 1 \end{bmatrix} \succ_1 \begin{bmatrix} 1 \\ 1 \\ 0 \\ 0 \end{bmatrix},$$

and those of the second agent by the relationships

$$\begin{bmatrix} 1 \\ 1 \\ 1 \\ 1 \end{bmatrix} \succ_2 \begin{bmatrix} 1 \\ 0 \\ 1 \\ 1 \end{bmatrix} \sim_2 \begin{bmatrix} 0 \\ 1 \\ 1 \\ 1 \end{bmatrix} \succ_2 \begin{bmatrix} 1 \\ 1 \\ 1 \\ 0 \end{bmatrix} \sim_2 \begin{bmatrix} 1 \\ 1 \\ 0 \\ 1 \end{bmatrix} \succ_\varrho \begin{bmatrix} 1 \\ 0 \\ 1 \\ 0 \end{bmatrix} \sim_2 \begin{bmatrix} 1 \\ 0 \\ 0 \\ 1 \end{bmatrix} \sim_2 \begin{bmatrix} 0 \\ 1 \\ 1 \\ 0 \end{bmatrix} \sim_2 \begin{bmatrix} 0 \\ 1 \\ 0 \\ 1 \end{bmatrix} \succ_2 \begin{bmatrix} 0 \\ 0 \\ 1 \\ 1 \end{bmatrix}.$$

These preferences are such that the first two commodities are perfect substitutes for both agents, and so are the last two commodities. In addition, the preferences are equal to those in the first part of this example.

Now, this economy allows the following four competitive equilibria:

$$_a\mathbf{x}_1^* = \begin{bmatrix} 1 \\ 0 \\ 1 \\ 0 \end{bmatrix}, \qquad _a\mathbf{x}_2^* = \begin{bmatrix} 0 \\ 1 \\ 0 \\ 1 \end{bmatrix}, \qquad _ap_2^* = {_a}p_3^* > 0,$$

$$0 < {_a}p_1^* < {_a}p_4^* < {_a}p_1^* + {_a}p_2^*,$$

$$_b\mathbf{x}_1^* = \begin{bmatrix} 1 \\ 0 \\ 0 \\ 1 \end{bmatrix}, \qquad _b\mathbf{x}_2^* = \begin{bmatrix} 0 \\ 1 \\ 1 \\ 0 \end{bmatrix}, \qquad _bp_2^* = {_b}p_4^* > 0,$$

$$0 < {_b}p_1^* < {_b}p_3^* < {_b}p_1^* + {_b}p_2^*,$$

$$_c\mathbf{x}_1^* = \begin{bmatrix} 0 \\ 1 \\ 1 \\ 0 \end{bmatrix}, \qquad _c\mathbf{x}_2^* = \begin{bmatrix} 1 \\ 0 \\ 0 \\ 1 \end{bmatrix}, \qquad _cp_1^* = {_c}p_3^* > 0,$$

$$0 < {_c}p_2^* < {_c}p_4^* < {_c}p_1^* + {_c}p_2^*,$$

$$_d\mathbf{x}_1^* = \begin{bmatrix} 0 \\ 1 \\ 0 \\ 1 \end{bmatrix}, \qquad _d\mathbf{x}_2^* = \begin{bmatrix} 1 \\ 0 \\ 1 \\ 0 \end{bmatrix}, \qquad _dp_1^* = {_d}p_4^* > 0,$$

$$0 < {_d}p_2^* < {_d}p_3^* < {_d}p_1^* + {_d}p_2^*.$$

As we can observe, each of these four competitive equilibria requires that the members of at least one pair of perfect substitute commodities do not have equal prices: for instance, $_ap_2^* = {_a}p_3^*$ and $_ap_1^* < {_a}p_4^*$ must hold, and these relationships are not compatible with the equalities $_ap_1^* = {_a}p_2^*$ and $_ap_3^* = {_a}p_4^*$.

The fact that an economy with unique commodities does not generally admit a competitive equilibrium, as shown by Examples A and B, is not, however, the single aspect that differentiates these economies from those with divisible commodities. Another point concerns the link between competitive equilibria and Pareto optima. For economies with divisible commodities we have (with other assumptions not discussed here) the following two properties: (I) All competitive equilibria are Pareto optima, and (II) all Pareto optima can be obtained through competitive equilibria, the resources being reallocated opportunely among the agents. Neither of these properties is valid if the commodities are indivisible.

The second property is not valid, as shown by Example A. In this example, already analyzed, we cannot obtain the allocation $x_1 = a_1$ and $x_2 = a_2$, which is a Pareto optimum, through a competitive equilibrium (no matter what the initial allocation of the commodities is, even if it coincides, as in Example A, with the Pareto optimum allocation).

The fact that the first property is not valid has already been shown in the literature,[8] assuming, however, that all commodities that are perfect substitutes have the same price. Since this assumption, as already demonstrated in Example C, is restrictive for the competitive equilibrium, it is convenient to examine the problem without this assumption in order to show by an example that a competitive equilibrium can exist that is not a Pareto optimum.

Example D. This is an example of an economy with only unique commodities, where there are two agents and four unique commodities, which shows that a competitive equilibrium is not necessarily a Pareto optimum. With the same symbols as in Example A, the initial commodity allocation is

$$\overline{x}_1 = a_1, \qquad \overline{x}_2 = a_2.$$

The preferences of both agents are such that, for any pair $x, y \in B^4$, if $e'(x - y) > 0$, then $x \succ_i y$; if $e'x = e'y = 3$ or 1, then $x \sim_i y$; if $e'x = 2$, then the preferences of the first agent are represented by the relationships

$$a_6 \succ_1 a_3 \sim_1 a_1 \succ_1 a_2 \succ_1 a_4 \sim_1 a_5,$$

and those of the second agent by the relationships

$$a_1 \succ_2 a_6 \succ_2 a_2 \succ_2 a_4 \sim_2 a_5 \succ_2 a_3.$$

There exists a competitive equilibrium given by the allocation

$$x_1^* = a_1, \qquad x_2^* = a_2$$

[8] Quirk and Saposnik [11, p. 134].

and by any prices that satisfy the following conditions:

$$p_4^* > p_1^*, \qquad p_2^* > p_3^*, \qquad p_1^* + p_2^* > p_3^* + p_4^*,$$

$$p_3^* + p_4^* > p_1^*, \qquad p_3^* + p_4^* > p_2^*,$$

for instance, by the prices

$$\mathbf{p}^* = k \begin{bmatrix} 2 \\ 5 \\ 3 \\ 3 \end{bmatrix}.$$

This competitive equilibrium, however, is not a Pareto optimum. In fact, the allocation

$$\mathbf{x}_1^p = \mathbf{a}_3, \qquad \mathbf{x}_2^p = \mathbf{a}_6$$

is preferred to the competitive equilibrium allocation by the second agent and is indifferent for the first agent.

Another point that is interesting to consider in the case of unique (or indivisible) commodities concerns Walras' law. This law does not hold in the narrow sense,[9] as in the usual analyses with divisible commodities; i.e., we do not have the relationship

$$\mathbf{p}'(\mathbf{x} - \mathbf{e}) = 0 \qquad \text{for all} \quad \mathbf{x} \in \phi(\mathbf{p}),$$

but only the inequality

$$\mathbf{p}'(\mathbf{x} - \mathbf{e}) \leq 0 \qquad \text{for all} \quad \mathbf{x} \in \phi(\mathbf{p}),$$

i.e., Walras' law in the general sense.

In fact, by varying the exchanged quantities of indivisible commodities, an agent may find it more convenient to exchange a commodity bundle, which is valued more at current prices, for another bundle, which is valued less but which he prefers, without the possibility of balancing its value, because of the indivisibility of the commodities.

Nevertheless, if a competitive equilibrium exists, all agents (this is relevant and not known a priori to the agents) choose $\hat{\mathbf{x}}_i^* \in \phi_i(\mathbf{p}^*)$ such that

$$\mathbf{p}^{*\prime}(\hat{\mathbf{x}}_i^* - \bar{\mathbf{x}}_i) = 0, \qquad i = 1, \ldots, m,$$

and, moreover, such that vector $\mathbf{p}^*$ and vector

$$\mathbf{x}^* = \sum_{i=1}^{m} \hat{\mathbf{x}}_i^*$$

[9] We have followed Nikaido's [10, pp. 262–263] definition.

represent a competitive equilibrium. In fact, since in equilibrium

$$\mathbf{p}^{*\prime}\mathbf{x}^* = \mathbf{p}^{*\prime}\mathbf{e}, \qquad \mathbf{p}^{*\prime}(\hat{\mathbf{x}}_i^* - \bar{\mathbf{x}}_i) \leq 0, \qquad i = 1, \ldots, m,$$

and

$$\sum_{i=1}^{m} \bar{\mathbf{x}}_i = \mathbf{e}, \qquad \mathbf{x}^* = \sum_{i=1}^{m} \hat{\mathbf{x}}_i^*,$$

we have

$$\sum_{i=1}^{m} \mathbf{p}^{*\prime}(\hat{\mathbf{x}}_i^* - \bar{\mathbf{x}}_i) = \overset{\bullet}{0},$$

so that for every $i = 1, \ldots, m$ it must also hold that

$$\mathbf{p}^{*\prime}(\hat{\mathbf{x}}_i^* - \bar{\mathbf{x}}_i) = 0.$$

3. COMPETITIVE PSEUDOEQUILIBRIUM IN AN ECONOMY WITH UNIQUE (OR INDIVISIBLE) COMMODITIES

The nonexistence, in general, of a competitive equilibrium in an economy with unique commodities can give the impression (by analogy with the case of the nonconvex economies[10]) that we could define a competitive quasi-equilibrium from which the economy under examination differs by a factor that becomes negligible in a large economy. With this objective, a competitive pseudoequilibrium is later defined by closing and making convex the already defined mapping $\phi(\mathbf{p})$.

In order to define the competitive pseudoequilibrium and demonstrate its existence, it is convenient to specify some sets and mappings. First, since the mapping $\phi(\mathbf{p})$ (like other mappings which are later defined) is homogeneous and of degree zero in prices (which are consequently defined only through their ratios), we can consider the vectors $\mathbf{p}$ as elements of the simplex S_n, which is the set of vectors of n dimensions that are semipositive and have elements whose sum is one: i.e.,

$$S_n = \{\mathbf{p} \mid \mathbf{p} \in R_+^n, \, \mathbf{e}'\mathbf{p} = 1\},$$

where R_+^n indicates the nonnegative orthant of the Euclidean space of n dimensions. Then, $T(\mathbf{p})$ designates the mapping that, among all upper semicontinuous mappings whose image sets are convex and include the image sets $\phi(\mathbf{p})$, is the one with the smallest image set. The mapping $T(\mathbf{p})$ is obtained from the mapping $\phi(\mathbf{p})$ through the two following operations.

---

[10] Arrow and Hahn [1, pp. 169–182], which includes a bibliography on this problem; Guesnerie [6].

The first is performed in order to determine the upper semicontinuous mapping $\psi(\mathbf{p})$ that is the most adherent to the mapping $\phi(\mathbf{p})$. For any point p of S_n we consider the subset $V_p \subset S_n$ including $\mathbf{p}$ (this subset can be composed of only point $\mathbf{p}$) for which $\phi(V_p) = \phi(\mathbf{p})$, where

$$\phi(V_p) = \bigcup_{\mathbf{q} \in V_p} \phi(\mathbf{q}).$$

[The subset V_p contains all points $\mathbf{q}$ of S_n to which an identical image set $\phi(\mathbf{p})$ corresponds.] We consider, then, the closure[11] $\overline{V}_p$ of the subset V_p. Let us now define the mapping $\psi(\mathbf{p})$ whose image set is obtained, for every $\mathbf{p}$ of S_n, as the union of all the image sets $\phi(\mathbf{q})$ that correspond to the points of the subsets V_q whose closures $\overline{V}_q$ contain $\mathbf{p}$, i.e.,

$$\psi(\mathbf{p}) = \bigcup_{\substack{\mathbf{q} \in V_q \\ \overline{V}_q \ni \mathbf{p}}} \phi(\mathbf{q}).$$

The mapping $\psi(\mathbf{p})$, consequently, is upper semicontinuous and is obtained by joining, for every $\mathbf{p}$ of S_n, to the image set $\phi(\mathbf{p})$ the smallest set necessary to obtain an upper semicontinuous mapping.

The second operation defines the mapping $T(\mathbf{p})$ as the convex hull of the mapping $\psi(\mathbf{p})$, i.e., for every $\mathbf{p}$ of S_n, the image set $T(\mathbf{p})$ is the convex hull[12] of the image set $\psi(\mathbf{p})$.

We shall now consider, for the previously described economy with unique commodities, in place of the mapping $\phi(\mathbf{p})$, the above-defined mapping $T(\mathbf{p})$. We define as a competitive pseudoequilibrium a pair of vectors $\mathbf{p}^*$ and $\mathbf{x}^*$ such that

$$\mathbf{p}^* \geqslant \mathbf{0}, \qquad \mathbf{x}^* \in T(\mathbf{p}^*), \qquad \mathbf{x}^* \leq \mathbf{e}.$$

The existence of a competitive pseudoequilibrium can be demonstrated by considering the following theorem, which is normally employed for this kind of problem.[13]

Theorem. Let us consider a point-to-set mapping $E(\mathbf{p})$, with $\mathbf{p} \in S_n$ and $E(\mathbf{p}) \subset W$, where W is a compact convex subset of R^n. If the mapping $E(\mathbf{p})$ satisfies the two conditions

(a)   the mapping is upper semicontinuous and carries every point of S_n to a nonempty convex subset of W, and

(b)   Walras's law in the general sense holds, i.e.,

$$\mathbf{p}'\mathbf{y} \leq 0 \qquad \text{for} \quad \mathbf{y} \in E(\mathbf{p}),$$

---

[11] The closure of a set is the union of the set and of the set of all its adherence points.

[12] The convex hull of a set S is the smallest convex set that contains S.

[13] Nikaido [10, p. 265].

then there is some $\mathbf{p}^*$ in S_n such that the set $E(\mathbf{p}^*)$ contains some nonpositive vectors, i.e.,

$$E(p^*) \cap R^n_- \neq \varnothing.$$

In order to employ this theorem, we define

$$E(\mathbf{p}) = T(\mathbf{p}) - \mathbf{e}.$$

All conditions of the theorem are clearly satisfied, with the exception of condition (b), whose satisfaction will be demonstrated.

As a condition of the agent's choice, we have

$$\mathbf{p}'(\hat{\mathbf{x}}_i - \bar{\mathbf{x}}_i) \leq 0 \qquad \text{for all} \quad \hat{\mathbf{x}}_i \in \phi_i(\mathbf{p}), \quad i = 1, \ldots, m,$$

and therefore also

$$\mathbf{p}'(\mathbf{x} - \mathbf{e}) \leq 0 \qquad \text{for all} \quad \mathbf{x} \in \phi(\mathbf{p}).$$

It follows that we also have

$$\mathbf{p}'(\mathbf{x} - \mathbf{e}) \leq 0 \qquad \text{for all} \quad \mathbf{x} \in \psi(\mathbf{p}),$$

since, if *ab absurdo* there were a $\tilde{\mathbf{x}} \in \psi(\mathbf{p})$ with $\mathbf{p}'(\tilde{\mathbf{x}} - \mathbf{e}) > 0$, then an adherence V_p of $\mathbf{p}$ in S_n would also exist such that

$$\mathbf{q}'(\tilde{\mathbf{x}} - \mathbf{e}) > 0 \qquad \text{for all} \quad \mathbf{q} \in V_p.$$

But, since $\tilde{\mathbf{x}} \in \psi(\mathbf{p})$ and since there certainly exists in every adherence of $\mathbf{p}$ some $\hat{\mathbf{q}}$ (which may be $\mathbf{p}$) for which $\tilde{\mathbf{x}} \in \phi(\hat{\mathbf{q}})$, we have also $\hat{\mathbf{q}}'(\tilde{\mathbf{x}} - \mathbf{e}) \leq 0$, which is a condition that contradicts the preceding relationship. Then, since $T(\mathbf{p})$ is, for all $\mathbf{p}$ of S_n, the convex hull of $\psi(\mathbf{p})$, we also have

$$\mathbf{p}'(\mathbf{x} - \mathbf{e}) \leq 0 \qquad \text{for all} \quad \mathbf{x} \in T(\mathbf{p}),$$

and we find that condition (b) of the theorem is satisfied.

Having demonstrated that a competitive pseudoequilibrium exists, i.e., a pair of vectors $\mathbf{p}^*$ and $\mathbf{x}^*$ such that

$$\mathbf{p}^* \geqslant \mathbf{0}, \qquad \mathbf{x}^* \in T(\mathbf{p}^*), \qquad \mathbf{x}^* \leq \mathbf{e},$$

it may be $\mathbf{x}^* \in \phi(\mathbf{p}^*)$ or $\mathbf{x}^* \notin \phi(\mathbf{p}^*)$. Now, if $\mathbf{x}^* \in \phi(\mathbf{p}^*)$, we have a real competitive equilibrium for which we will demonstrate that a vector $\mathbf{x}^{**} \in \phi(\mathbf{p}^*)$ exists ($\mathbf{x}^{**}$ may be coincident with $\mathbf{x}^*$) for which not only

$$\mathbf{p}^{*\prime}(\mathbf{x}^{**} - \mathbf{e}) \leq 0$$

but also

$$\mathbf{p}^{*\prime}(\mathbf{x}^{**} - \mathbf{e}) = 0$$

if all agents do not prefer lower quantities of the commodities (assumption of monotone preferences), i.e., if inequality $\mathbf{x} \geq \mathbf{y}$ implies

$$\mathbf{x} \succsim_i \mathbf{y}, \qquad i = 1, \ldots, m.$$

With this assumption, then, if there is a $\mathbf{x}^* \in \phi(\mathbf{p}^*)$, there is also a $\mathbf{x}^{**} \in \phi(\mathbf{p}^*)$ for which

$$\mathbf{x}^{**} \leq \mathbf{e}, \qquad \mathbf{p}^{*\prime}(\mathbf{x}^{**} - \mathbf{e}) = 0.$$

In fact, let us consider any vector $\mathbf{x}^* \in \phi(\mathbf{p}^*)$ for which necessarily

$$\mathbf{p}^{*\prime}(\mathbf{x}^* - \mathbf{e}) \leq 0.$$

If we have $\mathbf{p}^{*\prime}(\mathbf{x}^* - \mathbf{e}) < 0$, then there are commodities (indicated by index k) for which $x^*_{(k)} = 0$, $p^*_{(k)} > 0$ ($\mathbf{x}^*$ is a vector with elements that are integers, since $\mathbf{x}^* \in \sum_{i=1}^{m} \phi_i(\mathbf{p}^*)$ with $\phi_i(\mathbf{p}^*) \subset B^n$; it follows that an element $x^*_{(k)}$ of $\mathbf{x}^*$ can be less than one only if it is zero). For each of these commodities, let us consider the i_kth agent who owns it initially, i.e., for whom $\mathbf{e}'_k \bar{\mathbf{x}}_{i_k} = 1$, where $\mathbf{e}_k$ is the kth unitary vector (with all elements equal to zero except the kth one, which is equal to one). Since $x^*_{(k)} = 0$, no agent demands, in the competitive pseudoequilibrium described by $\mathbf{p}^*$ and $\mathbf{x}^*$, the (k)th commodity, not even the i_kth agent, i.e., we have $\mathbf{e}'_k \hat{\mathbf{x}}^*_{i_k} = 0$, where $\hat{\mathbf{x}}^*_{i_k}$ is the choice of the i_kth agent. The i_kth agent, then, cannot sell the (k)th commodity so that

$$\mathbf{p}^{*\prime}(\hat{\mathbf{x}}^*_{i_k} - \bar{\mathbf{x}}_{i_k}) \leq -p^*_{(k)}.$$

By the assumption of monotone preferences, however, the commodity bundle $\hat{\mathbf{x}}^*_{i_k} + \mathbf{e}_k$ is not less preferred than the bundle $\hat{\mathbf{x}}^*_{i_k}$, i.e.,

$$\hat{\mathbf{x}}^*_{i_k} + \mathbf{e}_k \succsim_{i_k} \hat{\mathbf{x}}^*_{i_k},$$

and therefore, since

$$\mathbf{p}^{*\prime}(\hat{\mathbf{x}}^*_{i_k} + \mathbf{e}_k - \bar{\mathbf{x}}_{i_k}) \leq 0,$$

$(\hat{\mathbf{x}}^*_{i_k} + \mathbf{e}_k) \in \phi_{i_k}(\mathbf{p}^*)$ also and, consequently, $(\mathbf{x}^* + \mathbf{e}_k) \in \phi(\mathbf{p}^*)$. Adopting this reasoning for every commodity for which $x^*_{(k)} = 0$, $p^*_{(k)} > 0$, we have $(\mathbf{x}^* + \sum_k \mathbf{e}_k) \in \phi(\mathbf{p}^*)$. When $\mathbf{x}^{**} = \mathbf{x}^* + \sum_k \mathbf{e}_k$, there is no commodity such that $p^*_{(k)}(x^{**}_{(k)} - 1) < 0$. Therefore, since $\mathbf{p}^*(\mathbf{x}^{**} - \mathbf{e}) \leq 0$,

$$\mathbf{p}^*(\mathbf{x}^{**} - \mathbf{e}) = 0$$

and

$$\mathbf{x}^{**} \in \phi(\mathbf{p}^*), \qquad \mathbf{x}^{**} \leq \mathbf{e}.$$

We have thus demonstrated that

(a) There exists a competitive pseudoequilibrium described by a pair of vectors $\mathbf{p}^*$ and $\mathbf{x}^*$ for which

$$\mathbf{p}^* \geqslant \mathbf{0}, \qquad \mathbf{x}^* \in T(\mathbf{p}^*), \qquad \mathbf{x}^* \leq \mathbf{e}.$$

(b) If there exists a competitive pseudoequilibrium for which $\mathbf{x}^* \in \phi(\mathbf{p}^*)$ holds too, and, if the assumption of monotone preferences is satisfied for the preference ordering of all agents, then there exists a competitive equilibrium described by a pair of vectors $\mathbf{p}^*$ and $\mathbf{x}^{**}$ for which

$$\mathbf{p}^* \geqslant \mathbf{0}, \qquad \mathbf{x}^{**} \in (\mathbf{p}^*), \qquad \mathbf{x}^{**} \leq \mathbf{e}, \qquad \mathbf{p}^{*\prime}(\mathbf{x}^{**} - \mathbf{e}) = 0.$$

Now, we must consider (when there is no competitive equilibrium) the degree of disequilibrium of the pseudoequilibrium in order to establish its relevance with respect to the size of the economy.

To every vector $\mathbf{p}^* \in S_n$ of the competitive pseudoequilibrium prices corresponds a limited number of vectors—described by set $\phi(\mathbf{p}^*)$—which indicate the commodity bundles chosen by all the agents at the prices $\mathbf{p}^*$. By using $_r\mathbf{x}^*$ to indicate the vectors of the set $\phi(\mathbf{p}^*)$, with $r = 1, \ldots, s$, where s is the number of the vectors of $\phi(\mathbf{p}^*)$, the degree of disequilibrium can be defined as

$$d = \min_r \mathbf{p}^{*\prime}(|_r\mathbf{x}^* - \mathbf{e}|),$$

where $|_r\mathbf{x}^* - \mathbf{e}|$ is the vector composed of elements that are the absolute values of the corresponding elements of the vector $_r\mathbf{x}^* - \mathbf{e}$.

The degree d of disequilibrium (for which $0 \leq d \leq m - 1$ always holds) may depend on all the data of the economy, i.e., on the numbers of commodities and agents, on the initial allocation of commodities among the agents, on the preferences of the agents and, if there is more than one vector $\mathbf{p}^*$ of prices of competitive pseudoequilibrium, also on the particular vector $\mathbf{p}^*$ under consideration. Although the degree of disequilibrium can be considered, wisely from a realistic point of view, a decreasing function of the number of commodities and/or of the number of agents, the agents' preferences must nevertheless satisfy, in this respect, some conditions (which concern, presumably, the substitution, not necessarily perfect, of the commodities[14]). Conditions based on the agents' preferences are necessary,

---

[14] With regard to this problem, the assumption adopted by Dierker [4] and Broome [2], which states that the number of (indivisible but not unique) commodities does not increase when the number m of agents increases (and the total endowment of these commodities does also), requires, since the units of each indivisible commodity are perfect substitutes for all agents, that each unit of a commodity has an increasing number of perfect substitutes.

since we can form examples where there is a degree of disequilibrium independent of the number of commodities and agents.

Recalling Example A, where there was no competitive equilibrium, we find a unique competitive pseudoequilibrium that occurs with the price vector

$$\mathbf{p}^* = \tfrac{1}{4}\mathbf{e},$$

to which corresponds a set $T(\mathbf{p}^*)$ composed of all the vectors obtained as convex linear combinations of the vectors

$$\begin{bmatrix} 2 \\ 0 \\ 1 \\ 1 \end{bmatrix}, \begin{bmatrix} 1 \\ 1 \\ 0 \\ 2 \end{bmatrix}, \begin{bmatrix} 0 \\ 2 \\ 1 \\ 1 \end{bmatrix}, \begin{bmatrix} 1 \\ 1 \\ 2 \\ 0 \end{bmatrix}, \begin{bmatrix} 1 \\ 0 \\ 2 \\ 1 \end{bmatrix}, \begin{bmatrix} 0 \\ 1 \\ 1 \\ 2 \end{bmatrix}, \begin{bmatrix} 1 \\ 2 \\ 1 \\ 0 \end{bmatrix}, \begin{bmatrix} 2 \\ 1 \\ 0 \\ 1 \end{bmatrix},$$

among which there is $\mathbf{x}^* = \mathbf{e}$. The set $\phi(\mathbf{p}^*)$ is composed of the four vectors

$$\mathbf{a}_7 = \begin{bmatrix} 2 \\ 0 \\ 1 \\ 1 \end{bmatrix}, \qquad \mathbf{a}_8 = \begin{bmatrix} 1 \\ 1 \\ 0 \\ 2 \end{bmatrix}, \qquad \mathbf{a}_9 = \begin{bmatrix} 0 \\ 2 \\ 1 \\ 1 \end{bmatrix}, \qquad \mathbf{a}_{10} = \begin{bmatrix} 1 \\ 1 \\ 2 \\ 0 \end{bmatrix}.$$

The degree d of disequilibrium is consequently equal to 0.5.

We shall now consider a first extension of Example A. In the economy there are still two agents, but eight commodities instead of four; i.e., $n = 8$. The initial allocation is now

$$\overline{\mathbf{x}}_1 = \begin{bmatrix} \mathbf{a}_1 \\ \text{----} \\ \mathbf{a}_1 \end{bmatrix}, \qquad \overline{\mathbf{x}}_2 = \begin{bmatrix} \mathbf{a}_2 \\ \text{----} \\ \mathbf{a}_2 \end{bmatrix}.$$

The preferences of both agents are such that, for any pair of vectors $\mathbf{x}, \mathbf{y} \in B^8$, if $\mathbf{e}'(\mathbf{x} - \mathbf{y}) > 0$, then $\mathbf{x} \succ_i \mathbf{y}$; if $\mathbf{e}'\mathbf{x} = \mathbf{e}'\mathbf{y} = t$ for $t \neq 4$, $t = 1, \dots, 7$, then $\mathbf{x} \sim_i \mathbf{y}$; if $\mathbf{e}'\mathbf{x} = \mathbf{e}'\mathbf{y} = 4$, then the preferences of the first agent are such that

$$\begin{bmatrix} \mathbf{a}_3 \\ \text{----} \\ \mathbf{a}_3 \end{bmatrix} \sim_1 \begin{bmatrix} \mathbf{a}_6 \\ \text{----} \\ \mathbf{a}_6 \end{bmatrix} \succ_1 \begin{bmatrix} \mathbf{a}_1 \\ \text{----} \\ \mathbf{a}_1 \end{bmatrix} \succ_1 \mathbf{b}_1,$$

where $\mathbf{b}_1$ represents each of the other vectors with $\mathbf{e}'\mathbf{b}_1 = 4$ and $\mathbf{b}_1 \in B^8$, and those of the second agent are such that

$$\begin{bmatrix} \mathbf{a}_4 \\ \text{----} \\ \mathbf{a}_4 \end{bmatrix} \sim_2 \begin{bmatrix} \mathbf{a}_5 \\ \text{----} \\ \mathbf{a}_5 \end{bmatrix} \succ_2 \begin{bmatrix} \mathbf{a}_2 \\ \text{----} \\ \mathbf{a}_2 \end{bmatrix} \succ_2 \mathbf{b}_2,$$

where $\mathbf{b}_2$ represents each of the other vectors with $\mathbf{e}'\mathbf{b}_2 = 4$ and $\mathbf{b}_2 \in B^8$. By reasoning analogous to that for Example A, we find that there is no competitive equilibrium and that there are competitive pseudoequilibria with

$$\mathbf{p}^* = \frac{1}{4}\left[\frac{c\mathbf{e}}{(1-c)\mathbf{e}}\right], \qquad \mathbf{x}^* = \mathbf{e},$$

where $\frac{1}{3} < c < \frac{2}{3}$. The set $\phi(\mathbf{p}^*)$ is composed of the four vectors

$$\left[\frac{\mathbf{a}_7}{\mathbf{a}_7}\right], \qquad \left[\frac{\mathbf{a}_8}{\mathbf{a}_8}\right], \qquad \left[\frac{\mathbf{a}_9}{\mathbf{a}_9}\right], \qquad \left[\frac{\mathbf{a}_{10}}{\mathbf{a}_{10}}\right],$$

for which the degree of disequilibrium again is 0.5.

Now, let us consider a second extension of Example A where the number of agents is also doubled (from two to four) in addition to the number of commodities (from four to eight). The initial allocation of the commodities is now

$$\bar{\mathbf{x}}_1 = \left[\frac{\mathbf{a}_1}{\mathbf{0}}\right], \qquad \bar{\mathbf{x}}_2 = \left[\frac{\mathbf{a}_2}{\mathbf{0}}\right], \qquad \bar{\mathbf{x}}_3 = \left[\frac{\mathbf{0}}{\mathbf{a}_1}\right], \qquad \bar{\mathbf{x}}_4 = \left[\frac{\mathbf{0}}{\mathbf{a}_2}\right].$$

The preferences of all four agents are such that, for any pair of vectors $\mathbf{x}, \mathbf{y} \in B^8$, if $\mathbf{e}'(\mathbf{x} - \mathbf{y}) > 0$, then $\mathbf{x} \succ_i \mathbf{y}$ (with $i = 1, \ldots, 4$); if $\mathbf{e}'\mathbf{x} = \mathbf{e}'\mathbf{y} = t$, for $t \neq 2, t = 1, \ldots, 7$, then $\mathbf{x} \sim_i \mathbf{y}$; if $\mathbf{e}'\mathbf{x} = \mathbf{e}'\mathbf{y} = 2$, then the preferences of the first agent are such that

$$\left[\frac{\mathbf{a}_3}{\mathbf{0}}\right] \sim_1 \left[\frac{\mathbf{a}_6}{\mathbf{0}}\right] \succ_1 \left[\frac{\mathbf{a}_1}{\mathbf{0}}\right] \succ_1 \mathbf{b}_1,$$

where $\mathbf{b}_1 \in B^8$, with $\mathbf{e}'\mathbf{b}_1 = 2$ and $\mathbf{b}_1 \neq [\mathbf{a}'_j \vdots \mathbf{0}']'$ for $j = 1, 3, 6$; the preferences of the second agent are such that

$$\left[\frac{\mathbf{a}_4}{\mathbf{0}}\right] \sim_2 \left[\frac{\mathbf{a}_5}{\mathbf{0}}\right] \succ_2 \left[\frac{\mathbf{a}_2}{\mathbf{0}}\right] \succ_2 \mathbf{b}_2,$$

where $\mathbf{b}_2 \in B^8$, with $\mathbf{e}'\mathbf{b}_2 = 2$ and $\mathbf{b}_2 \neq [\mathbf{a}'_j \vdots \mathbf{0}']'$ for $j = 2, 4, 5$; the preferences of the third agent are such that

$$\left[\frac{\mathbf{0}}{\mathbf{a}_3}\right] \sim_3 \left[\frac{\mathbf{0}}{\mathbf{a}_6}\right] \succ_3 \left[\frac{\mathbf{0}}{\mathbf{a}_1}\right] \succ_3 \mathbf{b}_3,$$

where $\mathbf{b}_3 \in B^8$, with $\mathbf{e}'\mathbf{b}_3 = 2$ and $\mathbf{b}_3 \neq [\mathbf{0}' \vdots \mathbf{a}'_j]'$ for $j = 1, 3, 6$; and the preferences of the fourth agent are such that

$$\left[\frac{\mathbf{0}}{\mathbf{a}_4}\right] \sim_4 \left[\frac{\mathbf{0}}{\mathbf{a}_5}\right] \succ_4 \left[\frac{\mathbf{0}}{\mathbf{a}_2}\right] \succ_4 \mathbf{b}_4,$$

where $\mathbf{b}_4 \in B^8$, with $\mathbf{e}'\mathbf{b}_4 = 2$ and $\mathbf{b}_4 \neq [\mathbf{0}_i'\mathbf{a}_j']'$ for $j = 2, 4, 5$. By reasoning as in Example A and its first extension, we find that there is no competitive equilibrium and that there are competitive pseudoequilibria with

$$\mathbf{p}^* = \frac{1}{4}\left[\frac{c\mathbf{e}}{(1-c)\mathbf{e}}\right], \qquad \mathbf{x}^* = \mathbf{e},$$

where $\frac{2}{5} < c < \frac{3}{5}$. The set $\phi(\mathbf{p}^*)$ is composed of the following 16 vectors

$$\left[\frac{\mathbf{a}_j}{\mathbf{a}_k}\right], \qquad j, k = 7, 8, 9, 10,$$

for which the degree of disequilibrium is again 0.5.

The same degree of disequilibrium results if we extend Example A to $4k$ commodities and two agents or to $4k$ commodities and $2k$ agents (with k a positive integer) by following the method used for $k = 2$ in the extensions of Example A analyzed above.

We can find examples with a nondecreasing degree of disequilibrium if a divisible commodity is also introduced: It is sufficient to recall Example B and consider its extensions analogous to those of Example A already analyzed.

REFERENCES

1. Arrow, K. J., and Hahn, F. H., "General Competitive Analysis." Holden-Day, San Francisco, 1971.
2. Broome, J., Approximate equilibrium in economies with indivisible commodities, *Journal of Economic Theory* **5**, 224–249 (1972).
3. Debreu, G., "Theory of Value." Yale University Press, New Haven, 1971.
4. Dierker, E., Equilibrium analysis of exchange economies with indivisible commodities, *Econometrica* **39**, 997–1008 (1971).
5. Frank, C. R., Jr., "Production Theory and Indivisible Commodities." Princeton University Press, Princeton, New Jersey, 1969.
6. Guesnerie, R., Pareto optimality in non-convex economies, *Econometrica* **43**, 1–29 (1975).
7. Henry, C., Indivisibilités dans une économie d'échanges, *Econometrica* **38**, 542–558 (1970).
8. Hurwicz, L., Radner, R., and Reiter, S., A stochastic decentralized resources allocation process: Part I, *Econometrica* **43**, 187–221 (1975).
9. Mas-Colell, A., Indivisible commodities and general equilibrium theory, *Journal of Economic Theory* **16**, 443–456 (1977).
10. Nikaido, H., "Convex Structures and Economic Theory." Academic Press, New York, 1968.
11. Quirk, J., and Saposnik, R., "Introduction to General Equilibrium Theory and Welfare Economics." McGraw-Hill, New York, 1968.

LABORATORIO DI ECONOMIA POLITICA
UNIVERSITÀ DI VENEZIA
VENEZIA, ITALY

New Results for a Competitive Equilibrium

Piera Mazzoleni

Let us consider a perfectly competitive economy at a fixed point in time. A good is characterized by its physical properties, by the time at which it is delivered, and by the place where it is located. Usually, goods available at different places and different points in time are considered different economic entities [3]. With each good we associate a real number, the price, which is the amount paid in order to have a unit of the good available at a given place at a given time. Let us individuate the time interval in which the economic activities take place and the corresponding space region. The time interval is subdivided into a finite number of unit subintervals, and the space into a finite number of elementary compact subregions. In such an economy the M economic agents are households $(j = 1, \ldots, N)$ and firms $(j = N + 1, \ldots, M)$; firms make production decisions, but households do not. Thus the economic agents are characterized by different decision criteria and by the constraints bounding their possible actions.

Let us consider the behavior of the households. Each household j chooses its consumption vector of goods $\mathbf{x}_j = [x_{j1}, \ldots, x_{jn}]^T$ in a feasible set $X_j \subset R^n$ in order to maximize a utility function u_j. Suppose the consumption set to be bounded above by the initial endowments $\bar{\mathbf{x}}_j$ so that, for the given price vector $\mathbf{p}$, the reduced feasible region is

(1) $\qquad a_j(\mathbf{p}, \mathbf{w}) = \{\mathbf{x}_j \in X_j : \mathbf{p}\mathbf{x}_j \le w_j\} = \{\mathbf{x}_j \in X_j : \mathbf{p}\mathbf{x}_j \le \mathbf{p}\bar{\mathbf{x}}_j\}$

for $(\mathbf{p}, \mathbf{w})$ varying in a suitable set $\mathscr{H}_j$.

301

For any point $(\mathbf{p}, \mathbf{w})$ in $\mathscr{H}'_j \subset R^{n \times N}$, where $\mathscr{H}'_j$ is the set in which the household problem has a solution, household j chooses the optimal consumption vector $\mathbf{x}_j$ on the set $a_j(\mathbf{p}, \mathbf{w})$, and a correspondence

(2) $\mathbf{x}_j(\mathbf{p}, \mathbf{w}): \mathscr{H}'_j \to X_j$

is determined, which represents the demand function.

Let X_j be a compact set. Then $\mathscr{H}'_j = \mathscr{H}_j$. Under the additional assumption that $a_j(\mathbf{p}, \mathbf{w})$ is continuous, the demand function $\mathbf{x}_j$ is upper semicontinuous in $(\mathbf{p}, \mathbf{w})$ and the optimal value function

(3) $v_j(\mathbf{p}, \mathbf{w}) = \max u_j[a_j(\mathbf{p}, \mathbf{w})]$

is continuous in $(\mathbf{p}, \mathbf{w})$. The same result holds for the aggregate demand function $\mathbf{x}(\mathbf{p}, \mathbf{w}) = \sum_{j=1}^{N} \mathbf{x}_j(\mathbf{p}, \mathbf{w})$, provided that the conditions above are fulfilled for any household j.

Now, set $\mathbf{y}_j = [y_{j1}, \ldots, y_{jn}]^T$, the supply vector for the jth firm, and $\mathbf{y} = \sum_{j=N+1}^{M} \mathbf{y}_j$, the total supply. The production possibility set is Y_j for a given j and $Y = \sum_{j=N+1}^{M} Y_j$ for the whole economy.

Given the price vector $\mathbf{p}$ and the production $\mathbf{y}_j$, firm j earns $\mathbf{p}\mathbf{y}_j$ and the objective is to maximize the profit over Y_j:

(4) $\max\{\Pi_j = \mathbf{p}\mathbf{y}_j: \mathbf{y}_j \in Y_j\}.$

Summation over all the firms gives the total profit $\mathbf{p}\mathbf{y}$. Let $K_j \subset R^n$ be the set of the price vectors $\mathbf{p}$ such that problem (4) has a nontrivial solution. For $\mathbf{p}$ varying in K_j we define the optimal profit-value function

(5) $\Pi_j(\mathbf{p}): K_j \to R,$ with $\Pi_j(\mathbf{p}) = \max\{\mathbf{p}\mathbf{y}_j: \mathbf{y}_j \in Y_j\},$

and the supply function

(6) $\mathbf{y}_j(\mathbf{p}): K_j \to Y_j,$ with $\mathbf{y}_j(\mathbf{p}) = \{\mathbf{y}_j \in Y_j: \mathbf{p}\mathbf{y}_j = \Pi_j(\mathbf{p})\},$

which is the set of the possible productions maximizing the profit.

Let Y_j be a compact set. Then $K_j = R^n$, $\mathbf{y}_j(\mathbf{p})$ is an upper semicontinuous function on R^n, and Π_j is continuous on R^n. Under the same assumption of compactness for any Y_j, the properties hold for the aggregate supply $\mathbf{y}(\mathbf{p}) = \sum_{j=N+1}^{M} \mathbf{y}_j(\mathbf{p})$ and the total profit $\Pi(\mathbf{p}) = \sum_{j=N+1}^{M} \Pi_j(\mathbf{p})$.

We shall now study the price system that allows mutually consistent actions for all the economic agents. For the sake of simplicity, let us assume that the consumers control the resources and, through them, control the firms. Usually, decisions will not be coherent with the available resources, and our problem is to seek the price system that allows an equilibrium. An equilibrium is an $(M + 1)$-dimensional vector $(\{x_j^*\}, \{y_j^*\}, p^*)$ such that

(a) x_j^* maximizes u_j for any $j = 1, \ldots, N$ on the set

$$\left\{ x_j \in X_j : p^*x_j \le p^*b_j + \sum_k \xi_{jk} p^*y_k^* \right\},$$

where b_j are the resources available to household j and ξ_{jk} is the fraction of the profit of firm k that j receives.

(b) y_j^* maximizes the profit p^*y_j on Y_j for any $j = N + 1, \ldots, M$.

(c) $x^* - y^* \le b$, where b is the vector of the total resources available to the economy.

By adding the inequalities

(7) $$px_j \le pb_j + \sum_k \xi_{jk} py_k, \qquad k = 1, \ldots, N,$$

we obtain

(8) $$px \le pb + py,$$

which can be written in terms of the excess supply:

(9) $$p(b + y - x) = pz(p) \ge 0.$$

Let us assume $\sum_{k=1}^n p_k > 0$ and restrict our attention to the simplex $\Sigma = \{p : \sum p_k = 1\}$.
Then the Gale–Nikaido theorem holds.

(10) Gale–Nikaido Theorem.   Let Z be a compact set in R^n and $z(p) : \Sigma \to Z$ be an upper semicontinuous function such that the set $z(p)$ is nonempty and convex and satisfies the inequality $pz(p) \ge 0$. Then there exists a $p^* \in \Sigma$ such that $z(p^*) \cap R_+^n \ne \varnothing$.

Proof   Let us introduce a perturbation function

(11a) $\delta_i(p) > 0$ if and only if $z_i(p) < 0$,

(11b) $\delta_i(p) = 0$ if $z_i(p) = 0$,

(11c) $p_i + \delta_i(p) > 0$ for any i,

which forces the existing price to approximate the equilibrium one. A very simple example of a function satisfying condition (11) is $\delta_i(p) = \max[0, -k_i z_i(p)]$ for $k_i > 0$, where $z_i(p) < 0$ means an excess of demand and the price adjustment $\delta_i(p)$ is positive. Then, for any i, $\delta_i(p)z_i(p) \le 0$. In order for

$\mathbf{p} + \delta(\mathbf{p})$ to belong to the simplex Σ, we normalize it and consider the new function

(12) $$\mathbf{q}(\mathbf{p}) = [\mathbf{p} + \delta(\mathbf{p})]/[\mathbf{p} + \delta(\mathbf{p})]^{\mathrm{T}}\mathbf{e},$$

where $\mathbf{e}$ is the n-dimensional column vector with all the components equal to 1. Also, $\mathbf{q}(\mathbf{p})$ is still a continuous mapping, and the correspondence

(13) $$(\mathbf{p}, \mathbf{z}) \rightarrow \mathbf{q}(\mathbf{p}) \times \mathbf{z}(\mathbf{p})$$

satisfies the Kakutani fixed-point theorem.[1]

Let $(\mathbf{p}^*, \mathbf{z}^*)$ be the fixed point. It is the equilibrium point we are looking for. Indeed, from the equality

(14) $$\mathbf{p}^* = [\mathbf{p}^* + \delta(\mathbf{p}^*)]/[\mathbf{p}^* + \delta(\mathbf{p}^*)]^{\mathrm{T}}\mathbf{e},$$

we obtain

(15) $$\delta(\mathbf{p}^*)\mathbf{z}(\mathbf{p}^*) \geq 0,$$

and the implication $z_i(\mathbf{p}^*) < 0 \rightarrow \delta_i(\mathbf{p}^*) = 0$ contradicts the definition of $\delta_i(\mathbf{p})$ in (11).

If we drop the assumption of pointwise location, we can consider the space an exchangeable commodity; that is, it is possible to sell or buy a zone of space or its use and refer the nonspace commodities to the point in space where they are available. In this way we can develop a general theory concerning the rent and the demand for the space [8].

Assume the economy to extend into region A, a compact set in R^n, and the vector function $\mathbf{x}_j(P) = [x_{j1}(P), \ldots, x_{jn}(P)]^{\mathrm{T}}$, with $x_{jk}(P) = \lim_{H \rightarrow P} x_{jk}(H)/$ measure (H), to represent the demand for a different commodity $k = 1, \ldots, n$ of the economic agent $j = 1, \ldots, M$ for P varying in A. Here $x_{jk}(P)$ is a real-valued function belonging to a Banach space X_k.

Let $\mathbf{p}(P) = [p_1(P), \ldots, p_n(P)]^{\mathrm{T}}$ be the price vector at any point P of delivery. Then for the purchase the total amount paid by agent j is

(16) $$\langle \mathbf{p}(P), \mathbf{x}_j(P) \rangle = \sum_{k=1}^{n} \int_A p_k(P) x_{jk}(P)\, dP,$$

while for the sale the income is

(17) $$\langle \mathbf{p}(P), \mathbf{y}_j(P) \rangle = \sum_{k=1}^{n} \int_A p_k(P) y_{jk}(P)\, dP,$$

---

[1] Kakutani theorem: Let f be an upper semicontinuous function of $X \rightarrow X$, where X is a nonempty, compact convex subset of R^n, and let $f(x)$ be a nonempty convex set for all $x \in X$. Then there exists an $x^* \in X$ such that $x^* \in f(x^*)$.

where $\mathbf{y}_j(P) = [y_{j1}(P), \ldots, y_{jn}(P)]^T$ represents the supply of any commodity k obtained from agent j. Here $y_{jk}(P)$ belongs to a Banach space Y_k.

For the sake of simplicity, let us assume there is only one extended commodity, the space itself. If we identify A with the unit cube $C_0 \subset R^3$, such a commodity will be represented as an element of the natural Borel field $\mathscr{B}$ on C_0. Denote the rent for the space by $\rho_1(P)$ and the purchase price by $\rho_2(P)$, $P \in C_0$, where $\rho_1(P)$ and $\rho_2(P)$ belong to a Banach space $\mathscr{R}_h$, $h = 1, 2$.

Thus, if the jth economic agent buys the use of set D_{j1} and the ownership of set D_{j2}, the cost will be

$$(18) \quad \boldsymbol{\mu}(\mathbf{D}_j) = \sum_{h=1}^{2} \mu_h(D_{jh}) = \sum_{h=1}^{2} \int_{D_{jh}} \rho_h(P)\, dP \qquad \text{for} \quad j = 1, \ldots, M,$$

while if he sells the use of E_{j1} and the property of E_{j2} he will earn

$$(19) \quad \boldsymbol{\mu}(\mathbf{E}_j) = \sum_{h=1}^{2} \mu_h(E_{jh}) = \sum_{h=1}^{2} \int_{E_{jh}} \rho_h(P)\, dP \qquad \text{for} \quad j = 1, \ldots, M,$$

where μ_h is a finite σ-additive set function in $\mathscr{M}$.

Let $\hat{Q}_{jh}$ be the quantities of space in the initial endowments of the agents satisfying the relationships $\hat{Q}_{jh} \subseteq A$, $\hat{Q}_{ih} \cap \hat{Q}_{jh} = \varnothing$, $h = 1, 2$ and $j = 1, \ldots$ M, $i \neq j$. Then sets D_{jh} and E_{jh} are defined as $D_{jh} = Q_{jh} - Q_{jh} \cap \hat{Q}_{jh}$, $E_{jh} = \hat{Q}_{jh} - Q_{jh} \cap \hat{Q}_{jh}$, where Q_{jh} is the quantity of space that the jth agent can use or owns.

Since in this model production requires the use and not the ownership of space, we assume $E_{j1} = E_{j2} = \varnothing$, $D_{j2} = \varnothing$.

Let us assume that ρ_1 and ρ_2 exclude both demand for and offer of use or purchase of the same set:

$$(20) \quad D_{j1} \cap E_{j1} = \varnothing, \qquad D_{j2} \cap E_{j2} = \varnothing, \qquad j = 1, \ldots, M.$$

If we distinguish households $(j = 1, \ldots, N)$ that are utility maximizers and firms $(j = N + 1, \ldots, M)$ that are profit maximizers, we shall have two optimization problems:

$$(21a) \qquad \sup\{U_j \colon \mathscr{H}_j\}, \qquad j = 1, \ldots, N,$$

$$(21b) \qquad \max\{\Pi_j \colon \mathscr{H}_j\}, \qquad j = N + 1, \ldots, M,$$

where $U_j = U_j[\mathbf{x}_j(P), \mathbf{y}_j(P), \mathbf{D}_j, \mathbf{E}_j]$ is the utility index and $\Pi_j = \langle \mathbf{p}, \mathbf{y}_j \rangle$ $+ \boldsymbol{\mu}(\mathbf{E}_j) - \langle \mathbf{p}, \mathbf{x}_j \rangle - \boldsymbol{\mu}(\mathbf{D}_j)$ is the profit. Assume that the production function $V_j[\mathbf{x}_j(P)\mathbf{m}\, \mathbf{y}_j(P), \mathbf{D}_j, \mathbf{E}_j]$ is concave with respect to all the variables.

Then the feasible regions

$$\mathcal{H}_j(\mathbf{p}, \boldsymbol{\mu}) = \Big\{ (\mathbf{x}_j(P), \mathbf{y}_j(P), \mathbf{D}_j, \mathbf{E}_j): \mathbf{x}_j(P) \geq 0, 0 \leq \mathbf{y}_j(P) \leq \hat{\mathbf{y}}_j(P),$$

$$x_{jk}(P)y_{jk}(P) = 0, \langle \mathbf{p}, \mathbf{x}_j \rangle + \boldsymbol{\mu}(\mathbf{D}_j) \leq \langle \mathbf{p}, \mathbf{y}_j \rangle + \boldsymbol{\mu}(\mathbf{E}_j) + \sum_{\xi=N+1}^{M} d_{j\xi} \Pi_\xi \Big\},$$

(22a) $$\sum_{\xi=N+1}^{M} d_{j\xi} = 1, \qquad 0 < d_{j\xi} \leq 1, \qquad j = 1, \ldots, N,$$

$$\mathcal{H}_j(\mathbf{p}, \boldsymbol{\mu}) = \{ (\mathbf{x}_j(P), \mathbf{y}_j(P), \mathbf{D}_j, \mathbf{E}_j): \mathbf{x}_j(P) \geq 0, \mathbf{y}_j(P) \geq 0,$$

$$x_{jk}(P)y_{jk}(P) = 0, V_j[\mathbf{x}_j(P), \mathbf{y}_j(P), \mathbf{D}_j, \mathbf{E}_j] \geq 0\} \qquad \text{for} \quad j = N+1, \ldots, M$$

(22b)

are convex closed. For any $\mathbf{p}(P)$ and $\boldsymbol{\mu}$, we individuate an optimal demand and supply functional for the nonextended goods and optimal multivalued correspondence for the extended goods.

Let us first consider [5] the optimization problems in terms of the decision variables $\mathbf{x}_j(P)$, $\mathbf{y}_j(P)$; at a second step we shall study the optimal choice for the extended goods [6], and finally we shall seek a system of prices and rents making the optimal decisions of households and firms consistent [7]. Let f and g be real-valued functions in a linear normed space $X, f: X \to R$, $g: X \to R$, and let a point $\hat{\mathbf{x}}$ exist at which f and g have Frechet derivatives.[2] The following theorem gives the necessary conditions of optimality for the problem

(23) $$\sup\{f(\mathbf{x}): \mathbf{x} \in X, g(\mathbf{x}) = 0\}.$$

(24) **Theorem.** Assume $\hat{\mathbf{x}}$ to be an optimal solution for the problem. Let $g: X \to R$ be continuously Fréchet-differentiable at $\hat{x}$ and $g'(\mathbf{x})$ to be a map from X onto R. Then there exists a Lagrange multiplier $\hat{\lambda}$ such that the Lagrange function $f(\mathbf{x}) + \hat{\lambda}g(\mathbf{x})$ is stationary at $(\hat{\mathbf{x}}, \hat{\lambda})$:

(25) $$f'(\hat{\mathbf{x}}) + \hat{\lambda}g'(\hat{\mathbf{x}}) = 0.$$

Under suitable regularity conditions on the constraints the result also holds for a subset $X_0 \subset X$.

In order to obtain sufficient conditions for optimality, we define pseudo-concave and quasi-convex functionals; a function $f: X \to Y$, where X and Y are linear normed spaces, is *pseudoconcave* on a subset $X_0 \subset X$ if it is Fréchet-differentiable on X_0, and for any pair $\mathbf{x}^1, \mathbf{x}^2 \in X_0$ the following implication holds:

(26) $$f'(\mathbf{x}^1)(\mathbf{x}^2 - \mathbf{x}^1) \leq \theta \to f(\mathbf{x}^2) \leq f(\mathbf{x}^1),$$

with θ the null element in X; a function $g: X \to Y$, Fréchet-differentiable on the

---

[2] See for instance [4, p. 175].

subset $X_0 \subset X$, is *quasi-convex* on X_0 if, for any pair $\mathbf{x}^1, \mathbf{x}^2 \in X_0$ the in-equality $g(\mathbf{x}^2) \leq g(\mathbf{x}^1)$ implies $g'(\mathbf{x}^1)(\mathbf{x}^2 - \mathbf{x}^1) \leq 0$. Then we obtain the following sufficient condition for optimality.

(27) Theorem. Let f and g be real-valued functions defined on a linear normed space, Fréchet-differentiable, f-pseudoconcave, g-quasi-convex, and quasi-concave on the convex subset $X_0 \subset X$. If there exist $\hat{\mathbf{x}} \in X_0$ and $\hat{\lambda} \in R$ satisfying conditions

$$(28) \qquad f'(\hat{\mathbf{x}}) + \hat{\lambda}g'(\hat{\mathbf{x}}) = 0, \qquad g'(\hat{\mathbf{x}}) = 0,$$

then $\hat{\mathbf{x}}$ solves our problem:

$$(29) \qquad f(\hat{\mathbf{x}}) = \sup\{f(\mathbf{x}): \mathbf{x} \in X_0, g(\mathbf{x}) = 0\}.$$

In the presence of inequality constraints, $g(\mathbf{x}) \leq 0$, we add the complementarity condition $\hat{\lambda}g(\hat{\mathbf{x}}) = 0$ to system (28). Moreover, if the solution point is not unique and the problem is convex, then the collection of the optimal solutions $\{\mathbf{x} \in X_0: f(\mathbf{x}) = \sup f(\mathbf{x})\}$ is convex.

Now, let us assume that the constraint set depends on some parameters $\mathbf{r}(t)$ belonging to a vector space $\mathcal{R}$. Then the problem individuates an optimum-value function

$$(30) \qquad F[\mathbf{r}(t)] = \sup\{f[\mathbf{x}(t)]: \mathbf{x}(t) \in \mathscr{H}[\mathbf{r}(t)]\}$$

and the collection of the optimal solutions

$$(31) \qquad G[\mathbf{r}(t)] = \{\mathbf{x}^* \in \mathscr{H}[\mathbf{r}(t)]: f[\mathbf{x}^*(t)] = F[\mathbf{r}(t)]\}.$$

Remember that a multivalued correspondence $f(x)$ is upper semicontinuous on a topological space X if, for any sequence $\{x_n\}$ converging to x_0 and $\{y_n\}$ converging to y_0, with $y_n \in f(x_n)$, we obtain $y_0 \in f(x_0)$; then the following theorem holds.

(32) Theorem. Let $f[\mathbf{x}(t)]$ be an upper semicontinuous real-valued functional on $\mathcal{R} \times X$ and $\mathscr{H}: \mathcal{R} \to X$ be a continuous correspondence with $\mathscr{H}[\mathbf{r}(t)] \neq \varnothing$ for any $\mathbf{r}$. Then the optimum-value functional $F[\mathbf{r}(t)] = \max\{f[\mathbf{x}(t)]: \mathbf{x}(t) \in \mathscr{H}[\mathbf{r}(t)]\}$ is continuous and $G[\mathbf{r}(t)]: \mathcal{R} \to X$ is an upper semi-continuous correspondence.

The properties we described above can be directly applied to the decision variables $\mathbf{x}_j(P)$, $\mathbf{y}_j(P)$ concerning demand for and supply of the nonextended goods. However, under suitable assumptions, they can be applied to the extended goods too. Indeed, suppose any set $E \in \mathcal{B}$ admits a regular parametric representation such as

$$T: x = \phi(u, v, w), \ y = \psi(u, v, w), \ z = \chi(u, v, w) \quad \text{for} \quad \zeta \equiv (u, v, w) \in C_0,$$

(33)

where ϕ, ψ, χ belong to a Banach space. Let $|J|$ be the Jacobian determinant of transformation T. Then the household problem with respect to space decisions,

(34) $$\sup\left\{U_j(E_j)\colon E_j \in \mathscr{P}_j, \int_{E_j} \rho(P)\,dP \le b_j\right\},$$

becomes an optimization problem in a vector space:

(35)
$$\sup\left\{U_j(\mathbf{\Phi}_j, \dot{\mathbf{\Phi}}_j)\colon \mathbf{\Phi} \in \mathscr{F}_j, \int_{E_j} \rho(P)\,dP\right.$$
$$\left. = \int_{C_0} \rho[\mathbf{\Phi}_j(\zeta)]|J(\dot{\mathbf{\Phi}}_j)|\,d\zeta = \int_{C_0} g(\mathbf{\Phi}_j, \dot{\mathbf{\Phi}}_j)\,d\zeta \le b_j\right\},$$

where g is a convenient functional and $\mathbf{\Phi}_j \equiv (\phi_j, \psi_j, \chi_j)$ is a vector function in $\mathscr{F}_j$, a family that corresponds to $\mathscr{P}_j$.

Now, let us consider the particular problem in which the extended goods are continuous surfaces with a parametric representation:

(36) $$\mathscr{S}\colon x = \phi(u, v),\ y = \psi(u, v),\ z = \chi(u, v)$$

for $(u,v) \in Q_0 = \{0 \le u \le 1, 0 \le v \le 1\}$. For any one of the projection mappings

(37a) $\quad T_1\colon x = 0,\ y \qquad y = \psi(u, v),\ z = \chi(u, v),$

(37b) $\quad T_2\colon x = \phi(u, v),\ y = 0, \qquad z = \chi(u, v), \qquad (u, v) \in Q_0,$

(37c) $\quad T_3\colon x = \phi(u, v),\ y = \psi(u, v),\ z = 0,$

we can define the extended Jacobian at a point P as the surface derivative at such a point of the set function $m_L(Q)$, $Q \subseteq Q_0$, which is the Lebesgue measure of the image of Q under the transformation T; i.e.,

(38) $$I_r(u, v) = \lim_{|Q| \to 0} m_L(Q)/|Q| \qquad \text{for} \quad r = 1, 2, 3,$$

where $|Q|$ is the corresponding measure of the set Q.

Assume any continuous Lebesgue surface to have a finite Lebesgue area and the plane mappings T_r to be absolutely continuous. Then, if we set

(39) $$I(u, v) = \left\{\sum_{r=1}^{3} [I_r(u, v)]^2\right\}^{1/2},$$

the following transformation holds:

(40) $$\int_{\mathscr{S}} \rho(x, y, z)\,d\sigma = \iint_{Q_0} \rho[\phi(u, v), \psi(u, v), \chi(u, v)]I(u, v)\,du\,dv,$$

and the decision problem of choosing the optimal surface $\mathscr{S}$ is reduced to the choice of functions ϕ, ψ, χ in a Banach space.

Let us introduce the optimization problem in which the decision variable is a set belonging to an assigned family. Let C_0 be the unit cube and $\mathscr{B}$ the natural Borel field. A function $e\colon \mathscr{B} \to R_+$ is convex if

(41) $\quad e(\varnothing) = 0, \quad e(D) + e(E) \le e(D \cup E) + e(D \cap E) \quad$ for $\quad D, E \in \mathscr{B}.$

We shall consider normalized convex set functions, with $e(C_0) = 1$. For such convex set functions, the first differences $e(D + E) - e(D)$ for D, $E \in \mathscr{B}$, $D \cap E = \varnothing$ are monotone increasing in D for E fixed, as a convex function of a scalar variable x satisfies the property

(42) $\quad f(x + \Delta) - f(x) \le f(y + \Delta) - f(y) \quad$ for $\quad x \le y, \quad \Delta \ge 0.$

A set $\hat{E} \in \mathscr{B}$ minimizes a function $e\colon \mathscr{B} \to R_+$ if relation

(43) $\qquad\qquad e(\hat{E}) + e(\hat{E}^c) \le e(\hat{E} + H) + e[(\hat{E} + H)^c]$

for $m_{\mathscr{B}}(H) < \varepsilon$, $\hat{E} + H \in \mathscr{B}$ implies

(44) $\quad e(\hat{E}) + e(\hat{E}^c) \le e(K) + e(K^c) \quad$ for any $\quad K \supseteq \hat{E}, \quad K \in \mathscr{B}.$

A set function $e\colon \mathscr{B} \to R_+$ is upper σ-continuous if

(45) $\qquad\qquad \lim_{E_n \uparrow E} e(E_n) = e(E) \quad$ for $\quad E_n, \quad E \in \mathscr{B},$

where $\{E_n\}$ is an increasing sequence. Correspondingly, we define lower σ-continuous functions.

Let $\{\mathscr{D}^\lambda\colon \lambda \in \Lambda\}$ denote a filtered family of partitions of C_0, $C_0 = H_1 + \cdots + H_{L_\lambda}$ and $\mathscr{B}^\lambda$ be the σ field generated by $\mathscr{D}^\lambda$. Then $\mathscr{B}^0 = \cup \, \mathscr{B}^\lambda$ and $\mathscr{B}$ is generated by the $\mathscr{B}^\lambda$.

For any set $\hat{E} \in \mathscr{B}(\lambda \in \Lambda)$ we define two additive set functions on $\mathscr{B}$ by

(46a) $\qquad \delta^\lambda_-(H^\lambda_i) = e(\hat{E}) - e(\hat{E} - H^\lambda_i) \quad$ for $\quad i = 1, \ldots, L_\lambda,$

(46b) $\qquad \delta^\lambda_+(H^\lambda_i) = e(\hat{E} + H^\lambda_i) - e(\hat{E}) \quad$ for $\quad i = 1, \ldots, L_\lambda.$

An upper and lower σ-continuous set function $e\colon \mathscr{B} \to R_+$ is *differentiable from the left* at $\hat{E}$ if the limit

(47) $\quad \delta_-(H) = \lim_\lambda \delta^\lambda_-(H) = \lim_\lambda \sum_{i \in I} [e(\hat{E}) - e(\hat{E} - H^\lambda_i)] \quad$ for $\quad H \in \mathscr{B}^0$

is a finite σ-additive set function on $\mathscr{B}^0$ (and can be uniquely extended to $\mathscr{B}$). Similarly for $\delta_+(H)$. Now, the following result holds.

(48) Theorem. Let e be a normalized convex set function which is also upper and lower σ-continuous. Then e is always differentiable from the right.

If $\hat{E}$ is minimizing, then e is differentiable from the right at $\hat{E}$ and from the left at $\hat{E}^c$. The corresponding measures δ_+ and δ_-, nontrivial for $e(\hat{E}^c) > 0$, satisfy the equalities

(49) $$1 - e(\hat{E}) = \delta_+(C_0) = \delta_-(C_0) = e(\hat{E}^c).$$

The definitions and results presented above are due to Rosenmüller [11]. From now on, a new theory is developed for convex set functions based on the results obtained by Rockafellar for functions of real variables and functionals [10].

A family $\mathscr{P}$ of sets in $\mathscr{B}$ is said to be *convex* if, for any pair $D, E \in \mathscr{B}$ that can be decomposed into $D = D_1 \cup D_2$, $E = D_1 \cap D_2$ we obtain $D_i \in \mathscr{P}$ for $i = 1, 2$, or, analogously if for any set $E \in \mathscr{P}$ there exist disjoint sets $\bar{E}_1, \bar{E}_2$, with $\bar{E}_1 \cup \bar{E}_2 = E$, $\bar{E}_1 \cap \bar{E}_2 = \varnothing$, such that $\bar{E}_i \in \mathscr{P}$ for $i = 1, 2$. Thus the convexity properties of the function e can be studied by referring to the epigraph

(50) $$\text{epi } e = \{(E, a) : e(E) \le a, E \in \mathscr{P}, a \in R_+\}.$$

The indicator function will be as usual

(51) $$i(E, \mathscr{P}) = \{0 \text{ for } E \in \mathscr{P}; +\infty \text{ for } E \notin \mathscr{P}\}$$

and studying the function $e(E)$ on the convex family $\mathscr{P}$ will be equivalent to analyzing the extended function $e(E) + i(E, \mathscr{P})$.

We know that the convex point functions are envelopes of supporting affine functions. Analogously, a closed convex set function $e : \mathscr{B} \to R_+$ can be represented as

(52) $$e = \sup\{h = m - a : h \le e\},$$

where h is an affine function satisfying the equality

(53) $$h(D) + h(E) = h(D \cup E) + h(D \cap E) \qquad \text{for} \quad D, \ E \in \mathscr{B}$$

and m is an additive set function in $\mathscr{M}$ and $a \in R_+$.

The collection $\{(m, a)\}$ can be regarded as the epigraph of the conjugate function e^* for e, where

(54) $$e^*(m) = \sup_{E \in \mathscr{B}} \{m(E) - e(E)\}.$$

$v : \mathscr{B} \to R_-$ is a concave function if it satisfies the relations

(55) $$v(\varnothing) = 0, \qquad v(D) + v(E) \ge v(D \cup E) + v(D \cap E)$$

so that $v = -e$ for a convenient convex set function e. Then the conjugate is defined according to

(56) $$v^*(m) = \inf_{E \in \mathscr{B}} \{m(E) - v(E)\} = -e^*(-m).$$

If we are interested in nonnegative concave set functions $w: \mathcal{B} \to R_+$, we apply the transformation $w(E) = v(E) - v(C_0)$, $v: \mathcal{B} \to R_-$.

Let us now define a subgradient inequality for convex set functions. Assume $e: \mathcal{B} \to R_+$ not to be differentiable. According to the inequalities

$$(57) \qquad \delta^\lambda_-(H) \geq e(E) - e(E - H),$$

$$(58) \qquad \delta^\lambda_+(H) \leq e(E + H) - e(E),$$

we can introduce an additive set function, a "subgradient" of e in E, such that

$$(59) \qquad e(K) \geq e(E) + m(K) - m(E).$$

Thus $\hat{E}$ is a minimizing set for e if and only if $\hat{m}$ is a subgradient of e in $\hat{E}$, with

$$(60) \quad e(K) \geq e(\hat{K}) + \hat{m}(\hat{E}^c) - \hat{m}(K^c), \qquad \hat{m}(K) - \hat{m}(\hat{E}) = e(\hat{E}^c) - e(K^c).$$

That being stated, let us introduce the following optimization problem

$$(61) \quad (P) \inf\{e_0(E): E \in \mathcal{P}\}, \qquad \mathcal{P} = \{E \in \mathcal{B}: e_i(E) \leq r_i, i = 1, \dots, m\},$$

where e_i for $i = 0, 1, \dots, m$ are proper convex functions.

$(\lambda_1, \dots, \lambda_m)$ is a Kuhn–Tucker vector for (P) if $\lambda_i \geq 0$ for $i = 1, \dots, m$ and the inf of the proper convex function

$$(62) \qquad L = e_0(E) + \sum_{i=1}^m \lambda_i [e_i(E) - r_i]$$

is positive, finite, and equal to the optimal value of (P).

Assume that inf $P > 0$ and that there exists a set $\bar{E} \in \mathcal{B}$ such that $e_i(\bar{E}) < r_i$ for $i = 1, \dots, m$. Then there exists at least one Kuhn–Tucker vector for (P). Moreover, let us define the Lagrange function

$$L(E, y) = \begin{cases} \{e_0(E) + \sum y_i(e_i(E) - r_i)\}^+ & \text{for} \quad y \in R^m_+, \quad E \in \mathcal{B} \\ 0 & \text{for} \quad y \notin R^m_+, \quad E \in \mathcal{B} \\ +\infty & \text{for} \quad E \notin \mathcal{B}. \end{cases}$$

$$(63)$$

Then $\hat{E}$ is an optimal set for problem (P) if and only if a vector $\hat{y} \in R^m_+$ exists such that the pair $(\hat{E}, \hat{y})$ is a saddle point for $L(E, y)$ or, equivalently,

$$(64) \quad \lambda_i \geq 0, \qquad e(\hat{E}) \leq r_i, \qquad \lambda_i(e_i(\hat{E}) - r_i) = 0,$$

$$i = 1, \dots, m, \qquad \hat{m} \in \partial\{e_0(\hat{E}) + \sum \lambda_i(e_i(\hat{E}) - r_i)\},$$

where ∂ denotes the "subdifferential."

If functions e_i, $i = 0, 1, \ldots, m$ are normalized and upper and lower σ-continuous on $\hat{E}$, the following sequence holds:

(65) $$\delta_-(C_0) = \delta_+(C_0) = L(\hat{E}^c, \hat{y}) = 1 - L(\hat{E}, \hat{y}).$$

By using the subdifferential of the function $L(E, y)$ with respect to E and y,

(66a) $$\partial_E L(E, y) = \{m \in \mathcal{M}: L(F, y) \geq L(E, y)$$
$$+ m(F) - m(E) \text{ for any } F \in \mathcal{B}\}$$

(66b) $$\partial_y L(E, y) = \{x \in X: L(E, \bar{y}) \leq L(E, y)$$
$$+ \sum \bar{y}_i x_i - \sum y_i x_i \text{ for any } \bar{y} \in R_+^m\};$$

then

(67) $\quad (\hat{m}, 0) \in \partial L(\hat{E}, \hat{y}) \quad$ if and only if $(\hat{E}, \hat{y})$ is a saddle for L.

For problem (P) we can develop a conjugate duality theory. As usual, we perturb the original problem:

$$p(x) = \inf\{e_0(E): E \in \mathcal{P}_x\}, \quad \mathcal{P}_x = \{E \in \mathcal{B}: e_i(E) - r_i \leq x_i, \quad i = 1, \ldots, m\},$$
(68)

where $x = (x_1, \ldots, x_m)$ belongs to a linear space X.

In order to have a feasible perturbation, the following inequality must hold:

(69) $$p(x) + \sum y_i x_i < p(0),$$

and for a Kuhn–Tucker vector $\hat{y} = (\lambda_1, \ldots, \lambda_m)$ no perturbation is feasible, so that

(70) $$\inf(p(x) + \sum \lambda_i x_i) = p(0) > 0 \quad \text{and finite.}$$

Let us associate the set $\mathcal{M}$ with $\mathcal{B}$ and the linear space Y with X. The perturbed problem (68) can be written in the more compact form

(71) $$p(x) = \inf\{f(E, x): E \in \mathcal{B}\},$$

and correspondingly the Lagrange function becomes

(72) $$L(E, y) = \inf_{x \in X} \{f(E, x) + \sum y_i x_i\}^+,$$

where $f(E, x)$ is a bifunction $x \to f(\cdot, x)$ such that at each point $x \in X$ associates a function $f(\cdot, x): E \to f(E, x)$ with $f(E, x) = e_0(E) + i(E, \mathcal{P}_x)$.

We can introduce the dual problem

(73) $$\sup\{q(y): y \in Y\}, \quad q(y) = \inf\{L(E, y): E \in \mathcal{B}\}$$

and link $q(y)$ with $p(x)$. Indeed, suppose $f(E, x)$ to be convex function.

Then, from equality $q = (-p)^*$ we obtain

(74) $$\sup\{q(y): y \in Y\} = \operatorname{cl} p(0) = \lim_{x \to 0} \inf p(x),$$

with $p(0) = \inf\{e_0(E): E \in \mathscr{P}_0\}$.

Vice versa, let us consider the dual problem and introduce a function $D(m, y): \mathscr{M} \times Y \to R_+$:

(75) $$D(m, y) = \inf{}^+\{L(E, y) + m(E): E \in \mathscr{B}\}$$

and $D(m_0, y) = q(y)$, where m_0 is the null element in $\mathscr{M}$. Then the perturbed form for the dual problem is

(76) $$r(m) = \sup\{D(m, y): y \in Y\},$$

which for the null element m_0 of $\mathscr{M}$ becomes

(77) $$r(m_0) = \sup\{D(m_0, y): y \in Y\} = \sup\{q(y): y \in Y\}.$$

Under the usual assumption that f is convex closed, we obtain $-e_0^* = \operatorname{cl} r$ and

(78) $$\inf{}^+\{f(E, 0): E \in \mathscr{B}\} = \lim_{m \to m_0} \sup r(m).$$

We can now conclude with the following theorem.

(79) **Theorem.** The following conditions are equivalent:

(a) $\inf{}^+\{f(E, 0): E \in \mathscr{B}\} = \sup\{q(y): y \in Y\}$;
(b) $p(0) = \lim \inf_{x \to 0} p(x)$;
(c) a saddle $(\hat{E}, \hat{y})$ for $L(E, y)$ exists;
(d) $r(m_0) = \lim \sup_{m \to m_0} r(m)$.

Let f be a convex closed function. Then $(\hat{E}, \hat{y})$ is a saddle for $L(E, y)$ if and only if $-\hat{y} \in \partial p(0)$, $\hat{E} \in \partial(-r)(m_0)$.

Thus we have proved that the classical results known for ordinary functions can be extended to convex set functions.

Let us define the constraint region in terms of some parameters and analyze the continuity properties of the optimum-value function $F(\mathbf{r}) = \sup\{e_0(E): E \in \mathscr{P}(\mathbf{r})\}$, $\mathscr{P}(\mathbf{r}) = \{E \in \mathscr{B}: e_i(E) = r_i, i = 1, \ldots, m\}$ and of the collection of the optimal solutions

(80) $$G(\mathbf{r}) = \{E^* \in \mathscr{P}(\mathbf{r}): F(\mathbf{r}) = e_0(E^*)\},$$

where $\mathbf{r} = [r_1, \ldots, r_m]^T \in R^m$, $\mathbf{e} = [e_1, \ldots, e_m]^T$, $e_i: \mathscr{B} \to R$.

Let I be a subset of R^m such that collection (80) is nonempty. The function $F(\mathbf{r}) = e_0[E^*(\mathbf{r})]$ is upper semicontinuous on I if, for any sequence $\{\mathbf{r}^n\} \subset I$

converging to $\mathbf{r}^0$ and such that the corresponding sequence $\{E^*(\mathbf{r}^n)\}$ increases to a set A, we have

(81) $\lim_n F(\mathbf{r}^n) = \lim e_0[E^*(\mathbf{r}^n)] = e_0(A) \leq F(\mathbf{r}^0).$

Assume e_i for $i = 0, 1, \ldots, m$, to be upper σ-continuous on $\mathscr{B}$. Then the optimum-value function $F(\mathbf{r})$ is upper semicontinuous and the results can be easily extended to a monotone subfamily $\mathscr{P} \subset \mathscr{B}$.

Let $\mathscr{P}$ be a σ-additive family of sets in $\mathscr{B}$ and let e_i for $i = 1, \ldots, m$, be σ-additive set functions. Then the feasible collection $\mathscr{P}(\mathbf{r}) = \{E \in \mathscr{P}: e_i(E) = r_i, i = 1, \ldots, m\}$ is closed with respect to any converging sequence of sets. And if we consider the problem

(82) $F(\mathbf{r}) = \sup\{e_0(E): E \in \mathscr{P}(\mathbf{r})\},\ \mathscr{P}(\mathbf{r}) = \{E \in \mathscr{P}, \mathbf{e}(E) = \mathbf{r}\},$

the optimum-value function $F(\mathbf{r})$ is continuous with respect to any converging sequence.

Assume $\mathscr{B}$ to have a topological structure. The collection of the optimal solutions $G(\mathbf{r}): I \to \mathscr{B}$ is upper semicontinuous if, for given sequences $\{\mathbf{r}^n\} \subset I$ converging to $\mathbf{r}^0$, $\{E_n\} \subset \mathscr{B}$ with $E_n \in G(\mathbf{r}^n)$, the limit set $E_n \to E_0$ belongs to $G(\mathbf{r}^0)$, $E_0 \in G(\mathbf{r}^0)$.

Suppose e_0 and $\mathscr{P}(\mathbf{r})$ to be continuous. Then $G(\mathbf{r})$ is an upper semicontinuous correspondence.

As a second case, we shall introduce a set function $v: \mathscr{B} \to R$, describing some particular properties of any Borel set $E \in \mathscr{B}$, as a parameter in the optimization problem

(83) $F(v) = e_0(E^*(v), v[E^*(v)]) = \sup\{e_0(E, v(e)): E \in \mathscr{P}(v)\},$

(84) $\mathscr{P}(v) = \{E \in \mathscr{B}: \mathbf{e}[E, v(E)] = \mathbf{r}\},$

where v belongs to a feasible family V such that the collection of the optimal solutions

(85) $G(v) = \{E^* \in \mathscr{P}(v): e_0(E^*, v(E^*)) = F(v)\}$

is nonempty. Function $F(v): V \to R$ is upper semicontinuous if, for any sequence $\{v_n\} \subset V$ converging to v_0 such that $\{E^*(v_n)\}$ is increasing to a limit set A, we have

(86) $e_0\{E^*(v_0), v_0[E^*(v_0)]\} = F(v_0) \geq \lim F(v_n)$

$$= \lim e_0\{E^*(v_n), v_n[E^*(v_n)]\}$$

$$= e_0[A, v_0(A)].$$

$F(v)$ is continuous if the property is satisfied for any converging sequence of sets.

Assume e_i for $i = 0, 1, \ldots, m$ and $v \in V$ to be upper σ-continuous functions. Then $F(v)$ is upper semicontinuous on V.

We say that the correspondence $G(v)$: $V \to \mathscr{B}$ is upper semicontinuous if, for any sequence $\{v_n\} \subset V$ converging to v_0 such that $E^*(v_n) \in G(v_n)$ for any n, the condition $E^*(v_n) \to A$ implies $A \in G(v_0)$.

Assume e_0: $\mathscr{B} \to R$ and $\mathscr{P}(v)$: $V \to \mathscr{B}$ to be continuous mappings. Then the collection of the optimal solutions $G(v)$ is upper semicontinuous.

The properties we have proved up to now can be applied to the household and the firm problems in order to obtain convexity and continuity for the optimum-value functions

(87a) $\qquad F_j(\mathbf{p}, \boldsymbol{\mu}) = \sup\{U_j \colon \mathscr{H}_j\}, \qquad j = 1, \ldots, N,$

(87b) $\qquad F_j(\mathbf{p}, \boldsymbol{\mu}) = \max\{\Pi_j \colon \mathscr{H}_j\}, \qquad j = N + 1, \ldots, M,$

and the multivalued demand for and offer of the nonspace commodities and of the space itself.

Let $\mathscr{P}_s$ be a compact convex subset in the nonnegative orthant of the normed linear space of prices and $\mathscr{M}_s$ be a compact convex set in the space $\mathscr{M}^2$ of the ordered pairs of measures. Assume that the feasible regions are convex closed and individuate continuous mappings with respect to the parameters. Moreover, let U be continuous and quasi-concave. Then the demand for and offer of the nonspace commodities are upper semicontinuous on $\mathscr{P}_s \times \mathscr{M}_s$ and, if multivalued, individuate convex collections. Analogously, according to the previous definitions, the demanded and offered sets for use or purchase satisfy the same properties. Referring to the aggregate demand for and offer of the nonspace commodities,

(88) $\quad x_k^*(\mathbf{p}, \boldsymbol{\mu}) = \sum_{j=1}^{M} x_{jk}^*(\mathbf{p}, \boldsymbol{\mu}), \qquad y_k^*(\mathbf{p}, \boldsymbol{\mu}) = \sum_{j=1}^{M} y_{jk}^*(\mathbf{p}, \boldsymbol{\mu}), \qquad k = 1, \ldots, n,$

the balance condition requires the demand not to exceed the offer:

(89a) $\qquad\qquad\qquad \mathbf{x}^*(\mathbf{p}, \boldsymbol{\mu}) \leq \mathbf{y}^*(\mathbf{p}, \boldsymbol{\mu}).$

Since the initial endowments of the agents contain disjoint sets in A $\hat{Q}_{ih} \subseteq A$, $\hat{Q}_{ih} \cap \hat{Q}_{jh} \neq \varnothing$ for $h = 1, 2$ and $i, j = 1, \ldots, M$, the optimal quantities of space the agents wish to sell,

(90) $\qquad\qquad\qquad E_{ih}^*(\mathbf{p}, \boldsymbol{\mu}) = \hat{Q}_{ih} - Q_{ih}(\mathbf{p}, \boldsymbol{\mu}) \cap \hat{Q}_{ih},$

(91) $\qquad\qquad\qquad E_{jh}^*(\mathbf{p}, \boldsymbol{\mu}) = \hat{Q}_{jh} - Q_{jh}(\mathbf{p}, \boldsymbol{\mu}) \cap \hat{Q}_{jh},$

are disjoint, $E_{ih}^* \cap E_{jh}^* = \varnothing$ for any $i, j = 1, \ldots, M$.

Correspondingly we can define the optimal aggregate quantity of space sold by all the agents as $E_h^* = \sum_{j=1}^{M} E_{jh}^*$, so that the following equality holds:

(92) $$\sum_{j=1}^{M} \mu_h(E_{jh}^*) = \mu_h(E_h^*) \qquad \text{for} \quad h = 1, 2;$$

but in general there exist portions of space that more than one agent wishes to buy or use, and sets D_{jh}^* are not disjoint. Let us denote by $D_{jh}^*(\alpha)$ the portion of set D_{jh}^* that $\alpha + 1$ agents demand to use or buy. Thus we can write

(93) $$\sum_{j=1}^{M} \mu_h(D_{jh}^*) = \sum_{j=1}^{M} \left\{ \mu_h[D_{jh}^*(0)] + \sum_{\alpha=1}^{M-1} (\alpha + 1)\mu_h[D_{jh}^*(\alpha)] \right\},$$

where sets $D_{jh}^*(0)$, denoting portions of space A that are demanded by only one agent, are mathematically disjoint, $D_{ih}^*(0) \cap D_{jh}^*(0) = \emptyset$, and lead to the aggregate set

(94) $$D_h^*(0) = \sum_{j=1}^{M} D_{jh}^*(0) \qquad \text{for} \quad h = 1, 2.$$

Finally, we can represent sets E_h^*, $D_h^*(0)$ as a sum of disjoint sets

(95) $$E_h^*(\mathbf{p}, \mathbf{\mu}) = E_h^*(\mathbf{p}, \mathbf{\mu}) \cap D_h^*[(\mathbf{p}, \mathbf{\mu}), 0] + \{E_h^*(\mathbf{p}, \mathbf{\mu}) - E_h^*(\mathbf{p}, \mathbf{\mu}) \cap D_h^*[(\mathbf{p}, \mathbf{\mu}), 0]\},$$

(96) $$D_h^*[(\mathbf{p}, \mathbf{\mu}), 0] = E_h^*(\mathbf{p}, \mathbf{\mu}) \cap D_h^*[(\mathbf{p}, \mathbf{\mu}), 0] + \{D_h^*[(\mathbf{p}, \mathbf{\mu}), 0] - E_h^*(\mathbf{p}, \mathbf{\mu}) \cap D_h^*[(\mathbf{p}, \mathbf{\mu}), 0]\}.$$

For the space purchased or sold for use or ownership, the balance conditions require the demand to be included in the corresponding supply and the demand sets all to be disjoint:

(89b) $$D_h^*(0) = D_h^* \subseteq E_h^*, \qquad D_{jh}^*(\alpha) = \emptyset \qquad \text{for any} \quad j, h, \alpha.$$

In the case of multivalued demand and supply, conditions (89a)–(89b) have to be satisfied by at least one element of the collection $G(\mathbf{p}, \mathbf{\mu}) = \{(\mathbf{x}^*, \mathbf{y}^*, \mathbf{D}^*, \mathbf{E}^*)\}$. Generally, conditions (89a)–(89b) are not fulfilled for any value of $\mathbf{p}$ and $\mathbf{\mu}$ and we must look for an equilibrium point $(\mathbf{p}^*, \mathbf{\mu}^*)$ that makes all the decisions of the economic agents consistent. Hence we can give the following definition of an equilibrium.

(97) **Definition.** A point $(\{\mathbf{x}_j^*\}, \{\mathbf{y}_j^*\}, \{\mathbf{D}_j^*\}, \{\mathbf{E}_j^*\}, \mathbf{p}^*, \mathbf{\mu}^*)$ is a *competitive equilibrium* if

(a) $(\mathbf{x}_j^*, \mathbf{y}_j^*, \mathbf{D}_j^*, \mathbf{E}_j^*) \in G_j(\mathbf{p}^*, \mathbf{\mu}^*) \qquad \text{for any} \quad j,$

(b) $\mathbf{x}^*(P) \leq \mathbf{y}^*(P), P \in C_0,$

(c) $\mathbf{D}^* \subseteq \mathbf{E}^*, \qquad D_{ih} \cap D_{jh} = \emptyset \qquad \text{for any} \quad j, h.$

The Walras law in a general sense takes the form

$$(98) \quad \eta(\mathbf{x}, \mathbf{y}, \mathbf{D}, \mathbf{E}, \mathbf{p}, \boldsymbol{\mu}) = \langle \mathbf{p}, \mathbf{y} \rangle + \sum_{h=1}^{2} \mu_h [E_h - E_h \cap D_h(0)] - \langle \mathbf{p}, \mathbf{x} \rangle$$

$$- \sum_{h=1}^{2} \mu_h [D_h(0) - E_h \cap D_h(0)]$$

$$- \sum_{h=1}^{2} \sum_{j=1}^{M} \sum_{\alpha=1}^{M-1} (\alpha + 1)\mu_h [D_{jh}(\alpha)] \geq 0.$$

Now, we are able to extend the Gale–Nikaido[3] theorem in order to prove the existence of an equilibrium for this new economy.

(99) Theorem. Let $\mathscr{P}_s$ and $\mathscr{H}_s$ be compact convex subsets in $\mathscr{P}$ and $\mathscr{M}^2$, respectively, and let Γ be a nonempty compact subset in $X \times Y \times \mathscr{B}^4$, with $X = \Pi_k X_k$, $Y = \Pi_k Y_k$. Moreover, assume $G(\mathbf{p}, \boldsymbol{\mu})$ to be an upper semicontinuous correspondence $G: \mathscr{P}_s \times \mathscr{M}_s \to \Gamma$ and individuate a nonempty convex collection for any $(\mathbf{p}, \boldsymbol{\mu}) \in \mathscr{P}_s \times \mathscr{M}_s$ such that inequality (98) is fulfilled. Then there exists a competitive equilibrium for the market.

Proof Let us define a response function involving the price system and the rent:

$$(100) \quad \begin{aligned} f(\mathbf{x}, \mathbf{y}, \mathbf{D}, \mathbf{E}) &= \{(\mathbf{p}, \boldsymbol{\mu}) \in \mathscr{P}_s \times \mathscr{M}_s \colon \eta(\mathbf{x}, \mathbf{y}, \mathbf{D}, \mathbf{E}, \mathbf{p}, \boldsymbol{\mu}) \\ &= \min_{(\mathbf{q}, \boldsymbol{\gamma})} \eta(\mathbf{x}, \mathbf{y}, \mathbf{D}, \mathbf{E}, \mathbf{q}, \boldsymbol{\gamma})\} \end{aligned}$$

for any $(\mathbf{x}, \mathbf{y}, \mathbf{D}, \mathbf{E}) \in \Gamma$, where Γ is a bounded set such that $\Gamma \supset G(\mathbf{p}, \boldsymbol{\mu})$, $(\mathbf{p}, \boldsymbol{\mu}) \in \mathscr{P}_s \times \mathscr{M}_s$.

Let $(\mathbf{p}^*, \boldsymbol{\mu}^*, \mathbf{x}^*, \mathbf{y}^*, \mathbf{D}^*, \mathbf{E}^*)$ be a fixed point for the correspondence

$$(101) \quad [(\mathbf{p}, \boldsymbol{\mu}), (\mathbf{x}, \mathbf{y}, \mathbf{D}, \mathbf{E})] \to [f(\mathbf{x}, \mathbf{y}, \mathbf{D}, \mathbf{E}), G(\mathbf{p}, \boldsymbol{\mu})],$$

that is, a point satisfying the conditions

$$(102) \quad (\mathbf{p}^*, \boldsymbol{\mu}^*) \in f(\mathbf{x}^*, \mathbf{y}^*, \mathbf{D}^*, \mathbf{E}^*), \qquad (\mathbf{x}^*, \mathbf{y}^*, \mathbf{D}^*, \mathbf{E}^*) \in G(\mathbf{p}^*, \boldsymbol{\mu}^*).$$

This is the equilibrium point we are looking for.

Indeed the following sequence

$$(103) \quad \begin{aligned} &\langle \mathbf{p}, \mathbf{y}^* - \mathbf{x}^* \rangle + \sum_{h=1}^{2} \left\{ \mu_h [E_h^* - E_h^* \cap D_h^*(0)] \right. \\ &\left. - \mu_h [D_h^*(0) - E_h^* \cap D_h^*(0)] - \sum_{j=1}^{M} \sum_{\alpha=1}^{M-1} (\alpha + 1)\mu_h [D_{jh}^*(\alpha)] \right\} \\ &\geq \langle \mathbf{p}^*, \mathbf{y}^* - \mathbf{x}^* \rangle + \sum_{h=1}^{2} \left\{ \mu_h^* [E_h^* - E_h^* \cap D_h^*(0)] \right. \\ &\left. - \mu_h^* [D_h^*(0) - E_h^* \cap D_h^*(0)] - \sum_{j=1}^{M} \sum_{\alpha=1}^{M-1} (\alpha + 1)\mu_h^* [D_{jh}^*(\alpha)] \right\}, \end{aligned}$$

---

[3] See, for instance, ref. [1, Chapter V].

holds for any $(\mathbf{p}, \boldsymbol{\mu}) \in \mathscr{P}_s \times \mathscr{M}_s$, and we can infer

$$\mathbf{x}^* \leq \mathbf{y}^*, \qquad D_h^*(0) - E_h^* \cap D_h^*(0) = \varnothing, \qquad D_h^*(\alpha) = \varnothing \qquad \text{for any} \quad j, h, \alpha.$$
(104)

Thus the proof is complete.

Assume that the exchange agents' preference ordering is monotone. In such a way, the Walras law holds in narrow sense; that is,

$$
\langle \mathbf{p}, \mathbf{y} - \mathbf{x} \rangle + \sum_{h=1}^{2} \left\{ \mu_h[E_h - E_h \cap D_h(0)] \right.
$$
(105)
$$
\left. - \mu_h[D_h(0) - E_h \cap D_h(0)] - \sum_{j=1}^{M} \sum_{\alpha=1}^{M-1} (\alpha + 1)\mu_h[D_h(\alpha)] \right\} = 0.
$$

(106) Theorem. Let $(\mathbf{p}^*, \boldsymbol{\mu}^*, \mathbf{x}^*, \mathbf{y}^*, \mathbf{D}^*, \mathbf{E}^*)$ be an equilibrium point with

$$\mathbf{x}^* \leq \mathbf{y}^*, \qquad \mathbf{D}^* \subseteq \mathbf{E}^*, \qquad D_{ih}^* \cap D_{jh}^* = \varnothing \qquad \text{for any} \quad j, h.$$

Then $x_k^* < y_k^*$ implies $p_k^* = 0$, and from $D_h^* \subset E_h^*$ we can infer $\rho_h^*(\ ) = \rho_\theta$, where ρ_θ is the null element in the linear space $\mathscr{R}$, identically on the set $E_h^* - D_h^*$.

Proof According to our previous assumptions, if at some point $\bar{P}$ a non-space commodity k satisfies the strict inequality $x_k^* < y_k^*$, we have $p_k^*(P) = 0$. Analogously, for $\rho_k(\ ) > 0$ we obtain a strict positive measure on $E_h^* - D_h^*$ and we contradict assumption (105).

Thus we have been able to find the classical properties for the new general competitive equilibrium model also.

REFERENCES

1. Arrow, K. J., and Hahn, F. H., "General Competitive Analysis." Holden Day, San Francisco, 1971.
2. Berge, C., "Topological Spaces." Macmillan, New York, 1963 (French edition, 1959).
3. Debreu, G., "Theory of Value." Wiley, New York, 1959.
4. Luenberger, D. G., "Optimization by Vector Space Methods." Wiley, New York, 1969.
5. Mazzoleni, P., "Problemi di Ottimo per Funzioni d'Insieme." Alceo, Padova, 1976.
6. Mazzoleni, P., Sull'ottimizzazione vincolata per funzioni d'insieme convesse, B.U.M.I., **B87**, 402–422 (1977).
7. Mazzoleni, P., Esistenza di un equilibrio concorrenziale per la teoria generale della domanda di spazio e della rendita, Rivista AMASES, anno I°, Fasc. 2°, 2° Sem., 15–33 (1978).
8. Montesano, A., La teoria generale della domanda di spazio e della rendita, *Giornale degli Economisti e Annali di Economia* **7-8**, 549–595 (1974).

9. Rockafellar, R. T., "Convex Analysis." Princeton University Press, Princeton, New Jersey, 1970.
10. Rockafellar, R. T., "Conjugate Duality and Optimization." SIAM Publ. No. 16, 1974.
11. Rosenmüller, J., Some properties of convex set functions. *Arch. Math.* (*Basel*) **22**, 420–430 (1971).
12. Rosenmüller, J., and Weidner, H. G., Extreme convex set function, *Discrete Math.* **10**, 343–382 (1974).

INSTITUTE OF MATHEMATICS
UNIVERSITY OF VENICE
VENICE, ITALY

ECONOMIC THEORY, ECONOMETRICS, AND MATHEMATICAL ECONOMICS

Consulting Editor: Karl Shell

UNIVERSITY OF PENNSYLVANIA
PHILADELPHIA, PENNSYLVANIA

Franklin M. Fisher and Karl Shell. The Economic Theory of Price Indices: *Two Essays on the Effects of Taste, Quality, and Technological Change*

Luis Eugenio Di Marco (Ed.). International Economics and Development: *Essays in Honor of Raúl Presbisch*

Erwin Klein. Mathematical Methods in Theoretical Economics: *Topological and Vector Space Foundations of Equilibrium Analysis*

Paul Zarembka (Ed.). Frontiers in Econometrics

George Horwich and Paul A. Samuelson (Eds.). Trade, Stability, and Macroeconomics: *Essays in Honor of Lloyd A. Metzler*

W. T. Ziemba and R. G. Vickson (Eds.). Stochastic Optimization Models in Finance

Steven A. Y. Lin (Ed.). Theory and Measurement of Economic Externalities

David Cass and Karl Shell (Eds.). The Hamiltonian Approach to Dynamic Economics

R. Shone. Microeconomics: *A Modern Treatment*

C. W. J. Granger and Paul Newbold. Forecasting Economic Time Series

Michael Szenberg, John W. Lombardi, and Eric Y. Lee. Welfare Effects of Trade Restrictions: *A Case Study of the U.S. Footwear Industry*

Haim Levy and Marshall Sarnat (Eds.). Financial Decision Making under Uncertainty

Yasuo Murata. Mathematics for Stability and Optimization of Economic Systems

Alan S. Blinder and Philip Friedman (Eds.). Natural Resources, Uncertainty, and General Equilibrium Systems: *Essays in Memory of Rafael Lusky*

Jerry S. Kelly. Arrow Impossibility Theorems

Peter Diamond and Michael Rothschild (Eds.). Uncertainty in Economics: *Readings and Exercises*

Fritz Machlup. Methodology of Economics and Other Social Sciences

Robert H. Frank and Richard T. Freeman. Distributional Consequences of Direct Foreign Investment

Elhanan Helpman and Assaf Razin. A Theory of International Trade under Uncertainty

Edmund S. Phelps. Studies in Macroeconomic Theory, Volume 1: *Employment and Inflation.* Volume 2: *Redistribution and Growth.*

Marc Nerlove, David M. Grether, and José L. Carvalho. Analysis of Economic Time Series: *A Synthesis*

Thomas J. Sargent. Macroeconomic Theory

Jerry Green and José Alexander Scheinkman (Eds.). General Equilibrium, Growth and Trade: *Essays in Honor of Lionel McKenzie*

Michael J. Boskin (Ed.). Economics and Human Welfare: *Essays in Honor of Tibor Scitovsky*

Carlos Daganzo. Multinomial Probit: *The Theory and Its Application to Demand Forecasting*

L. R. Klein, M. Nerlove, and S. C. Tsiang (Eds.). Quantitative Economics and Development: *Essays in Memory of Ta-Chung Liu*

Giorgio P. Szegö. Portfolio Theory: *With Application to Bank Asset Management*

M June Flanders and Assaf Razin (Eds.) Development in an Inflationary World

Thomas G. Cowing and Rodney E. Stevenson (Eds.). Productivity Measurement in Regulated Industries

Robert J. Barro (Ed.). Money, Expectations, and Business Cycles: *Essays in Macroeconomics*

Ryuzo Sato. Theory of Technical Change and Economic Invariance: *Application of Lie Groups*

Iosif A. Krass and Shawkat M. Hammoudeh. The Theory of Positional Games: *With Applications in Economics*

Giorgio Szegö (Ed.). New Quantitative Techniques for Economic Analysis

In preparation

Victor A. Canto, Douglas H. Joines, and Arthur B. Laffer (Eds.). Foundation of Supply-Side Economics

Murray C. Kemp. Production Sets